RESPONSIBILITIES
THEN RIGHTS

AN ECOLOGICAL VIEW OF HUMANITY AND MIND. BELIEFS, CONCEPTS, IMMAGINATION, CONCERNS, ANALYSIS, SUGGESTIONS, DISCUSSION, AND EMERGENT BEHAVIOURS.

"There is an almost organic living process and strength which enables all and any to change for themselves for the better, within their mind, in the light of fact with reasoned ideas."

BY *ROBIN HOWAT*

Tellwell Talent
www.tellwell.ca

ISBN
978-1-77302-200-0 (Hardcover)
978-1-77302-198-0 (Paperback)
978-1-77302-199-7 (eBook)

Table of Contents

FORWARD

The true nature and reality of Human Rights are seen when observing their effect on the powerless and impoverished.

Human Rights are seemingly in place in Western Societies but obligation and responsibility appear to have too often become forgotten. These need to come first if the will to properly ensure principles of rights stands a chance of becoming a general reality rather than so much wind.

Just because a pronouncement is stated by a person in authority does not make it true. When intentions are placed alongside their consequences, then the reality is made apparent. A pronouncement can simply indicate an urgent need for greater thought and closer examination of a situation to clarify any unclear guiding motives and influences that may be hidden. Anyone could say that there are Human Rights, or even that pigs could grow wings, but lack of evidence leads to disbelief. Further, exchanging one supposedly victimized person for another fails to fulfill a duty of care. Similarly, the term Democracy refers to far more than just periodic elections. This freedom of choice needs to be 'evidenced' and evidential in speech, in media processes, and in that choice to participate and behave responsibly while displaying mutual respect through a fulfillment of Responsibilities. Those who deserve the protection of Human Rights are those who have fulfilled their Responsibilities. Manners, which are accepted codes of interpersonal behaviours, make the society.

Casuistry occurs when moral-ethical concepts are officially enshrined within a decision framework. This calls for a structural contextual approach that extends beyond mere rules or regulations. Good law is seen to benefit and take account of the context which surrounds a situation. Within contexts often associated with "The Law", process-lists and charts have evolved which may be referred to but hopefully also lead to specific and personal additions and amendments: they are not intended to be set in concrete. Past problems outside of their historical context will most likely not apply in the same way today, thus requiring interpretation with regard to the present situation. The implementation of Human Rights and Political Correctness seem to be a far cry away from a reasoned thoroughness which would ensure the inclusion of an established background and the fuller social context. Just as what is believed to be acceptable and right in History can change based on time and circumstance, so can fixed written Rights.

A Psalm of Life

By Henry Wadsworth Longfellow 1807–1882

*What The Heart Of The Young
Man Said To The Psalmist.*

Tell me not, in mournful numbers,

Life is but an empty dream!

For the soul is dead that slumbers,

And things are not what they seem.

Life is real! Life is earnest!

And the grave is not its goal;

Dust thou art, to dust returnest,

Was not spoken of the soul.

Not enjoyment, and not sorrow,

Is our destined end or way;

But to act, that each to-morrow

Find us farther than to-day.

Art is long, and Time is fleeting,

And our hearts, though stout and brave,

Still, like muffled drums, are beating

Funeral marches to the grave.

In the world's broad field of battle,

In the bivouac of Life,

Be not like dumb, driven cattle!

Be a hero in the strife!

Trust no Future, howe'er pleasant!

Let the dead Past bury its dead!

Act,— act in the living Present!

Heart within, and God o'erhead!

Lives of great men all remind us

We can make our lives sublime,

And, departing, leave behind us

Footprints on the sands of time;

Footprints, that perhaps another,

Sailing o'er life's solemn main,

A forlorn and shipwrecked brother,

Seeing, shall take heart again.

Let us, then, be up and doing,

With a heart for any fate;

Still achieving, still pursuing,

Learn to labour and to wait

PREAMBLE

Responsible treatment of the largely powerless may benefit from drawing upon both social and educational theory and experience. Unacceptable behaviour and the resulting need to establish norms through firm but fair support and practices are equally valid for the adult as for the child. For this reason these theories and 'good' practices can and will be reflected here. Within the vast worldwide human nation, its many forms, languages, customs, and beliefs have produced long established common threads in standards of hospitality, decency, and respect. Ascribed to these are **expectations** regarding our own actions designed to support our families and those who are experiencing difficulties, hardship, and pain within our communities and our nations. These are also what makes Canada and what makes Canadians be Canadian. In short, we have Responsibilities which must be freely accepted. These Responsibilities were established, felt, experienced, and relied upon long before the invention of Rights. Most people understand that there is a right way to behave and there is a wrong way to behave. This understanding directly follows honourable and freely accepted Responsibilities and Obligations. An ever expanding humanly devised system of legalistic Rights, which are given so much funding, power, and attention, shows that this easier surgical legalistic-style is preferred by both big corporations and politicians. Similarly, the same funders promote the election of the powerless who are advanced to become the powerful: either you are in the legal loop or you are out. An 'out of the loop' situation is one which our War Vets and needy elderly experience firsthand. For example, fifty-nine survivors of warfare who were suffering from Post-Traumatic Stress Disorder (PTSD) were directed to go through so much shock and horror, for Canada. In final desperation resulting from wretchedness and lack of adequate support they decided it was better to take their own lives: this is nationally shameful. These are victims of war as much as those who have been blown apart physically. The fact that neither adequate resources nor the necessary administrative Governmental understanding were available is deserving of our genuine tears. The very expensive Rights-Steamroller shows a clear need to rethink and return to inner understanding and empathetic response. Nebulous concepts of Human Rights failed to be of any use to these lost souls. If a system is 'broke', then mend it or discard it. This Rights process could logically provide after-empowerment and protection for all who honestly shoulder their Responsibilities as placed within a devised written framework of laws, and with such beneficiaries having first demonstrated their social focus to their community by actively meeting their obligations and Responsibilities first. Further, understanding which activities are supported by empathy and considered appropriate for sympathetic response is a learned habit-skill which needs to be birthed and nurtured in the young and then exercised ever onwards. One supposes that this learning is a major role of both religion and organized education, but is it?

Actions do speak louder than words: legalistic or otherwise. Meanwhile, *absolutism* remains the curse of humanity: it is both unforgiving and un-listening, being self-assured of its virtue, despite any and all contrary evidence. Further, a new set of commandments seems to be replacing belief systems.

One system is Human Rights, the belief system supported by a single new autocratic world order and government.

In essence, the focus of this book disagrees that all people have full Rights, irrespective of what they do in society and what they do to society and especially when their deliberate actions cause grief or shortages for others and in so doing inflict avoidable and selected harm. This piece should have been written by a more expert 'wordsmith', but that is life. We must follow where our personal inner calling tells us to travel. I feel passionately that this debate is long overdue; political correctness be damned! Time is running out.

. . . .

The accredited source of the term Political Correctness appears to be the result of advice given in the lead up to Wold War II surrender of the Japanese, September 1945. President Harry S Truman was in communication with General D A Mac-Arthur. Mac-Arthur was rather basic in his description of the Japanese and said so. He asked for last minute instructions regarding the surrender procedure. President Truman was concerned with Mac-Arthur's potential choice of language, especially when speaking to the press. He apparently wrote :-

.....some of your remarks are fundamentally not politically correct.

Mac-Arthur replies that both he and Chester Nimitz:-

..... are somewhat confused, [and asks] exactly what does the term politically correct mean?

The US President reportedly replied:-

Political Correctness is a doctrine, recently fostered by a delusional, illogical minority and promotes a sick mainstream media, which holds forth the proposition that it is entirely possible to pick up a piece of shit by the clean end!

(The source is suggested as from someone at the Truman Library and Museum, Missouri)

. . . .

DEDICATION

I dedicate this book to all those sincere and selflessly kind people who battle for others. I have written this book for the generously kind and responsible; for those who are tirelessly working for better more 'civilized' conditions for all, irrespective of religious belief, colour, tribe or nation; irrespective of sex or nonviolent orientation; irrespective of political preference or change; irrespective of social preference; and for those who support and encourage a freedom to speak openly. Generosity of spirit goes beyond wealth or lack thereof; it is demonstrated by worker or employer and by those who are brave enough to be different and to think differently. Such people live responsibly and at peace; it is from <u>responsible individuals</u> that a better future will spring.

No piece of work comes as a result of a single person's efforts or energies, but rather at the end of an *effort chain*, thanks to so many others. That my wife, Bev, believed in me and put up with my myriad of notes, bits of confetti-like paper, open scattered books, sudden ends to conversations, and the subsequent writing or typing, is, to say the least, a testimony to her strength, balance, and support, and is not always easy.

- Thanks go to Janet Powney, OU Tutor, Lecturer, and Author who showed such inspiration and primary belief in one of her students; to Pauline Minnis and her logic and determination who showed how the unorganizable could become organized, with her humour and patience. Thank you to both for never giving up on me. Gratitude is owed to these and to many of the Open University, UK lecturers and tutors I met, especially Glenda Jones, when all seemed doomed to failure - they would not let me sink! I extend my heartfelt thanks for sticking with me, encouraging me, and accepting last minute submissions. I also owe my thanks to a young member of MUSE at Nottingham University who pledged with me to work towards our separate goals during an extraordinary three-day workshop based upon that very personal-rebuilding theme that year. This lead to my starting towards and ultimately gaining my MA Ed., with the OU. Thanks Chris!

- To London University I offer thanks for their 'night watch' courses in Psychology, Sociology, Sciences, Art Teaching, Geography Teaching, History Teaching. Computer Maintenance, Computer Programming, and even the relaxing fun of making jewelry and stained glass at Barnet College. Further, I am thankful for my experiences in Maths, a number of Business Management Courses, and gaining 'Investors in People Status' via Southgate Technical Collage. I learned from Science Teaching with Care 'beyond the call...', Psychology of the Disturbed Child, teaching Methods for Geography and Art with Sociology Diploma courses at LONDON Ex.Mural. There were also very many courses run from the BMA building ranging from the Anger Management of Others to Mind Mapping, Circle Time, and The Accelerated Learning Method. The very logical and successful fresh approach to learning to read and spell, generated by the

THRASS Training Courses, was truly illuminating. I recall Honey's memorable pamphlet pointing out the disservice of many modern trendy teaching approaches to the subject of English Language, with their far less structural approaches and the subsequent detrimental effect upon student prospects. THRASS works well and is both fun, informative, and well-formed. Further fresh historical insights were gained due to those changes caused by and through World Wars I and II. This study enabled a deeper appreciation of the breadth of human contributions with their sacrifices for others all encompassed in a four-year OU History Diploma Course. Finally, many thanks to fantasy author, Terry Pratchet, for gymnastics in lateral thinking with so many good relaxing laughs and not just a little wisdom.

My deep gratitude goes to Ian Rowlandson, my dear friend, who put up with years of my 'blathered-thoughts' and rambling ideas as he took the time to discuss them and cared enough to tell me honestly and kindly when he thought I was wrong; to Dr. Lakhani for his help and understanding; and to Reverend J. Scott who gave such an interesting and informative year of lessons on The British Constitution at Senior School Forest (UK). Thanks also goes to Vergotsky, who sadly died far too early but fired the concept of human emotional and process learning through *scaffolding*. Further particular gratitude to a seemingly undervalued hero, the Canadian Blatz, who opened a clear appreciation of the role of others in our development with simple but workable stages of *security development theory*.

I fondly remember a vicar at The Anglican Church in Frinton, UK., when I was about 10 years old who preached a sermon on the meaning of Jesus' 'crucifixion and cross'. He asked us kids, who were sitting on the carpet up at the front, what the cross on the altar said and meant. We all came up with logical answers, which he praised, but we did not guess his.

He unforgettably stated that it was the word "I" crossed out: "so go think of others and care for others as Jesus' example shows!" he said. WOW! I am grateful for the guiding power he taught and trust that my responses have done some good. Grateful thanks with fond memories, of Betty Alwyn Howat, nee Compton, mum, an uncompromising Dad, Bill, to their friends and many acquaintances with their accounts of influence. Somewhere I should fit in The Three Horseshoes but I am not sure how and where. Finally to my editors and guides at Tellwell for untangling the tangled and greater focus where required, with plenty of encouragement.

This written work, for it has been work as well as a fun-filled journey, is concerned with what I like to call *Responsible-Democracy*. My work is dedicated to the successful and lasting care and consideration of others through our active involvement-choices. This certainly does not need to be to our own detriment or loss of health. Instead, democracy can be viewed as the raising of conflict from a physical to a mental level.

> *On our own we could ....but together, so much more, we will...*
>
> *A Human Right ignored often goes unnoticed whilst a Responsibility ignored is seldom unfelt. [R]*

INTRODUCTION

In order to achieve real meaningful success, we need to believe in what we are attempting to do. Unless we believe that what we do is right and for the best, there can be no real satisfaction, mental peace, nor completion. Without the knowledge of generous wellbeing, life becomes a downward spiral of take, take, and more take. Result is loss. People, as individuals, cannot do it all alone. We need each other's support. Such support and respect, if genuine, are obviously not a product of force, be it legalistically or otherwise imposed, but are born from within ourselves. Support and respect follows experience and reason.

How we choose to take up a position on any Human Right is much like the varied concept of progress: going downhill or going uphill. Both are forms of progress but with very different outcomes. Progress of the Social Family will be varied: difference may lie in aim, achievement, self-interest, or personal perspective. Fixing words does not fix their meanings; it is what surrounds words that does that. The meaning becomes fixed through a context. The word Progress is a personal viewpoint: it can be confused with views of Human Rights. Both are personal viewpoints. One danger is the creation of an almost idolatrous worship of 'rights'. Success in this can produce financial reward and a source of much craved-for power(s). It could also be a source of escapism through the blaming of others: symbolism versus actual reality. Here again is an outcome of the 'rule of two' being a yes or no. Is it their fault or is it mine?

> *To be responsible we need discussion:*
> *to have rights we demand laws.*

Rights simply refer to a 'right way', an indicator, or a guide, but not a judicially enforceable power. That power may be added. The right way is simply one of many possible 'ways' that results from an expectation of a 'right behaviour' capable of producing a 'right outcome'. A responsible behaviour is both a behaviour responding to self and a social consensus. It is a working part in a perception of direction: a cog within the social machine.

What makes a life worth living? For some, sadly, it is undoubtedly the experiencing of conflict. Some clearly enjoy watching or producing conflict situations. They may well use whatever means are available to them, and Human Rights may be some such means. Others wish to achieve a surer and better opportunity for security and fulfilment by using sense and reason with reasonable social pressure, possibly supported by collective agreements, arranged in a structure of perceived Rights and Responsibilities.

What is love? Here is just one aspect and opinion regarding one slant on the topic: love is an extension of self to others. It concerns itself with fullest regard to and for this wider whole. As with the Community, the broader whole matters more. Beneficial approaches ...... long-term ...... are success-fully living with and amongst others with love, friendship, understanding, co-operation, and respect for difference, which I would term individuality. However, the 'manipula-tive controllers' of life assert their existence and value by and through maintaining their controlling powers, which may go well beyond the practical and so become thoroughly destructive. This is seen regarding overprotective 'Helicopter Parents' and paternalistic governmental departments acting in the name of loving concern but not in fact.

The powerful rule. O.K?

It is a truism oft quoted that with power comes Responsibilities: it does not take a leap of imagination to appreciate that following the acceptance of Responsibilities there are certain conditions and expectations which may be labelled by those Responsible as Rights. Acceptance of this approach empowers others by making their task easier to intimidate and enforce, thereby leading to a new brand of leaders coming to the fore. There are many more outcomes beyond and around the simplistic design of a list of rights which are not always good or beneficial to the Social Family. Such a list is a form of summary, creating a fog of ideas. The Ten Commandments in the Bible may quite easily be recognized and considered an interlinked list of reasonable behavioural expectations. Some could argue their acceptance is partly the result of familiarity and time. Where they are not apparent, the outcome has not been for the greater good. The Ten Commandments and Responsibilities became observable in social norms and traditions. For example, simple courtesy and good manners, if they are applied consciously, will come from within us, just as a Gentleman needs to be a gentle-man as an ongoing way to be: not a soft man, but so much beyond requiring depth and strength of character. Consideration and intent are crucial. Likewise, an honest awareness and need to behave responsibly grows from within the individual's own reasoning powers. This inward or else outward generated behaviour is a dichotomy which has been the cause of much conflict and unhappiness. The question has become whether the outcome is caused through nature or nurture, rather than a question of whether the outcome is one to be desired and worked for. Accepted codes of behaviour and 'good manners' enable separate social units to mix, work, and interact together far more easily and amenably than if each were to follow a purely personal path. Clearly what some feel as obvious and clear others reject as not specifically stated or cloudy: just so courtroom conflicts abound and may well be a construct with intent but not with Justice at the centre. Instead of people working together by using reason, experience, and cause to find a sure and calm way and establish reasonable expectation, too often something else occurs. Unexpectedly a growing natural harmony can become a discordant clash. Lost is any hope of achieving peace as an outcome nor of predictable effects: the very limited words used in 'rights' when legally enforced can so easily become a Dictator rather than a facilitator of progress. That should neither be the intent nor an acceptable outcome.

It is sad that the illusion of Human Rights exists as some benchmark, a collection of axioms and fundamental truths. Are they not more like nuts and bolts within the social machine's structure which are artificially highlighted through a quasi-legal perception? Because their existence is agreed upon and they are a special focus, they clearly are a part: however, they are not the whole. They have acquired an importance but are not the most important. They appear to be 'active-able' and protectable but only in *a society already benefitting from strong social and civil cohesion*. In a society accepting a whole raft of pre-existing social Responsibilities and norms, where many so-called rights are already built into peoples' belief systems, they 'fit in' well. They do not create the society; rather, society recognizes and formalizes them. They may be viewed as almost a form of pre-existence leading to and establishing an outcome called belief. However, beliefs vary with time and condition.

There is a priority, a choosing, a greater need, and a 'greater good' for safeguarding our futures. That pedophiles gain legal protection under interpretations of Human Rights has become nonsense. Children need to be protected from such corrupt and insane predators. Why should such a known criminal be permitted to live near a school and remain anonymous! Getting such things right is the social priority and the Responsibility of all in society. The young are the future and the future needs forms of protection. A person who ignores all the agreed upon tenets of decency and sanity having chosen to indulge in such totally socially abhorrent planned activities as child abuse must be controlled along with those who indulge in what some mistakenly call "adult sex". That others rape, assault, commit ruinous fraud, theft, or murder, all need containment. Can and should these be afforded the same protection through Human Rights, or is this a nonsense both to the detriment of its victims and society? The courtroom witness-stand should never become an avenue for further 'attack' upon the victim, any more than 'formulated', tick-list early release from Jail.... an unjust non-sense which needs to be cleaned up and swept away. Those who live by their Responsibilities deserve the fullest powers and protection of any agreed legal structure. It is hoped that this structure has been established and developed to defend and protect <u>proven</u> members of the deserving and the innocent.

One may well ask who the deserving actually are. Or maybe one should ponder upon the possible challenge: "To define who or what are the deserving!" Any asking who these are as if ignorant of the accepted Social Family norms are a major part of the problem. With minimal intelligent thought they could differentiate, yet they choose not to.

I can have no loving duty towards those intent upon the destruction of my Social Family. They have chosen to use their God-given free will to feign ignorance and to attack as their preferred path, and I have my own chosen path to resist and defend.

On our own we could, but together, so much more, we will ...

The law's power mainly stems from being written down; it is therefore consistent and benefits from the full support of the state. If the law is broken, restitution, if relevant, can be made. Compensation is one such form of restitution. Cut and dried. Exact and surgical. But look beyond: observe what happens. There is the Bill, the Act, the Right, and so on. There is great care to exercise equality under the law. However, experience shows that the more a person owns or has influence the more the law either works or can be circumnavigated to legal advantage........blown away. The law then becomes injustice. The power to plausibly change 'what is right' can become an ability to create right from what is clearly wrong. Consequently, those most able to do exactly that have become some of the most highly paid and influential people. Another phrase for this is 'to become successful' bringing with it social recognition and social reward. Nice, eh! As Brakenreid says in Murdock Mysteries ... Bollocks!

There once was a time ...and do believe it .... when it was the Feudal Lord's Right to 'enjoy' the bride-to-be of a serf, before the wedding day, having the power to prevent the wedding..... and far worse, slack lime thrown over you in a pit is not a nice way to go.

There are inevitable excesses of power exercised through loopholes as a result of faulty law.

To try to bring the discussion to a gentler key is now difficult due to the clear existence of excesses which have been enabled through 'faulty' laws, no matter how well intentioned the initial concept was. One of the problems with 'wordage' and its eloquent practitioners is that it provides the illusion of a balanced and correct word-led direction, which can in turn upset and reduce what is right: not to be confused with 'a right'. Some of those with wealth and or real power chose to and are able to both select and manipulate actions regarding 'Human Rights' and prescriptive law, specifically to work for THEIR benefit: in doing so, Human Rights are adapted to become a tool of their ambition.

Human Rights Concepts are most productive when successfully countering inhumanity and the abuses by the powerful. For example, the French Syndicalist movement leading eventually to the more moderate right to form trade unions is one example of many. The self-restraint and forward planning of The Fabian Society (UK) in the promotion of reform and Rights is another. However, that new situations can allow for the growth of new social and national bullies is a regrettable fact of life. Vigilance is the wiser course. Interest groups through collective action gain power for good or for evil. We need to protect our environment, but there are those who will exploit for their own ends worthy concepts such as the Ontario Environmental Rights. Further, in Sweden, the use and omission of the invented non 'sexist' word, that sounds like Susu, rather than using him or her, can be, no doubt, aggressively and harmfully insisted upon.

This sort of 'newthink' does not deal with serious regional issues such as endangered people, tribes, or races; persecution and or elimination of religious groups; the murder, oppression, slavery, and subservience of women; child recruitment and abuse; homelessness, starvation, and illness; nor the destruction of ecology and the planet. We need to focus on the essentials and not the self-interested call for more regulations by pressure groups and lobbyists. Deregulate to obviate suffering and injustice. 'Justice for all' requires accepting our individual and collective Responsibilities with personal, regional, and international obligations being met by all. That in our present age there continues an international trade in the body parts of albino native Africans shows just how far we still have to go; in fact, it should rebalance the him/her debate. Further, provision for the dispossessed and individuals at risk should use all optional funding such as paid grants for parades. Let those wanting the street parades go back to fundraising and paying for their own parades rather than soaking up much needed tax dollars. From a moral standpoint, prioritising funding to actually meet the physical demands of the needy should replace the political vote buying through municipal or regional grants for parades and other such less important activities. This is another debate.

CHAPTER 1:

Education and Government

It is one of the primary remits of the Government to train and provide citizens who are willing and able to provide life essentials in the form of farmers, doctors, nurses, and teachers while also enabling employment and protection of both citizens and their property....Otherwise why TAX?

The greater variety within city-life enables more employment opportunities with niches which can be more easily entered and filled by minorities. With their variety and diversity cities have become more liberal in outlook. This is particularly so in times of peace and plenty which attract a greater influx of new people. The role of Urban Life and 'City Design' is to promote the secure and 'good life' for many.

SOCIAL EMPATHY: Beliefs and quality of life

'Guilt can be a difficult but useful emotion' to help us avoid

similar mistakes ....
SS Voyager (TV)

A problem caused by *imposing* standards is due to their very perception and source. These come from outside and so can intrude upon our personality: we can chose to `give in` and feel dominated or reject these standards and so push back to maintain our self-image. With negative force, even another`s actual and active agreement can result in and become inactive by "disempowering". However, suggestion/advice/observation and reason may lead to more permanent good. A form of `fellow feeling` is needed: being able to empathetically visualize being in the other person's shoes. To project our thoughts and to feel as the other person(s) could and probably would feel will consequently help us recognize when we are wrong through, for example, a guilty feeling which becomes one way of correcting regret. To change and improve is a gift, strange as it may seem at the time, and is born of insight.

The beliefs expressed by the teachers of various religions that lead to treating others kindly and with constructive-consideration are both centrally human and are found in original teachings in various faiths. These show an underlying base of social awareness focusing on constructive kindness. However, later corruptions of ideals through misinterpretation by some who followed after the `inspired one`, the Teacher, seem Historically almost inevitable. These corrupting 'follow-ons' are the curse of religions, for they serve their proponents' own selfish ends rather than the Social Family they claim to support and cherish. They may be labelled insights, or interpretations, or visions. Proponents set aside their Responsibilities in favour of their appetites and lusts for things of this world including wealth, comfort, power, revenge, and so ever on. The desire and insatiable appetite aimed to gain the power to control others is a real human curse. The fact that many promoters of good have been murdered either openly or through involved and twisted planning with elaborate tales illustrates well the corrupting power of a few determined and evil minds. They claw their way to power, to control, to domination. So many men and woman use what could be good to cut and tear using manipulation, misapplication, misinterpretation, and mistruth to pervert what had been fine ideas and ideals all for self-interest, for their own sorry and sick benefit. By promoting so called ʻRightsʼ, some have been able to promote themselves within their own home-grown organization which having reached a point of ʻcritical massʼ they begin spreading like a virus throughout society. They self-fulfill their words, they orchestrate and cause problems, and they upset, cause real pain, and even death with no feeling of remorse or guilt. "The end justifies the means", but only for them. If they had some honest guilt to guide them, how much better off we all could be. So many problems would not remain unresolved or better still would be un-begun.

The possibility that measures can be devised to establish and ensure quality of life is debatable but possible. Simply put, such a Quality is subject to our believed perceptions of possible rewarding conditions and gaining them over a period of our lives. For each individual will differ greatly depending upon experience, awareness, education, and realistic expectations to name a few. There can be no ʻFit Allʼ solution to a Life-goal concept. To suggest otherwise is a deception. However, certain living conditions are needed by all citizens: enough food, heat, and shelter, appropriate education; security; and good health care. We all have the responsibility to see that attainable conditions are there for ALL members of our *Social Family*. That the UK has reportedly over two million malnourished individuals, unknown numbers who are both homeless and cold in winter, means that we are not focusing upon the priorities sufficiently. If these needs were better met, it is quite possible that much of the funding thrown at prisons and law enforcement could be put to far better use. Children are bullied in schools, some commit suicide, and others leave incompetent in the three Rs: this need not be. Further, there can be a lack of opportunities in the arts, moral development, and healthy sporting for all during schooling. These outcomes suggest containment and incarceration rather than education. For an appreciation and realization of 'quality of life', family and education must be at the forefront rather than placed behind lesser matters being promoted due to hysteria and emotional imbalance. More of education and moral development later.

In Cuba there is apparently a saying:

"Die facing the sun, not facing the dirt."...

*This says a lot about the
vagaries of their life.*

TRUTH, Freedom, and Power

Truth is not the sole preserve of the wise or wealthy, though they might like to pretend that it is. In fact, a person's 'wisdom' or knowledge can be so one-sided as to obscure truth from her or him. Emotion is particularly effective in the obscuring of truth. This has been exploited through the ages by some in all religions, by politicians, teachers, the legal professions, and so on. Some parents are blinded to their own children's (literally) dreadful behaviour by a self-embracing attribution of love and care for their child, despite the evidence. Understanding is within its own bounds: these are the boundaries of perception and the boundaries of individually accepted truths. How one may choose to 'fix' those boundaries or frame them in words or place them within a perceived reality may well be irrelevant to what is fact... the actual outcome. But for a Fact to be a fact it cannot be negotiable. Rights must be understood through clarity and plain language. They need to be grounded in experience and therefore relevant to personal experience. We are all imperfect beings and so can get things wrong. Learn to live with it! Mistakes are made, but there is no reason to compound them, for example, by not learning from them. However, the search for power and consequential ignoring of wisdom and understanding in order to gain that power are especially injurious to a healthy Social Family. Why should four billion dollars be acceptable for a presidential election campaign: how can that be right or defensible in a country with the sick unable to afford care and with so many who are homeless? This implies that wealth makes the presidency while lack of wealth excludes most other worthy candidates.

How often does tragedy follow when humans speak of 'God's words' in order to give a supernatural edge to a chosen Earthly way? Misuse of God's words are employed to confuse personal preference and wishes for what is true, what is right, what is necessary, and also what is ultimately good. The evils of the inquisition and their perpetrators; the attacks upon and persecution of Christian pilgrims on their journey to Jerusalem; the resulting barbarity of the crusade (the first one against such as the Cathars); and the Intellect of Suleiman and its betrayal are just some of Humanity's ungodly actions. Pol Pot of Cambodia; terrorist attacks by a few IRA; brutalities committed by some of the Black Watch in the name of law and order; terrorist organizations in Europe, Russia, Asia, the Middle East, and Africa; Zionist Assassins; glen clearing Scots landlords; Stalin; Hitler; and more recently ISIS are just some of too many inhuman and ungodly focused Social Family tumours, as their actions have proven. These can have the pseudo legitimisation of being the Elected or appointed Government, but their actions demonstrate otherwise. In this way, 'GOOD' seems to be as subjective as Right. Vicars, priests, incumbents, politicians, teachers, mullahs, and so on can all be wrong and frequently are. Truth can be misunderstood, manipulated, rationalised, and misapplied. The Koran states at the start of each chapter the following (translated): "In the Name of God, the Merciful, and the Compassionate." Wonderful words! Since the followers of God know these are the characteristics of God, namely mercy and compassion, then as God's creation these characteristics should be followed by humanity to the very best of each person's ability. There is here, yet once more, evidence and hope of a peace to come.

Years of studying, in and of itself, do not make one right. Honesty; valuing of truth; genuine, caring concern; and a balanced view of responsibility are clothed and extended by the process, practises, and products of study. If the start is evil, then study will make it more so. Study is not of itself a magic spell which will give the answers to life. Instead, study furnishes what is being sought. Good finds good and evil finds evil: inner awareness with its ambitions are truly from the mind and emotional 'heart' and will work towards that inner preferred goal.

Lord Salisbury said, "Education without religion simply creates clever devils."

A self-proclaimed philosopher with an equally easily chosen title of "Prophet" means nothing if the deeds and words fail to match: when such a person speaks using only a babble of erroneous utterances, good could not be its outcome and consequently produces misery and harm. Evil intentions and actions highlight evil people irrespective of what they or others choose to call them. Advocating murder, theft, rape, and child molestation is real evil in action. Further, when a person spouts rubbish, it remains rubbish no matter what she or he has elected to be called. This is equally true of Company Chairpersons, a so-called Holy Man or prophet, disciples, relatives of the wealthy or 'great', and could sadly be true of us all. The greater tragedy is when we believe we are right and delude others to believe likewise, causing them to take in the words but neglecting the reason and consequences. The deluded are blind to ambitions and counter arguments and take no time to consider possible outcomes out of hand. With time and situation-based boundaries, we can be fooled. Can it really be so 'now and here' as it was 'so then and way over there'! The trick is realizing, recognizing, and not simply accepting blindly. Despite a long history and belief of others, it may still be false: these two beliefs and time on their own are not sufficient. When a mistake is made which has become the accepted *new knowledge*, it still is wrong. Acceptance only based on time and hearsay is insufficient. The harder and more demanding challenge is to take the time to responsibly seek out and weigh the 'pros and cons' so as to better understand which direction to go or which new initiative to take....... or not. "By their works you will know them."

TIME

There is a content utility in key words as well as the opportunity to abuse. But what is time, actually, and what is its significance?

Time certainly CAN govern our lives. Does it exist as an invention in its use; is it a reality? It can be constructive or destructive; it can be instructive and repressive; and it may be encouraging or fearfully discouraging. Is it reality, or is it imagined - like that ghost under the bed? As with so many concepts time is a matter of how it is perceived and used......
like Rights.

Just because there is a word for it does not mean it exists. Some people 'believe in' dragons. The word time is a result of a functioning idea which does exist. However, an idea does not ensure existence other than as an idea. Just because people are affected by the idea 'of it' does not confirm that it actually exists. That simply is an indication of their ideas and idea-outcomes, as with Rights.

So, what is Time?

Time is exact moments; time is a progression; time is a measuring system; time passes from one state to the same ....
but is thought of as a different moment, stage, or state, as with something which actually follows on. Time is unseen; time cannot be tasted or felt. Time is not alive but it is rather an idea which flows within an almost nervous communication of producing and enabling calculation. It seems to me that time is whatever shade of colour you wish it to be, being an invention, and so time is a child of the inventive mind. Time is really nothing at all other than one form of description subject to and dependent upon the moment and events. Good timing three hundred years ago with its cogs and wheels would not be sufficient for today's needs: good time varies.

I believe we all understand that there are shades of grey in life. What we think or believe can be equally nebulous: there is appearance and there is reality and the two don't always meet. When trying to find social reality, how can it be identified within such a varied and changeable landscape of multi inter-active minds and very differing lives? Also, with this problem, how can we ever know its opposites and defend against them? The *condition of living* is a sharing of interpersonal relationships in which limited norms (accepted ways) of how we act and the expectations so produced emerge. These periods of social stability include a 'regional agreed upon' set of obligations and Responsibilities. Relocate, and one may have to start over learning new 'basics' again. International mobility, by its very nature of contact with unfamiliar norms, destabilizes. So often what is not understood is feared and resisted: not good social glue!

Understanding enables co-operation, forgiveness when appropriate, and healing opportunities since they lie within accepted and permitted forms. Cultural format is a facilitator towards a stable interacting society with its inevitable many 'off moments' which could too easily cause conflict. One of the key skills in life is that learned ability to listen and com-prehend other peoples' points of view. We may not agree, they may in fact be wrong, but we need to appreciate their position if understanding and cooperation are to proceed.

It could be said that a listening society is a learning society.

To impose upon the unwilling is clearly the way of the dic-tator. Interestingly it is not uncommon to hear one *interest group* speak of another opposing group as fascist while at the same time demanding obedience to their preferred way.

Kevin Domean in *The Diagram Book* restates the truism that words 'can be and often are abused'. His work shows ways to clarify and open up meaning and data through diagrams which may be easily interrogated. Intentional Confusion of meaning may use an abuse of words to cover a real intent with an implied other goal. Constructive social discussion requires open discussion as an aim and reality - freedom of speech tinged with a sensible measure of self-control. This is preferable to the self-promotion and bile of lobbying interest groups who seem to deliberately work toward complicating matters through confusion, confrontation, and obscure linguistic form. Words can clearly be placed so as to cause inappropriate associations and consequently can be given *add-on meanings*. The words themselves can be accepted as truthful, but they are a lie. Ascribing attributes is one skill of advertisers. A variety of Interpretations of two words can illustrate this such as freedom and rights, right to freedom, rightly free, and so on. Place them together at an opportune point and they can easily combine and become intermixed in the mind to project a hidden but nevertheless internalized message: an unconscious and subconscious learning process. One may wish for freedom, but freedom has to be gained and then protected. Freedom is not achieved necessarily as a right. Too often erroneous interpretations by others of differences between individuals are accepted as truth without full and reasonable factual knowledge. Rumour can be a powerful tool of harm and even destruction. Conversely, factual details clarify and inform. Verification of validity is a skill which can be trained and learned. Only the individual can be self-aware: all others use imperfect understandings and so need time, caution, and care (TCC). To judge the words or actions of one individual by another is fraught with dangers, especially in heated exchanges. One's judgements relate to and are informed by personal experience, memories, preference, emotional state, (hopefully) sound research, and frequently aspirations. Further, one person's honest joke can so easily be another's insult with the misunderstood intent relating to their prejudices further complicated by differing levels of maturity. Prejudice can be equally strong on both sides of a confrontation to form inverted prejudice. Emotion rather than mature thought may so easily be manipulated to produce an unjust outcome. Rights need more reason, much more reflection, and less reflexive reaction.

Defining Sin and Harm

SIN is a failure to do what is known to be right and or to actively intend to do harm.

1. The breaking of a religious or moral law ... especially through a willful act

2. An offence or fault (Collins Pocket English Dictionary – CPED)

HARM is 1. Hurt, injury or damage

2. Morally wrong (CPED)

A. Is it reasonable to encourage citizens to put themselves at risk by permitting and so encouraging the Citizen's Arrest? Or conversely:

B. Is there a RIGHT to defend and protect one's family, friends, and property and if necessary to use force in doing so?

Realism is on trial here: YES<-or->NO. This has the appearance of a straightforward choice but is far from it. How would the results of a Referendum on A. differ from B? Or would it?

Every violent act precipitates a response and reaction. Violence should sensibly be the last choice as it ensures the next problem, but it may become "necessary".... or PROVE necessary. The power of words.

EMPOWERMENT (opportunity) Versus ENCOURAGEMENT (words)

Laws alone do not cause change but they can open up relevant opportunities to do so: such openness to change is not always appropriate. A collective accepting attitude enables fine ideas, ideas which are hopefully behind a law, to take root and successfully grow. Time, understanding, and collective agreement are needed to make change actually work. Just as important are the true purposes and objectives behind the formulation of each section of Human Rights? How did each come into sufficient prominence and how was each lobbied by whom to become enforceable through Law? To achieve consent of the people, this important information needs to be generally understood and accepted as both accurate and beneficial. Clearly openness is a major facilitator for general agreement and fully enabled adoption. The next stage would seem to be "check what you get." Make sure each is operated and works as intended.

Varied concerns will develop. If Rights are to be truly beneficial, then they need to be experience-based, provable, and acceptable due to a knowledge base. Rights cannot just be emotional. The greatest danger is bias and misunderstanding leading to precipitous action by one party against another. Some use blame with its underlying purpose of self-protection; this is a smoke screen strategy. When a person says "I know" in a loud confident voice, it is not necessarily true. Truth, viewpoints, and values vary. Values are a 'bias' developed due to life's lessons, and they are probably functional and goal directing. A 'good' bias could be essential to safety as a beneficial prejudice towards a particular course of action to achieve a worthwhile and safe outcome. However, bias and prejudice have developed into labels with a specific perceived negative goal implied. This need not be and often is not the case.

Personal labelling is fraught with the dangers of misunderstandings also with fallacious additional information applied by others who are generally unaware of the complete picture.

A human label is one perception out of many possibilities, but the question remains as to whose perception is more valid and how to both differentiate and know. Misinterpretations and exaggeration, which are both understandable and avoidable, may frequently be based on some emotional misconception which itself may be hidden beyond an individual's awareness. These may be exploited to entertain harmlessly through humour. The old mother-in law jokes are full of these. This is where maturity and responsible behaviour should be evident with maturity of the listener and responsibility of the speaker. So whose reason should be perceived as acceptable? That both are, seems clear. If the intent is clearly not malicious and the format used is responsible, then hopefully all can enjoy the humour. Comedy, humour, and leg-pulling are part of being human. Often the giving it and 'responding well', or giving it back, opens a greater unity between individuals, even friendship.

There need not be unpleasant recourse caused by jibes or taunts. A balance learned in home, school, and society at large is needed. 'Anything' does not go. There needs to be a responsible attitude developed in us all. The sanction against breaking the norms of decency should be temporary social isolation, not socially funded imprisonment. Sadly there is an appetite for an overload of unacceptable behaviours. These are seen in huge pictures in street advertising, on television, and in film: public support has been developed to such an extent that these aberrations are part of a multi-billion dollar money tree. The sexual, sadomasochistic, violent subjects feed and grow a public appetite which in turn grows in financial value, while also proving that such imagery does indeed affect people's behaviour. It is opposite to and opposing of healthy and moral growth. How can pornography, drug taking, blood lust, and desire for both paranormal horror and violence be the way of humanity? This can only lead us backwards in time to a violent and brutal world. Indulgence of this form is weakness of purpose and intent. It is not freedom but rather the growth of a new pernicious bondage to wrong-minded things beyond just one individual.

References for Chapter 2

Helen Fisher, *Why We Love*

Strathclyde Report (August 2011)

Terry Eagleton, *Literary Theory ...An Introduction* ISBN 0 631 13259 7

Yury Lotman, *The Analysis of Poetic Text* (1972)

Allan Pease, *Body Language...How to Read Others' Thoughts by their Gestures* ISBN 0 85969 406 2

Daniel Goleman, *Emotional Intelligence. Why it can matter more than IQ* ISBN 0 7475 2830 6

Bill Rogers, *You Know The Fair Rule* [Easier] behaviour management in school ISBN 0 273 63277 9

CHAPTER 2:

SOCIALIZATION and Government

*The successful learning and use of
signs is part of socialization.*

Where there are people, individuals interact. An interacting population is a society that is either orderly or chaotic and all the stages in between. How the individuals interact affects the quality of life for each member as well as the whole. Within any population there will be those who form groups for various purposes and focuses. These "interest groups" will have a structure based upon the group's purpose and personality. That structure will vary with their goals and also as a result of outside occurrences. Agreed patterns of behaviour will evolve to become traditions which may well be 'protected' by laws. Most agreed upon behaviours will need little enforcement. Common practice of these behaviours enables stability, security, and harmony within society. This state of being will generally be perceived as right. Since that is the preferred way, methods of perpetuating this 'right way' will develop to standardize certain central behaviours necessary to support the 'right way'. Further, these methods will often become institutions such as religious political forms and educational processes. Those refusing to conform will appear to be right or else wrong resulting in appropriate Social Family response or responses. Interactions will depend upon sense-data, emotional impact, and ideally reason. Reason follows patterns of thought. These can generally benefit from knowing about experiences of others and standard relevant 'truths'. Reasoning is a learned mental process developed through perception and exploration.

Interestingly, it has been said that 80% of human input is visual. Obviously this is not so for the blind. Naturally scent and smell play an important role in the processes of recognition, with some forms being more important at a particular time than others. For example, it has been suggested that the condition of the immune system may provide information to others and so affect their reactions at a primitive level. What is sensed is compared with previous information and thereby affects 'gut reactions' as well as attraction or repulsion. How this plays out regarding bonding with or rejecting babies or meeting others is a matter of study, as is the dissonance or more effective focus blindness which may be produced (*Why We Love* by Helen Fisher). To what extent must a feeling of security be required for our well-being? The personal acceptance of a society as one's own provides identity, membership, and attachment. This adds to our feeling of security, as does our sense of nationalism, and so having a national identity can reduce the feeling of vulnerability and encourage group cooperation and even self-denial in emergencies. The immigrant has to *find a way* to deal with initially being 'outside' this security. When social harmony exists and is accepted it brings racial and cultural unity. The unscrupulous break up this perception to gain and build support which they can use to manipulate, dominate, and steal through their version of a 'security form'.

What should be focused upon first? Should this focus be upon the adult or the child? Primary 'Sociality' relates to doing as one is instructed by following dictated behaviour patterns. These grow out of learned behaviour. Obedience and self-discipline are crucial learned behaviours which are more easily learned during childhood. The rewards or outcomes of successful internalization of these learned behaviours and self-control are security, confidence, independence, opportunity due to co-operative activity, and peace of mind.

Antisocial attacks by rabid forms of humanity within Britain led to the Strathclyde Report (August 2011) on Scottish youth gangs in Glasgow. This report shows a significant difference from those dangerous gangs further south. In Glasgow there was frequently found to be both a lack of criminal intent or a need for gang leaders for a gang to exist. By organizing social remedies, the appearance of dictatorial and autocratic leaders of gangs had been considerably reduced, the report states. So young gangs need neither be criminally motivated nor controlled by a central leadership. Why this difference? Could it be social, belief based, a national self-perception, or what? It would be more than useful to identify and establish the role of education, family structure, and local and national leadership through evaluation of traditional and religious inputs.

Educational practices will inevitably play a significant part in building social partners. For this reason theory needs to be more generally discussed and more fully understood not just by so called "experts", but as our collective objective experience. Personal experiences can be used in a sense to verify their contribution and concept validity. Validation is simplified through provable experiences in studies and reports. For example, the Canadian Blatz put forward a simple account of the essential progression of levels of personal development. To simplify, each must achieve the previous level in order to be able to progress to the next. Through this progression dependence, insecure dependence, dependant security, through to independent security are easily observed. Recall your own previous development or study of developing children and these stages become obvious. The beauty of this format is its ability to be used to help and advance those who are 'stuck' at a particular level, fearful to move on. Vergotsky, the great Russian educational researcher and theorist, is a beacon in this area. Tragically he died prematurely many years ago. What else he might have achieved if spared! One example of his work is his scaffolding theory where the 'expert' works together with the learner by providing support which is gradually withdrawn. The learner becomes increasingly proficient and self-confident when using the new knowledge and skills. Similarly, Montessori built upon providing confident use of knowledge through combined relevant sensitisation (sight, shape, feel, colour...) of related sensorial experience linked to learning objectives. As shown by Blatz and Vergotsky, repetitive tasks greatly assist this confidence building which allows for a controlled 'wandering' of interest and will, so typical of the young, but with purposeful and focused structure.

It needs to be the responsibility of society to ensure future parents have a far sounder understanding of developmental processes than what exists at present. This writer believes firmly that parenting should be part of our educational process, as should financial planning. Both would not be wasted resources, but would rather enable insight. How easily we plug children in electronically while leaving them unplugged socially! Parental 'scaffolded' support needs to be provided and consciously informed through observation and planning, instead of unconsciously as a matter of chance or circumstance or as a need arising through some random action, display of attitude, or use of language. Parenting needs to be a part of the school curriculum. It would be prudent to expose the actual parents to curriculum content first. The addition of visual electronic aid can add benefits effectively. However, just because it flashes and looks good does not necessarily mean that it will be of benefit to the child. Adults have a responsibility to call on reason, to plan, to observe, and to adapt constructively. One could go so far as to say, tongue in cheek, that it is the child's right to have parents behave in this way.

Learning to read is an important skill for individuals to master, with the freedoms it brings. People can survive without, but literacy will enable a fuller life with greater constructive self-respect. OLSON's work here is illuminating, to say the least. We adults have forgotten over time how it feels to start finding those reading skills. Olson has a neat reminder by guiding us through experiencing letters and words as the illiterate child does. This makes one more appreciative and responsive to the non-readers' feelings. Adults placed in the non-reader's world are unable to recognize the symbols in front of them. Next, they are progressively introduced to strategies of success. Symbols are linked with pictures. Words, after all, are a type of pictures for sound structures (see examples of the excellent THRASS approach available on the internet). These semiotics (using symbols for ideas/words) become easily understandable, just as hieroglyphics were once understood. The Chinese language uses associated symbols as writing. These are in picture form representations which work as bridges to meaning and are just as easily understood for any of the dialects of Chinese or English once the picture form is mastered. They could bridge a multitude of different languages.

Information and ideas are transmitted through signs which C.S. Pierce, the American founder of *Semiotics*, identified as existing in three basic forms:

1. *The sign* resembles what it stands for (*The Iconic*) such as the photograph or picture identifying your Facebook page.

2. A picture form is associated with a meaning such as the road cross sign indicating a cross-road (*Indexical Form*).

3. The *Symbolic Form* is linked only by the sign's meaning, such as in Scouting where I seem to remember that a small round stone sitting on top of a larger round stone was invented to mean 'I have gone home'.

It has been established that there is a *Body Language* which transmits certain ideas (Allan Pease et al.). Allan Pease's book is an interesting read regarding this concept which is centred on Western ways and culture.

These signs are understood as following rules and so are able to provide meaning. Possibly music would be an interesting inclusion here. Some (*Polysemic*) signs have multiple meanings. A group of signs may all replace each other and transmit the same meaning (*Paradigmatic*). Others may need to be linked together to produce their meaning (*Syntagmatic*) and so on. Sadly, these vary with background and societies and so can lead to confusion and even enmity. A person from a different culture would indeed do well to be able to cope with this and other communication challenges to better feel 'at home'....true on both sides.

Some common form of cultural behaviour that is expected in one society can be considered rude or insulting in another. Some examples are the manner of sitting in an open group, the Inuit greeting of sticking out one's tongue, the reputed Arabic expression of satisfaction for a good meal being loud belching, a hello kiss, and shaking hands to name a few. The fact that a person may feel insulted following any of these behaviours might just simply be due to lack of information. The correct knowledge would produce an opposite effect. **Lotman** saw in poetry a concentrated transmission of meaning through form, patterns, and sounds produced by words and phrases. As he observed, the transition of an earlier meaning may only appear at a later stage. How easy it is to misunderstand, especially if we respond too soon. **Mukaroversusky** highlights that some meanings are clear because they are, for example, of vision so seen- (*Material artifacts*). A statuette and others exist only in how the individual feels about the object (*aesthetic object*), for example: 'my dead mother's favourite statuette'. Since we are not mind-readers, missing the point and misunderstanding during interpersonal interaction may only too easily occur. It is suggested here that <u>responsible reasoning</u> prevents this from not occurring more frequently. Successful learning and use of signs is socialization, having successfully responded to taught patterns of behaviour and behaviour validation.

There are no Human Rights other than national beliefs and preferences.

In some children's books, pictures are used to replace key words or ideas and can help increase confidence in the mastery of reading. Words and sound shapes (er, ow, Ash, th....) often repeated become recognized "friends", thereby aiding confidence in an insecure environment. Words become recognized letter-pictures in combination and spelling becomes repeating these word-pictures when writing so that essentially they look right: spoken spelling requires a different set of skills. It seems unlikely that illiteracy would be anything like the problem it is if educational practice was mastered by parents for a selected number of key skills. What could be more natural? Could is the operative word. Is teaching these key processes to all not a responsible action to take for our children, their parents, and the needs of our

Social Family? Though it may not be a right, it is clearly a Responsibility to be taken very seriously.

The word 'rights' needs to be placed in the context of the traditions and conventions which spawned them: they follow; they should not be permitted to lead. However, how often in places where written Human Rights gain a measure of respect and real power (legal teeth) do they act mainly to the benefit of 'aggressive' pressure groups and other bullying organizations? Further, big business may be able to squeeze out smaller less wealthy competition being better able to afford the short term costs and changes under the guise of Rights or Health and Safety which they may later be able to safely reject elsewhere. Eliminated competition carries no threat. Believe it or not, formalized rights can operate to the detriment of natural justice, common sense, and respect for independent thought. Freedom of speech is essential to democracy, as is its intelligent and respectful use. Reportedly Charlie Murder, a computer role-play game viewed in 2010 only to be re-vamped and re-launched in 2013, does not permit even a small measure of racial "humour", contrary to the life experiences of Irish, Scots, and Newfoundlanders. It left a 'Scar' on some sensibilities. Elsewhere, the offensive depiction of a Prophet is irresponsible but seemingly permissible to media and entertainers despite the upset it causes to millions. This deep-seated upset inflicted upon some is inexcusable. The depiction of Jesus as a homosexual was apparently equally acceptable to the BBC despite the serious distress that this caused to some. Contrarily, calling an escaping single thief a black bastard is not and leads to disciplinary action; calling him or her white trash is seemingly acceptable. Calling all Welshmen Taffy (after the South Welsh River Taff) is acceptable, while calling a Pakistani a Packi is not; taunting a redhead with abuse and the name "carrot top" appears to be far more acceptable than the label applied to Africans from the Niger River region as Niggers;

all Scots it seems may be called Jocks, and so it goes on. Grow up, people! Where do these controllers of such nebulous shadows come from: more exactly and more importantly, why? Too often these inconveniences are adopted and adapted to suit growing powerful self-interested groups to promote their view of life and to submerge other points of view both for and against. Exploitation is no new problem. They can equally be used to ascribe value where there is little or none. Too frequently these pronouncements of absolutes are manipulated and manipulative. Far too often they may be the tool of hidden forms of abuses. Strategic, yes; right, no.

Identification photographs of active paedophiles near a school or nursery may not be provided nor circulated by the police in the UK, because this would be considered an offence against their privacy and human rights. Not even the Principal nor gate staff may be shown such identifying photographs. Anyone with that sick habit should have lost such 'rights' because he or she failed to respect the 'rights' of the most vulnerable in our human family, the right be an un-abused child. The police should be permitted to exercise fully their Responsibility towards the protection of the vulnerable rather than having to protecting the heartless exploiters. A mother, who is trying to rid herself of a brutal ex-husband, wishes to travel. She wants to change her son's or daughter's name only to find that her new address and the child's school are listed on the document which is sent to the father (England, 2010)! How can that be right, reasonable, or responsible? Meanwhile in Canada (2015), private data collected about individuals for political party data banks do NOT have to be made available to these people. So much for rights of privacy and also transparency.

It is one of the ironies of politics that autocrats take on Responsibilities, for better or worse, while the people of democracies give their Responsibilities away. There are too many candidates in both categories ready to abuse the freedoms and Responsibilities handed to them. Rights are dictated and backed up by processes of state and law and tools of fear and punishment, while active Responsibilities are rationally accepted: fines and prison on the one hand and discussion, and tradition and reason on the other. Personal choice and development results from accepting Responsibilities. Rights arrive via externally imposed dictate, though they sometimes provide a valuable additional source of protection.

For many or even most, the essences of Rights have already been agreed upon. Imposed rights do not demand the same level of social and personal development: rights come from 'them' (external) while Responsibilities are 'mine' (internal). Further, there is a danger that the absolute nature of rights can and does harm the 'socially immature' or naive. Laws are specific; therefore, it is hard to adapt laws to circumstance. Responsibilities are more free, adaptable, and regulated by conscience and tradition as well as local and direct experience. Is that a good thing? Freedom of conscience is a two-way cutting blade, for with it comes the freedom of association. For this reason, support for developing a ground of responsibility is important: appreciation of actual Responsibilities requires a large measure of directive experiences.

Human Rights should promote and facilitate respect and human dignity. They need to imply agreed upon and accepted obligations rather than decreed regulations. Dictatorships, once established, jealously and closely guard their powers and extend their petty regulations and laws through cohorts of self-interested administrators who use and frequently abuse that power. Traditions and respect are crucial to a functioning and contented Social Family. These are passed on by the example of those we have learned to respect. They grow out of, through, and because of very personal experience. Daniel Goleman termed this Emotional Intelligence:

Calm down and think through a problem. Formulate it into words to express what is being felt . Identify a "POSITIVE" outcome. Think of as many ways as you can to achieve this outcome. "Think ahead to the consequences". Decide upon the best plan and go for it. (276)

Our schooling builds us since it adds to our experience and world understanding. It builds upon earlier experience, innate qualities, and following life. Individually, we need to understand our own feelings and behaviour. Yet this is impossible in a school without 'good' discipline and is further complicated by a school with "too many" people being 'bottled up'. We are the result of the building blocks of our personalities shaped by our experiences: our Lego-like emotions, our Lego-like knowledge, and so on. Class sizes should not exceed 20 and schools should hopefully be comprised of about 200 students divided vertically into social teams (Houses in the UK) with a senior student of each social team overseeing their three or four teams and being directly responsible to a Team leader teacher for each team. By graduation all would have experienced being most junior to most senior; held real Responsibilities as Team Seniors, organized teams and events; and been involved in group competitions with the enjoyment of cooperation and the excitement of competition. All would graduate with appropriate behaviour patterns. Participants would have agreed to 'following rules' and experienced the benefits of responsible social order. Further, home life and family would benefit. Inept parenting and schooling damage would be much reduced. Without such a school system, bad upbringing can destroy empathetic experience and confident development and waste away its rewarding Social Family membership. As a side point, our children become part of their own experiences. Parents, workers, and teachers pay for the schools: they are the source. The fact that children are subjected to our bussing system as an economic convenience just does not cut it, despite dedicated drivers. Bring the children home to their communities, where they are known. Feed them properly and responsibly. Shrink the class sizes, lose the busses, and demand quality education. Stop blaming the teachers. It is we who must act and demand for our children's sake and the sake of their futures. Since we accept the current malpractices, it is we who are to blame.

An admirable aspect of Japanese society appears to demonstrate that having central beliefs and being culturally aware may, can, and do merge. Clearly there is a strong and creative culture of respect in the majority of Japan. To treat people with respect encourages them to treat others with respect in turn. This shows so markedly in how Japanese culture honours the elderly, despite their frailties, while highlighting their contribution to 'the now' through their involvement in constructive pasts. They are recognised and sometimes honoured with the title of "national treasures": a worthy goal.

A man or woman is as good as their word. Children need to learn and 'feel' this, and so this truth NEEDS to be taught and encouraged.

<u>Predatory People</u>: Make *your list* with identifying behaviours

TABLE 1

Name or Title	Associated activity or action(s)
1. Bully	Shouts, behaves menacingly, uses violence, screams or threatens in order to control another <u>for some gain.</u> A violent person seeking control of others.

<u>TAXATION</u> for a Caring Role

Following a democratic election, governments gain the right and power to require taxes. This is by virtue of assuming that powerful position as a direct consequence of the so called free vote of The People. Upon election it becomes both their right and responsibility to collect such income because of real need. Through time collective needs replace elitist needs. Representatives for those needs were established by loosely following the traditions of the preceding power structure.

There are needs which justify specified activities. For someone to take money from our wage packet to pay for their pension, luxuries, protection, and health care would seem ludicrous, but we accept this action of governments as part of our social responsibility. This is not called theft, though it can feel like it at times. The pacifist has part of his or her tax used to prepare for and fight wars. The homeless remain homeless while huge amounts are spent on crumbling castles and historical locations. An absolutely honest taxpayer pays for the housing, shelter, food, and additional provisions in prisons complete with medical care for the rapist and murderer. All these are accepted as what should be done by a civilised Social Family.

The collection of funds is ENABLING by its nature, as it enables planned goals to be reached in the promotion of a fulfilling and happy life for all in our Social Family. The achievement of this good life for all, as suggested here, is the purpose and so should be the ambition of successive Parliaments. It is incumbent upon us to establish exactly what these needs are and what this boils down to, and then we must prioritise.

Safe and dependable food supplies, secure shelter, health care, and education enable us to build for ourselves the achievement of a secure and fulfilling life. It is the last of these which demands the greater imagination, variation, and protection. The implications of a fulfilling life have led to establishing a list of finite and simplistic rights. This is a step, but in which direction on the benefits scale? Is something better than nothing, or are these rights the absolute limits and the final goals within the Social Family?

Without safe and wholesome food our health, energy, and life quality are damaged. Thus, those who provide our food needs could be viewed as social heroes. Yet this is not so, for taxation and exploitation abound. How true and how often ignored is the call from the agricultural communities within our Social Family that "Farms Feed Cities!" It would appear, for example, that they receive less protection regarding their production than financially bloated industrial companies who so often supply and support the very members of parliament who have been given the responsibility to protect our food requirements: consortia/conglomerate profits appear to supersede those which the 'all weather' farmers deserve AND need. There seems to be no specific Right to protect farmers, despite their vocation being essential to the wellbeing of us all.

The provision of vast numbers of safe, secure, and comfortable homes in several parts of the world has been a modern miracle. Our homes attest to the skill, imagination, and hard work of the designers and builders. Why then have so many in our society become excluded from this essential resource? Surely equal research, planning, and design for these disadvantaged people is a governmental Responsibility and a right of the dispossessed. Do the disadvantaged no longer matter? Are they not also children of our Social Family? Is their poverty, mental state, or family rejection somehow an eraser of their need and of government's remit to enable protection – what some would class as their right? Does our society not have Responsibilities towards the disadvantaged? Yes, many are very different, but the insides of our homes attest to safety and security for each of us. Why have some been allowed to spiral downward into despair and real poverty? For these disadvantaged people, rights do not equally and actually exist.

The champions of security try to keep our homes and ourselves safe. The police, the armed forces, and the fire services are there for us. Workers in these fields know that their lives may be put 'on the line', but this is the life they choose. For their vocation they gain our gratitude and respect: they serve and sacrifice for the Social Family. Sadly, we too often hear accounts which lack full and reasonable care and equipment provision for these forces with their having paid the price for their dedication and the agents of the government having failed honourably to pay the 'tab', our tab.

HUMAN BEHAVIOUR

Human Behaviours Interflow

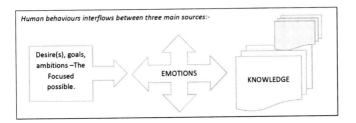

Human behaviours interflows between three main sources:-

Desire(s), goals, ambitions –The Focused possible.

EMOTIONS

KNOWLEDGE

The web of social interaction is a deliberate human construction.

Resonance of communication and mood results from two or more people working together effectively and successfully. Resonance promotes unity and hence achievement. *Dissonance* of mood results from confused communication. This confusion generates a climate of blame or distrust which in turn blocks effective progress. Perception relates to experience and valid awareness coloured by emotion, which in turn affects our goals. When a goal or object is valued or prized, its possession takes on a power. This adds to and builds confidence. Shared confidence even makes trade possible. Knowledge with wisdom empowers the ruler; it is the basis of effective power (PLATO). The strong harmonious group prospers.

If one accepts that standards are necessary for a strong Social Family, then standing up for standards - from small to large - is significant (e.g. manners, letters of thanks, honesty, trustworthiness, clear handwriting, justice, cleanliness, truth, family, and the valuing of life). Adopt, adapt, and improve are what life is about, but vision is required first. Then analyse, plan, and evaluate followed by taking action. Seizing the realistic moment requires a certain maturity: observe, think, act, and be patient.

One may usefully consider to what extent Health Education is central and positive to health care. It seems that health education is only reasonably practical with the stability of wealthy nations where ironically there is often a great lack of exercise and a great weight of anxiety. Apparently, many Polynesians were originally exceptionally healthy thanks to their good weather and plentiful food sources: they did not depend upon planned education or gold reserves, as reported by Captain Cook and other early explorers. We search for the ideal, listening to the persuaders. School uniforms are seen as levelling class differences, as are School House Team Sports, while encouraging a feeling of belonging and co-operation. Uniforms are seen as an aid to constructive voluntary self-discipline by helping people to appreciate and identify with a 'group-identity' and work together constructively. One could surmise that the experience of good schooling could maintain and encourage a greater feeling of responsibility. Taking part in maintaining the quality of a school environment can positively contribute to and spill over into a will for neighbourhood and hospital cleanliness, recognition of the values regarding being trustworthy and efficient, encouraging a sense of responsible co-ownership, and possibly even establishing the basis of healthy food consumption. My experience of supervised dinners at school saw teachers at the ends of every table initiating all sorts of conversation and enjoyment in a calm though noisy environment. Should this be promoted, as the liberals say, to produce 'Change that Works'? Further, my turns in providing weekly playground supervision were comprised of showing students 'new' games, sorting out problems before class time, getting to better know and understand current and prospective students, while also spotting new skills or potential problems and being there to take appropriate action.

HEALTH CARE

In Norway it appears there is one very popular provider of "chilling out" viewing, namely Ambient TV. This following of a ferry for a week with ever-changing views and changes of location, sounds, and impressions was popularly viewed without any demands entailed. Viewers simply soaked it up. Later, watching a long train journey through the mountains proved to be just as popular: a shared mood of peace and progress. This probably supported the improved mental health of viewers. In Canada there are plenty of resources for this kind of relaxed viewing.

A 'happy' life is more assured with good health, which should better enable contentment and a probability of self-fulfillment. One proverb states that:

> **"To be of use in the world is the only way to be happy."**

Usefulness is greatly advanced by good health. This health needs to extend first to the mental state since the mind colours all else, remembering also that the state of the body greatly affects the state of the mind.

A balanced mental state is crucial for cooperative communal action and is supported by visible respect. Governments have a primary Responsibility to provide full health provisions so as to enable all to play a useful role. This does not refer to the low cost of fulfilling day-to-day needs such as cotton wool or aspirins, for these are inexpensive for almost all. Rather, this responsibility is for the otherwise costly care which is too often late in arrival, guarded by form fillers, or denied on grounds of cost or age. Those elected to represent us and protect our interests levy taxes upon necessary medicines and health provisions. Some treatments are placed beyond the reach of a few, and other treatments are placed beyond the reach of many. The withholding of treatments results in continued ill health and absence of necessary care. This seemingly acceptable and 'permitted situation' is a direct consequence of funding. Meanwhile, restoration to full health or improved condition is possible via an alternative treatment. For example, the taking of a pill form medication as opposed to the injected form, the pill being a new improved medication to fight cancer, was compared by the UK Ministry of Health. The less effective standard treatment requiring injections was continued. The pill failed to be funded simply because it failed to fit the previous definition of the treatment: injection. This denied the sick a better proven treatment. Which Rights were denied there!

Child safety is a matter close to most hearts. For this reason, a strong supportive home protects youngsters. Beyond the home-environment, this becomes a very different matter. Child safety becomes increasingly the responsibility of law makers and law enforcers. Currently in Canada and beyond, air flight has yet again come into focus. The practice of restraining seats for youngsters on airplanes is being hotly reviewed. It would be interesting to learn how many problem flights involve infants each year, including how many accidents occurred and if there were any fatalities. These details are relevant. The spin-off could be to highlight a deeper more fundamental problem regarding irresponsible parenting. Next, let us move on to an area which has been seemingly left alone with the status quo maintained. It would be a useful exercise to establish exactly why this area has been ignored. Children travel to school every school day on busses without seatbelts. As they travel, they are able to move around, argue, and even fight. How the poor drivers cope in many instances is a mystery and of great credit to these women and men. The questions are ones of comparison. How many children travel on school buses daily and annually? How many accidents have been reported each week and each year? How many are injured and how many die? Are the children who travel daily on yellow school busses any safer than those who travel on those deeply scrutinized occasional plane trips? Who is expected to pick up the bill for "improvements"? This may well offer a clue: often answers revolve around the availability of cash.

The imbalance between cost and price is related to the demands and wishes of corporations, their profits, and their unseemly bonus structures which appear to be politically protected: the very real power and cost to us of political lobbyists. If so much of our Social Family resources were not wasted on non-essentials, inflated prices, the greed of both the powerful, some of the general public, the idle, and the provision of care to some of the people from abroad, then the total result would provide far more for those deserving fuller help and support but who currently lose out. Again, the weak suffer. Less taxation wastage would lead to less objections and so hopefully less taxation avoidance with the fulfillment of its finer intentions. The system needs to be better understood and observed as fair to any wishing to check this outcome. This goal remains for the future. There should be no significant difference between quality of care or education for the rich and poor which means investing and improving where proven necessary and not simply abolition or removal of a problem by renaming it or closing it down.

Society needs involved, active, and physically and mentally healthy 'People Units'. Trust, which is crucial to a feeling of wellbeing, both encourages and is indicative of mental health. Constructive listening is a factor of and is related to trust and self-respect. To listen and act in a balanced trusting way, rather than dictatorially, signifies personal and social maturity. However, listening and producing balanced responses are skills we learn. Our society values freedom of speech which is a central factor of working democracy; consequently, this needs a 'give and take' compromise in the pursuit and defence of other rights. Constructive calm rather than angry hysteria is called for to achieve balanced and long lasting success. We therefore need to operate a reasonable and responsible approach to both and all.

DIAGRAM 2: Appetites battle with mind

Appetites Battle with Mind.

PREFERENCES		Versus		GREED
DEMOCRACY ⬌	RIGHT ⬌	NATURAL INCLINATION	+	RESPONSIBILITIES ⇨

Payback time for political funding should be less about profit and more about right being done with improved corporate images. The nurses wish it, the doctors wish it, the people need it, and the government has a Responsibility to provide it - no excuses. There seems to be very little reason why this social priority of health care cannot be greatly and quickly improved. Affordable dentistry needs to become a Canadian fact rather than just a dream. Long term care and support need to extend to those championing our security if injured, including those in the military, policing, or firefighting: better still if fully adequate protection, equipment, and manpower were in place. Part of too many failures result from too much administration with their insatiable appetite for time, papers, and resources. Sometimes there exist too many restrictions, demands, and qualification requirements. Further, the high costs charged by many providers of supplies to medical 'centres' reduce the amount of available funding and resources the overworked practitioners have to offer. Maybe a percentage of voting shares in such companies needs to be allocated to the health service itself as the leading buyer, rather than investors, which would provide income from dividends and voting powers on the company boards, even ownership. Less expensive care would require less expensive pension provision and support or rather better support and services for the same cost to people. It is sobering to realize, as quoted by CBC in November 2015, that over 300,000 people use the Ontario food banks weekly with 35% more elderly users…. and winter was very late! There is an imbalance within society: the see-saw of life is too high on one side and far too low on the other.

DIAGRAM 3: Power and the Popular

Control …..Consensus.

| Control | Interference | Consensus | Support |

FINANCIAL POWER.

VERSA / Opposed to Popular Preferences

AGREED? Action Taken

FORMING SOCIAL GROUPS
and Anger Management

Bill Rogers, *You Know the Fair Rule* ISBN 0 273 63277 9

*"No one should be without peer support." (**Rogers**, 6)*

Isolation of individuals or groups causes fear, reaction, dislocation, and even violence. We all need to belong and will find ways of achieving this (*positive reactivity*) or force ourselves into view through antisocial means (*negative reactivity*). Isolates will form distinctive links which may never have occurred without the pain of isolation. Antisocial groups grow, merge, and wrap around themselves the trappings of subcultures such as anti-language, calls, gestures, and chants. They may easily slide into a confrontational position having decided upon their opponent group or groups with inevitable outcomes and self-justification (*supportive fabrication*) playing its pernicious role. Social groups are an all participant mutually valued construct. They are the result of 'give and take' with basic hard core accepted and recognizable behavioural patterns with some fundamentally shared beliefs. The cohesion of social groups lies in an established consciousness along with some subconsciously shared feelings and beliefs which enable an ongoing and 'productive stability' through belonging. Successful attacks upon these, should they prove destructive and over aggressive, could probably result in the group either restructuring if it is strong enough or breaking up into smaller groups and thereby restarting the cycle in several new forms (*adaptive survival*). Consensus and agreement are at the core. Through changes within the group's logical expectations of itself and beliefs, the unsettling of core concerns will induce instability, conflict, and adaptive reactionary change. Through overcoming conflict we become stronger people, but not so when a conflict is manufactured. A society, being a much larger group, will have additional expectations and demands beyond those of smaller and less formal groups: levels of formality will probably depend upon what sort of group goals prevail. Some form of 'historically identifiable' membership recruitment is common which entails shared experience and aspirations as well as statements of belief. Specific 'codiformes' of interaction, called traditions, may play an important role. Traditions need to be understood and allowed as an accepted interference to some individual positions. Membership of a group follows some researched 'evidence' of specific behaviour-outcomes or logic sets. So within the group are preferred accepted mind sets which are inherited, discovered, or imposed. Imposition, it may reasonably be suggested, is the least likely to produce the desired long term affect due to a probable negative reaction to force. Perception and 'sense' play their part. However, the power of what may be sensed and the reality of what is sensed may be at variance and will later cause harm to the group and beyond. Openness and truly free rational discussion is one way to better avoid such dangers and better achieve acceptance.

There is no such thing in nature as Human Rights, but there is an aspect of citizenship in artificially devised law. This distinction is significant, no matter how it is termed. Laws need to be the product of accepted human practice and expectations. These need to rest upon their society and its values, which consequently <u>add</u> the necessary legitimacy, strength, and will to laws for the necessary processes to be effective. It is best if such law is part of the outcomes we wish for, which happily ensures better compliance and acceptance to law. Power will play its part whether welcomed or not. Those who can exercise power through the letter of the law may not consider what 'best serves justice'. Corrupt practices can succeed with the power of finance or blind belief, thus removing the luxury of free choice. Further, obligations can be crowded out by the co-option of attitude prepared to use - or rather misuse - money, law, or politics.

DIAGRAM 4: Forms of Idea Infusion:

Influences Upon Decision.

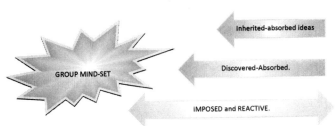

A belief in not belonging, with its isolation, makes breaking the rules and physically attacking the surrounding social form not just probable but the only relief. Groups and individuals who are seriously wishing to be accepted and to enjoy the society which they have joined need help in understanding the accepted norms of that society. They need mentoring and support (Vergotsky's Scaffolding), for it is highly unlikely that they will be able to value the alien behaviours and customs before becoming isolated. To avoid this pain of isolation and insecurity, 'settlement clusters' become established and grow in neighbourhoods. This tendency leads to displacements, suspicion, and scapegoating acted out by the previous unified majority. This state of *Insecure Dependence* (Blatz) needs addressing, for it prevents integration. This causes judgements being made regarding outward appearances and word-sounds: a less than constructive process of getting to recognize and know people from their outside rather than taking the trouble to constructively view the inside character.

Values list: Bill Rogers

Promoting the right environment, access to opportunity, clarity of regulations, and responsibility

Self-discipline, Self-control, and Self-responsibility; *Self-esteem, Self-respect*; equality of treatment, dignity, worth, fairness, justice; *consideration of others, respect, courtesy, tolerance, teamwork, trust, honesty*; pride, effort. (p. 123)

`It would be useful to refer to Rogers' book:

+ Notice the key nature of "Self-" also that... '*humour can defuse tension and help people feel a little less stressed....*' (Rogers, p. 113, L.15).

+ Diagram of "*The framework of our behaviour policy*" (Rogers, p. 133, figure 4.2). An interplay of concepts of Rights over rules, relationships and responsibilities tied in with security, communication, and problem-solving.

+ A Summary Diagram on Holding Accountable (Rogers, p. 156, figure 5.1) in which fairness, responsibility, valuing self-respect, and repair are discussed.

It would surely be both kind and sensible to insist that anyone taking up permanent residence in a new country would in every case commit to learning and using the local language. How can a people communicate, reassure, or support new arrivals who fail to understand what is being said in their daily interactions? To get a feel for this problem, try watching a foreign tongue film without the help of subtitles. Then imagine this situation being a daily experience. It is little wonder that misunderstandings, fear, isolation, and failure to achieve **independent security** result.

CHAPTER 3:

OBLIGATIONS

The sweetest and the strongest creative forces are the ones which are openly and willingly accepted. These should demonstrate fairness, reality, harmony, and confidence. Using the concept of friendship as an example, there is a meeting of minds, a coming together from somewhere else, and give and take are central. It is almost as if the activity of friendship uses some extra energy source and thought process. Consider the logic. Friendship really is an illogical condition, for it demands so much of the friends who have freely entered into an almost total emotional contract which is both demanding and time-consuming. Operating upon levels of mutual support and mutual respect, friendship may well keep self-interest away from any detriment to others - and so it is sacrificial. Friendship is frequently seen to be selfless, empathetic, supportive of a 'good', but also both strongly and sensitively critical. A friend is thoroughly dependable during times of crisis and need. To have a 'true' friend is to be a millionaire. This is one definition of a miracle, but these miracles happen frequently. Both parties know and accept certain obligations and acts of loyalty. Friends are not lost but can be misplaced due to circumstance, only happily to be found again later. To a lesser extent, maybe, this is true of our Social Family.

So who is this 'friend'? Well, it is not simply someone we 'hang out with'. It is not simply someone we go to events with, it is not simply someone we get drunk - or other - with, nor is it simply someone we talk and laugh with. No, friends share an understanding, a mutual bond, and an existence in which both parties are a crucial part. Friendship is not a position of isolation. A friend is a person who cares so deeply for our well-being that they are at peace with us and vice versa, especially when all life seems to be in good order. Friendship has no bearing on colour, religion, or race; it goes far beyond. Friends can share emotions 'freely' and in total confidence. Friends recognize and encourage our strengths and equally recognize our weaknesses and failings. They know how to constructively criticize and repair. A friend avoids anger and helps build confidence and happiness with a security that enables mutual concern for others. Friendship expands our experiences and our understanding. This is a form of mutual belonging.

Human Rights need to be empowered and promoted with more humanity and gentle persuasion which they too lack. Rights tend to become the hammer used to crack the proverbial nut. Sometimes it is the avenue chosen by some individuals to get themselves noticed by the launching of a platform for themselves beyond the expected. When they are imposed, Human Rights exist artificially from the outside. Human Rights need a living environment of agreement to be created so that they may exist within most individuals, through their free agreement, to be fully effective. That does not mean that they are in essence wrong, merely that the view, or the perception of what they can basically force, is wrong. The method needs reviewing. A fully effective

Right needs to be internalized. It needs to be felt. It works when it is a natural part of our personality and belief system: neutrally powering a self-initiating awareness and acceptance. Rights work for those who already exist in an environment which respects the ideals which have already been accepted by the community in general. If willingly embraced, rights successfully instruct their accepted and active adoption in others. Hopefully their need, over time, will shrink and fade. They, like common law, could evolve through free interpretation unfettered by confused emotion. They need to be consistently applied to achieve consistent outcomes. Most people understand the basic requirements of living a lawful life as well as a rightful one. One may reasonably follow one's conscience and informed beliefs through an appreciation and acceptance of current Responsibilities. Without this, rights cannot be enforceable through lack of acceptance.

Obligation = the personal chosen path

Fulfilling our obligations is an act of social recognition of our part in life's play. This is for the courageous, the strong-minded, and the intelligent and so becomes the essence of our 'social glue'. Obligations are the product of group experience, tradition, and awareness, and acceptable and accepted social pressure with a directing internal force.

Responsibilities are the obligations accepted by each individual and group to act in specific ways to achieve specific outcomes for the benefit of the individual and the community. One part rests on group-Responsibilities which relate to the 'value' placed upon carrying out each obligation by the individuals within the group. Such learning is also a function of education and moral teaching. Many Responsibilities are entrusted to Government, with the institutions they promote and manage for us.

Legalistic Rights are the use of legal power in a specific time and situation to address and enforce agreed upon social priorities. These may become redundant or even inappropriate with time as perceptions, needs, and beliefs change. Legalistic rights are specified and fixed, but they cannot be complete. They are summaries missing important details.

Government is the servant of the people directed by group obligations and Responsibilities with these being expressed in each manifesto of promises and law. A belief in natural justice is an advantage but not necessarily practiced. Governments need to have a primary focus upon the three Hs:

> *Housing* – security, a base
>
> *Health* – energy, fitness, and nutritious food
>
> *Head* – leadership, education, and reflective logic

These are the basic requirements to forge a secure and happy life through and because of governmental activity.

DIAGRAM 5: Emotions and Balance.

Emotions and Balance.

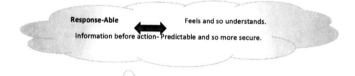

Response-Able   Feels and so understands.

Information before action- Predictable and so more secure.

Obligations and so Responsibilities

SOCIALLY RESPONSE-ABLE = Responsible: To be reliable and trustworthy, also able to react to other people's needs and thus dependable. This requires a conscious mental state which follows reflection and mature soul searching. It is consistent and strong.

A responsible person is exactly that. A responsible person at times requires action and must be a leader to avoid inappropriate action. Responsibility, which comes from within our minds, allows us to make thoughtful choices and take constructive action.

Before something is achieved or produced, a course of action must be decided based upon some knowledge and knowing. One must know that the problem is able to be resolved, and then carry through the practical plan by following appropriate checks and reviews.

The 'sovereignty' of <u>one</u> specific right can too easily be assumed and asserted without proper thought for other Responsibilities and rights. It is almost like a first past the post situation where the first to call upon their right wins over all other later claims. So, if you assert one Right first, you win. Further there are those self-appointed 'defenders of rights' who fail to appreciate that their actions can cause interference, be counter-productive, and can even cause harm. Let the people speak for themselves when they are able; by all means get involved if they are incapable of doing so. Such is the Responsibility of us all to help the weak be free of injustice.

Socially we appear to be looking out for everyone else's well-being. All are truly part of the whole. Weakness in any part weakens the whole; therefore we need to care about values, cultures, feelings, as well as historical worth. However, this does not mean that we forget our own. As an Anglo-Saxon, European product I need to recognize the vast progress, yes progress, which Europe has enabled throughout the world's north, south, east, and west. New ideas, either within our personal culture or beyond, need to be understood, accepted, and embraced over time to better promote good outcomes and to stick. All cultures and people make mistakes. We have to learn from these mistakes and move on while also celebrating past successes. All cultures bring their gifts.

Industrial Consumer Responsibilities

Manufacturing Producers bring safety and quality Responsibilities with specific and well publicised Health and Safety measures in place. So many possible carcinogenic harmful emissions from production must be dealt with, but not through irresponsible outsourcing to third world countries without education or protections being in place. If this occurs, then the public is honour bound to boycott such products, manufacturers, and associated companies. Government action, litigation, and fines remove the crushing burden of seeking justice by the individual. Unfortunately, since some occupations involve risk, sufficient insurance or else tax money provisions need to be in place so as to be automatically made available to safeguard workers' and their dependants' security at times of loss or injury. Three examples of risky occupations are asbestos sheet installation removal, armed forces, and the police.

'Workers' in offices or in workshops should not be expected, prompted, or permitted to place themselves in situations of risk unless they are in exceptional circumstances where they are needed to voluntarily protect others or to rescue those who are already greatly endangered. Such is the trained calling of the rescue fire department. Further, there is an obvious need in all forms of employment for adequate rest time, free time, special family time, health protection, and safe machine operational training and checks. It is no surprise that the work requirements of some lorry drivers, reps on the road, and those working all hours holding down two or more jobs cause accidents. Here legal protection is essential which requires the active support of consumers. Workforce Responsibilities extend further than what may be fully appreciated with a duty of reasonable care. Further, some may rightly wish not to join the workforce at all, being needed to daily ensure the wellbeing of others such as young children or the elderly without opposing pressure from feminist or other pressure groups.

Since available resources are limited, there is also a question of natural justice: not in the legal sense of a 'right to be heard' on both sides and a fair and impartial trial, but in the sense of what is morally and defensibly the right course of action to be taken. Yet again the formalities and dictates of Law produce tensions. Outdated laws can cause failures of 'natural justice' until a completely intolerable train of events demands changes in legislation. The use of Rights without common sense and flexibility can too easily produce situations of unfairness and harm. Discussions aimed at doing the right thing can be aided greatly through an instrument of 'greater responsibility'. So, to which is the greater responsibility owed: the mentally ill; the comfort level of criminals; effective use of limits 'for the benefit' of the elderly, young, and infirmed; Green obligations; lifespan products; or primary producer income, e.g. milk or affordable justice for all? There is a 'duty to act fairly', but how do we define and settle that? "To act fairly *dependent on the context*" (Canada) seems a clear enough starting point.

In the context of the examples above, one can quite easily select an example which <u>deserves</u> full help and support while another does not. This is referred to as 'necessary prioritisation', 'social prioritisation', or more delicately, the taking of selective and decisive action to act fairly. The deserving get as the deserving should, period!

Sequences of events demonstrate an underlying pattern. Legal Statutes intentionally 'fail' to have the flexibility that is required for 'naturalistic' justice. Although the starting point may be seen as admirable, where does it finish up and after what sort of journey? Life is a continual process of improvisation. Interpretation is key and misinformation is the stumbling block. So, add up the meanings both seen and unseen, the clear and the "spin offs", and then act if you must but with a sound foundation of consideration. Discussion is clearly a good way to start sorting out ideas. Remember that we all talk rot from time to time, as does the law. Since anyone cutting off conversation uses an action which is final, minds can no longer meet and explore and consequentially they become insular, brooding, and isolated. So, for the intelligent there is a responsibility to continue conversing to produce those *idea patterns* recognizing useful *idea clusters.* Within a communicative approach lies many keys to positive progress. When unheard, who can be the expert in such an ever-changing process? Who makes visible the silent and sometimes dark aspects of an uncommunicative society, a community of seeming secrecy, with its actions remaining hidden in fact? It is so much more constructive to be socially interactive and supportive to change. For example, how else are family failures to be addressed? Disconnection is the enemy of the Social Family, as it opens the door to anger, isolation, and extremism. If disconnect occurs, how can we assess and discover which form of help is needed to offer positive support? Too much anger is out there in the world due to 'social disconnect'.

Beliefs, race, age, ability, language, body language, social interaction, or tradition, to name a few, can all be the cause of a disconnect. If an individual is not welcomed or accepted as a meaningful partner in the Social Family, what else can we 'reasonably' expect? How inexcusable is the 'in your face' attitude that rejects the language, costume, and traditions of a host nation and so becomes self-harming? Every time we lose a member of our community, we become weaker for it. We need to encourage individualism, diversity, and variety and so stay connected. Since the world is formed by our communities, we need to be active members of our own 'adopted' community to help maintain its strength. We adopt social norms because we need a conscious choice to belong and so to feel we belong. If all do so while being aware of the beneficial agreed upon interconnections that are needed, then society will become so much stronger, mentally beneficial, and healthy. Because division is such an effective negative force, it is best avoided.

TOLERANCE: Multiculturalism Versus Extremism with Assimilation and Acceptance

I was very lucky to have grown up in an exciting age of social experimentation, but the world is still paying a heavy price for the resulting disconnect that this period caused. More than just experimentation, this period produced action. A brash confidence of new hope led to the review, revision, and rejection of tradition. A period of building was followed by consolidation. Symbols and signs of individual character abounded. While these could have been so valuable and constructive, sadly they ran like a derailed steam train: very powerful but also destructive.

'Compulsory Miseducation' was a focusing book title available when I was studying. The Untried became adopted in several forms of infectious academic madness. One entrenched view abused the other and the battle of titans was allowed to ensue. Our Responsibility to provide secure consistency to the young was forgotten. Then came "Real Books": Oh please! Academic and political names were made through the 'un-understandable' while too many valuable tried and tested moulds were allowed to be broken.

Respect needs to be mutual. However, different cultures, experiences, and expectations will 'understand' and interpret behaviours differently. The baselines of behavioural certainty in each separate group will differ. Here lies the difficulty and the need for mutual respect, namely trust, through which are formed better abilities to achieve clarity of communication and respect. So, we all need to step back and permit a give-and-take approach if we are going to AGREE to live together, rather than join in battle. Together is a good word. Having friends and acquaintances who are Christian, Jewish, Bahia, Muslim, Buddhist, Sheikh, Jains, and Zoroastrian, I never once found we could not interact happily together until the inverted prejudicial and arrogant politically correct, self-appointed thought-police arrived, in the guise of a sane and sincere man or woman and convinced in their being without prejudice: absolutely right, and so uniquely qualified, by themselves, to be a self-proclaimed defender of the oppressed and abused. Get a life, person. Interferers need to respect that these good people are not weaklings. They can do life for themselves; they are not so sad and weak that they need you to put in your destructive oar! Yes, sometimes people need help and support, but not from someone who is intent upon causing an emotional storm to break over it all!

Social Responsibility

Anne Marie Fermenti (CBC- 8.30, March 18th, 2010) reported conditions following Indonesia's tragic Tsunami in

2004. Workers were trapped and unable to return home. In the "reconstruction efforts", hired labour was subcontracted out and reportedly some were treated as slave-labour. The Red Cross made cash payments for legitimate help, much of which failed to reach these unfortunates. Their 'rights' were not met because there was no acceptance of Responsibilities in place. The administration must therefore be seen as either being misrepresented by reports, ignorant of their duties, criminally corrupt, or profiteering gangsters. There are those who uplift people whilst others are evil 'glue downers'.

This internationally permitted harm and abandonment of civilized and civil standards has no bearing on any Human Right. Such rights had long been realized as obligations and Responsibilities and were in place long before. They fully existed; they were and are there. Without individual Responsibility, no right is worth the paper it may be written upon. Responsibility is inherent to internal standards and accountability. Rights are a formalising of our interpersonal Responsibilities, a sort of external book of rules. Without accepting our Responsibilities to each other as members of the Social Family, rights count for nothing and are just so much wind. Further, without the checks and balances of fully considering the broad range of active Responsibilities, excesses in Law cannot be avoided or prevented any more than the harm caused by self-interest. Using the law through Human Rights trials can too easily yet again become the proverbial mallet used to crack a nut. Interpretation relevant to time, place, and circumstance is wise and right. So, during a time of conflict, which reaction has dominance, rights, or circumstance with an appropriate response?

Enlightenment has been suggested as an illumination of awareness, but it could equally

be shown to have been blinding oncoming
headlamps at night, on full beam!

Facial expressions clearly communicate emotions. Facial movements display personality and emotions and may precede action. These 'recognitions' of facial expressions relate directly to our memory and experience. A smile to one person is a welcome; to another a smile is a 'come on'; and to another a smile is criticism. In this way the same facial expression can mean very different things to different people. How we respond to the facial expressions of others is an outcome of our own mental state, character, experience, and expectations. Similarly, interpretation of rights can be misapplied beyond what an individual right expresses: truer to the words rather than *the spirit*. Responsibilities can achieve similar spiritual ends but from a different source. In both Responsibilities and Rights, awareness and education are of considerable benefit providing that the proper emotional balance is there. An awareness and discussion of broader implications linked with experiences is useful and needs to be both encouraged and developed. However, it is too easy just to quote Rights as if that were the end of the matter. Use your brain before resorting to the dictates of brawn!

Imagination is a journey into the
possible, arrogance is the closing of it.

War, Terror, and Refugees

Sadly the oldest profession after the forager-hunter may well be the fighting man. With that, the refugee soon followed. The tragedy of those forced to leave all they have built, those they love, and the places of their most cherished memories continues. The madness of warfare grows due to the madness of science, the powerful and the persuaders, and those seeking both wealth and 'position'. This madness continues because awareness of our 'humanity' with its Responsibilities and obligations has become lost and submerged. Seemingly the aggressive will always be with us, but it is when they combine that the strongest response for self-defence is called for. If the responders seem to have no hope of success, then 'relocation' is probably is the best of three evils: suffer, submit, or flee. In 2014, 2015, and into the future the evil has grown around Iraq, Syria, and regions of Africa with millions dead, without hope, displaced, and broken. These crying souls are mentally placed beyond words of comfort and action is required, as it has been in the Congo for decades. We mention these people in conversation as THEM: they are apart. However, THEY are part of the 'we' of the human race and the Social Family. From before Alexander 'the Great', otherwise known in several regions as 'the devil', we may go beyond Old Testament Genocides, persecution of Christian minorities (victims of earlier crusades in Europe), 'The Terror' of the French Revolution, clearing of the Scottish Highlands to replace people with sheep, famines, droughts, Stalin, Hitler, Pol Pot, Assad, ISIS, and maybe Putin (which time will show). The abuse of society has developed with growing implications. The damage to our Earthly Ecology by so many 'scientific' wars will probably remain incalculable. The same is true for the price of business conglomerate 'warfare'. However, the hidden suffering and hopelessness can be unearthed and clearly seen due to the concern, selfless bravery, dedication, and professionalism of individual 'real' reporters within the media. We can no longer plead ignorance, for only the emotionally dead can avoid being aware of and feeling deep sympathy and empathy for these suffering people of all ages.

Yes, the able could stay and resist by fighting back, but like the brave people in a Northern Nigerian village they would find that knives and working tools are no match for heavily armed deranged aggressors. These Nigerians made a bold stand, but they lost. The cowards they faced knew well they would make their warped beliefs prevail through rape, torture, and theft. The aggressors' murderous progression was only through the bad luck of the victims . The equipment the terrorist thugs had planned for and silently gathered, with the support of lunatic arms salespersons from elsewhere, enabled this inhuman garbage to grow. Sadly many idealistic and fine people were to be deluded, infected, and dragged down by their words. Scum collects scum with the unwary. This is not only a news story from Africa but an agonising historical account of reality.

Floods of refugees wash the shores of Europe: some are dead while most others are alive, or half-alive. Some have walked for seemingly eternity, in all weathers and with all forms of shortage, to lands where a walk to the shops can be thought of as a chore, even driving there in a car! What can be done and what should be done? How do we ensure their survival? How do we create those necessary conditions and powers to do so in a happy cooperating future? This is our responsibility to plan well and to demand well beyond mere Rights.

The need for a Truly New-formed United Nations which is active in their resolve to finally stop the slaughter is essential. Different national traditions will in their own time converge. Imposing our ways can do and has done more harm than good. Convergence needs time and patience. Regional, linguistic, and international co-operation and understanding have succeeded in many countries and this is growing. Political and national mergers are happening. A reformation of this body of United Nations, or of some other body, needs to become a reality and not just an ideal. In Syria the people's call should from a moral standpoint have produced a very different response from its leaders and from the world. Too much self-interest and too much 'thoughtless' opposition were seen to effectively create the current conditions. We know societies evolve and change, and Syria is no exception. Predictably, such a viewing led to reviewing Syrias's History and that of the region. Similarly, the even greater earlier sufferings of the Chinese people under Mao and his followers might not have come to pass if the displaced legitimate predecessor to the last ruler had been able to follow through on his wish to emulate the British Constitutional Monarchy. If this had occurred, the new Empress - the last monarch of China - would probably never have arrived in power with the support of those more powerful. History is made, as well as rewritten, and there can be a way for the world to settle the question of malignant dictatorships. Wave your magic wand, I hear some say. Yet there is no such hope. The first stages were begun long ago. Good will and imagination are required to continue this task which could be termed the Third World War. This war for human dignity, freedoms, security, and happiness for all is currently mostly needed in poorer nations, till we join them. We are one family with two primary Responsibilities: to each other and to the Earth's ecological future.

Permitting refuges to arrive at the unknowable without a recognition of the need for action to heal the cause is at best sheer stupidity. Their situation, in our world of mass communications and data banks, is one of never being able to place their experiences behind them, and likely not for generations to come. Further, the remaining memories for those left behind will linger. Dispossessed descendants of Highlanders of Scotland who settled in Eastern Canada still recount their sad histories. The Palestinian situation seems forever irresolvable. For these and many other situations there seems no imminent termination, no peace. The 'histories' passed down suffer from embellishment and fact confusion. There is many a settler's descendant, in Canada, who confuses their story of ancestral free choice to relocate with that of others who were forced to relocate. An example of historical confusion is of an uprising in Colonial Boston USA that was started by an English soldier killing a settler. This appears to have been two Irishmen who had engaged in an earlier argument and it could well have been an opportune settling of the score, in a later stand-off situation, by the serving soldier who was one of the pair.

Refugees clearly travel away for good reason, or else why would they bother! The return of refugees to their homeland becomes more unlikely over time. The economic migrant Viking, for example, remained in England, Scotland, and Ireland. The Huguenots fleeing from religious intolerance did not return home either. Putting down roots is not usually a temporary situation: the further those roots go the more unlikely a change. It seems reasonable to envisage that most of the people living within Western Democracies have at least two to three times the quantity of what they need. Some of this affluent waste could be channelled to those in desperate need. As both demand, disorder, and dislocation increase, how soon will it be till this is rebalanced through lack of natural resources, overcrowding, war damage, the spread of epidemics and worse? Many constructive solutions are needed, but all will fare far better if they are born from firm convictions and belief in Responsibilities rather than coercion which so easily leads to growing violence. Blessings are extended by those more fortunate world citizens who welcome and help support new arrivals in their more fortunate countries, but this sadly will change with numbers, stories, and misunderstandings. Such welcomes need provisions and reassuring smiles with the new hope they can bring. However, another huge task being asked of shell-shocked, exhausted, and sceptic refugee people is to understand and fit in with a totally different way of life and new thought-processes they can have no way of knowing. The hardest battle will be when the personal 'locational' goal is achieved and understanding the ways and mindsets of the host people begins, especially when they are further isolated by language. Time is fast running out.

In summary, following is an outline of a plan for better integration of refugees.

> *A Refugee is a member of the Human family trying to escape from too many unacceptable experiences with their associated emotional and often terrifying consequences. Some choose regional relocation, others choose relief via belief systems, while yet others rationalise acquiescence with the opposition.*

Even at this tragic time, a refugee's entry into another political region is not a right. Rather, it is an obligation or responsibility for the receiving community to care for humanity as members of the Social Family. To force residency in another's house or homeland is an act of aggression. Being dictatorial is an invasion of person and property with the strong forcing themselves upon the weak. Just because one is a refugee does not mean one is necessarily weaker than those beyond who are being affected. Being the weaker in one situation does not necessarily mean that one is the weaker in another, as History teaches. How then to create the condition with a reasonable prospect of success and peace?

There needs to be clear agreement, from the start, between the two parties regarding clear actions and obligations. This is a realistic position and one which garners a better chance of proceeding well. An 'Open House' is a nice idea but unrealistic if peace, order, and a happy outcome are to be achieved.

The use of force constitutes an invasion: no less.

PRINCIPLES OF IMMIGRANT ENTRY IN EMERGENCIES

1. Upon arrival of immigrants, plan for reduction of trauma through counselling, safe care, and dwelling provision.

2. Establish recruitment and training of immigrant members of security and supportive personnel available to those arriving after a set period of time for immigrants to personally readjust. They have suffered greatly!

3. If there are language differences, daily provision of language classes in speaking, reading, and then writing should be available. Language and literacy skills are deemed essential for both males and females.

4. Medical clinics run by doctors and nurses should be provided with the majority of personnel at all levels fluent in immigrants' languages and, if possible, containing significant numbers from the same cultural backgrounds.

5. Plan for weekly entertainment typical of the host nation and region. Hopefully these activities are both fun and constructive.

6. Provision of a planned community familiarisation program of the welcoming country's customs, expectations, and traditions in which newly arrived immigrants take a respectful role.

7. Following the above, in time no residency should be granted without proven language and cultural knowledge of the host country.

8. Time of remaining to become 'resident' for permitted legal residency, which may relate to certain conditions rather than a fixed timescale, clearly explained and understood with any other available options provided.

*The eventual outcome is the reality
and not just in a flood of words.*

• • • • • • •

CHAPTER 4:

THE WORLD

Maud Barlow, *"Blue Future"* (Ends of the Earth series)

Maud Barlow speaking in Yellowknife, available on YouTube.

COUNCIL of CANADIANS - Hydrological Cycle concerned with Social, Environmental and Health of our Democracy.

Target Outcomes and Ecology

The search for what makes life worthwhile is a search for processes ensuring quality of life both for mind and body, assuming the body survives.

The purity of the air we breathe, the quality of the food we eat, unpolluted ground and seeds we use for agriculture, and the seas we fish exist for us, but then again, maybe not. These essential intakes are what build us, forming our very fabric. Our health directly depends on these materials. Society rises and falls as a result of these. Far too many millions have died as a result of our abuses and irresponsible practices which will do away with countless millions more: forget any Rights. We do not have an automatic right to a future; conversely, many Responsibilities and Obligations will need to be fulfilled if there is to even be a future. There is not just *the web of life*, or an ecological interconnectedness, but also a <u>web of society</u>. Playing with nature is a game of Russian roulette which produces either relief or death. Fill the air with poisons, and what else can result but death? Turn up the thermostat of our planet, and what else can result but death? Alter scientific research and change genetic structure to improve *profitability*, and what else follows but death?

Disregard for water conservation reflects the apathy of ignorance. We cannot survive without water and so we should value it as much as good air quality, but we take both for granted and so will pay the price in time. Wasteful taps rush water into sinks faster than necessary as industrial processes, intensive farming, and vast pipelines and containers reduce the availability of clean water. Electricity is used wastefully to light up areas downtown at night when no workers are 'in house'. Street lighting makes them safer, but the lighting installed often goes well beyond what is needed, thereby blocking out a beautiful soul-rewarding view of the stars. Domestic dryers and blowers raise the use of fuels. Considerable quantities of irrigated wasted foods get tipped into black bags or other forms of disposal. Lorries rush here and there when trains would be more efficient for the long haul. Resources are squandered, with our future the victim. I shudder to imagine what future generations will think of our criminal negligence.

In Yellowknife, Maud Barlow, Chair of NWT Council of Canadians, speaks clearly and logically about the obvious danger to the world's fresh water prospects in the future. Our elected governments do have a clear obligation to us all to protect our natural resources, particularly clean air and water. In the global south a child dies every three seconds due to water problems and water pollution. Barlow uses the example of USA Detroit in which 80,000 to 90,000 people had their water cut off by the companies as they were hit by unemployment and poverty. That many politicians renege on their Responsibilities is a sad fact. Water is being sold as a commodity by investors and big business, for example Switzerland's Nestlé. This privatisation of water is spreading quickly to benefit industrial and commercial demands. By the year 2050 it is predicted that there will be between nine and ten billion people needing water along with the associated growth in farming and industry. China reported over 50,000 rivers in 1960, but this number has now dropped to under 23,000 with demands placed upon those countries nearby. In time, rivers starting in China will not survive to flow beyond. Further, those flowing into China will become the focus of conflicts. Flood farming replaces large areas of dry farming when ground water is available. There is a huge underground water filled aquifer in the western states of the USA, or rather there was, with over 20,000 bore wells which enabled flood farming methods to supply the USA and significant parts of the world with its produce. Production has already fallen by some 50%, Barlow reports, and will be eliminated in our lifetime (prediction of the USA Agricultural Department). Barlow focuses upon the once huge Aral Sea/lake, in Russia, which has been reduced to 10% of its original size. If similar use were made of the Canadian-USA Great Lakes, it is predicted that they would be bone dry in 80 years. I believe that this would cause a horrendous effect upon our Canadian climate. Regarding the rise in sea levels, Barlow states that one-quarter is due to "displaced" land water. Barlow further makes the point that water pumped out of the ground is doubling every 20 years. There is little to be optimistic about in the future, bearing in mind the piping of "Canadian" water to the USA and the growing Oil Fracking developments with its demonstrable injury to local health, ground water contamination, and beyond.

Vast quantities of pollutants, or poisons to use the *avoided* term, have been spread and continue to be spread around the world with the help of shipping, for example. Some pollution is air borne, some is water borne, others have gradually formed, and much is birthed in factories and our homes. Whole ecosystems have been dangerously reduced while others have been pushed to the edge of extinction and beyond. Industrialism seems to be saying we have the Right to do so. Our Obligations and Responsibilities seem to be absolutely clear here. Our very web of life is being destroyed thread by thread, by us! Each is doing their destructive bit in almost every home. The food chains we require are only temporarily meeting our needs, but depend upon conditions in nature which must be able to repeat themselves. Currently an alarming quantity of plastic micro particles are increasingly appearing in our food and disturbing our continuing food chain. This Echo of life needs to be valued, understood, and maintained. Once it maintained itself, but now it is less so. As Lois Little said, "…water is life."

With vast acreage of cash cropping, the massacre of nature has evolved into a downward spiral from balance and sustainability towards who knows what: the stuff of science fiction becoming science fact. By building over some of the best farmland, our chances for survival are being buried brick by brick through this squandered resource. Cleaner rivers will not alone revive a sickly ocean world. In too many of Canada's beautiful lakes, particularly the big five, poisonous chemicals make it very unwise to eat the fish from those waters. During storms with their onshore winds, one wonders how far inland we must go to be absolutely safe from possible danger from the fine spray. We have been informed that over 30% of pollution build up is from shipping in the last ten years. Sulphur pollution of the air in many places is over 1600 times greater due to trucking fumes and cargo ships. CBC reported in one programme that there are 62,000 Canadian registered ships from fishing to cargo. Over 90% of the pollution is from the larger cargo ships and cruise liners. So, what is the priority here? What is to be done? The cost for cleaner fuelling is immense and would have to be passed on with a possible rise of 30%, if 2008 predictions are correct. Maybe the return to local shops with local farm production is the inevitable clean future. Possibly the slogan will change from Farmers Feed Cities back to Farmers Feed Villages. It would be interesting to check out how much of what we have in our homes is nice but not really essential, despite what the advertisers wish us to believe with their "I Want That" slogans. The rise and fall of gas prices tells us nothing about the cost of pollution and its effect upon our climate and everything else. Destruction of jungle, wetlands, hedgerows, breeding stock, and interference with DNA all promise a hideously unpredictable future which will deny our descendants countless as yet unrecognized or undervalued benefits – with everything simply swept away and lost forever. With a more Active and Responsible attitude there might be a good future ahead to replace a very worrying and unpredictable one at present, despite its Rights to things which then may be impossible to secure or even hope for.

It would be useful and instructive to carefully consider what happiness actually needs and is. What makes for contentment and quality of life? For which losses and for what gain? People who think differently are often viewed with concern, amusement, or even fear. They are `odd-balls` rather than individuals; `cranks` rather than visionaries; spreaders of `doom and gloom` rather than early warnings. It would probably be wiser to look for value in our eccentrics and their eccentricities which may be relevant to life and survival!

Adam Gobnick fashioned the phrase: "Raising our children is our second life"; however, this may no longer be relevant due to the actions of the past three generations and ourselves. Our descendants should have a right to survive, so let us do it right for them as a responsibility and an obligation. Further, it is their right to not be saddled with a Politically Confused, also termed incorrectly politically correct, world. To exist in a world where we may make mistakes is more natural. We would understand and respect differences, be able to abhor and shun the bully, and actively protect the weak. We need to get back to simpler happier times. This return to past ways might help us restore the right to be young, to play outside, to be provided with the security of appropriate known and fair discipline, and to have safe boundaries. All of this is achievable by viewing empathetically and intelligently 'Through the children's gates with their gaze' - a nice turn of phrase by Adam Gobnick. One strong possibility with full mechanisation, robotic labourers, and falling world populations becoming standard is subsidised parenting for those parents who are brave enough to take on that responsibility. This would enable a parent or two to remain with their own children and mentor and support their development.

•

Defining an expected outcome for almost any relevant action requires a vast process of planning, fact gathering, and interpretation. Jumping in too quickly with a target decision without either looking for or considering the relevance of what has been defined as centrifugal (outward moving) or centripetal (inward moving) factors and forces is to encourage bad judgement and a probably wrong outcome. What influences a situation could be termed *the line of information*. Part of this line includes any relevant *emotional content* which will have its *influence of bias* and will skew the resulting decision. Identify the ways in which a specific situation is being influenced and address how these are key factors of the almost organic quality of 'happening'. Simply quoting and insisting on the basis of rights alone is to use a bench saw for eye surgery! Activities are permitted as a right, irrespective of the danger from misinformation or inappropriateness. This is not a good way to achieve an objective, no matter how seemingly "lord-able". Balanced and accurate information is crucial to factually forming the broader consequences of conscience, Responsibilities, and chosen `moments` to act.

Continued global warming and an industrial treadmill for humanity seems inevitable right up to extinction. Vast population growth fuels ecological costs and an ever growing dependence on industrial output, energy, and process. We must come to our senses regarding both industrial production and exploding populations. The destructive certainty of both need not become humanity's end, but is the most probable outcome. Rights will count for nothing in the coming battle for living space and resources as this species and most others tramp downwards to termination. We have so much and learn so little, but we are not powerless puppets dancing towards inevitable doom. Recycling is an essential step and works also as an educator for the whole population. However, we have come to a time when we must do far, far more. Built-in obsolescence needs to be seriously revised. Factory output and work times could then be reduced with less annual time spent heating and lighting indoors. Energy needs and raw material demands would fall. Establishing local production where possible would provide employment, mass transportation would be reduced, and quality of food would be better fitted to purpose. Redirecting advertising focus and sales pressure would result in falling demand, waste, and industry. Growth in local production and greater use of repairs rather than replacement would stabilize the population as well as production. Such a combined strategy would bring carbon emissions and pollution more quickly under control while improving the quality of life.

EXAMPLE: *Cars Production and Human Costs* → worker twice daily cars travel →

Unproductive travel time → Congestion ← Transport fuel → Exhaust fumes → fatigue, etc.

PRODUCTION:

Inputs: ←steel, plastics, electronics ←workers' cars + discount ← R&D Research and Development ← inventory

Cost: training → plant → factory site and tax → raw materials → fuel extraction → purification → storage and more transportation

Inputs: ←workforce + international foods = extra production costs ← manufacturing and energy costs ←expensive package and storage + energy ← trees and paper + printing ←water + relocated inside foods ← pesticides (industrial)← transport

The fuel problem is one full of possibilities and choices. It would be interesting to find a 'rule of thumb' method of working out the wasted fuel in traffic jams and also per 10 kilometres/hour increase in speed. Toronto could boast the highest level of "fuel use without progress" every day in Canada: the 401 Highway alone from 3:00 to 7:30 PM must add up to an astronomical amount of wasted fuel and unnecessary pollution. Now multiply that twice a day and all around the world! If car speeds were reduced to a maximum of 50 kilometres per hour, then rail and bus transit travel would become economical, destination hire car firms would greatly prosper, and dependence on importing fuels and commodities would shrink. Further, electric or hydrogen cell cars would be able to travel further and the journeys would be far safer. Less cars on the roads would reduce congestion, road-kill of all sorts, and truck problems........all achievable for the common good.

Carbon dioxide and methane gases produced by livestock farms are a concern regarding their contribution to global warming, or possibly a goodly number of this persuasion are 'active' vegetarians! Whatever the cause for concern, current trucks, trains, ships, abattoirs, fast food outlets, shops, and factories achieve very many times more than the animal carbon output. There is also speculation about promoting genetically manipulated protein farms which would necessitate huge fuel requirement: would this reduce carbon footprints, or would it cause huge cash crop farm estates with greater transportation `costs` and higher profits for relevant consortia? We are told that whole tower blocks is the future for reducing the heating costs of buildings. This form of suggestion needs to be clarified, for if these enclosed buildings have to cope with periods of sunny warm days in summer following winter fuel use, the overall fuel demand will increase and may not provide any savings. Further forced air flow spells more trouble. Will there be health risks and other costs due to these closed environments? The people and workforce within will become accustomed to almost tropical temperatures year round and their home temperatures and energy requirements will increase. Energy reduction need not be so drastic.

Street lighting could be designed to be 'sensitive' to the ambient light in the sky and relevant to the numbers using our roads and sidewalk pavement. Is there a reasonable case for a slower vehicle night time maximum speed requiring less lighting? Every other street light could be on one of two separate circuits so that lighting and energy consumption could be reduced between, for the sake of argument, one and four a.m. Many villages and country highways and roads manage with no street lighting at all. What would the savings be?

Home or local drop-off point incinerators, with smoke filters, could be developed to burn off trash waste, thereby reducing the need for frequent heavy diesel using trash wagons/dust cart collections. Smaller, more efficient local machines could become the norm with a stronger recycling ethos to generate financial resource for local governments, including energy output. An insistence could be placed upon more eco-efficient goods travelling over a maximum specified distance, with other goods being sent most of the way by train. This would be better than a system of long-distance trucks with their road damage, policing vehicle upkeep and maintenance, and air pollution! Yes local loading and unloading bases/depots would be needed. Potentially a number of currently unemployed workers could staff these centres. Local delivery in efficient electric or hydrogen vans could operate from the rail collection depots. Smaller is better, as local is more lovely. However, the future will dim if we do not accept our Responsibility to ACTIVELY support environmentally aware organizations like the 73 Chapters of the Council of Canadians. If not, this freedom to squander Nature and permit Investor State RIGHTS and 'land-water' grabs will continue on an accelerating downward spiral to disaster: we are a passenger-filled airplane intent on flying straight ahead despite the mountain in our way. This is little to do with Rights but a lot to do with survival. The pace of change can be equally socially destructive.

Avoidance, Waste, and Decay

Alvin Toffler, *Future Shock*, ISBN 0 330 02861 8

Disconnect from society can be achieved intentionally or through wrong (unacceptable) habits. According to Toffler, this is "A disease of too rapid change". Conversely, disconnect from society can be a useful part of relaxation and recuperation. However, if overdone, disconnect leads to a reclusive and isolationist way of life that is divorced from reality and constantly avoided Responsibilities. To be an effective Social Family member, an individual needs to firstly understand and prioritize their own needs. With thought and action, the most effective people are able to achieve this. Avoidance obviously does not achieve this. Since an effective individual has a greater chance of experiencing self-fulfillment and happiness, that is the better way to go. With effective interaction it is easier to face up to life by drawing upon a sensible blend of realism and optimism. Television can promote this constructive and fulfilling journey. However, television is a child too long out of control.

There are a number of forms of avoidance in which Responsibilities are ignored. All around us people are cutting themselves off from their communities for greater percentages of their lives. Television has largely replaced family evenings, music making, and discussion. Fast food removes related cooperative home activities. MP3 players and headphones shut out an unwanted world, while going out socially to sporting events, playing a sport, and visiting the theatre and even the cinema are interactions only infrequently enjoyed together. The infamous couch potato lives in a personal and probable self-centred bubble of 'watching the box'. If married, the couch potato is less of a partner and is ever increasingly growing apart. Both bodily health and mental health suffer. TV producers quote audience viewer figures, but these do not show value or benefit. Some of the most "popular" programs are based on hysteria or spite with no long term enjoyment. Real social interaction is necessary for a healthy empathetic society. Ours is becoming isolated and brutalised.

Basically we all operate in similar ways until we choose how to make a difference by how we behave. Reality can easily be replaced by all sorts of fantasy. Spite, violence, and abject stupidity become focusing human traits. These in television are experienced without the consequences needed to modify behaviours. Individuals and groups simply stray into observed patterns of taught behaviours. Such visual learning is quick and sadly efficient. Much of comedy has become gratuitous spite typical of the bully: it is often loud, unsubtle, intellectually un-illuminating, and appealing to the baser forms of life and mind. The appetite for these baser appetites are increased with every form of sad and sick minded role model portrayed. For every one portrayed on the box, many more are born of the box. Where people would probably never see a murder, abject cruelty, horrific violence, and the worst forms of human behaviour and interaction, all of these are experienced and internalized daily - often even glorified - under the name of 'home' entertainment. No wonder there are so many neglected and disenchanted youngsters. No wonder there are so many violent and ignorant people. You get what you check! Unfortunately, the behavioural rot is contagious; and sadly, it even seeps into the most caring of families from outside. Education has been diluted and rendered almost helpless with all forms of bad behaviour left unchecked. What hope have our emasculated teachers, and what hope have their more dedicated and so worthy students? Education is our society: compulsory mis-education is destroying it.

Dumbing-down rather than raising up seems to be the order of the day. Some responsible reporters and writers valiantly battle to direct us towards higher ground. From such higher ground we could be able to perceive a better world, but the opposition and the seemingly more general growth of stupidity seem all too likely to continue well into the future until total chaos throws up strong leaders with the necessary number of followers to restore sanity.... or else oblivion.

The family needs to be a strong entity. Each is a building block from within. Porous and fractured bricks crumble and will fall. Equally divisive living styles and divided families do not build a sane and caring Social Family. Governments have a responsibility to enable the family to be a strong unit, and this is not helped by allowing excessive prices to develop regarding housing, health, and food. A strong family is only possible if health, home, and nutrition are secure. That mothers <u>have to</u> place their children in nurseries as they work to help pay the bills is a matter of 'regret': it should be a matter of choice. Increased greed (need for the unnecessary) and unforgivable negligence can spin off this situation. That far too many children attend school in which they become dispirited, brutalised, or suicidal is unforgivable. That there are teachers, nurses, and police who keep their jobs despite being totally unsuitable is unforgivable. That food practices and conglomerate manufacturers cause huge body growth, ill health, and even terminal depression is so avoidable. The care and comfort of the elderly is far too frequently totally inadequate with their quality of life miserable - this is both uncivilised and unforgivable. These could be remedied, but not by maintaining the current dominant self-centredness of blunted emotions and a throw away culture. It comes back again to each one of us, the family, and education.

People need to feel usefully occupied, which is one reason why having work is more than just a matter of income. This work should be organized so as not to be an unreasonable burden. Ideally all should be able to pursue their talents and a fulfilling future in their <u>chosen</u> form of work. Developing the powers of reason and analysis informs choice and supports satisfaction, contentment, stability, and one would hope a happy family life. Good education counts many times and ways. Every day there needs to be a clear period for thought: no cell phone liable to sound. It should be a human right to not have to respond or reply to work demands while away from work, but many are not allowed such reasonable peace. Over five out of every ten with mental illness are so because of pressure from work: it was reported on CBC that some unfortunates received between 200 and 300 cell messages a day all of which had to be acknowledged to avoid punishment! Working weeks vary from 47 to 71 average hours depending upon the nation surveyed. Then add in the tyranny of the cell phone! Researchers have found that more hours did not produce more efficient and productive output. It should be asked if less hours produced more stable and happier families. Loblaw's Chain-Stores, Canada, stops internal e-mails by shutting down its server each Wednesday. This action must provide many worker and organizational benefits well beyond any temporary problems caused. Stress and depression have risen in 14- to 24-year-olds. This rise has been accompanied by increased suicide cases. It is also now known that increased illness results from depression's effect upon the immune system.

It is good and healthy to have time to relax!

Standards

Karl Popper provided one scientific process or instrument for establishing a new theory. This process is used to find out if the theory may be considered scientifically sound and correct. The object is to find provable objections to the theory. When a new theory is proposed others must try to find a way to make it not work. By 'falsifying' the theoretical statement, that statement then falls. If the statement cannot be falsified, then it stands. Showing an 'idea' and conclusion does not work when another appropriate situation shows it to be wrong and false. If established scientists who are skilled in a related area of understanding or field are unable to 'falsify' the finding, then it becomes accepted .... until, if ever, it is disproved.

A system for reviewing standards has far greater validity and implications than stating or suggesting some fixed inherent nebulous condition. Also, the spirit of reasoned discipline and accepted self-discipline encourage strengths within society to better protect a constructive concept of validation.

STANDARDS ↔ ATTITUDE ↔ PERSONALITY = > CHARACTER = > ME ^ THE SEPARATE PERSON

Deciding to relate, to join with, and to belong to each requires a personal introspective decision. A similar process can enable or result in an 'excluding individualism' which leads to dislocation and isolation. How we chose to use our controls can be an avenue to happiness - like simply creating via baking - or the opposite. Too much control can easily produce a reactive nonconformity which may be picked up by creative minds spotlighting areas ripe for improvement, change, and advancement. The divine qualities of creativity are its promise from within of producing something worthwhile without, but sadly creativity can become corrupted.

Quality of life as a concept needs to have a more central educational and administrative position in planning and decision making instead of a preference for productivity and textbook processes of production. A nearly wasteless society is an ideal, but this cannot be built upon obsolescence and redundancy. Where is the sanity in paying fit and able people not to work through the establishment of a benefit system: spend to create employment? The mom or dad at home running 'the family business' does darned hard work for which more help is needed with preparation training in school: 'early-years home-keeping' needs to be seriously researched and taught with the aim being to better encourage successful family growth. Creating, contributing to, and caring for a family are no easy tasks. The social processes are taught and caught and not biologically produced. Such education would and should make the provision of a successful home environment and life less instinctive with its hit and miss learning. It could make a significant difference and life would be better and more fulfilling for children and for the Social Family. Those strong and well balanced families would collectively make for a strong and well balanced Social Family. The standard of family life can be enhanced by the subject of family living playing a greater role in its members' schooling. In early 2013 it was found that over 50% of family businesses had growth exceeding 15% - the conglomerates would like to be in their position. The family business approach is more resilient, it seems. This is probably due to shared understanding, shared values, shared background, and shared consequences. If the standards are reasonable and maintained, then the outcome should be most beneficial for all involved.

CHAPTER 5:

RIGHTS

Rights: The Roots of the Tree

We have a responsibility to live righteously, as discussed in detail throughout the Bible (New Testament, New International Version). Also review Romans CH. 2. 14-15: The outcomes of doing right and right actions being written in the heart. CH. 12. 6-11; 12: That we should use our natural gifts for good, such as encouragement, generosity, forgiveness, patience and hate of evil. CH. 12. 18: That goal of trying to live in peace with others. This living by doing what is considered right makes sense and matters greatly, not necessarily just because of any religious significances.

Living 'righteously' is active at point of contact and is connected with the concepts of an achievable ideal. There is not only one fixed way to live righteously, which allows room for a modicum of difference. Rights promote ideals concerning specific behaviour patterns: these are actions and rules of consequences, but for whom? We are all different and will respond differently through life. Enabling constructive communication between the different social parts encourages both sympathetic and empathetic responses rather than imposed rights backed up by force with inevitable alienation and disconnect. The sad outcome of ISIS's descent into barbarity is that in all probability it was initiated by fine ideals. Certainly it was a brave attempt, particularly in Syria, to counter the barbarity taking place at the time. Slavery, child soldiers, forced 'prostitution', and mass murder appeared with the arrival of 'disciples': not an unheard of occurrence. The brutality of the Congo goes ever onwards. Many religions have descended into such degenerating self-proclaimed acts of 'justice'. The Boston Marathon Murderers knew exactly what they were planning and doing. The younger man (brother) could have chosen another course, but being a coward and fanatic he did not. He has no excuses which stand inspection. Sadly, some were invented for him placing their inventor(s), now his co-conspirators after the fact, in the same category of violently abusing the state. They too chose their way though they could have chosen otherwise. The vile killing of nine good black church members by a mentally deranged isolated white youth in the USA shows again, if any doubted, that any grouping of humanity can throw up degenerated subversions of humanity. Meanwhile, guns remain too easily available, as they are considered a right, with no training or testing before its owner is let loose on the world. Madness!

The mind is a collection of active and participating processing units. Of its nature it develops and passes through stages which may be crudely summarised as follows:

> innate processing potential ↔ sensory input ↔ recognition ↔ input processing and comparing ↔ intel-

ligence development regarding thought application ↔ application with emotional self-controls ↔ growing social awareness ↔ conformity from understanding ↔ social and personal discipline

Some of the above may occur together and others apart. While one is developing another may slip into the background during that process. War and brutality can disrupt the whole developmental process preventing progress to the next stage.

For many there is an assumption of a passive 'other' who will respond and react in a passive way without pre-set goals or design of outcome as merely a catalyst enabling better fuller awareness and understanding beyond. For others still it takes a disadvantageous involvement justified by an inverted prejudicial view of 'the other' which dictates and shapes the possible alternatives. Such like to use the words prejudiced and bigoted towards opposing positions as an insult and personal self-justification and excuse for their weak logic and loss of position in debate. They fail to be aware that the two words best reflect them: they are limited.

The Jewish peoples, just like the Scots and the Quakers, have produced so many wonderful thinkers that they rightly have much to be proud of. The former two have suffered conquest and occupation while all have suffered persecution. Yet this failed to diminish them nor their quality. Ashley Montague was born Israel Ehrenberg on June 28, 1905, in London, England. He rose above and beyond the vicious spite he experienced as a Jewish boy growing up in the East End of London. His actions were to become battles of liberation. He acted constructively and therefore successfully in improving conditions and bringing hope to sufferers of racial and gender subjugation. His gifts will last. Further, by championing an improved position for the handicapped, he enabled the development of a whole new world of hope and opportunity. It would be safe to say that his faith in humanity bore considerable fruit. He appears to me to be at base an optimistic realist. His book, *Elephant Man*, opened the eyes of the cinema world to the appalling distress and limitations caused by attitudes towards the innocents smitten from birth with disability: as a result the world lurched into a new and ever expanding compassionate mindset. This great mind affected surgery, the gender question, and the continuing battle for balance in racial questions: thereby annihilating the racial superiority belief. Hopefully in the future there will be no more questions and battles. Rather, there will be accepted kindness, decency, and universal justice. His belief in the power of love rather than hate as a changer of social conditions has proven well its effectiveness.

Law and Justice are not necessarily the same.

Rights as expressions of social values, a so-called normative form of rules and principles, are a guide for behaviour and decision making, but are dependent upon an agreed upon code of morality through the processes of reason. These would better stem from collective experience, memories, beliefs, and testimony: each would therefore be recognized as a worthwhile variable both in outcome and process. The background of one person's sense will be different from another's. Seeking and uncovering different information will inevitably produce different conclusions amongst people. The occurrence of differences would not be seen as unreasonable or necessarily wrong understanding - an abstract work of art can be to some an inspiration while to another an object for derision or despair. The same object can and does produce very different reactions, arguments, and outcomes, as do human responses: each being personally right and valid. Such is the danger of extremism, idealism, and their proponents. Calm consideration is needed based upon what is, with all those associated distractions from the variable natures of personalities and their perceptions.

One most useful function in experiencing guilt and honest regret results in that sincere inner need to change oneself. The use of raw coercive power leads ultimately to destruction of the once powerful. Why so? It may reasonably be argued that once fear and anger reach a threshold level, consequences are replaced by thoughts of action, good planning, and a decisive reaction, all in the expectation of change and/or a return to a previous state. Some are empowered or generate this empowerment to coerce, and in so doing sow the seeds of future problems. It is better to gain free and more secure agreement than to coerce. There is no inner strength or anything Macho in destruction, just the evidence of lost decency and lasting evidence of lost self-control.

A system of rights is by nature closed and restricted. However, before rights first evolve, there is the concept and feeling of responsibility. These are more open and adaptive and stem from conscience drawing upon reason, empathy, sympathy, and custom. These are part of the social form and so usefully inform our feelings. Our sense of responsibility dictates from within us, through our own choice, rather than being imposed from outside ourselves. Responsibilities are almost organic, for they grow and adapt in their awareness of change while benefitting from personal experience. Rights may be set aside, but this is not so for Responsibilities with their tie to family and experience and with our concepts of humanity. What value and benefits are drawn from having Rights if those people who respect and act responsibly by accepting their duty are not in a position of power or influence to make them happen? Arguably these are actually privileges being granted rather than automatic rights.

Rights are often approached somewhat along the lines of the Laws of the Medes and Persians which cannot be changed.

The implication is that a Right is fixed for all time and should always be followed, but it is suggested here that a Right must rest upon the condition and circumstance of each occasion. The result of following a direction of absolute infallibility is wrong. Outcomes are unpredictable. What a Right entails could easily be affected by political considerations, the media, or a referendum. Such variation suggests that rights are malleable and may morph and reform into a new shape. If a 'sanctity' of rights is accepted, the implications to interpretation and fallibility are clear. Further, it is better to establish personal individual self-controls and social norms than to depend upon laws. Let's be quite clear: these controls come from clear and fair discipline in the family, supported by friends and reinforced in our educational establishments.

Just as those engaged in Wars need controls, Human Rights Laws demand clear checks, balances, and lines of accountability. Rights proliferation is social manipulation, or alternatively social warfare. Both of these attempt to impose a collection of beliefs operating through a position of superior power. The use of these powers needs to be shown to be valid and morally sound if they are to meet civilized social standards. Checks and balances with the accountability of those exercising this power need to be able to prove or disprove the validity of the cause. Retrospective legislation is anathema to fairness and right. Further, social awareness is not instantaneous nor can it be uniform in all social settings and districts: interpersonal communication and problems will vary greatly from place to place. To suddenly introduce a sweeping series of statutes and paint this injustice with the 'nice' word Rights seems deceitful and wrong, for the 'nice' word fails to make wrong action acceptable. All judgements operate through the BIAS of personal experiences, beliefs, and preference in a condition of insecurity and conflict. The blunt hammer of NEW and unrefined laws is not the way to solve a social problem; rather, it is a sure way to deepen and extend social issues through discontent. Social outcome must repeatedly measure the value of this Rights structure and monitor and compare the intended results against what is occurring in reality over a variety of areas. From what I have seen and experienced in education and tragic social rebellions such as Broad Water Estates in North London, UK, rights were not the issue regarding the actual outcomes that day. The arrival of intransigent subcultures causes almost intolerable difficulties due to the number and breadth of changes being forced on the indigenous society. In education I found that no race with which I had dealings was unreasonable or bad when the correct 'give and take' occurred, following reason and the will to be aware of reality rather than myth. In fact, a number of different culturally based adults and children were found to be both delightful and caring members of the Social Family from whom I could learn. Back anyone into a corner and expect resistance. Stay at home mothers, in a new land, need the instruments to understand and adapt as a minority. Too easily offence can be caused through differences in tradition and unawareness of their sound historical significance. All mothers should be able to speak the local language as should all members of any group. This needs to be a requirement demanded of any making the brave and worrisome move from a familiar culture to an unfamiliar one. Rather than being prejudicial, this is sound sense and enables all to better find a working and acceptable way. After all, we are all of the same human race, but have grown up with different conditions, advantages, and disadvantages to cope with. Tradition can often be a significant part of this ability to cope. In a less safe environment than most Western nations, to what extent has the notion of Human Rights reduced or prevented deaths, torture, and illegal imprisonment? Dictatorships are frequently shown to have little regard for Human Rights. People in power in The West generally respond to accepted standards of decency and accept the Responsibilities of civilized conduct. This leaves the issue of rights violations as a small matter involving the fine tuning of specific small areas of abuse generally brought on through ignorance, misplaced or abused standards, and misplaced acceptance of codes of behaviour and personal responsibility. In Stalin's Russia, Hitler's Germany, Pol Pot's Cambodia, Burma of the Generals, and current Syria (2012), to name just a few, rights have not been of use nor any real protection. The excesses of powerful people occur despite any system. However, when religion, family, and society 'marinate' each developing individual in reason-led universally accepted Responsibilities, then the evil have little success in gaining power and soon lose what powers they may have stolen. If reason, courage, and responsibility rests with both the majority as well as each individual, that will provide real lasting protection for the Social Family. As huge industrial empires are grown on the debris of individual and small scale economic entities, these huge conglomerate corporations take control of the means of promoting our political leaders. So, the next round is gathering power to dominate and inevitably destroy opposition, no matter how justified. Sadly the next young international bully is most likely growing fast into adulthood, with little care for the 'family' model of society. Within there are also the irresponsible 'political gamesters' who play the field to get their kicks.

One sure sign of the Social Adult is that they take their Responsibilities and 'rights' seriously and provide for the young, the old, and the needy. Responsibilities are equally understood to apply to young and old alike and each adult to the other. Rights are a part of the framework but are not THE framework.

One may ask if Responsibilities are formalized in rights or conversely are a very different thing altogether. Often rights are implied within Responsibilities, but rights are too inflexible and too narrow. Responsibilities are a matter of conscience which often relates to tradition, while rights are generally a product of the law or they become the law. Rights are over-formalized conventions which become petrified, rigid, and inflexible. Where a rights 'infringement' is the question, a tribunal may well provide the avenue for filling in the details and so such a precedent becomes the way forward. Wisdom comes with greater understanding and such understanding is the stuff of responsibility. Assumptions can be refuted through evidence and may also be upheld by the power of evidence. Rights operate as a paradoxical paralysing system called justice, too often through precipitous action. If we believe the Law is absolute, then each nation's laws are absolute, no matter how they differ from each other. That is illogical. If Human Rights are absolute, then each nation should accept them. Already we have a conflict.

In China the telephone service is controlled and private conversations can be lawfully intercepted. This is used to control. We have learned that this also happens in Russia, Britain, and the United States. So much for this 'right'! Newspapers can, through intrusive reporting in the name of the almighty sales figures, make some people's lives miserable based on the hollow excuse of freedom of information, etc.

Do newspapers have a responsibility to defend our freedom, liberty, and so on? It would be useful here to read *Dial M for Murdock* if you have not yet read it. Many ask the question if there is an enforceable right for and of privacy. While following the Murdock Disgrace, one sees the ineffective nature of rights. Surely a well-developed perception of Responsibilities would have been a better guarantee of justice and fair play rather than circulation numbers, bonuses, and shareholder dividends. One does not wonder for long if money and the addiction to power make the suspect actions of a few leading police, politicians, judges, business people, and even ministers inevitable. It must be quite clear to nearly all that the concepts of civility, honour, and chivalry are more important to humanity and the individual than raw financial power.

Equally suspect is the acceptance in misnamed 'professional sport' with the miscalled 'professional foul' which in reality is breaking the rules intentionally or in other words cheating. Such actions show that the user is not competent enough to succeed legitimately. Fixing sports results displays the lack of morality. Such a flawed attitude naturally goes beyond just sports, into wheeling and dealing, and using insider information in banking and commerce. The good legal representative fights to ensure right prevails as an outcome of The Law. The corrupted use law's failings, weaknesses, and 'loopholes' to make money and serve ambition.

Art and science take known elements, move them about, and create something new in the crucible of the mind. Human Rights are elements also, and their use and value need to be built up. They are an 'intentional construct'. Their value lays in an ongoing and constructive nature, rather than punitive reaction. Responsibilities are the filter through which rights need to pass, to be processed, with due respect shown to traditions and local culture. Fulfilling expectations via understandable predictable outcomes with desired social structures should be reasonable, predictable, and deliverable by legal systems. The function of a machine's moving parts, when well understood and designed, makes for a better machine which properly fulfills the goals of its designers. To the artist, the colours in a picture can be seen in so many more different tones and values than simply quoting a basic colour. Rights are the colours within society. A painting depends on going well beyond mere elemental colour, as it is more about their relationship and the influence one colour has upon another. This is a crucial part of the pictorial dynamic: an ecological interaction. Equally so, the relationships and influences one human right has upon another comes from an active dynamic, not a stagnant notion. Responsibilities are the starting point, as they contain the goals and form the touchstone for judging how to apply rights and determining how appropriate to the whole that application would be. Rights cannot be permitted to dictate the 'end game'. The manner of application or 'style' is important: it is not just the words which matter or the simple meanings of those words. This goes beyond and comes from the wellspring of Responsibilities within our Social Family.

When to let go in disputes is always the meat of an interesting debate and a sign. Letting go needs to follow sufficient information with well thought out alternatives and reasonably expected outcomes in mind. In the absence of the possibility of balanced awareness and agreement, there is then an argument for Raw Law, a primacy of the Human Right, but the exception would highlight the essential value of Responsible Interpretation.

DIAGRAM 6: Broadening Awareness and Understanding= Open Discussion.

Broadening Awareness and Understanding = Open Discussion.

Some Need — Debate — Progress — Absolutes, when introduced.

Building discussion — Can too easily BLOCK agreement

Since there always needs to be a healthy opposition to test validity, there should be a facility for constructive criticism. When there is an examining procedure, fresh ideas and innovations are less likely to be lost. There needs to be a Reason Able balance regarding Human Rights. This is expressed in the imposition of new Canadian contracts for individuals and teachers in 2013 for 2014. This imposition has caused dissent and promoted conflict.

What is intellectually preferable now is not always possible or even desirable due to the wrongs that may be caused by precipitous action. Sensible consideration, planning, then prioritization are advisable for achieving long term success. The Responsible goal is to achieve good which through consensus of agreement maintains stability. What is right and correct and required is not only the responsibility of the government but is rather the Responsibilities of us all. An impermanent solution, due to progress and change, can never be a satisfactory "end result" from action. More is needed. Social change is difficult and demanding of all, as it is often fraught with dangers both real and imagined and may seem impossible on occasion. That's life. Again, the question of untold numbers of influences and variables make prediction almost impossible. To act too quickly, with poor research and thought rather than with responsible planning, will prove counterproductive and slow down progress - or worse, it may precipitate destructive counteraction. Lasting social change is not achieved by legislation but rather by general acceptance. This is both enabling and empowering. Social change needs to be a call willingly answered, not enforced.

Worthwhile consideration provides a constructive message which is sensitive to different points of view and belief. Implementation of a quasi-autocratic law may achieve a short term desirable outcome only to ultimately precipitate a violent response at a later date. ISIS seems to be a case in point as an initially understandable reaction against the excesses of a permissive western lifestyle. Sadly, with ISIS arrived the excesses of the dictatorship of fundamentalism and so the closure of rational debate. Agreement and mutual respect, through understanding, is necessary for calm decision making followed by clear public consent. These are absent. As DeToquville summarised, "it is better to count heads than to crack them." ISIS seems unable to grasp this reality: the world reaction is following.

A definition of a halfwit:

Those which have the arguments but lack the necessary morality.

Euthanasia

Euthanasia is not an easily resolved discussion. The medical calling is committed to the reduction of suffering, to knowingly do no harm, and to healing the unwell. Health and safety inspectors are committed to better ensuring safe structures and safe practices. Judges are committed to upholding the letter and spirit of the law. School teachers are committed to the advancement of those in their care to become both responsible citizens and constructive participants gaining satisfaction with regard to their lives in a safe and caring community. Medicine can seemingly ensure an unending road of suffering; buildings and bridges may need to be demolished; judges can be mistaken and biased; many children fail, never reaching near to any of their several potentials: that unfortunately is life.

Life is often an imperfect affair. Insistence upon an idealistic but cruel principle cannot be right nor considered a human right when permitting and extending suffering and misery. This sad condition is only too real for some tortured souls. Having watched a dear friend slowly being eaten alive by cancer, which had grown from a melanoma beside her eye to take over the eye, the nose, the mouth, and beyond, I wonder how such suffering can be confused with 'a principal' sanctity of life! She hated the progression of her disease and suffered so. There can be no justification for refusing her a peaceful and dignified end, a few weeks earlier. Yes, her friends and family were there, but they had also been there earlier when she was afraid but 'healthier'. We could laugh and chat with her then: not later.

The war against pain and suffering goes ever on. Medication which could be prescribed is sometimes 'unavailable'. Such administrative decisions seem close to criminal negligence with the front line troops being under attack from an enemy with superior force and weaponry. What is more, this enemy has a habit of torturing all its victims: they are tortured to death, with no hope of escape! Shouldn't properly administered euthanasia with 'adequate' safeguards be a moral responsibility? Those who are generally in good health themselves may claim that intentional aided "release from life" is wrong, and is murder. But such release is merciful, since otherwise the sad alternative allows and prolongs continued pain and unbearable suffering. The removal of the fear and experience of lingering pain is not just justifiable but is also responsible "intervention". Period. Again, the question needs to be asked: What constitutes injustice and whether the law itself can be unjust?

Since the law is the law, and assuming its safeguard mechanisms during implementation have been used, then it must, by definition, be just. It is impartial and unbiased. Evidence was sought and presented, both defendant and accuser spoke freely, witnesses spoke, precedent was followed, and professional advice was assured so that any lack of legal knowledge was accounted for. What could go wrong? But allowing continued suffering with no hope of relief or cure is "knowingly to do harm". To imprison a person who is mentally ill due to lack of finances to make proper health provision is to do wrong. To place people in a new country who are unable to even communicate their simplest of needs or fears is to cause harm. To indulge a child in such a way that its social future is in ruins is to do irresponsible harm. For the entertainment industry to suggest that what the majority consider wrongful behaviour is acceptable is to do wrong. Oh yes, often the workings of the law may not display a lawful presence.

When law is lawful, then the police, medical doctors, systems of justice, and armed forces act as they do because they believe in the benefit that the law imparts...... not the harm. Outcome is its measure! All or in part a law either fulfils a purpose or it does not. Effect is the outcome of process and so exists 'because of.....' Indirect effects sometimes indirectly cause something other than that which was intended. Rigid application of regulation is well able to cause that! Training and arming resistance movements in the Cold War days have certainly borne fruit, but not that which had been envisaged. Afghanistan is one sorry example, and Iran is another. Divisions and borders artificially created in the Middle East demonstrate the path of good intentions. So-called positive discrimination is a good thing, but who is being discriminated against as a result? Can the outcome of intervention be known, or even realistically be envisaged? There may seemingly be a good predicted outcome which only later results in the emergence of awful ramifications due to a shortfall of vision, knowledge, planning, assumption, publication, or reasonable establishment of safeguards. The trick is in knowing HOW to ensure what is best for the public AND the Social Family, and how to KNOW what will be the best means over a period of ever-changing times, generations, and numerous unpredictable events. Intervention to enable free choice, with a mind to create and ensure staple, consistent behaviours, is more like Russian Roulette than assuring desired progress. Consequently this will probably result in those 'best laid plans of mice and men...' with matters made worse rather than improved. Social change needs adequate time if it is to succeed. It is through true consensus and agreement that change is reliably established.

"What makes life worthwhile?" is the leading question. One person's good may well be another's bad, as clearly elaborated by Baruch de Espinoza (more usually called Spinoza), the excommunicated son of Jewish Refugees. To do the right thing needs to be relevant to what is understood in this concept as *the goal of life*. What "to do right" demands needs to be established, along with the recognizable outcomes of the application of a Code of Right-Outcomes, both visible and hidden, to demonstrate conclusively that good has occurred. The application of a Code of Rights should cause, support, and promote the Harmonious Social Family in all of their varieties. Sadly, the result of *use of force*, no matter how applied, makes clear who holds the power and is insisting on using it. This produces intransigence, resistance, discord, suffering, and more conflict. Consequently there is a need to carefully and sensibly decide which conditions of 'good', amongst the many options, are best for quality of life and are actually achievable.

People from war torn countries of violent social conflict frequently become brutalised through their experiences: many become cynical and quite naturally and understandably look for escape routes taking their new emotions with them. Relocation to escape fear and danger involves people arriving who are desensitized in several areas of their minds while extremely sensitized in others. Residents of the 'chosen' new peaceful location can have no full understanding of these newcomers. From this position, each becomes readily prepared to take many different and previously not even considered approaches to their thoughts and actions. Society becomes increasingly fractured, unpredictable, and extreme as its units search for greater peace and security than they believe they have. Each apportions blame in one way or other which leads to a sudden decision as to who is to be blamed and for some quite possibly imagined reason. This whole situation can provide a need to escape from this state of fear, shame, and degrading insecurity. The insane murderers on campuses, in theatres and restaurants, or at holiday resorts justify their inadequate and sick response to events.

The mass murder of 77 people in Norway 2011, by Anders Breivik, occurred because he felt that his was a justifiable political response to promote his manifesto. His "European Declaration of Independence 2083" was electronically publicised by him at that time. The text opposed Islam and Muslims being in Europe. Feminism was another target for its supposed emasculation of men. Within his writing he called for all Muslims and 'Cultural Marxists' to be deported from Europe. His parents had divorced when he was one year old: mother was a nurse and father was a Norwegian diplomat who served in London and Paris embassies. Mother remarried a Norwegian Army officer to divorce again when Breivik was twelve years old. He went on to become a member of a Hip Hop activist group. His was a prolific outpouring of graffiti art. He was known to the police regarding early mental health issues. He was a self-identified Fascist and National Socialist and claimed Odinism as his religion. By following a role play with repulsive computer SIMULATIONS, reality tragically replaced possibility when eight died as he detonated a Van Bomb in Oslo's Governmental Regjingskvartalet district. He then moved on to the Workers Youth League Summer Conference camp on the island of Utoya where he cold bloodedly slaughtered 69 people who had been enjoying the festivities. So many people died at that Labour Party camp. It seems impossible to the secure that such killers can justify what they do, but they do exactly that. All these horrors occur within an environment of law which fails to have any effect on protecting the public from these deluded and brain deadened killers.

Any value in law depends entirely upon the actions and belief structures of those who are more powerful than that law. Terrorists survive and wars are lost by both sides following the destruction of so many souls and despoiling resources built up over years. No one wins. Documented Rights are an expression of force. Those controlling the force invent and shape the Rights. For every force there is an equal and opposite force. What is taught by physics is probably true of society. Without that human will or instinct to overcome, our race would not have survived. Survival is and will remain the key. A battle has been started by the establishment of force. This situation is not the same as if an idea had been discussed and accepted as a reasoned and responsible direction to choose. The demand for obedience to Rights, which if acceptable need not demand but through making demands will by its very demanding nature produce conflict. Force threatens, it demands, or rather dictates - a situation guaranteed to be opposed. Garbage put in: garbage comes out. Conflict put in: conflict comes out!

The idealistic outcome is generally unobtainable but when actually achieved takes plenty of time and care. This goes beyond simple hopes and aspirations to an ideal state. When there is much variety, as in human thought and belief, there can be no one quick way: what is ideal is diverse; it is not singular. The ideal takes many forms and focuses. The only way to avoid significant conflict is through consensus. Gaining this consensus is the trick of good politics and good politicians who are only too aware that life is in constant change, so they review and change their position as they deem necessary. The idealist way is the seeking of a good, a new good which comes from moving to meet the ever-changing events. As with financing there are many more and varied possible outcomes from so many targeted projects. Borrowing is a gamble with hoped for outcomes being encouraged by 'due diligence'. This diligence is an analysis of the known to better predict what will emerge from the unknown. Individual freedom does not and cannot usefully be defined, encapsulated, or frozen in the form of a system of 'Rights', especially when dealing with evolving communities. Law stands as a pretty simple set of basic ideas and principles; it is nothing like rocket science. However, it does contain extremely complex arguments and rulings which become precedent for future rulings. It is the interpretation of the law which takes into account specific events and conditions which can become too involved. The French 'Crime of Passion' is a very reasonable short-cut through a potential quagmire. The French common sense trumps again.

A Better Tomorrow

Rights have become the coin of politics and a source of intransigence as well as limited and limiting discussions. Creating a sort of `holy cow` out of Rights is less than informative or instructional. The proposal is that Responsibilities are the better social currency or coin. More than a right to fly to our holiday resort, this needs to be measured against our responsibility to low lying third world countries. IF beliefs regarding the cause of global warming are accurate, then this human cause threatens a considerable rise in the sea level threatening cities and settlements, such as Christ Church New Zealand, London UK, New York USA, and coral island dwellers: this is Pollution Power! We can afford taking time off for holidays, but we do not need to travel long distances to enjoy ourselves. This travelling further adds to endangering the habitat of island and coastal peoples. Interestingly, much of Florida is predicted to eventually be below the waves! We have nurtured a need to acquire, to own, to gain 'things': aggressive advertising sees to that. Ownership is suggested as our empowering right, and is often viewed as an indicator of our success and social progress. Dragon Demand continues its rampage through nature, causing topsy-turvy destruction in every direction. One of the outcomes is an ever growing loss of farm land. This affects both the intensity of production and production growth. Intensive breeding and rearing systems endanger us. All of this imbalance is due to industrial provision for our artificially created demand with its lower percentage of necessities. Once again, maximising local production would be the saner and happier way. As they say in painting pictures, "Less can be more".

Rod Andrews in his seven-year book of research entitled *Cooling Down Planet Earth* places the blame squarely on humanity's removal of those natural factors which help cool the planet. Nature provided ecological interactive instruments which aided balance and repaired damage. Shading, water directing, and water holding trees are crucial to our survival, yet a staggering 90% of trees have been removed in recent ages. The unshaded landscapes with fast runoff of precipitation have resulted in more water in the seas, thereby adding to the sea levels. With melting ice from ice fields and mountain glaciers with snow not being replaced, the starving of billions, not millions, becomes a real possibility as transnational rivers and lakes disappear and wars rage. One example is the Aral Sea in Russia: Google to see an example. We await California's problems with exhaustion of its underground Aquifers. What of our Great Lakes? What we think we know will prove just part of the sad story of shortages and growing conflict.

The powers displayed by our governments should make us more concerned than we are. For whose benefit was the change of weights, measures, and coin with the cost and loss of wasted financial resources? Trade dominated the conversation: so back again to the giants in trade, the banks and corporations. The purpose of any group is the wellbeing of the individual parts. Move away from that purpose and everything deteriorates. The tragic financial position of our recent world crisis demonstrates the power of irresponsible actions and sheer greed. There are clearly more occasions when referendum use is both right and proper to decide our future. *Big business has a greater say in the future than the population as a whole.* Not included here is the highly successful entrepreneur who well deserves the rewards of vision, passion, development, and success. Rather criticised are the bloated bank directors and corporate bosses, the bonus parasites, the blood-filled leeches feeding off the body of society and thus the Social Family. Dishonesty causes financial crisis as much as stupidity and greed. "They all do it, so why not me?" is the antisocial mantra! All are guilty. Truly discovered 'Responsibility' does not allow for irresponsible actions. Yes, it is the Rule of Two again: either it is right or else it is wrong.

The modern world's move away from the support and strength of an open meritocracy is a further tragedy. Millennia of progress, growth, development, and skill are being eroded and thrown away. The quality of language through its demise affects the quality of intellectual development. The trite and speedy outcome replaces craft, skill, and style. The cool 'half cooked' replaces the well prepared. Thinking further and thinking beyond are the nerdish tendencies of the swat, the uncool, the shunned. Without contemplation and intellect, there can be no secure future. Quality of education needs to again focus upon the development of mind and sound reason based upon principles of quality, achievement, and understanding through persistent effort. These have been and are still being undermined. Emotional tinkering and second-hand excuses for the failings and sorry lost opportunities of much modern education seem to be preferred instead of a return to a respect for the pursuit of excellence which is currently looked for and expected in ice hockey players and athletes. Quality and excellence are needed within our education. What should be the educational priorities? What is the present outcome? Who suffers? Parents, stand up and demand quality, depth, and discipline for your children and remember to support those who honestly try to provide your children with these gifts. Students, you are the clients and have a Right to demand the same: it is your future that is being downgraded.

Humanitarian effective concerns enable access to full medical facilities. This happens for prisoners with ample food, shelter, and warmth. This is good, this is right, and this ennobles the Social Family. However, at the same time the denial of provisions by general practitioners to many good citizens is evident not just in Canada. Elderly die of hypothermia; too many homeless freeze to death in the wintery streets of cities and towns; cancer sufferers are denied oral medication; scales and subjects of medical charges appear to be arbitrary; dentistry moves beyond the pockets of many; insurances seem inadequately applied. It could be concluded further that the wealthy and multinational companies win because of the lawyers they can afford. Some have found that they are able to do abroad what would be unthinkable in their mother country! One could be forgiven for thinking that in this phenomenal age of communication, these much interconnected blessings are being manipulated, 'data dipped', and resourced primarily for the benefit of the few.

Folks, there is the overriding right of freedoms WITH the responsibility towards others, especially the disadvantaged and weakened. Questions need to be considered regarding the reported incident in the Daily Telegraph (UK) 49119 TAP 30 13 where it has been considered that "prisoners *had* been *stripped of their rights* to watch TV." Wow, what a terrible thing to not be permitted to watch television because one had been "naughty!"

Shame on you, prisons. Such BS!

Vital Sensitivity and Development

The Arts promote sensitisation by awakening and instructing a 'greater vision' and awareness within. Creativity and vision are crucial for humanity to move beyond the immediate. The Arts extend mind and language skills while teaching patience. What better way to achieve this than through the fine arts and experimental sciences? Learn to see and feel beyond the now. Go there within the mind: a journey into the unknown and imaginary. Next, go outside into the world, but this time feature the senses at work linked with memory and the mind. Too often if we take the 'creative' Arts for granted, we miss so many opportunities to feel and learn. They have a way of relating our collective mindsets and behaviours; they can freeze-frame a moment and liberate. The Arts are the expressive mind; they provide the open mental window so we can go beyond. Art is viewed by each individual and destined to benefit many. Art's output simply bubbles up; it erupts out of awareness and a combination of both experience and emotional responses to life, yet for a time we may not understand why. By the evaluation and critical analysis of "Works of Art" we continue to learn: thereby extending our mental elasticity. Perceptions based upon information from others deepen our awareness and understanding while sharpening our perceptive powers, language use, and creativity. In consequence we are sent forward: we innovate and adopt. Each creative approach takes things (elements) from outside us. These elements initially wander, unfixed, next they may focus, summarize, and express newness of things through which we may go beyond. Heightened sensibilities extend empathy and insight.

Freedom of Speech and being responsible

Freedom of speech carries with it Responsibilities. Jesus taught this so well and so bravely, as he was selflessly and fully aware of the dangerous outcome. True personal freedom provides the option to do right or to choose wrong, but the guide which overrides such freedom is accepted responsibility. Confusion between what is said to be 'cool' instead of the reality of being cruel demonstrates how a subjective approach can disrupt the essence of a situation. Interpretation can negate accurate recognition. My distaste for the bog-standard program, The Royal Family, shows how confused we can become over Rights and wrongdoing. That any family should be subject to such abuse and ridicule begs understanding. That it also is an attack upon Britain's National Dignity cannot be denied, though it will be by some. In Canada on the cash aisles of our superstores those waiting to pay are subjected to The Enquirer and The Globe publications which are seemingly too often dedicated to misinformation and lies: in Britain they call it the 'Gutter Press'. Anyone who has achieved a position of recognition and fame seems to be considered a just target because of their position. It seems immaterial if they have behaved badly or have tried to lead productive and constructive lives. The question must surely be faced whether this 'licence' to print filth and lies about people is a vital part of freedom of speech or rather a total corrupted view of that essential process. This question needs discussion using factual information and debate. The argument rests upon the protection of our democracy and the individual: creative lies and misinformation are the enemy of all that. With this goes the associated confusion (to use modern parlance) … "To be Hip act like shit!" Cool instead of Hip fits in here just as well.

The gift of free thought is like the gift of alcohol, to be used with due care.

Creativity in the graphic arts is as significant and as important to free thought as pictures painted by words. Society
should be a unifying force. It needs give and take to be beneficial to us all. There are sound arguments for moderation
in what we say publicly which become more important for
opinion leaders, "persuaders", and celebrities who need to
accept certain Responsibilities and restrictions. Ability to
speak out reflectively, following analysis, enables a reliable
focus which may benefit those magical gestalt moments.
I imagine most would not have allowed Adolf Hitler's
speeches or the freedom to make them, if they could have
been contained. There are times when the boundaries need
to be pushed and tested to right injustice, to offer hope for
the righting of wrongs, or to highlight just how far accepted
thought has gone astray by causing deep harm and hurt.
Clearly outcomes may not be knowable at initiation, but
an appreciation of responsible care is known. Even inspiration is subject to decency and an *expectation* of responsible
outcomes. Moments of inspiration are not unusual, but they
by nature are different and can be easily wasted. Beliefs or
traditions may highlight or state that a specific belief or
experience infringes or conversely supports a Human Right!
Some will be introduced, though they are irrelevant. If one
perceives and agrees that there are dangers of manipulative
political or class censorship in place, then that topic must be
considered open to review. No matters nor incidents involving the public which go beyond impartiality, whether old or
new, should be allowed to force their way through reasonable checks. Then again, who decides? Who evaluates an
idea's value and whether or not it deserves equality? Who
considers if an idea has a harmful side? What is important
is that freedom to ponder afresh, to be able to consider
and be aware of all alternatives, only possible with thought

freedom rather than thought restriction. This has nothing to do with a conclusion which rejects some alternative for good reason. With manipulative censorship, neither fine tuning nor additional caveats may be added. All becomes closed and securely protected from any other emotive or thoughtful alteration. Such restriction of insights and visions may become blinded and produce 'blind followers': an education through active implementation without any effort of further critical thought. Un-researched but fully accepted ideas can too easily become wrongly established as traditions in time containing a dictatorial requirement which expects and demands acceptance as a restrictive and restricted discipline of thought. Religious inflexibility and tyranny, without the advantages of debate or proven benefit of practice, holds down rather than uplifts. Sterile edict, terminally clouded by quasi legal threat, denies inspection; being without sensible introspection so denies inspiration.

As with so many aspects of racial, religious, and cultural difference there needs to be a reasonable accommodation which must operate on 'both sides'. To succeed harmoniously requires calm and the equal exhibition of respectful and respected positions. This is not a right but a human obligation and responsibility of the civilised and the social. This is not achieved through the arid repetition of 'mantras' but by the exercising of free choice and the intellect. Indoctrination, particularly of the young, is a product of arrogance and the autocrat. These are never the friends of freedom nor a promotion of intellect.

CHAPTER 6:

BELIEFS WITH THEIR SHADOWS

SPIRIT BUILDING BELIEFS
and Gaining Energy

Love is a formidable driving emotion, for it is a background-energy for existence, the energy of the universe, and the energy of a belief in a God. With love's satisfaction is found good humour, optimism, confidence, and vision and so stability thrives. Logical processes are supported by intuition guided by that same energy, the interconnectedness of all - they may simply 'float' in our ideas but they are also drawn together. Life questions come initially from experiences such as those related by our parents or parent substitute - they are authority figures - and through our constructive experiences they hopefully lead us forward - we are the next step and so of itself evolving. Smaller early questions serve, address, and lead to the larger 'life questions'. These result in 'hunches', intuitions, and so on to the next step. Finding the right question most likely leads to the right answer, and the opposite applies. What we allow into our minds consequently builds our minds, thus affecting the whole of our lives. How easy it is to exchange one form of religious oppression for another: to mistake blind servitude for moral growth. The autocratic slavery to excessive extremes of orthodoxy turns off the power of the mind, reason, and constructive observation, and as a result replaces the need to think and decide with meaningless railway tracks of living. No pressure, no pain, no gain.

The fabric of a positive society is built by the willing fulfillment of Responsibilities while the aspirations and vision of that society are expressed in its culture and view of what is right and wrong. These need clarity and agreement. However, diversity may result in a present 'right way' being squeezed into the form of fixed laws for supposed clarity. On the other side is excessive so-called freedom. Licence (a random haphazard form of freedom) leads to a gluttonous tyranny of indulgence and sensory stimulation. The outcome eventually is disgust and reflection, and if one is fortunate licence is replaced through rejection by finding a calmer, simpler, happier, and less 'free' way.

Gaining 'Spiritual Energy' by a focus on the 'machinery' of the environment, its players, and surroundings connects us with our fundamental source of being. Our focus then centres upon the positive and honest feelings we enjoy. We all benefit from being positively aware and exhibiting 'good sense' with unclouded senses. Then when all is especially good and joyous, with colour, plants, and being positive, one reason for life seems more attainable: this is an inner illumination. This then encourages a feeling within of being connected to all 'creation' - being in it - being part of creation and being trusted to fulfill our Responsibilities to creation. "Breathe in WITH it". Breathe in that connective idea of an energy: that feeling of euphoria, joy, and buoyancy. Experience the growing closeness of things and their connectivity. See the glow! Breathe in deeply the good and enjoy again, appreciating that all we do and experience are so importad to us. Then some form of collection bucket circulates.

Freedom's meaning: Such a wonderful concept and experience. However, with freedom comes decisions and consequences. Freedom brings the need for self-regulation; it is a state of opportunity and options which can cut both ways for good or for bad. Freedom can too easily become an enslavement to trends suggesting free will but resulting in the loss of it: drugs, drink, violence, and excess of many kinds. Late viewing of television every night can lead from problems of fatigue to depression - the balance needs to be struck by the individual self-imposing the restrictions. The exercise of self-control is generally initiated by earlier restrictive influences be they fasting, time restrictions, or some other 'code of behaviour'. With excess 'freedoms', individuals can soon find themselves bound up with commercial and political pressures, unhealthy stimulations, uncensored and avoidable repulsion, and mass thought with minimal consideration. One of the main aspects of freedom is the need for reasoned self-control coupled with generally identified responsible behaviours.

Every life event is significant: each adds knowledge. They provide answers as each event arrives, even if there were no original question. 'Find its silver lining' can be a useful practice of staying alert for insight even from coincidence, and consequently consciously evolving oneself. These events may 'jump out' at us with new implications in a 'gestalt moment'.

GESTALT MOMENT: A realization of a form, pattern, or structure awakened as a perception by a 'course of events', prompted by experiences and produced in and by the mind. A single sense experience may awaken this vision, concept, or awareness. How it works is unknown….. as yet. An inspirational moment.

Compare a story of dreams to an account of life. Thoughts, dreams, and daydreams all give us a view/insight of what could be. They can prepare us for that option of what could be, so we need to become observers of these to become usefully aware of them and question the thought. It seems sensible that 'fear images' need to be faced to be better understood, halted, or controlled. It would be more constructive to achieve this as soon as they appear so that a more positive and useful image can replace it. Hate, paranoia, greed, and xenophobia are just a few destructive examples. Destructive ideas are exactly that since they can produce destructive reactions. We need to direct our insights into a better way of being which is social, supportive, and enjoyable. Discovering the remedy for these problems comprised one area of S. Freud's and K. Jung's work.

There are levels of awareness beginning with new and then becoming familiar and unconcerned. Next awareness becomes emotion or harmony, else conflicting or dissonant thought. From these a reactionary dogmatic insistence may arise being severe, concerned, or insecure.

Truth and Reason

Trust is essential to security. Without security fear and mistrust grow. Terrorists use this insecurity and fear: they promote both deliberately to advance their hold and power over people and communities. The atrocity in Boston at the

2013 Marathon; the IRA in Northern Ireland; The Baada Minehof Group, called the Red Brigade, in Germany; and the killing of Israeli Olympic competitors are just some of the 'disabling' and cowardly examples of the socially sick: mad dog groups intent on their own ideological self-advancement of achieving their concept of position through imposing their will via the instability and fear they produce. The extent of their social sickness is seen in their acceptance of the madness of hurting the totally innocent! Sadly the less extreme of these groups suffer the loss of the potential support they undoubtedly could gain from thoughtful people regarding clear explanation of some real problems they are trying to reduce. Meinhof stated:

> "Resistance is when I ensure what does
> not please me occurs no more."

Those in power can too easily use the extremes of terrorism generally without fear of personal suffering until matters have gone beyond the realms of hope. Terrorism is not justifiably used against civilized people because civilized people work together and do not blow each other apart. To be civilized is the co-operative promotion of the common interest, whether in Borneo, the Amazon Jungle, or New York. Loyalty to leadership, mutual support, and a singular group identity are all in place. Those who have funded and still fund terrorism, fully knowing what that will cause, are in the same category of the devils' workers: dogs of war is one description and scum of the earth is another. The "nuts and bolts" of a social life produces social cohesion, group co-operation, growth, security, and happiness and these nonhuman funders of violence do not.

People need to meet and mix. A good and kindly Christian, Jew, Muslim, Zoroastrian, Buddhist, Hindu, Bahia, etc........ are all expressions of good. Good supports are constructive. Good people give freely of their time and resources to the benefit of others. They listen and think. What they can believe in may well be beyond their own self-interest. This outlook is supportive to those in need and will promote trust. Trust is a bonding between individuals and helps blend groups: it is a bridging between differences. This blending is essential for acceptance and so through agreement can result in real integration with various parties accepting change. Where large groups are involved it is realistic for a smaller group to accept that the larger group will not change. Why should it lose its identity! The smaller group, wishing to join with the larger, needs to respect this or find an alternative location where a dissonance will not be experienced by them and others. The terrorist or rabid forms of immigrant 'clergy' shouting for their hosts to transform and become them are both deluded and destructive. Theirs is a socially avoidable danger which needs to be removed. The last thing needed is for a "them" and "us" situation to evolve and be intentionally developed: a situation which these dissident closed minds thrive on, feeding their self-importance and power. When something or someone is noticeable, it is better that they be noticed because of being constructively noteworthy rather than because of an alternative negative condition. The following is my take upon one part of the religious position:

> *There is no single knowledge, no other path, no certainty but what is right and good for those unable to gain good for themselves. God lives in giving good to those needing goodness. Since God is the creator he created a multitude of people-types to populate very varied regions of a diverse planet. Since God is a God of love and justice he will love all forms of his creation, including plants, insects, animals, and the very scenery we live in.*

Beliefs and Argument

A strong society has arrived at a position in which it is uncompromising with regard to its core belief structures. Fortunately the modern world facilitates people moving to a society whose beliefs broadly reflect theirs. We are our beliefs. Beliefs are not the same as ideas or notions, as they have grown over a period of time: they are structurally part of the linkage within our experience, the memory streams, and our past. They are our consciousness. They are what we are. Individual people will always differ from one another. This is why the rearing of our children is so special, for we are participating with society in building what they will become - for better or worse. Society only exists strongly in unity and co-operation. The world is an interacting whole, whether we like it or not. We are a single people: we are one Social Family, a global society. Our interconnected interdependence encourages this unity, or it should. It is only the ignorant and the 'brutalised' who reject this inevitability. They are either for us or against us. The anti-social strikes are against us all. The racist and extremists of so-called religion attack us all. The call should be, "Come in and join in or get out", but this joining in is more feasible in smaller communities locally. How to envisage this practice in a world-family? There appears to be no way to avoid this "them versus us" attitude appearing, developing, and then becoming a destructive and self-defeating conflict. We see this in current fundamentalism in North and Central Africa, the Middle East, and even that so-called land of freedom, the United States. If there is disagreement, then an intelligent approach needs to be sought rather than a belligerent one: a matter both of choice and preference. Discussion will hopefully lead to fuller understanding and balance. However, the Israeli/Palestinian conflict shows how difficult this can be, as does the conflict between North and South Korea. Being rational in an irrational context is a tad difficult. Yet Quebec has managed it, thus showing the way to others: French good sense prevails again.

The moronic response of "If you think like that then I won't talk to you anymore," leads to a number of problems and negative conclusions which simply multiply:

> Such talk will never allow those 'offending' opinions to be challenged!

> If there is a misunderstanding, which is not infrequent since we all come from different *experience-networks*, it will never be resolved with such an unintelligent attitude. Further, the limp-minded 'other person' will be allowed to remain ignorant of the real point and counterargument which could have afforded some enlightenment, assuming there is one.

> However, if the other's point of view proves to be really offensive and spiteful, it should not be left unchallenged.

> Finally, by one withdrawing from discussion, the other wins by default.

> Through withdrawal, that person suggests a lack of faith in their own viewpoint and position and a feebleness in it or any associated debate.

> Following a full discussion, to agree to disagree is a different outcome since the debate has been allowed to run its course with the different viewpoints being clarified.

Agreement to differ is a different thing altogether, for at least it is an agreement. It is also a recognition of both points by both parties with an acceptance suggesting a certain respect for the other person's position despite disagreement, which may only prove to be a single point out of many. It may also be a reasonable alternative to inappropriate conflict. Many fathers and families would have a happier life if they followed this path, as would their sons and daughters for recognizing the same.

Myth is different again, as it is not a reality but only calls upon some. If myth is perpetuated over time it becomes stronger than reality, being faith-related, especially if accompanied by an emotional element. Good and bad luck illustrate this phenomenon as they cause people to irrationally modify their intended behaviour.

The perception of what should fall within the remit of our self-interest will not stop there. There is always a beyond. Also, since value and worth are subjective concepts, greater and broader experience encourages us to search further and more deeply - thus bringing the need to overcome a discovered problem of what now could and should be. The action(s) which are initiating those important opinions of our peers have a huge effect, either positive or negative. This quite naturally extends later into the economy and social realm. One example is the financial black market of 'cash in hand' which affects us all, self-justified by such reasoning as "they all do it so why handicap myself by not doing what they ALL do?" Realistically, thought through theft is theft and social theft affects all. How to rebalance a rational imbalance?

The love of reason needs to be above and beyond the search for power. Those seekers of reason are so very diverse one wonders how, at base, they could be searching for the same thing, but they do. They are searchers for truth. Sadly there is no one fixed truth. That would be convenient but is too unrealistic. Rather, social truths are often dependent upon changing circumstances which affect emphasis, balance, and direction of what is and what could be. Philosophy approaches these convergences and divergences. Many insights seem to be inevitably time-bound. Every measurement ensures there is another beyond. It is formless, like fog, which produces occasional recognizable shapes and motions. These shapes come and go being very much dependent upon the interconnected conditions of the time. Truth can be somewhat like that due to its general subjective interpretation. Because of the changeable nature of thought, axioms are sought and found, only to be undermined by newer thoughts. Beware of those who speak of absolutes, of fixed right ideas, for there is always variety, tone, shade, hues, and change in our thinking and so-called knowledge: that cascading knowledge of what is right.

Ideas, like the forces of electricity, have many manifestations and applications. It is the living application which needs to be watched and the outcomes of the ideas' implications need to be studied. There is always an abstract feature to be aware of in association with the less obvious beliefs supporting it. Recent awareness of the indefinable but useful properties of atomic sub-particles demonstrates how we can KNOW nothing without being ready for change!

Going Beyond a Design of Rights

Sound medical practices and standards better produce a cure. Sound proven educational standards, rather than guesswork, better facilitate the building of the mind and society. Western education is not just western. It follows universal principles but also has add-ons, including unwelcome additions glued on due to political misconceptions of rights. It promotes Responsibilities and both directs and inverts prejudices. Education needs to build a positive outlook rather than a cluster of negative memories and attitudes, though it is wise to be cautious. Food standards and healthy practices need acceptance and adherence to grow and maintain a fit body for the mind to use. Likewise, well thought out building standards are needed to achieve safe housing. Good laws based upon sound practice, drawing upon full and not assumed information-gathering, protect individuality, liberty, and society and make justice a fact.

In this sorry time of celebrating mediocrity, it is hardly surprising that there is confusion regarding real skills, competences, and quality. The broadcasting media through its embrace of inappropriate recorded audience responses is close to indoctrinating their viewers and listeners into a new wave of response. The unfunny receives dubbed laughter support and applause, and the trite passing thought is rewarded with pre-recorded cheering and more applause. In this way shrunken standards of quality become adopted and confused. It is more than just likely that there will be positive standards as well as negative standards which pretend to be positively submerged in the world of the 'creative mind'. We can well create our own realities. Training, brainwashing, and indoctrination all recreate this presence, this belief in a reality. However, what can be the touchstone to prove a conclusion's quality? There needs to be ideals or models and those standards need to be protected and defended so that only the strongest of the 'new creative' wins through: the rest are rejected. To continually add to or subtract from the inch would create a nonsense of the practice of measurement. By accepting and supporting group standards, society is enabled to happily 'dance to the same tune', live in harmony, and limit the causes of friction, confrontation, and violence while promoting progress and development for the common good. It also enables the identification of the unsocial and crass. Such is the action of the strong and intelligent. Though it is not easy, it is preferable. The cults of selfishness, self-interest, self-indulgence, and sheer arrogance need to be physically opposed and such 'practitioners' need to become outcast and ostracized to reduce their damage, unless there is evidence of them having changed to a better way. Now there is the problem of how to eliminate these selfish, self-centred factions. It is a seemingly impossible task to find remedies that can be suggested and formed into a collection of positive activities to actually achieve this end. To many, quite rightly, the thought of social engineering by elites is anathema. However, this may be the direction which succeeds. History is paved or rather littered with misery and the blood of the victims of extremists, purporting to have the good of the masses or their souls central. Such altruism has been used as the excuse for their brutality. A system of reasoned flexibility is needed. The absolutes of the law need a new model or branch. If indeed an adaptable and fully caring society of strong individuals is possible, then greater flexibility should be our goal. Are there any examples of such? Rousseau certainly thought so. Hume believed through our intellect and minds that it could be so. The Buddha likewise placed faith in the development of clearer thought and self-control. Jesus showed us the possibilities that real loving care can open up and so redeem others as he died for us, which reinforces that opportunity to follow a new and better path. Some Polynesian groups seemed to have found the key to not upsetting or belittling members of the group to such an extent that trying to get them to play soccer was impossible since letting the other team have the pleasure of achieving goals somewhat upset the ethos and purpose of the game. Beyond this we must decide what exactly the cost to each of us will be if beliefs are not taught, both as an individual and a group member. Where their undermining becomes acceptable is where hope's lead becomes questionable. The alternative choice is not to teach clear beliefs or conversely to accept a set of general beliefs and enable their continuity through dissemination by teaching. There are always costs, and these need to be weighed: the positive versus the negative. The system of rights, Human Rights, is such an imposition. However, it needs to be asked if the outcome is working well, if the outcome is simply working well enough to justify its continuation in its current form(s), or if the outcome is just limping on in some continuous deep dark mountain mist.

The CBC programme "Shame" on 5th January 2014 illustrated the ineffective nature of supposedly imposable rights. If belief and responsible attitude are vacant, they become impossible rights and cannot work. CEDAR is concerned with feeding and foods for the young in new economies and beyond, but the purity of the ideal is interrupted by political and social realities. Aid comes with interest charged and trade deals locked in. For example, UNICEF has been portrayed by some as a 'Betrayer of Africa'. The neglect goes beyond betrayal. Internationalism has a responsibility to protect individuals' most basic expectations of justice with which I trust all civilised people agree. Unbelievably, over 60% of rape victim cases are reportedly being neglected! Such matters demand a new system of and for justice. The continuance of this and other very different problems of neglect continue and so are permitted, since they continue in spite of all Human Rights!

Gender

Present times are throwing up a plurality of gender groupings wrapped up in a maze of letter acronyms, or as I call it, alphabetic soup. It is constructive to start with the straightforward and then move on. Here goes! Gender is a matter of biology. It is a fact of nature and therefore not of mind: a rock is a rock. There are many varieties of rocks. As mud may be classified as a rock, so a gender is definable. There are plants and there are animals with each meeting certain descriptions related to the physical; this leaves out the microscopic forms of life, some of which can be either plant or animal or both.

In the same way, gender is a matter of being male or female at its basic level. These descriptors are plural in their form. There are some who BIOLOGICALLY are born both, as happens in nature. None is better than the other; to think otherwise merely reflects a subjective preference. The suppression of women is derived from a form of opportunism and can be seen as 'slave' making. It may also be the outcome of ignorance, primitive fear, brute strength, and the corruption of belief systems. It has no place for those who purport to represent mankind, humankind, God, or use intelligent analytical thought. While opinion is one thing, suppression and cruelty are quite another. It cannot be justifiable to oppress, subjugate, bully, manipulate, and even destroy people through the vagaries of birth. Justice through laws needs to be meted out to the violent and dishonest, and not be subject to birth. Reasonably this also refers to age. The child needs its parents, and the elderly need their families. This is the primary and more illuminated position. I imagine mental illness will continue to be a significant human challenge far into the future. Socially- or industrially-caused mental illness demands action now as a Responsibility to those at risk and should not be blamed upon gender, race, or belief.

It is a matter of personal belief and observation that women generally possess specific abilities and gifts more often and more pronounced than those found in men, and men also have their forms of *gendercentric* other gifts. These gifts tend to be present in both genders and all its variants but with differing focus or concentrations. I will not enter the nature-nurture debate here, as a wise and just society needs to value both equally. With these 'special' gifts are human traits common to both men and women. Both can learn skills; absorb knowledge; and exhibit tenderness, empathy, and gentleness as much as outright courage. The subtle differences are most probably why we have survived and developed over millions of years and why we have many more yet to go as humanity continues to develop and evolve with the help of its more constructive inventions.

We repeatedly and sadly learn how amongst the 'defenders' of our rights and laws are found far too often those who can be bribed; those who are narcissistic, bigoted, and corrupt; and those who are neglectful of their Responsibilities. Those who govern at any level need to be of such a character and clarity of mind as to be able to withstand the 'temptations' of power. To put a gender factor here is nonsense. Proven ability and worth will better serve the people than the very necessary safeguard of a voting system. Further the operation of positive discrimination of its outcome will make that voting discrimination redundant. Too many of the most suitable and most moral are too frequently swept aside by wealth, prejudice, organizations, pressure group activities, lobbyists so often with blinkered prejudices, corporate investment yet again forcing their ambitions, crime syndicates, and insane religious fanaticism. There can be no reasonable argument put against fully Socially Responsible individuals representing 'the people' no matter their sex, personal orientation, or belief if they are proven efficient, intelligent, empathetic, and caring. The violent destroyers of social cohesion, the greedy polluters of land or families, and the screamers, shouters, and abusers of power need to be excluded. They just don't get it!

Certain aspects in life go above and supersede the letter of the law. Unfortunately those who operate with an 'in your face' approach currently seem to come out on top through sheer noise and belligerence: they become successful. These are called 'pressure groups', but are more accurately dangerous social nuisances. I angrily experienced the intentional interruption and hijack of a Shriner's Summer Kingston Parade, arranged to entertain families and children, by a Gay Rights group, with some members grossly gyrating, cavorting, kissing, and cuddling while throwing condoms around. This may seem amusing to a certain mentality, but it was hardly socially constructive nor did it promote understanding or respect. They were grossly out of order! It was clear they were there to shock. No free choice for the waiting families. Also, this was undoubtedly not the preferred way of taking part by some gay paraders. By such selfish disrespect and unintelligence they achieved a weakening of their original position, which is often supported. Yes, we are as we are. Live with that fact. That two people may responsibly wish to spend their lives in each other's caring company is a matter which needs to be defended. Likewise, arranged marriages need to be freely agreed upon with <u>both</u> parties fully aware of the implications, but only when old enough and financially independent: one form of this is through computer dating. Further, that the vagaries of the law would leave a surviving homosexual partner dispossessed of the shelter and finances they had before the death of their partner was then and is now indefensible. That a woman's property became the man's upon marriage through an active 'law' was and is theft. The law cannot change that. That extra taxes must be paid to the government upon the passing on of assets at death is death theft and also fraudulent following its World War I inception with the assurances at that time. That two people living permanently together can fail to receive the same allowances and protection as another two people, since these less protected are of a different religion, colour, sexual orientation, or sex, is monstrous. It seems impossible to find powerful enough words for the above in the light of all the misery, despair, and anger this injustice has caused and still causes.

Regarding belief and gender, what possible reasonable argument may be made to justify a small rabid section of women of the broader 'liberation' movement for their attack upon 'home moms'? What business is it of theirs: such intolerable insolence! Also the attacks upon women wishing to fulfill a personal image of femininity and style: such spite-filled arrogance! These are people who talk unendingly of their rights, but they are hypocrites. Equally mind-blowing is a concept that there can be such a thing as a short-term/part-time extra wife. Having an affair is what it is, having had such an affair, should he and she both be stoned? The list is almost endless.

Discussion and Consensus

PARTNERSHIP is working and planning together. MARRIAGE is partnership following special measures intending to create, grow, and support a family in addition. Dominant is not love, rather common goals are achieved through discussion and consensus: similarly within society success comes from consensus. Love is a harmonious, free, and caring union of minds and intent. Ultimately, when two or more personalities are involved, their language use, meaning, and intent are largely predictable and easily interpreted. These very personal interpretations of meaning relate to how the choice of words are experienced, remembered, drawn upon, and so understood. Assumption rather than knowledge can creep in to displace discussion and consensus sometimes with direct conflict the outcome. It would be unrealistic to suppose total agreement is possible. Enforcement sadly cannot create a positive mindset within the enforced party. The aggressive enforcement of Rights works against the establishment of consensual agreement. Too easily force ultimately works against its own goals.

Exemplars of Behaviour Promoted through Media and Story

The media exports ideas. What we see, experience, read, and listen to form what we are and what we become. We let these things into our minds via the senses. The mind's job is to recognize, sort, and store information. This can be good mental stimulation, instruction, or *mind-pollution*: all will have their influence upon us. How obviously better it is to follow good possible options and examples than to waste time and mental energy on the product of irresponsible thought. Lift up and sharpen rather than drag down and deaden. We have too few hours for enjoying life to waste them on mind-pollution. Knowing about injustice and remedial action is, however, a social duty.

A burning question is the beneficial outcome of totally removing from the media anything which aggrandises antisocial behaviour since there will be those who will wish to copy. Media communicates and so presents and teaches ideas. A healthy shock response to 'wrong' is necessary in a just society. Suggestion is a powerful force, because "I can" has never automatically meant "I should". What is viewed or read can plant the unwelcome seed of a corrupting idea. Conversely, "I should" infers that an action which needs to take place probably won't. So, "I can't" suggests that "I should" cannot apply. Positive social glue does not theorise in coulds, shoulds, and can'ts; instead, its focus is upon "I will and I am and I can". The attitude is both the driving force, the will, as well as the Social Glue. We need to be on guard to protect our societal attitude and every action with our belief structures rather than accepting mere preferences: we are what we do and what we permit.

What we want is not necessarily the same as what we need or get and this is an age old problem. Advertising frequently perverts and confuses judgement and can be really offensive, even in the name of information. Indeed, that may be what is intended by much of it. These promoters of ideas and emotions (advertising agencies) like to view it as an art form. Some advertisements are exactly that since they can inform, uplift, and amuse. The gutter-advertisers have other objectives associated and attended by poor moral development, naivety, ignorance, cynicism, and greed. That many societies, fraternities, co-operatives, businesses, conglomerates, and politicians support these parasites speaks volumes about their paymasters. They spread all sorts of mental excrement which sticks and is difficult to remove.... that is their plan. What we really need is warmth, water, food, shelter, health, safety, and honest knowledge. In all races and religions there are people who have a good presence. When we come in contact with them we feel that strength and support in their smiles, handshakes, and hugs of friendship. We resonate with them as they transfer a feeling of unity. On the other side of the coin are those who are the opposite as they pursue isolated self-interest in stark contrast to those who generously give of themselves to and for the benefit of others. These 'givers' are the human blessings within our world which can and do offer so much.

Appropriateness

Every social construct has outcomes and consequences which may be appropriate, inappropriate, or even ineffectual. Objects and groups appear for a reason: some accidentally and other by design. *Made for purpose* or appropriateness does not always produce the desired outcome. Purpose can fail due to design and cause a shortfall in the reality of putting something imagined into practice. All the right elements may be present, but how they are assembled, linked, and applied may not be. This is similar to some socks made with good soft thread which are well-coloured, firm, and not too tight but sadly have the toes-end stitched. Because they are not seamlessly woven, they result in extreme discomfort, blistering, and ultimately need to be worn inside out if at all. Application of Human Rights can be like that. Appropriateness of design and implementation is the key to successful adoption.

Human Rights are a collection of flags to rally the troops when absolutely necessary. They are the verbalisation and formalising of some ideals. Their language is time-bound while their essence may not be. These are the legal weapons used against authoritarian governmental, legal or corporate tyrants, and bullies. Their more constructive use is on the big stages of life, but overexposure through needless repetitious quoting in "small case" situations should be avoided. They are always there if a reminder is needed. One or two individuals do not operate with sufficient power to justify cracking each nut with a two-pound legal hammer. Further, using Human Rights inappropriately devalues them and even generates unnecessarily negative outcomes. Understanding and appropriateness are crucial.

There are three levels of awareness

I am borrowing from several theories.

The Outer is the conscious and observable. Being so many sensory responses can be confusing and divisive, thereby necessitating balance and selection. The outer 'awareness' is adaptable to observable situations and the frequent external changes taking place. Personal rational confidence makes this a more powerful and useful level.

The Inner is the hidden which can only be imperfectly observed and which is far too often pronounced upon erroneously, by others. By being hidden, clarity is to say the least problematic. So partial awareness or understanding is how it is experienced and can fail. It is the nature of this 'inadequate' and imperfect experience to be introverted, protected, and withheld: the inside thought or emotional response.

The Deeper Hidden is the unaware and lost until possibly emotionally released as an uncontrollable impulse. It is the sound and fact of our working awareness-machine working within us. Existence based upon survival and actual life provides body processes. This can be highly unpredictable, irrational, passionate, and even dangerous if 'triggered', causing sudden tears, outbursts of joy and anger, or dulling despair.

The awareness state is the person's 'performances' which are displayed to others. It is the person as wished or self-sought. It is selected, chosen, imagined, and consequently progressively built. However, other aspects of our awareness are transitory. They appear and disappear seemingly without reason: though there is reason, it is submerged. Response and apparent awareness can frequently seem irrational or a barrier to an undeniable, ultimate goal ..... the imagined, conceptualised, desired, felt ultimate goal. The reasoning mind is a feeder, for it can and does feed the other reasons while also being fed by them. Our individual concepts of ourselves are the result of a balancing act between memory and sensory inputs. When calm the body's back-up facilities are relaxed and working using a periodic random sample mode. These then move into possible violent mode when suspicions threaten: being impulsive stems from some insecurity and reactionary behaviour probably relating to previous learning experiences. It is reactive, probably illogical, and more emotional. So if one accepts this model, then the outcome of coercion and restriction generates the emotional! The irrational nature of the terrorist fits in here.

JUSTICE and ETHICS: W. Durant

Chapter 1 focusing upon the ancient Greek philosopher, Plato.

> *"A handful of might is better than a bagful of right." (Durant, p. 17line 4)*

This sadly is often 'a fact of life' while also seeming to pull us down when we drop our guard. Failing to succeed itself produces personal problems.

> *"The shame of one's own inability." (line 21)*

More constructively we need to be aware and understand the growth achieved from recognizing inabilities and classifying these as irrelevant or else in need of remedial activity. Further, it is easy to neglect what is good and right with the acceptance of the following:

> *".. the strong do what they can and the weak suffer what they must." (line 3)*

If this is to be the meaning of life the question becomes:

> *"....so... Is it better to be good or to be strong?" (line 38,)*

Society is a collection of individuals acting for very personal reasons. This intended action becomes organized collectively via political activity. Greed, ambition, and envy are too easily developed into destructive forces which produce aggressive competition with the weaker individuals or identifiable groups and victims becoming victims.

In business, corporate competition generates the growth of the advertising industry. To inform and establish brands, the advertising industry takes on psychological theory and subliminal messaging forms. Often it seems the primary goal of advertising is to create desires rather than to inform: this generates impulse buying. The corporate conglomerates feed upon each other and us. Such 'feeding' is achieved at the expense of others encouraged through greed fuelled by rivalry with market division being the outcome. What is best for the people often seems far from their mind: many ethical questions remain unasked with the dominant influence of stockholder votes and dividends payments produced. There is a greater responsibility to stocks and shares than to the public or workforce. BBC internet news published an interesting article concerned with violence against parents (BBC 05/12/2015). The clear suggestion of this article is not that these violent children are a result of experiencing and learning violence within their homes but rather that equal attention must be paid to such violence experienced through television, violent computer games, sick films, and the irresponsible reporting of news "stories". One assumes that further overemphasis on sexual matters is just as influential in its own way.

Previously enlightened leadership unfortunately moves on to POLITICAL rivalry. There is a division of the spoils accommodating a form of social warfare fed by greed (Durant, p. 19, paragraph 1). The politicians look to gain from the divisive concept of The Majority and the masses, but:

"Mob rule is a rough sea for the ships of state to ride." (Durant, p. 19, line 44)

Democracy is in constant danger of becoming the rule of the manipulated mob through an autocratic manipulator. In such situations there is too little consideration for the Common Good as the human vultures feed. How we behave as a society, with regard to accepted obligations and Responsibilities, builds our way of life, for truly:

> "States are made out of the human natures
> that are in them." (Durant, p. 20, line 25)

Democracy evolves and changes in stages, for example with the growth or Meta-democracy of the controlling big power financiers and the money emperors or rather corporate empires interacting. As each grows ever bigger, and as they absorb the 'weaker' of their numbers, one wonders what comes next! Will there come a time when business conflicts become global? If such were to be permitted to occur, then there would be little concern regarding what is right as military mercenaries learn to dominate - possibly as they did in the Hundred Years' War.

. . . .

CHAPTER 7:

THE FAMILY

Dominating Engines of Trade and Breakdown

Business makes two main forms of investment, specifically investing plant with supplies or 'things' and investment in people's labour, processes, and skills. Both need to be used and cared for properly. The assumed lay purpose of industry is to serve the needs of the people and the needs of future international employment levels which must be protected as long as employment is the basis for personal and social provision. There is a time approaching with the possibility of a race of slave robots functioning for a human race at play. Humanity in this situation would meet their needs via processes of gathering from robot output. The implosion resulting from the absorption of companies with their assets will further build up the conglomerates which are unhelpful to social need. The resulting losses will be apparent sooner or later through instability and shrinking populations. These 'greater nations of corporate interest' will dominate all while their concentration will become focused in fewer and fewer locations and require less people. Population growth with shrinking resource availability could well result in the driving engine of corporate trade rationalizing any need for our present levels of growing world population. Rationalizing this position would soon follow. In time one should ask how many people - who will have lost their means of self-provision via work - are needed. The outcomes can only be guessed at. With industry and jobs requiring lower 'manpower' needs, the powerful will only depend upon their serving robot-thinkers. Currently we see work being transferred abroad, with outsourcing resulting in local establishments being shut down and unemployment rising. There seems to be little if any corporate regret. Efficient 24-hour workforces of machines will prove their worth and inter-corporate competition will have its own ambitions. There may conceivably come a Science Fiction time when surplus populations need to be culled or neutered.

The container ship, lorry trains, and rail are how such industrial focus can develop and move location. The fact that statistically two huge ships sink every week of the year shows the cost advantages this system must be able to provide, even if there is only one loss per month. However, the less visible human loss cannot be so easily measured. The closing of large areas of timber production in Canada, for example, is to the advantage of timber exports from the States. Surely this cannot be progress. What worked well and supplied jobs has disappeared in many locations: the means of life relocated. Excessively sized fishing trawl nets that could surround a number of Boeing 747 airplanes explain why fish shortages have developed with the loss of a lifetime's work for smaller scale inshore and offshore fishermen. This smaller scale was better fitted to society's requirements, as is fishing for local need. That fruit, vegetables, and fish can be sent to China to be processed, packaged, and returned is nonsense when considering fuel consumption, ecology, and the future.

Huge companies in pursuit of unnecessary over-production are diminishing resources for future generations. Huge amounts of energy and natural resources are transformed, only to be wasted daily and land in garbage landfills. Mountains of food are discarded because they are past their 'peak' sell-by date not to be found in food banks for those in need nor processed into a new product for distribution abroad in areas of need. The power of advertising, like the excessive use of fertilizers, give 'The Haves' even more to waste, throw away, or exchange for newer models, etc. Advertising companies function to create demand rather than fulfill real need, except almost accidentally. One only has to look at the unnecessary clothes we have, the jars and potions in our bathrooms, the tins and packets of food forgotten in the corners of our cupboards, freezers, and even fridges to appreciate the overkill of modern living. How many ways do we need to smell good or have a yogurt? Whatever exists now, more is on the way! Advertising increases wasteful production, appetite, and greed on both sides of the store counter.

We are informed that Canadian lobster fishermen and women export on average 90% of the year's catch. Their boats cost over $28,000, thus saddling them with a huge debt. Our government allows them to catch in their own area of the sea once they have purchased an expensive permit costing $1,400 (2012): verifying this figure is correct has proved problematic to say the least. For this livelihood the fishermen and women risk their lives and limbs. Instead of the catch mostly being processed and packaged here in Canada, it is sent outside the country southwards with a large part being packaged and sent back for sale. Consequently other members of the Canadian side of the family are denied the benefits of working in this industry. Obviously these lost salaries, which often were jobs for other family members, cannot be used to reduce debt, upgrade the boats, and patronise local businesses. How long till the lobster numbers go the way of the cod, despite safeguards? There are a number of government videos and research summaries on this topic available on the internet.

Housing Costs

Housing is essential, especially here with our Canadian winters as they are. Surely housing is a governmental responsibility! However, there are far too many Canadians, Britons, USA citizens, and beyond with no home to protect them from rain, wind, or snow. What a disgrace while finances can be found for so many inessentials. In many countries and locations the cost of a house has been permitted to go through the roof! An intentional overly free market approach seems intent upon enslaving all but a fortunate few parents to endless work to pay for homes, often by taking on a second job, while development in business and industry is reducing work job places that provide the essential opportunity to work and be paid. Even greater tension regarding jobs centres upon immigrants as a result; it is not their fault but is their pain. Meanwhile the percentage approach to payment for realtor services does nothing to encourage stable pricing regarding rent, lease, or sale: the motto could be believed to be 'hike the prices and earn more.' As with used cars there could be a scaling put into place for housing, a governmentally-backed initiative to have fixed price levels using location to potential work opportunities, size, age, state of upkeep, shops, schooling, and area. Government initiative seems the only way a workable 'buffer' period of readjustment could operate while a workable alternative is found. Further, we seem to be returning to shrinking opportunities for work and a period when one member of the household bringing in income will be the most that the majority can hope for, thereby encouraging "closed shop" employment for family and friends.

ETHICAL DUTY of Care (services and manufactured goods)

There are telephone companies which allow shatteringly high bills for tens of thousands of dollars to build up. These companies may argue that they cannot know or be expected to care what the personal requirements of users are, but they have the means to do so and seemingly choose not to. Yes, there may be less to spend upon directors' bonuses on top of outrageously high salaries, but why not legislate to ensure safeguards are put in place: is that not what governments and the Law are for? Could this not be seen as a right as well as the right way? Ignorance of technical matters is not a reasonable excuse for causing real human pain! Hopefully this neglect of information would not be allowable for gun owners. The shock and horror caused by roaming cell costs in other countries and huge telephone bills generated by children and youths are well documented. To have young salespersons not knowing the facts about the contractual obligations and costs is unethical, unjustifiable, irresponsible, and even criminally negligent. Since governments legitimately taking on corporations have major problems, what chance do you and I have for justice here? The salesperson could be unaware that the sale of a gun or a knife will produce tragedy, but if adequate safeguards are put in place then tragedy can mostly be avoided. Simply to say that a person did not know that the gun was not a toy and could fire real bullets does not remove the responsibility of reasonable care from the manufacturer, salesperson representative, or new owner. Manufacturers are as responsible as the boss of a firm sending out employees to do outside work. Furthermore, the mental stability of a purchaser is of overriding concern. To vacuously repeat "It is my right and EVERYONE ELSE'S to own a gun, under the Constitution," is to demonstrate the depths of stupidity some will pursue. Change the circumstances only a little and a right can become a glaring wrong. If a part of the Constitution has passed its 'sell-by date', then change it through due process with all of the relevant safeguards. I wonder how many suicides were contributed to by cell phone charges suddenly appearing, changing bad financial positions into seemingly impossible ones. I heard of a woman travelling through part of a drug-crazed area of Mexico who was tracking her seven-hour 'taxi' journey on the satellite of her phone to ensure she was taken in the correct compass direction. She was completely unaware of the looming charge, and that cell-phone logged up a bill of over $19,000. It may be suggested that a profile of use can quite quickly be established over a few months leading to a progressive and gradual general creation of safeguards of and for the user: by law if necessary. Changes to that established norm could be notified and thus save huge costs. Also with the technology available it seems ridiculous not to show a running call charge displayed on the cell-phone screen during calls. The telephone company Virgin does so after the call, which is a help, but why not during? Why not all cell-phone companies? Costs I hear called out from afar: profits I reply. Here there is a reasonable and practical <u>duty of care</u>, on behalf of the user, to show running call costs provided by the telephone companies. I believe they can monitor for crime and pedophilia should the need arise, so why not adopt this to a running cost as standard? With general inclusion of this 'service', the first phone would become the market winner and costs would quickly fall with development.

Likewise, a duty of care already exists regarding food quality, medicine, safe transportation, shoes, swimming pools, home cooling, phones and wall electric phone fittings, sound levels, air quality, use of fertilizers, herbicides, makeup quality, avoidance of allergies, peanut free chocolate bars, and endlessly on..................... So, why not display both cellphone and home telephone charges? That seems an ethical choice for providers to make to reduce the problem!

Unknown but knowable cost can be found anywhere. In the case of heavy metal contamination of the soil this can be due to overuse of fertilizers producing an excesses of lead. Interestingly, these dangerous excesses have recently been found to be reduced significantly with the planting of Canola. The increase in lead is as much a worry as the increase of mercury in the Great Lakes. Windborne health hazards also result. Consequently it has become the right course of action to reduce such problems.

ETHICS: A pursuit of what is morally right

ETHICS: 1. The study of standards of conduct and moral judgement.

2. The code of morals of a particular person, religion, group, profession, etc. (CPED)

"Ask questions about accepted moral opinions and never stop doing so!" SOCRATES

"Ethics is complicated because our morality is an odd mixture of received tradition and personal opinion" (Introducing Ethics by Robinson D & Garratt C –P5)

"Let youth practice filial duty......give itself to being reliable....let it be particularly fond of manhood at its best...." (**CONFUCIUS,** in Ware JR.-P22)

What is "eternally" moral, not subject to circumstance, and therefore considered correct? What is the nature of moral duty, and with which obligations? All of us experience moments of decision which frequently touch upon the concept of right versus wrong. These may well produce moments of personal greatness. They determine our character due to and through our decision and so define our personal quality.

When considering society and life, one of the abiding and deep seated problems is that individually we are too small to achieve meaningful change, no matter how strongly we may believe in that change. This is unfortunate because it exhibits exponential negative outcome, a wilting and sorry form of negative growth. Although the first step taken can be the hardest, it is essential: other steps follow. People recognize truth. We have a basic appetite for goodness with a wish and a will for improvement. We all have this drive within, but we need to value and cultivate it. Many are blessed with the ability to pass the message on, not just to one person alone but rather to many, who will exponentially do the same. 'We' seem too ready to compartmentalize what we can and cannot do even with regard to the betterment of our Social Family. We accept we can change the look of our home with significant investment of time and money; we are confident it can be done. The far lesser effort needed to write a couple of letters; to make a couple of phone calls on behalf of others;

to join together with others to make our point known; or to contact the newspapers or broadcasting companies are some of the simpler ways to help promote change. People usually seem to feel that the effort is not worthwhile, and so the idea becomes remote. To feel is to be aware and through our awareness we recognize how we are able to cause improvement. To feel is to care. To care is to be a healthy minded member of our Social Family. As varied as our life experiences and background belief systems are, they come together in a richer variety of possibilities. These will be expressed and focused upon differently for different changes because they stem from different people with their relevant experiences. Such differences may be seen also in our working habits, not so much for change but more about maintaining personal standards and the effective group. Differences can highlight specific needs for active imaginative processes of development.

Professionalism was once an appellation awarded for demonstrating quality, thoroughness, and high standards. We all expect these qualities from people who call themselves professionals, despite the absurdity of calling cheating in sport a professional foul: how unprofessional! Imagine if this mentality was applied by a general practitioner or surgeon; solicitor or attorney; the Bank; our child's teacher; or social worker ..... I won't even go into the expectations for a priest. Horror and anger are rightly the outcome of such betrayals. But is this not true of all forms of employment? In all areas of our labours we must try to do our best as employer and employee. Every one of us is a working and moving cog in the Social Family. According to chaos theory and butterfly wings, no matter how small we may view our activities they collect and influence outcomes. Each action has an influence which ripples across the still pond of life. Thinking of human rights, what right has any group to ruin my long planned and eagerly anticipated holiday through strike action? That action clearly harms me. Their reason? So they can get at 'The Management' who keep their jobs running. No wonder the travesty and social criminality of bonuses for 'failure bosses' is able to flourish. Why should sports fans have to pay such unjustifiable fees and costs to watch their favourite game or to buy an extortionately priced souvenir shirt or scarf of their team, that team which is there to serve them, that team which exists because of them? Their lack of gratitude to be able to play a game they love leads them to almost impoverish some of their most loyal fans as they obscenely grasp vast sums of money, every week, from these fans. They do it because they can and not because it is ethical and right. Then follow that up with the sad use of the "professional fouls": this is actually cheating and so much for expensive professionalism!

With such role-model-serving of self-interest and dishonour, no wonder there is a rise in fraud, crime, and unprofessional behaviour. The social glue has simply gone in too many places, replaced by arrogance, greed, and pride.

A Culture of Blame

What should come first: control from within ourselves, or control from outside?

The primary decision is that we accept we are all global citizens and members of a global Social Family. People will move from place to place as a result of local or personal conditions. An individual may disassociate from their immediate family for whatever reason, but that leaves the biological reality totally unchanged. All sorts of fears, both real and imaginary, can dislocate the social unity, but in that very disunity it is shown that the primary link remains. There is no necessity to be all the same in every way: it is clearly impossible as well as undesirable. This was well discussed In Michael Enright's CBC discussion with his four guests on Sunday, January 18th, 2015. There needs to be a meeting of minds to identify the key values, which are apparent to the most cursory of observations, in accepting diversities rather than turning diversity into a problem or threat. The highlighting of some personal preference can create a condition of antagonism or could equally be one of enjoyable diversity. Tourism clearly recognizes the fun and enjoyment of the latter. Those bright festival costumes are enjoyed while the cultist costume does not gain a similar universal reception. The Scots' national dress is generally accepted and viewed with pleasure, along with the bagpipe band, but few would chose to adopt it outside that community or occasion, especially in our Canadian winter. The carrying of the claymore (cutlass) has necessarily been discontinued......a reasonable concession. What was once the norm need not remain so following reasonable and sensible thought. So, identify what the key needs and values really are. Mutual understanding and clear respect help in this *adjustment process*. With the understood benchmark values remaining in place, one can agree to alter what is less essential. That certain groups choose to continue to maintain disconcerting or separatist costume is an indication of stubborn refusal to compromise and so to be separate in fact. Isolationism denies the reality of the global Social Family but cannot remove the fact of its existence. Furthering this very isolation is a problem that needs to be faced, rationally discussed, and addressed. It is just a little difficult to hold a conversation in silence. Stubborn 'separatism' is not community or socially constructive and sows problematic seeds. Failed integration will throw up the fears and excuses of an inevitably decaying condition which is promoted and extended through ignorance and isolation. There is a certain muddle mindedness and confused logic borne of emotion rather than logic which will support any and all differences whether appropriate (working well) or not (causing problems). Our identities are much more than costume and are better not fettered to mere rags on our backs. Mutual respect is necessary for successful assimilation and willing co-operation which reasonably accommodates differences. The forces of disunity focus upon justifying people's own inadequacies or problems, if permitted. It seems foolish to help them in this. Annoyance easily turns to blame and an ingrained culture of blame that is not to be confused with any reality. Further, values are not fixed, for they change and evolve. A seemingly fixed value mindset may become totally impractical with changing conditions. Reason and uncommon sense need to prevail through rational analysis and thought.

Moving onto the question of 'public health and safety', it seems reasonable enough to again accept the greater responsibility for monitoring our own actions and organizing ourselves safely. For those structures, machines, and situations over which we have no individual control the need for 'health and safety' agencies exists. Then comes the inevitable question as to whether our self-regulation is adequate or 'professional' enough. Thinking of a recent incident (2015) where a law case is being threatened against a Nature Reserve because a tree branch fell upon a camper's tent, one wonders nervously if that party has a driving licence! Rule 1. Don't pitch a tent in a dry gulley or on a cliff or quarry edge. Rule 2. Don't pitch a tent on a flat farm road, under a big tree, or beside a leaning barn. If this example of 'safety blindness' grows, there will have to be a licence issued following both written and practical tests for campers.

There appear to be two categories to consider first with regard to safety processes:

Suggested additional standards

Demanded standards

These may have to change with time, in all probability, due to changing conditions. Interpretation of the very nature of interpretation enables flexibility. Accepted old standards are seen as reasonable. Standards needing to be imposed have lost the agreement battle. With statutory regulation there needs to be an allowance or flexibility allowing for differences and pressure of commitment to responsibility. Inflexibility is a weapon of bigots, neglect, prejudice, amoral sociopaths, as well as extremism and terrorism. One can see examples of this weapon with the perverse use of quotations taken from the Bible, Koran, Upanishad, and so on in which the blessings of the written word are transformed into aggressive dangerous dogma. As with alternative strategies of complaint and blame, these would better benefit from listening and learning.

Social Readiness and Family Harmony

FREE, open information courses with a balanced home-living foundation can be a product of our education, confident in its approach toward discussions within school, which would significantly help achieve the respectful behaviour of parents, siblings, and children. Better understanding leads to better processes and broadening discovery rather than guesswork, supposition, and continuing prejudices. School support should help reduce the future conflict of dysfunctional families. Even a brief experience of school "Quality Circle Time" in the UK (see the supportive work of Jenny Mosely) and the "....Fair Rules" of Bill Rogers have proven the value of open talk accompanied by reason and balanced discussion. Further, seeing both school and our society as a 'moral supportive community' builds security, wellbeing, group identity, and co-operation. Lack of this may be why so many care so little for social decencies, are socially immature, and cause disharmony. This is illustrated by litter, loud intrusive music from cars and buildings, graffiti scribbled on walls and rail carriages, prejudice, and argumentative behaviours. The individuals who can conduct a sensible discussion demonstrate their evident maturity. Complexes of linguistic garbage, rather than straightforward talk, suggest insecurity: a hiding behind words rather than the free flow of ideas and communication. In short, one does not need to have "swallowed the Oxford Dictionary" to conduct a reasoned discussion at depth. Technical subjects require the necessary descriptive names as tools of theory and understanding whereas conversation and discussion require clear communication of ideas between the parties and not the fog of verbose obscure language.

Clearly society and its avenues of education both need to outline and define roles and Responsibilities, as well-voiced as the specifics relating to the expected Social norms. Smaller sized classes enable a necessary group identity to grow with more possibility for individual interaction. I see 'Factory Schools' with their reduced quality of interpersonal interactions and relationships causing social problems and a huge waste of resources through antisocial activity and crime. George H. Mead showed how our behaviour is a response to and through our social experiences and explained how they affect our lines of behaviour and thought. It is an amazing and welcome outcome of good family development that there is not far more antisocial behaviour, but the family cannot do it all. The family can be undermined by a reaction caused by a cold, mob-ruled, dehumanizing system. Following discussion, research, and a broad national debate, education processes and structures need to be revised with a visibly articulated central planned introduction of clear values, discipline, and social awareness. These need to be formed into written records to enable clear discussion and promotion without the vagaries of outlandish personal interpretation and invented priorities stemming from pressure groups. Once established with the goal to form, hone, and ensure both simple and clear enunciation and transmission, it is decision time. Most of the product will already be in place but would benefit from a new clarity throughout to support them: a clear and available social guide. These were previously achieved through religious teaching, team games, and firm, fair school rules.

Outcomes: Fuller understanding and agreement produces balance, broader social maturity, awareness of our valuable personal contribution, and consequent growth of unity and harmony. It is more than probable that the huge costs of crime would shrink significantly due to greater agreement, awareness, and community support.

Formal explanations of Social Family Traditions rather than inferred long-winded strategies or operations, being simpler, have a greater chance of success. In time it should be clear to each the core base of traditions. Clarity will be achieved regarding bi-national or multi-national roles: these drawing on wider traditions as opposed to the purely national roles and Responsibilities. The inevitable idiosyncratic customs and national characteristics could even become a source of interest and celebration. This awareness should promote the necessary will to co-operate. The development of Human Rights is an attempt at this. However, too often abuses can appear to be the direct result of a too strict interpretation and subsequent leverage being abusively applied. It is very hard to co-operate or even understand due to the covert intentions guiding some Rights-guided activities. This failure of purpose, recognition, and implementation affects the whole and easily leads to hostility, intentional bad manners, and even 'racial' or group-centred threat. Misunderstandings, for example, are seen in differences in interpretation of body language which sadly demonstrate examples leading to conflict. As an outcome of interpersonal experiences, as well as substantial individual needs, people change their position and priorities. What is perceived we believe. These beliefs affect and alter expectations, planning, and actions. Perceptions causing responses may not be correct. Consequently, with failure there comes the need to reassure and explain in order to re-establish that necessary feeling of security by drawing upon and re-establishing some shared values and awareness.

Language needs to be used as a facilitator of integration. Its importance cannot be overstated. People needing to integrate have both a responsibility as well as a pressing need to communicate at some depth: to speak the same language as those they need to interact and integrate with. A difference of language too easily leads to mistrust, mistakes, division, and even exploitation.

Faith-based schools and ethnic schools can be a national treasure adding new aspects of the human spirit to a society. This is a waterfall contribution rather than a flood, but in the wrong hands these can become hate-based schools offering an education of division. Isolation is not constructive to socialization and is not intended to be so. Intent is the key with awareness of isolation as a tool of manipulation. For groups to accept and respect each other, they need to meet and frequently interact in a positive and mutually rewarding way. Why not, when both have so much to offer! Building requires planning to better be a sound structure. Socially we require mutual respect, aspects of conformity, and acceptance of 'rules' since these form important parts of the structure. The 'finishing polish' is supplied using creativity and free-will which come to us naturally. Unity of social understanding and purpose will bring ever greater success to a happy society.

The world changes, so humanity needs the skills to adapt and adopt. A fixed rigid system will act and "fight" against necessary change, which is its designed function, and so eventually will cause rather than prevent harm. Learning from the past is useful but we need to avoid remaining within that past rather than moving forward with the future. With modern travel opportunities there is an ever growing need for accepting differences in people. We cannot know exactly which differences will be most needed in the future. Also, we need to accept that it is the nature of people to be different, warts and all: such is being human. To pre-judge outcomes and changes in behaviour patterns is fraught with danger, especially when based upon a narrow and biased batch of personal experience. Rule changing because of the past affects the future and there is no way of knowing ultimately which one way will prove to be for the better. So, emphasising empathy, reason, and adaptability raises the prospects of survival in adversity.

Growth Achieved Through Failure

Too often we are overly fearful of failure and not getting what we had hoped for. Accept it: failures happen. With a constructive view of life it is hard to look back and think of having had a failure that has not had a positive learning side: setbacks can often lead to successful steps forward. Social failures which involve many people do not generally have a similar happy ending. Each person's bad experience adds to the pool of social disharmony and so further disconnect which can be exploited by the ambitious. This form of learning produces a downward spiral of despair. Growing anger and mistrust extend isolation. Questions remain unasked and so unanswered. Confidence and security are needed to encourage constructive questioning. For some a feeling of powerlessness leads to a powerful negative response: violence.

What society should be about is promoting confident positive learning behaviour(s). Failure for the insecure cuts while failure for the secure is more an annoyance or an avenue to positive adaptation.

A preferred outcome should not necessarily lead any discussion. Instead, the principle of what is right, constructive, and productive of that elusive better outcome, should. Minority pressure groups (small in number) through unity and boundless energy frequently succeed. Lobbyists are well paid because they are successful. Interference opposes good governance; open discussion improves understanding; ignorance and lack of relevant experience confuse discussion and promote failure. Failure tells a clear moral story and can be the first step to success.

Family Life and the Free Gifts

When it is said simplistically that nothing in this life comes free, one wonders where courtesy, kindness, family care, and loyalty fit into this cynical belief. There is much which is freely given, particularly by those who value the Social Family and consequential positive interpersonal interaction. With the family membership comes Responsibilities which support the family and its individual parts. So much in family life is freely given, and by being expected it is no less free. Love, warmth, support, instruction, tradition, security, and life itself are all freely given as are the responsive reciprocal gift of respect, co-operation, honesty, and the sharing of tasks. When these virtues and gifts are disparaged, it does not diminish them in any way at all for those who respect and follow the family arrangement. Mocking, disrespectful, disparagers are the losers: sadly their imagined security, if one can call it that, is increased by the destruction they inflict upon others, but destroyed also are their social beliefs and social buffers. What is right will remain so and one needs to hold firm to those principles through all battles and assaults. Remember that any organization needs a consistent decision-making chain if it is to succeed.

There is currently an insane permissiveness regarding the freedom and liberties taken by some adults who immaturely relish attacking working beliefs and traditions. As well there are the young, too often singled out simply because of their age, inexperience, and in some cases unwise but relevant honesty. Frequently we are encouraged to forget that in social situations our actions are not isolated and so benefit from learned self-discipline. Currently excessive permissiveness is confused with love or caring or even rights. Youth by its very nature is lacking many experiences and life-lessons. The young need guidance and safe boundaries to kick against if they must kick. Silly but safe. If not, they too frequently find or rather fall into the dangerous path: and allowing and encouraging such is not love nor is it reasonable care. Guidance and consistent discipline are not easy but they are essential for safe development. Current permissiveness is not freedom but rather licence. Instead of proving reliable and thoughtful maturity, notoriety becomes more attractive and sought. This then extends to the older 'big children' believing themselves to be 'adult' who exhibit even more crass forms of indifference and unsociable behaviour. It is not character building, but rather life endangering and alienating. Self-marginalisation produces self-inflicted problems. Dress, language, anti-custom, and 'having fun' may all contribute. Freedom benefits from virtue, unlike the liberties taken to the detriment of self or others. When being able becomes the deciding choice, although known to be wrong, stronger minds will resist and the immature will fail.

There is currently an unhealthy obsession with youth. This precious and transient age is spoiled with available forms of violent gratifications dressed up as entertainment of all sorts, including law-breaking and dangerous recklessness being glorified and culminating in assaults, irresponsible chases in cars, and endlessly on. Tender behaviour towards and with others is degraded in sexual explicitness which is classed as 'adult entertainment' rather than emotional infancy. In some this behaviour prompts and feeds the sexual drives while leaving the youth unfulfilled and thus dangerous.

Respect is undermined using questionable humour or characterisations by lesser intellects. Some use the term "Adult Theatre", but when many of the products are looked at critically this reveals a different view of social immaturity, sexual deviancy, and even pathological malevolence: a far cry from maturity and intellectual development. The CBC (midday 14: 07: 2015) reported that the Entry Age for pornography (called adult entertainment by some) is not adulthood but rather eleven years of age! It stated in the report that in <u>every</u> new study the age is 'getting younger every time.' Knowledge brings an appetite for more knowledge. Access to this new knowledge is easier with portable electronic communication devices and other forms of online perversion. The report continued by stating that this unhealthy trend begins in elementary school as curiosity often evolves into compulsion and then develops into addiction resulting in errectional dysfunction and other problems later in life. From age eleven to fifteen research shows the brain 'enlarges' within the **excitement areas.** *Last to develop are areas of Judgement* such as delayed gratification. Ever younger teaching and learning of sex education, with its recent inclusion in a political-correctness sense, may be the wrong approach and a cause of further problems. At a course on primary teaching about the Holocaust by one who had years of experiencing those terrors and fear while protected in a one-room workshop and surviving Nazi searches, the speaker finished by stating that he strongly believed that such should be taught later in schools when a greater maturity, empathy, and understanding had developed. Why, one may ask. His point was that only then could the implication be understood. Since there was only "one time" this human inhumanity could be brought fresh to the young mind, he believed it needed to be done at the more appropriate older age so as to be understood properly and effectively. I agree and suggest the same for explicit sex education.

Necessary for social harmony and a satisfying life is an accumulative garden of customs and pleasant behavioural patterns that work. These are instructive and do not necessarily become intuitive, but that does not diminish their essential nature of forming the glue both for family and the perceived community. Their traditions and behavioural patterns encompass the strengths and values of awareness, understanding, and necessary self-controls. They move the human animal beyond that state to a better level and the possibility of a happy, fulfilled, and more secure existence. We are animals at base. An animal lives, feeds, and reproduces. It is capable of independent movement and decision making. In the 'higher' animals aspects of right and wrong behaviour are taught, often with a gentle slap, as with apes and lions. Higher still are those animals which respond with new behaviours, use of materials, transferral of one situation to another for a new application, and the display of concern and conscience regarding other entities.

This does not mean that the young cannot be right or cannot discover a better way. If mutual respect is present and honest examination is possible, youth can become a source of constructive change:

Regarding a decision for change, what are the specific goals?

To what extent are these outcomes reasonably predictable?

What is the reality in them and what is just hope?

Will outcome be personally positive or negative and for whom?

How to check outcomes?

Is this a sensible position or simply a power play?

What part is personal identity playing, and is that significant regarding the decision?

Is a positive attitude being developed or a self-destructive, overbearing, argumentative, and anti-social one?

At the more public level a balance needs to be struck between civil liberty, civil safety, and security.

Family Health and the Elderly

Care of the elderly, as with all family care, will depend upon family attitudes, values, wealth, and interaction. Respecting and caring for the elderly is a duty, a responsibility, and an action of gratitude for those who came before and did their best for those who followed. Hopefully we, when it is our turn, will deserve loving care.

The few Canadian care-homes I have visited 'nocks the spots off' the UK's Old People's 'Places', which are called homes. The stench, overcrowding, dirt, neglect, use of sedation, and lack of privacy and meaningful stimulation, too frequent in the UK, speak volumes as to what is thought of these vulnerable people and how their rights are considered. Hopefully that has greatly improved out of responsible decency: a view of Human Rights certainly has not achieved this. It would appear that to have any rights respected there needs to be the clout or teeth already firmly in place. If Responsibilities were truly accepted, then how could this situation be able to continue? That the carers are often badly paid and from much of my experience badly managed exacerbates the dire situation. The caregivers, aware of the high fees charged and poor food, would excusably feel anger and inadequacy to the task. Like the inmates, they become trapped in an unwelcome workplace with their wish to do good being frittered and squandered. If conditions were at an acceptable level then probably both client and carer would be far happier and contented. What greater gift can be given to someone towards the end of their hard working emotion-filled life than to feel comfortable, safe, secure, and appreciated? Surely that should be their Right! Further, to add to their suffering, keeping our 'loved ones' alive artificially is cruelty when these poor souls are in excruciating pain and incurable distress. This can't be from love, as the conditions often fail to show that. Further, the necessary information that is required for a family's decision is too often absent or withheld, thus leading to distress for all worsened by lack of real understanding with its consequences.

There is a powerful imbalance between the medical practitioner's powers and those of the family. The family should be the expert regarding their elderly relative's feelings and emotions. They need to be strongly involved rather than all powers resting in the hands of a mere acquaintance who too often presumes very much so as to know what is best. If nothing can be done to cure the pain and distress, then medical advice is pointless. If intervention prolongs suffering, then that cannot be justified. When others can't be helped sufficiently due to lack of funds and space, then how can it be justifiable to deny the one who can be helped by forcibly keeping the terminal sufferer in a prolonged artificially supported state of misery? Further unwanted use of support staff and medication removes resources from where they are wanted and needed. One example is the 'savings' made by bureaucratic procedures leaving sufferers of Thalidomide uncared for due to a loss of medical records in a hospital fire. One would think that deformed limbs might provide the necessary evidence to set support in motion, but apparently not in Canada.

Diagram 7: The Basic Human Needs Machine And Its Beakable Cogs

Food, water, safe shelter, warmth, and now world trade.

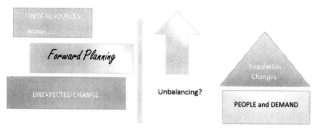

Much of our food production is dependent upon an insect: Bees. If these small insects ceased to exist, then much of our food would be no more. Yet bees worldwide are suffering "Colony Collapse" in which masses of the bees die. Farming practices may be a major cause. Mite spray killers, antibiotics, mono culture (single crop), and insecticides conspire so that the Bee has reached its survival limits. Short-term problem solving, with pest control for example, could promote and result in agricultural collapse. As with many human failings it seems to revolve around a mindset problem (Mark Winston "Bee Fellow" In Michael Enright CBC).

*Adversarial remedies Versus
Collaborating with Nature*

A necessary portion of Buddhist 'mindfulness' seems called for here: proper thought and care to achieve accumulative goodness, thus benefitting our all-important world of inter-dependent nature. As individuals we too easily may forget just how much good or harm we as the group have achieved and will achieve. It is better to have analyzed more generally a learned skill, and from discovery improve. What is now needed is not rights but a more responsible approach to agriculture which may well mean a return to some older ways and smaller scale rotational farming. Sustained and sustainable development is required with a rethink in farming circles. Farmers need far more say and control with their industrial and financial partners. A fresh attitude with improvement more in tune with nature than 'science' is clearly called for. Group contribution with their collective outcomes seems to be the sane way forward rather than lone voices, even if they are huge conglomerates doing their own thing. There can be no substitute for assured healthy food supply. The next level of food processing development is long overdue for a rethink throughout. Again, smaller may yet prove better.

Writing of his time in a concentration camp, Victor Frankl wrote:-

"Humour was one of the Soul's weapons in the fight for self-preservation"

sadly humour is only too brief for many. (in Bill Rogers, p. 113, L.10). If ever there was a time of terror and starvation, that was it. What this illuminating quotation says of the human spirit is amazing. It demonstrates what a wonderful gift we each have hidden away inside ourselves. We need to have greater faith in humanity's strength and ability to survive disaster. Further, we need the wisdom not to encourage and bring on disaster: we are our food's product.

A Different Viewpoint

A form of WikiLeaks of the advertising industry and advertising companies' intentions is needed. Those advertisements designed to cause insecurity and lack of self-confidence and which promote and sell brand goods for the wrong reason(s) should be identified and then made public. Ascribing and 'dressing up' products through the phoney aura of portrait or personality-cult is irresponsible advertising. Advertising needs to be factual, instructional, and/or informative so as to have customer value rather than simply corporate value. Value comes from need and experience: the past informs the present, thereby making a better future. That which is perceived as contributing to our community automatically benefits society.

If we have a true democracy, then we probably believe that the elected officials - paid for by the public's gift via taxes - are acting on our behalf. They are there to responsibly administer our <u>public</u> properties, services, and resources. As employees of the people's Social Family, their duties include protecting and extending the people's building stock as necessary, providing services, and ensuring personal protection. These officials have no authority to sell off, give away, or end any of these without clear public agreement through some sort of discussion and clear and unequivocal approval: for example through referenda now possible via the internet.

The city as it has become is the cause of many problems. Its growth was enabled by the powerful, big business interests which too often act to the detriment of the quieter and more peaceful majority of citizens. This was and is in contrast to country life as well as the production-centred smaller scaled rural norm. Corporate activities are designed to ensure and grow their dominance beyond any reasonable entitlement or wisdom. The giving over of powers to administrators and some minority interests enables these to manipulate and enforce social processes to their own financial and hierarchical advantages.

In the 1990s elected powers decided that the banks needed to be rescued. Significantly, an important number of USA governmental advisers came from those same banks. The governmental obligation is to try to effectively treat such institutional "illness" and its consequences so as to protect its people, the electorate and their dependants. There was a need to heal the banks, but not to reward them. A period of panic fused out reflection. Action seemed to not fully extend to the newly dispossessed people, but certainly shored up the perpetrators even to their bonuses seemingly paid for causing the financial chaos which was throwing dispossessed people of all ages out onto the streets. The problem eased only to return in 2008. How were governments able to take the actions they did? However did they persuade The People to put up with it? Hope is a wonderfully powerful emotion. It enables individuals and groups to achieve what could have been seen as impossible. People believed that support for the financial institutions would return us to stability. Did the promises from the financiers bring the desired much needed stability? Had we all learned from experience?

Here we are in 2016: nothing seems to have changed for the better. Wealthy Britain could be chosen as a financial barometer. Their *Daily Telegraph* newspaper reported on Tuesday 29th of March 2016 that 60,000 families a month are affected by Negative Equity and so looming eviction from their homes as financiers 'reposes' their properties. There have been 80,000 applications to take possession of homes over the past six months out of which 19,000 homes have been taken. The numbers continue to grow. The *Daily Telegraph* predicts this financial crisis will affect more home owners than the 1990s crash with its massive pay outs to financial institutions. Standard and Poor predicts 26,000 more homes will be worth less than their mortgages needing to be paid from January to Apri2016.

The actual numbers harmed by negligent and seemingly profiteering banks is not known, but it should be established. There is a wait time for actual figures to be collected and resulting data studied to produce useful conclusions and publications, unless tampered with. However, other information could have been made available as data which might have informed better action. One wonders why direct personal support of those victims of what clearly was a corrupted system were apparently not directly considered instead of handing banks and financial institutions huge wedges of cash. Individuals could have had help stabilising their mortgages which had been administered by those same banks. Cash would have been injected where it was most needed: at the individual level. It is interesting to consider if the costs would have been less with financial social stability being re-strengthened, neighbourhood commerce (shops) benefitting, as well as reducing unemployment with workers paying more to the governments in taxes from their rescued work, wages, and salaries. This was not to be. Further, it would seem apparent that The People no longer own their currencies: the banks and corporations do.

CHAPTER 8:

INDUSTRY and CORPORATIONS

*Good deals are nice, but good
people are even better.*

There are parasitical organizations which feed on others in order to grow. Like a tapeworm, within the gut of society, they consume what has not been gained through their own effort and thought. Society is blessed through diversity. Small may in one sense be more costly....but it tends to be 'more beautiful'. Where there are many providers in their own area, rather than a bulky few dominating, they have their clients ever uppermost in their minds. They custom build and innovate. The conglomerates look to shareholders and banks and make use of The People. In contrast, 'smaller' providers need the support of day-to-day clients, with their good will. Far more often the customer is or becomes personally known with needs and preferences being met. Smaller providers can be more easily trusted rather than having successfully networked with the self-promoting and feeling-less conglomerate. Huge corporations exist beyond anything the people can research or defend themselves against. They rely on international balances. These providers should be most concerned with providing quality which fulfills needs, rather than manufacturing unhelpful self-serving devices to rake in vast amounts of extra cash. Industry or people: who should serve whom?

It may seem a small point, but why not standardize the heads of screws so that only one set of tools is required? Why not standardize cell-phone chargers? These are just two examples of the ridiculous and wasteful duplication in our world forcing up costs and pollution. With less duplication, shops could be smaller with their energy needs reduced. Advertising and display shelving could be greatly reduced. Production costs would decrease and workforce knowledge could become more relevant to customer needs. Delivery would be less fragmented and cause a smaller 'carbon footprint', and those offering advice would be more relevantly knowledgeable. What possible social value is there in having so many 'mirror-object products', varying only in the factory, workforce, and brand name? Reducing duplication would also make sense as it would reduce the waste of finite raw materials and fuels with both industrial time and output. The current overproduction, including food production, demonstrates that our best interests are not being considered by industry. The main argument for many production units is that they are smaller and more local and so serve a far more interrelated community-focused block. There are many other examples of customer exploitation. The Quarter Masters Store comes to mind. Computer printers are a nightmare as the manufacturers spew out new ink cartridges with each new model. So piles of computer inks are wasted, all to raise production profits with a sprat and mackerel philosophy. This situation could be fixed by new models with significant innovation built around a standardized cartridge to increase sales of available design instead of old stocks being wasted and thrown away, as planned for production redundancy. This wastage should be a Green priority and action.

The development of improved digital photographic cameras, like computer printers, has seemingly built in an unusually short work-life. I was informed in various shops that cameras were manufactured to last for about two years and printers for about a year and a half, 'depending upon use'. Such is criminal waste, as the only partly-broken goes to Refuse Disposal. For some it is the power source, for others the power contact unit, for others the display, and so on and on. From my experience, it is the printer roller-pickup that fails: surely this is a simple replacement fix! But one is told that the roller can't be replaced or would cost more than a new (subsidised) printer! Do they think that the world is a vast unending infinite source of resources? What is manufactured needs to last as long as it can, but this is not to the benefit of hungry corporate business and the almighty shareholders. Here is another interesting question as to which shareholders actually do count and have a meaningful voice. For users or backers, there is no Democracy there.

Some exemplary businesses go to extraordinary lengths to be constructive in our shrinking world only to be sadly lost to the devouring predatory and more profitable corporations: the price of caring 'too much'. Their products cost more since they did more and gave more back. Then ask how the great human public rewarded them when that cheaper international corporate competition set its sights upon their assets and sales. Will we ever know the full story of Nortel and BlackBerry? Both became tragic examples of how the scene of security can change company fortunes almost overnight: possibly as a tool of takeover or removal of competition. The workforce is hit en mass with mortgage planning, family dependants' provision, personal plans, and obligations all in tatters. However, company leadership is generally cushioned through accumulated benefits resulting in better security, their financial rewarding bonus system having added well to their 'wages' though they are still company 'workers'. Other workforce members who had produced the actual continuing wealth were, by outside standards, better paid but less well-cushioned due to outsourcing! Retirees achieved their seemingly secure pensions while those with disabilities and health problems were beneficiaries of company schemes - while they remained in place. All were funded by production, but then it came to an end. The company assets were still assets, but the producers of company wealth could no longer actively earn or provide the surpluses which took care of those no longer working. However, administrative workforce, including directors and the like, could have legal contractual security with even some instances of bonuses providing sufficient funds which had been safely set aside. This state of affairs did not 'trickle down' in anything like equivalent value. So much could be improved in the safeguards and Human Rights of the majority of the workforce. What had gone so wrong with those obligations and Responsibilities of the administrative workers (directors etc.) to affect so many of the Social Family which they had every obligation to protect? Directors were happy with severance pay.

The CBC in its usual way brought to the fore a glaring example of a current problem of conglomerates. The CBC certainly knows how to investigate and use a smaller example to highlight much broader ones. One huge corporation appeared to need to be broken up because of their daily active growth with their absolute power. These corporations are financially bigger than many countries and no doubt will, in time, take their place as the Government: a tad autocratic and definitely not democratic. Unless they are stopped, these conglomerates will effectively rule the world - that is, if they do not already act as a quasi single world government.

Tobacco: A simple and jolly social and enjoyable word until the toll in life and misery is added up with a $50 billion profit shown for one corporation. It has been estimated that this works out to $10,000 per death (Toronto University). This figure is very many more than deaths on the roads, which to be reduced requires very costly policed measures. Laws have been put in place demonstrating that this road carnage is not regarded as one of choice or a Right. Further, regarding road safety, Rod Andrews' revelation concerning the danger caused by car windscreen wipers brushing the rain in the wrong direction causing failed vision in heavy rain, which continues uncorrected, is presented in his book entitled *Cooling Down Planet Earth*. The ensuing tobacco death toll is also more than the present members of forces killed in the many wars around the world. How many deaths does it take to become a matter of Human Rights and to be afforded adequate protection? Thomas Boughey presented a frightening depiction of corporate powers, used by BA Tobacco, when nations such as Canada, Britain, New Zealand, and Australia decided to try to encourage their citizens to give up the habit. 'Giving up' the habit at an early age, as proven by research, generally results in full recovery. Governments use tax and health warning regulations to promote this end. In recent times trade agreements have taken on an added role as the conglomerates threaten or actually start using planned well-funded reserves to fight such anticipated activity. Such legal action is taken against nations on the grounds that their identification logos are not able to be prominent as is their right due to the legally required health warnings put in place, for example. Their company tax problem was attacked by their provision of 'no tax brands'! In Canada, for example, cheaper brands became available from Native American trade posts. Less popular cheaper brands made available on the borders in one country, but popular next door, have greatly reduced the number of charges leading predictably to their increased sales over the border being so inexpensive, loss of tax revenue as a penalty for the government, and less than the expected reduction in health care costs.

Poor countries can ill afford the costly legal confrontations even if they had the necessary skills, as Uruguay has discovered and Namibia is currently discovering. However, the strong pro-smoking counterattacks go beyond the poorer nations. As the trading post move demonstrated, Canada lost that battle, as did New Zealand. Australia also lost an earlier fight, although the blessed Aussie spirit shows its strength again as in 2014 they again faced the companies Head On, in a full legal showdown which promises success. We await the outcome in hope. Since Tobacco giants have 'promotional budgets' bigger than many national reserves, it is sure to be a battle. Hopefully, despite current setbacks, the hundreds of thousands of annual deaths will soon be shrinking dramatically: it certainly would benefit China and India as giant tobacco consumers. The Human Rights issue relating to a healthy lifestyle, particularly regarding smoking and alcohol, appears irrelevant through law, but the responsibility sticks.

FINANCES, BUSINESS, INVESTMENT, and FINANCIAL AID

What we want and what we actually need can be two very different things, yet advertisers like to cloud this issue. There is nothing wrong with reasonable wants, but needs must be met first and it is the responsibility of government to facilitate and enable these needs to be met by their citizens without creating greater problems. One responsibility for compulsory education is critical encouuraging thinking to establish a general ability towards an "understanding" of wise or reasonable practices, especially regarding spending and savings. These life skills are the 'reading and writing' needed for financial and social success. Current governments permit a form of Bank Lead Theft called Interest Payments well beyond what is reasonable and honest. They even enforce death theft of monies and assets for which full payment in taxes etc. had been made during a lifetime. The dead have a convenient habit of saying very little! We all need to accept that there is a need to spend and save sensibly, to provide for the future, and to give away less to the banking money shops. Credit can be useful if wisely used as a constructive financial tool, but it becomes useless and harmful to those who cannot and will not control the credit and themselves. Life can and too often does becomes a nightmare to the 'spender': a downward spiral of debt with the misery and absolute despair which ensues. Loan sharks move in! Banks generally do not seem to help or care despite the havoc they may well have promoted. The key to *responsible debt* and lending is that the means of payment are there within a responsible timeframe and amount. The weak need to be protected. Often loans are about 5% interest. Some advertise a $100 loan for just $10, which makes it 10% interest with any additional interest...... sweet! This is allowed by government and the Law. And then comes the Store Cards with their huge interest rates. During times of financial difficulty the temptation and necessity is to add to Bank Credit Card debt which will incur huge interest payments and costly letters being sent by the bank, when these loans are not swiftly cleared. Enter 'The Single Parent Bank' undercutting these others and giving far longer for repayment...

It is both wrong and avoidable that so many are lacking in disposable cash due to bank and lender practices that cause unending debt. Despite the will and ability to work with a paying job, individuals become heavily indebted, and not through gambling. This is a social disgrace. All should be in a position to create and maintain a meaningful 'rainy day fund' having seemingly been taught how and why through factual past crises. Certainly those times of shortage will arrive for most. Equally dishonest but more easily recognized as such is the practice, disclosed in 2010, of corrupt financial practices in a number of Canadian Keep Fit Establishments. The aim of joining one is to maintain heath and reduce the fear of costly dependency. However, following termination of membership many members of the public continued to have money taken from their accounts through double and triple billing. This is fraud, and must be the responsibility of both police and law to pursue and eradicate. But no, the practice continues (2014) ... while a "suitable agency" is reportedly being sought to deal with this. Fraud is not a novelty.

Banking, Stocks, and Insurance: THE BONUS culture has been perverted; it eats into potential assets and benefits like some form of social leprosy. Rather than a constructive way to award good practice and service, as originally intended, it has been built in as a contractual engine powered by some forms of output trigger that do not have to reflect the best interests of, for example, customers. The bonus incentive has frequently degenerated into vile and criminally corrupting practices: a vehicle to carry forward higher reward and a magnet for successful greed as non-customer benefits initiated with *Staff Points Systems* are used as a means of encouraging silence below towards wrong doing above. Duplicity thrives amongst those who should know better. It grows with 'Executive Bonus Bandits' being the first to protect their "money cow" as opposed to ensuring responsible action to both protect and respect the general public - their unlucky clients. 'Lucrative confusion' established purposefully through misinformation and downright misleading projections is put forth and used for investor recruitment. These plausible inventions unsurprisingly produce more investment and so trigger bonus thresholds and other rewards for those in command. These bonuses have too frequently been proven to be incentives towards the irresponsible!

The Worker, the Day, the Vision

Because of mechanisation there could be a shorter working week. Just four working days could have an equal or higher productivity. The Netherlands has the shortest working week and Italy has the longest. France has about 36 hours on average. What is 'Normal' is nationally variable (2013). For work to be relevant, it should meet our needs and fulfill our wishes. The New Economics Foundation (UK) researches current economies and beneficial economic change. Anna Coote asks what makes us happier. This foundation researches the following:

i. *What is wrong with the current economy?*

ii. *How can it be better?*

iii. *Demonstrably putting our ideas into practice*

iv. *Working internationally to build a movement for economic change*

David Suzuki suggests that we need to 'think globally while working locally'. In this way we can inspect what has been personally achieved and through these results be encouraged that we are walking the right path. Unfortunately, too little attention is paid to the evidential research and the unseen and unforeseen outcomes of our activities. Celebrating success is too infrequent. There is a tendency to become fixated upon the concepts of a larger and broader outcome while underestimating the importance of our combined smaller contributions. Our role is not irrelevant. Admittedly ours may seem to be a small part, but many small parts are needed to build into the whole - like the steel bonding rivets which enable a ship to travel the world.

What is the essence of Free Markets? How free is free? Free from what and why? With whom to benefit? The removal of protective tariffs enables the easier movement of produce, goods, and services. This enables vastly increased sales and resulting transportation. In time, demand calls for economies and wage disparity beckons the corporations to land with cheaper wage bills, further encouraged by financial 'gifts' from those governments. Gratitude seems boundless. The very workforce, who initially sustained the success of manufacturing, is now at risk. Rationalization of production costs means getting it done on the cheap while taking over other businesses and using relocation while selling assets. What the conglomerates are doing is buying into higher profits as they take over another business with its customers and reduced total costs. So governments negotiate their own electorate's demise. Because of the home country laws and industrial justice, won due to ever watching unions and Human Rights Groups, Governments and employees are now at a disadvantage and are no longer in a bargaining position. Yes they are free, but they are free from hope regarding this bargaining. They become 'free' to become powerless or unemployed once the link and distribution mechanisms are in place and out of reach, because a cheaper less 'troublesome' labour norm has been found, with and as a result of earlier governmental approval. Being cynical, this could be explained by arranged bonuses. So could the appeal for negotiating officials within the relocation process becoming so very much wealthier be called market forces? Consequently a worker who for years, through loyal work seems to have earned a job for life loses it, along with his workmates, to better enable the "free movement of trade". Does it not seem untenable to believe that something has gone badly wrong here? There seems to be little concern either for Human Rights or for human decency. Money rules, OK! So in addition were Wall Street 'Death Bonds' chickens coming home to roost! Folks, we are so lucky to live in a democracy and to live next door to "God's Own Country". You believe that!

By their works and what they do you will know them.

Outcomes speak louder than words......

A stitch-up in time makes someone wealthy-er.

Corporate kindness is close to invisibility.

Empty banks make the most noise.

An oft-played record is played again ... and again .... and again!

The road to truth is hidden by a multitude of words.

Hunger is now your kitchen.

Trust is the hope of fools.

Hope springs .... and drops on its face.

What are they doing to OUR world? Democracy yet again is corrupted by those who are exercising power and those who are sponsoring them: fortunately this is not true of all politicians and all who are wealthy. We are of a common life-force and depend upon each other. Some rule, some create, some maintain, but we can all contribute and we all eventually die. There must be a way to make existence better, more fulfilling, and happy for all and not just for some. More mutually acceptable ...... a human-right way produced through an all human following of Responsibilities, FREELY accepted and acted upon by all: of free will; of personal choice. Money cannot buy this condition of mind. Only the mind can realize it through a mental state that is attuned to reasoned concepts of justice. Justice is a balancing act in life, not of extremes, not of intimidation, not of confrontation, not of force, but freely chosen because it is right. There must be a common good in justice not subject to the whims of extremism, money, and power. The conflict between economics and political vision need not be perpetuated in an international conflict of interests. How brave and just if we all wanted less so that others with less could enjoy more. That should be their right and our choice. In fact many do choose to give freely of time and resources. The Social Family need not be in conflict because we often wish for some different condition. Some would hate to command but enjoy the exercise of skill and creativity. Others feel fulfillment in service or entertaining much more so than the alternatives. Some enjoy physical work and being outside, while others delight in exercising the mind and problem solving. All are important and all are needed. Providing the work is not an undue burden, it would be best to follow our preferences promoted by a more personal and relevant educational experience. The administrator, who feels 'on the top', is an employee like all the rest. These directors are traffic wardens of industry. They play an important role, but no more important than the rest. Meanwhile too many deliberately soak out of their employing structure much of its financial blood which could be better spent upon research, development, and community projects. Why they should expect and receive such vast amounts extra as an employee defies sense and decency. It is a defect which evolved through historical stockholder greed and has nothing to do with Human Rights. Rather, it has everything to do with Responsibility betrayed. Administrators might believe it is because of their greater intelligence which may be one of intelligence's manifestations. But their ability with one handful of tasks does not go far beyond that, and no doubt "lower level" employees could achieve similar results. One important truth highlighted by G. Dryden and J. Vos regarding Multiple Intelligence theory is the following:

"...we all have the ability to improve and expand our own intelligence: it is not fixed."

All should be in a position to acquire both the necessities of life with some pleasant extras as a result of agreeing to play a full role within the Social Family: one works with all. Why not include property and make affordable rental for those not wishing that responsibility of home upkeep? Cadbury's Bourneville and Saltire are two cases of such justice way back in time. Surely this is not beyond our modern industrial giants' imagination and use for 'surplus' capital! Bill Gates and Warren Buffett have grasped this concept, but there again they built their own dreams rather than being employed as a traffic warden of industry. The accumulation of wealth is a functional form of protection from insecurity as well as speculative investment: it enables a certain *secure dependence* (W.E. BLATZ, 1966) and does not necessarily result or stem from antisocial actions or belief. Their greater personal ownership could stabilize and secure most members of society, with the matter of creating demand and the necessary conservation of finite resources having been adequately dealt with. Team building is an acquired skill as are those concerned with planning and dissemination. Sadly we all probably have personal experience of the workplace well-poisoner busy at work with innuendo, hint, and criticism all aimed full of bile and destructive intent. They don`t like the well and wish to poison its water for others by pretending to be on the side of the workforce while gaining personal satisfaction in the process but to the detriment of that same workforce. In contrast, Jenny Mosley's "Wells" which "give you energy" are:

COGNITIVE WELL: ideas gleaned from others, discussion, and planning

EMOTIONAL WELL: recreation, family and friends, openness, discussion, and support

CREATIVE WELL: hobbies, art appreciation, and involvement

PHYSICAL WELL: right living, physical exercise, diet, and relaxation

SPIRITUAL WELL: Sense of 'wonderment and awe', renewal, mentally going beyond, and setting time aside specifically for this purpose. (adapted from Page 24, *Quality Circle Time* in the Bibliography)

· · · · · · ·

Students' *mastering* of the school material is manifested in goals reached to achieve the necessary grade, but since we all work at different learning rates and use different learning processes, some need to "redo" and "retake" sections. A good method may work well for one student and not another, though the latter could prove the better agent of and for application of the same knowledge following a different approach: an argument for the identification and provision of different educational approaches in the same classroom: using varied styles: there is here a good case for arranging smaller educational units to better respond to different behavioral types. The shy will respond so very differently from the outgoing and active. There are so many more variations to consider such as befitting the introvert and extrovert: group activity is not the way to go for all. In educational matters society must decide finally what are the key aims and how to achieve them. Difference enriches humanity but sadly may be swamped and submerged because of political Rights and educational short sighted dogma.

Since education is now exceptionally costly, there is a social obligation by the student to make an honest effort to 'cope' efficiently with variation before they have the experience or maturity to easily do so..... such as coping with those over-indulgent parents. Each needs to take sufficient rest times, take on the implications of socializing, and not accept the avoidable loss of standards. These are huge tasks for the young BUT they can be up for this challenge and go well beyond, as pupil charitable efforts prove again and again.... Our young are not as immature and unable to cope as some may possibly believe. Hall Denis Report (Ontario) echoes much of the far earlier Plowden Report, UK. Consistent unchanged assessment standards in an ever-changing world is no easy matter, especially with changing interpretations. The key is quality and depth of understanding which enable flexibility and performance, and this rests on value-judgements as well as base knowledge and personality. Further, redefined standards and parameters become "new data/information/statistics" for 'watch-dogs' and government agencies. These changes are difficult to compare with the old data due to the 'happenchance' changes........Indulgences in the careful manipulation and cherry picking of data-information, with careful selection of presentation-format, can *appear* to improve by reshaping an outcome or seeming to maintain it ....the purpose being to 'move the goalpost'.....! No surprise there, just warped ingenuity.

Is Canada ahead of the pack? Which descriptors are selected and aimed to produce which effects? Understanding, namely successful idea-absorption with the ability to correctly use and reuse it, hopefully results in logical linking, broadening awareness, and a willing additional absorption of facts. Application and combination will follow enjoyable successful learning. Nothing succeeds like success! So learning takes time to work, ferment, and produce the final product: that product can often be simply a beginning. Topics being taught successfully build essentially upon secure previous understanding achieved at younger levels, thus making essential earlier learning and skills preparation the keys to growth.

Injury to progress is assured following 'grade inflation': some examples of verbal overkill are the use of the word 'genius', and 'wonderful' and 'you are a star', which need to mean a lot more than getting early work right. Simplifying tasks to reduce accountable records/data 'failure' figures will have an inevitable result while placing an unhelpful extra burden on the educators at a later stage directly due to those earlier failures. There seems to be an early loss for that greater expectation of higher results at more advanced levels. Language handicapping has almost become a science in itself. Details matter. Loss of articulation and ability in formal English is allowed to handicap at increasing levels and over the professions so dependent upon meaning transmission. Yes, here standardization is very necessary for the more efficient exchange of ideas.

Language is thought and greater language skills enable ease of interpersonal communication and therefore greater levels of intellectual engagement.

"NO-SPEAK" Phrases and Purposely Caused Confusion:

Malpractices: The public depends on moral professional investigative journalism for its safety and freedoms. With the discovery and reporting of what one party viewed as *malpractices* with other concerns, according to interview all was seemingly met with little action and large expanses of hollow words of contrition. Phrases abounded such as: '*We are doing a lot of work on ....*' and '*Things will become very straightforward ......*' (BBC Radio, UK., April 3rd 2013). J. Humphries' revealing and informative interview followed a 10 million pound Ombudsman fine reportedly taken from a £2 billion floating fund put in place by the culprit company, in case of such an eventuality. This preparation proves an awareness of a hazardous situation. Huge corporations can prepare for these by setting up such sums paid for by their public. Furthermore, their strategies of defence can be built in advance. In such situations words alone are of little value other than 'buying a little time'; time will tell what the next avoidable tragedy will produce!

Personal Time and Relaxation

Peter Skinner, in his PowerPoint Investors In People Course (UK) entitled *Managing The Individual*, underlines the successful nature of consent and agreement to successful business practice. This is seen in what he classed as Theory Y (Douglas McGregor). A realization and appreciation that individuals will decide for themselves how they are going to participate in the workplace relates to their needs, wants, and goals. This was established by Victor Vroom (1964). It appears that McGregor would encourage a climate of agreement and cooperation rather than a climate of *"direction and control"*. He suggests that:

> *"physical and mental effort at work*
> *are as natural as play or rest."*

He continues by stating there are better incentives than coercion; *commitment to successful objectives is self-rewarded*; under the right circumstances most will not only accept responsibility but seek it; and there is plenty of creative imagination to be "utilised". He states well the point that since all workers are productive and could have useful input for an organization, it would be sensible to sort out ways to help this process.

Planning time to relax to ensure sufficient 'down time' will assist cooperative work involvement, he advises, especially if the place of work is seen to promote this benefit. The same may be seen as an outcome of planned time for physical exercise. The action of planning itself demonstrates that an activity is important and valued. Planning our holidays or any building or home decorating projects improves probable results and can maximize opportunity: likewise, better exercise outcomes will result from planning.

Encouraging greater concern leading to investigation validates impressions rather than permitting the preferred or imagined to dominate. It is necessary to properly inform sound judgement. A rested mind is better able to achieve this. From such analysis we develop trustworthy awareness and information. An appreciation for the lessons of history and geography provide instruction concerning actual examples of human development; these consequently have important roles to play in deepening understanding, just as the arts can promote deeper breadth of reason and appreciation of both beauty and skill. Competitions such as the annual CBC Literary Awards empower, encourage, and enhance awareness and discussion. However, one may wonder if such discussion can be too easily hampered and manipulated by some political animal following some hidden agenda.

The achievement of willing worker participation is a sign of both a healthy organization and personal attitude. Wickens focused upon the increase in motivation and commitment by those who participate in deciding targets,

> *"Particularly if they are kept up to date*
> *with relevant outcomes and findings."*

He points out that with initial success there is a greater incentive to progress, be it in regard to goals or needs. Active participation is more than likely to be positive and constructive, as music or poetry as part of events heightens emotional involvement and creative input. It is the antithesis to passivity and so is well worth encouraging from a young age. There is only one of us, so let us make of ourselves the best we can. Our lives are a flow or current of action and experiences. One of the joys when getting older is knowing one has been productive and being able to appreciate that we truly will be leaving this world a better place because we were here and chose to participate to the fullest of our ability: time well spent.

Social Training and Informative Education

Early life is the time for putting plans into action aiming to allow and promote meaningful constructive exploration. The mind is less cluttered in the young, and by being surrounded by warm love and affection one can more securely simply accept what is appreciated as right or wrong behaviour. With the future in mind both self-discipline and confidence are developed, but the balance can be difficult and no two children are the same. This is an area of learning for both parent and child. Ability and development tables can mess with - or rather confuse - the mind. They are rules of thumb at best. Further, a child may well appear to forget one learned skill or several because so much focus is being placed upon acquiring a new skill, only for the previously evident skills to return later. The benefits of accepting a prevalent social base of behaviour is not harmful but necessary for successful assimilation and identification with the local Social Family. If any remedial action is taken right at the start and is maintained, kindly and consistently supported by reassurance and warming response from others, then fuller friendship can grow this security. Vygotsky is again a useful read here. Presenting a positive image of society is constructive, experiencing it is essential.

A clear idea of what should be the *inevitable consequence* of education will enable more verification and thus effective activity. To produce truly educated individuals, these will need to become experienced, informed, literate, numerate, analytical, concerned, hardworking, respectful, responsible, and thoughtful. A similar warm and caring experience, as with the family, is required. "Factory sized schools" are not the way to achieve this. The educational firm but fair experience should result in a clear appreciation of the value of all individuals; a preference for positive interaction and loyalty; and a determined drive towards the achieving of group and personal goals. To achieve these the young need to have experienced and successfully overcome setbacks with each accepting responsibility to oneself and others. At the same time, the young must develop a clear appreciation of the value of both justice and strength of character with that essential readiness to listen and learn.

This miracle may be achieved first through the exercise of thoughtful self-discipline, respect, and constructive experiences designed to confirm and produce the desired outcome. It is a structured approach which builds upon the good in all humanity. This cannot be widely achieved with overcrowded classes, idle or disheartened teachers, spoiled or uncooperative children, or absentee or foolishly protective parents. Yes, the adults need to be educated first. Here the government's Responsibility is obvious and pivotal, for everything stems from Governmental actions, their honest determination, their lead, and both the laws and systems they introduce. All need to feel and know that they are 'stakeholders'. Fine details need the outcome of group decision advised by the active educators in the classrooms, for they will be making the all-important daily decisions and adjustments. No child should be able to feel isolated due to class overcrowding. Augmenting educational funds from industrial profits could be used to support this arrangement. The appalling decline of general education and general attainment with an inability in basics and behavioural standards is not due to teachers, parents, or pupils: this decline is due to what the politicians have changed our Social Family into. So much good has been discarded and so many young lives have been spoiled or ruined as a result. No wonder adolescence is seen as a time of rebellion rather than joyful and uplifting success. Plan and give <u>meaningful</u> projects for adolescents to be actively involved in which are possibly linked with their interests in exciting ways that allow self-expression (force). Perceived as irrelevant, school days become damaging, spiteful, and fearful which are factually too prevalent. If this were not so, then the bullying, graffiti, litter damage, and destruction would not happen, nor would teachers and pupils be attacked. Yes, it is that simple: standards beget standards while lack of them and reasonable and fair controls encourage brutish behaviour, filthy language, violence, and worse for that is the outcome of loss of self-control and self-respect. The young frequently have every 'right' to feel let down by exploitative industrial money, media corruption, and governmental self-interest and degeneration. I know of an autistic (UK) child who was *frequently* 'banished' into a 'separating' school room all day, totally alone, because of behaviour. Was this isolation ever going to improve the situation? Change is not just needed; it is essential with the active Social Family to ensure and establish that fair treatment and justice may return to their rightful place. Home and school can harmoniously share their overriding goals, or else why would we have both? I understand Karl Marx was all for breaking up the family and removal of property. This would prove to be the worst steps taken as communism and history show. Smaller secure units are needed where the child can develop a caring and secure self-image. Alternatively, the destruction of family and ownership would send children and adults in opposite directions from that which is desired. Educationalists are concerned with the child evolving to adulthood with 'good' character. This needs to base itself on clear beliefs and understood behaviour. If fear rules, a belief will be centred upon reaction and survival and all that this can lead to. The need is to encourage *responsible action* and so what is discussed and illustrated must identify most clearly where the focus of 'this responsibility' lies and what it entails. When this is in place, then so-called rights can logically follow on by using a firm base of values explored and understood by the developing personality. This membership of ideas and ideals builds community and safeguards citizenship.

Established standards being known and applied can produce written checks and balances to be read and appreciated in general, not least of all for minorities placing the information they need in front of them. It seems ridiculous the level of hysteria regarding Black Knights, black sheep, Tin Tin in the Congo, mean Scots, and other such minor annoyances. There are far worse priorities to make than these minor irritants. Matters of health, safety, and life threatening conditions and/or diseases desperately need attention. The best of good reporting using black print in 'good newspapers' both uncovers and reports the bigger case for focusing on action needed to protect inner city young from drug sales and gang culture; children killed or injured from 'old' but still active mines; AIDS in infants; the many more killed by filthy water; the curable problem of malaria; child exploitation and pornography; slavery; child soldiers; and mothers banished from family home and village due to appalling bladder injuries from bad birthing of their children. And that is just the start. How dare people waste our time with minor annoyances when there is such rampant injustice, poverty, and pain to be dealt with! Each nation should first deal with its own major problems, and from a place of strength enable their freed resources to support the actions of those still in need: it could be done. How much was found for the self-infliction by banks during the 1990s and 2008 financial Crisis; how much financial potential is wasted for each and every election campaign; how much is found to go to war; how much is spent on TV snacks and fashion clothing? Priorities.........

Flexible Less Formal Legal Tribunals Are Needed

Since industrial matters can too frequently fail to remain calm, as with day-to-day interpersonal contacts, disputes will inevitably occur which will need some strong, supportive, and impartial instrument to resolve. Fewer disputes need go to court, magistrate or otherwise, and many could be resolved by a speedy, fair response. There is a clear need for simpler and less costly ways to achieve settlements. It seem reasonable to conclude that with the growth of population density, an increased number of conflicts come before a system designed for a 'quieter' time. Swift action better reduces the probability of a buildup generating an outcome of even worse emotional decay, which can be avoided as long as a process is known and believed to be fair. I imagine that some conflicts would be better served by anger-managers and straight arbitration. With the huge cost of law, a less expensive way may be preferred by those directly in conflict. Such a development would not be easy, but that is no excuse for failing to try to innovate and hence meet this need. The finances placed in government hands are 'in trust' to be used for the good of the Social Family. This collective and collected wealth is justifiable only on the grounds that it enables the wellbeing of the people through support of existing provisions and the introduction of new or improved ones.

Full Health and Home Support

The ability to live in sound home-bases, with good individual health care, is the responsibility of government. All citizens should have a home. Even if they opt-out by preferring to live on a mountain, there should have been available the clear opportunity and provision to do so. The question arises of how to pay for this. The cost of one jet fighter plane would go a long way. Subsidies for industry could include a demand to build housing for the workers included as one of the provisions necessary to achieve financial awards or concessions. This strategy worked well with permits to build railway lines in the UK. Taxes upon profits could be held to ensure provisions can be provided even in an emergency. Local work-related housing would reduce transport problems, long commutes, and fossil fuel use. Less pollution would encourage better health and lower medical costs. With the loss of our industry, the pressure to move and relocate adds to housing and health problems. Stability in industry and workplace provision is necessary for relevant social planning and community development. That industry is permitted to relocate needs a planned and empowered set of strategies to resist. This problem has been allowed to develop and must be addressed. Local production is less costly than the problems being generated with all of the associated and inevitable emotional, environmental, social, health, and financial consequences.

· · · · · · ·

CHAPTER 9:

RELIGION AS AN ENABLER

There needs to be in place a general belief in the legitimate choice of whether to worship or not, in one's own way or religion. This could possibly be expressed as a Right that in no way should allow forced harmful or unwanted painful primitive practices causing intentional and unintended harm to others. This goes back to a hierarchy of rights that should be in place within law but is not. I am a Christian and feel fortunate in what my faith brings and offers through Jesus's invaluable teachings and examples promoting what is right. I also study other religions, for they too have so much insight to offer. What is there to replace the basic ideals taught by religions regarding personal conduct and personal behaviour in the form of 'contact points' within society? Through a belief-base there can emerge a stronger will to exercise self-control and discipline. Feelings can prove to be somewhat chaotic and so can greatly benefit from regarding accepted needs with agreed upon and internalized patterns of behaviour. This balance of forces can be achieved constructively by each individual, rather than reacting in a defensive way due to external coercion, imagined coercion, or threat. Perverted practices develop from human minds and not God's ways. If conditions are seen to be a fair, responsible, and successfully working system, then how much easier they are to accept and promote: for if they work well, then why not use them! No place exists for the incontinuities and anger of 'extremism' here. The human race won its way and so arrives at now. Its natural inclinations, order, and awareness has achieved this. Totally ignoring extremist forms may not be the more productive way forward to achieve continued survival and to advance.

True belief in any positive deity will include a desire for self-improvement, honesty, and kindness and help toward others. This will not succeed if one is weak and manipulated. To use one's gifts for the good of the Social Family and to look for the good rather than the bad in others promotes cooperative advancement. However, when the bad has been identified, it needs to be confronted and dealt with. We live walking on those stepping stones to God. In different religions, with the same touchstones of working for the good, action, - like awareness - is a process of learning. One may start from a 'multi formed' polytheistic faith focusing upon the multiple layers of life, but in the end it is personal and singular. The Hindu faith enables an easier focus upon the plurality of life's many forces. Zoroastrianism develops the concept of a single deity creator opposed by evil, while Judaism provides clear rules to enable a better 'style' of life. Buddhism helps understand the development of a fuller appreciation of our personal responsibility and ability to develop ourselves with our self-control. Loss of self-control cannot be remedied after the fact nor by legal action. Christianity develops the need to be thoroughly honest about inner feelings with honest concern for all others, while providing the keys to the future, as taught by Jesus. Islam also demands those actions consciously designed to help and not harm others and emphasizes the centrality of God and an obligation to perform good works. Admittedly mine is a very simplistic and subjective selection, but hopefully it shows religion's value to humanity and thought. Being so different, we all will draw differently from these and the other religions. Our different approaches do not mean we are doing something wrong. Rather, by being different people we have different needs - be they in the form of mental images, explanations, or reasons to exercise self-direction differently. It is my belief that the creator made us all different for good reason. Assuming there is this divine purpose, then we are meant to be different. This in turn is provided for through different philosophies and beliefs. Different roads may eventually arrive at the same destination. One person's belief will be another person's certainty and yet another's dependence on faith. The biggest problem is those corrupters of their own self-proclaimed faiths intentionally and unforgivably turning their beliefs into a force for evil: this is definitely not the good that was intended.

Evil people have selected their confined area of evil and have honed and perfected the evil they exude. This is one of the leading arguments for swift action to prevent that honing: nip it in the bud. At its simplest, true and worthwhile religion is positive and operates by looking outward for the inward benefit, all resulting in group development. It must support the needy and encompass and improve society if it is to be a constructive aid to the survival of the Social Family. We must realize that we all do some wrong, and we must address this issue. Down the ages great women and men have influenced the thinking of those around them. Some have been called prophets, others have been called teachers, others have been called enlightened ones, and another has been called The Savior. They have often been signposts of example, providing the individual a better world image and thus a better future. Too many of their following interpreters of such visions were less constructive in their personally-constructed visions and contributions. Some were arrogant and self-seeking, and some were plain evil. However, despite their destructive nature, the evil that has been viewed as acceptable by the generation of that time can be relied upon to be less well-received or considered completely wrong by those generations who follow in a different time with different immediate memories. Religions tend to provide a continuity of direction for far longer periods of time and to provide a platform through which these ideas may be passed on and even defended, en mass. Tragically, religion can also be manipulated by self-seeking cowards and social lunatics to gain power, settle grudges, and try to remove something which they interpreted as objectionable, having been examined by their shrunken and deformed intellect.

New ways of thinking may be called 'up to date'. Others may be considered just modern or simplistically promoted as a better or middle way, but they may and too often do cause harm and unhappiness to many. Poorly examined dogmas are equally liable to be corrupt and corrupting. Old ideas, dressed up in new clothing, do not make for new ideas even if they are called New Age or something else. Furthermore, new ideas can be just plain wrong. The old saying, "If it ain't broke don't fix it" can frequently be proven only too right in positive situations, but sadly that would tend to be inevitably in the light of hindsight, loss, and tragedy. Understanding does not come from nowhere: it is searched for, thought about, and tested. When exposed to open debate, religious leaders in society - without the benefit of the fullest and broadest forms of education available - are not worthy of that name. They are mud-filled chasms into which the ignorant, inadequate, angry, or just plain lonely fall and are drowned. They are even more dangerous than the deluded fanatic, for they gain power through creating doubt and then controlling their 'victims'. The gift of oratory was given to both Hitler and Ghandi; Jesus and Stalin; The Buddha and Lenin: by the outcome of their words they are known. The gift of oratory may be heaven-sent or evil inspired. We can all appreciate the difference between Ghandi, Jesus, or Buddha and the works of Lenin, Hitler, or Stalin. History is littered with this human trash and their sorry followers as well as those fine opposites intent upon the good of the many. In general, power achieved through force and intimidation is a good indicator of their lack of worth, be they Pope or Mullah, King or Leader, politician or civil servant. Too frequently we see these evils manifested in entities disgracing their own religions and our combined God using their perversions, half-truths, superstitions, lies, and even murder. A religious person recognizes that the great God-given gift of thought is given for good in all, with reason and inquisitiveness both deeply imbedded within. These God-given gifts are best valued when well-exercised. They need to be enabled and encouraged through respecting the subject and exercising strong and reasonable self-discipline. This self-discipline is copied from the example of others, from its consistent use, and it is not perverted in the false name of freedom or as a descriptor of adult behaviour (in reality arrested adolescence), Human Rights, or - weakest of all - free personal choice. Religions often form the guide towards understanding, consequently teaching where and how to apply 'discipline'. The State can step in when and if matters move beyond the remit of any religion. Religious directions can be a formula for constructive civil behaviour. However, we need to guard against religion becoming part of the institution etched into an active State System of intervention: so please promote self-control more than state control. If religion takes on political powers, then it is wrong and loses its 'right' to 'preach' (offer advice), for by accepting overriding powers of government it has opened itself to the abuse of its primary Responsibilities. This is not to be placed on the same shelf as administration, which is a whole other 'can of worms'. Religion therefore needs to be of the people, for the people, and amongst the people, while government sadly seems to often be self-isolating despite all of its protestations to the contrary. Too frequently it is because of its isolation that Government can be seen to be descending into either a quasi or absolute dictatorship and closed government.

True religion is centred upon the development of an awareness of Responsibilities towards a better self and community; the promotion of those related attributes of thinking, reason, and care; and an awareness and concern for matters within and beyond our community: in short, a specific future for all people in all lands. That is enough for any one collection of people. Government should be left to a separate body or administrative bodies. Government is organization and right provision and not a theological watch-dog. Governments serve, not teach. Further, the sheer diversity of these Responsibilities could well explain why there are different religions and what such variety has to offer a world of so many different personalities, cultures, economic conditions, and preferences. Things religious are not, and never can be, the sole territory or preserve of a 'religious' people or organization. Those who have not taken up the gift can later find/discover and so accept personally the illuminating promise religion could bring. Religions advise, suggest, and support but should never dictate: this is not God's mind, but rather a structure through which we learn, experience, and grow spiritually. Their gift is too personal for that if it is to be of lasting or even eternal value. Religions singly cannot "know it all", for after all they are or have become subject to human addition and constructs relevant to specific and local experiences.

Religions are one of the greatest influences for good because they sensitize us more and more to the needs and feelings of others with those outside our direct experiences as well. Such empathy brings with it a fuller understanding beyond us. The gift of life is to live, and this life entails so many differences. Life is about success and happiness, failure and despair, and all those shades that lie in between. One major key to successful development is the mental outcome called discipline or *constructive purposeful organization* of thought. This focus entails predictive action towards perceived worthwhile goals. Actions (ways of being) when followed by appraisal and adaptation when required are most likely to achieve balance and therefore contentment.

SINS: Defined

Sins Defined.

1. The breaking of religious or moral law especially through wilful act
2. An offence or fault
3. Rebellion and alienation from God [rather than] a crime; a violation of civil law. *Collins Pocket Dictionary*, P782
4. **Christian:** Falling short of the will of God [through the human failing of original sin - Adam and Eve]
   4a. there being Institutional sin ... in Church and society
   4b. as well as personal sin
5. **Muslims** view sin under two headings....
   5a. a fault or shortcoming which happens inadvertently......(e.g. Adam and Eve, there is no original sin in Islam)
   5b. a willful transgression...which is a matter of intent rather than accident
in **Christian tradition,**...........Social and community The 7 ... sins....pride, covetousness, lust, envy, gluttony, anger, and sloth...The fundamental vices thought to underlie all sinful actions.
Pg. 487& Pg. 471, *Dictionary of beliefs and Religions*, Wordsworth Reference Series, (Ed. 1995)

Individual Versus God so Versus Community

Personal Sensory Experiences Versus the Unknowable Hope

Versus What Supports Both

Experience Versus Hope Versus Support

Religions and Beliefs

"There are two forces, those for good and those for evil and we live and drive between them ."

(*Andromeda* -TV Sci-Fi Series)

Service towards others is not a matter of rights but rather a matter of decency, humanity, and responsibility. This follows a belief that such in itself is right. We need our beliefs which inform and form us into what we are, a situation we too often neglect to consider. At crucial moments beliefs play a major role. So much of life is ever-changing and uncertain but an understanding of Responsibilities with their often flexible and personal natures enables a more situation-specific choice to be made with the likelihood of a probable satisfactory outcome. Just as the computer enables the internet to be accessed, so the system of belief and Responsibilities enables constructive situational interpretation with creative social interaction. This is not always possible following the letter of rules and laws. Furthermore, the essence of each may be perverted when they are used as a tool of the ambitious, thus resulting in their being put to bad and even evil use.

Still the mind that is content and so at peace

While all around discard in disarray and grief.

Do take notice of those who so display respect

That calms their manner,

So passing one good moment to the next...............
(Unknown author)

God has and is giving the one humanity every permutation of variable to enable humanity to each find a way to become one with God - believing and serving willingly, happily, and in joy.

Extremism

The tragedy of religions is the seemingly inevitable arrival together of misinterpretation and the extremist. Where the most unhappiness and cruelty are seen, there is the most error. Extremism often shows itself in a form of Rabid *Orthodoxy*: an animal-mind takes over. Any difference or variation from their own becomes viewed as wrong and a danger which must be eliminated. So runs the mad authoritarian mind. Enter Hitler, Stalin, and many others from vicars to popes to mullahs to priests. Consequently, too many are somewhat tragically tarred with the same brush since they too are popes, vicars, priests, and mullahs despite their demonstrating good. All are viewed with the same distrust and fear as those evil examples; all are painted with the same brush to be viewed by strangers. Consequently, some wonderfully caring social leaders who give up so much of themselves so selflessly for the benefit of others and their community are lumped wrongly with the cowards, bullies, control-freaks, and ceremonial 'nut cases'. For me, a creator God is both rational and caring. Only a mentally defective individual would seek to destroy its own creation. God is not that. The creator of so much beauty, symmetry, and visual splendour is the Creator and so cannot be the Senseless Destroyer. That countless numbers of recognized and forgotten saints have died in all religions in their attempt to further peace and the good of humanity, goals learned thanks to their religions, shows what a difficult and dangerous road they have travelled. That they died at the hand of hatred demonstrates the disregard such murderers hold for their creators' work. That destruction is true sacrilege. Such people are outcast from God, and hell is when they realize they did it all themselves and have to exist forever in shame and pain, unable to join their ancestors and family members who are remembered fondly for having kept themselves so much less tainted and dishonoured. We do not know what fate awaits such leaders of evil intent, but in accord with Biblical prophecy how much greater will be their guilt and self-flagellation for eternity. This is a personal concept.

Better to repair rather than revenge. Greg Mordiston's book entitled **Stones into Schools** demonstrates true greatness, not just his own but that of the village leaders who were involved in the inclusion of girls in education. From our childhood and early social encounters we learn to regulate and understand emotions while developing valuable empathy. Conversely, a drive to punish or avenge perceived slights and hurts could however become the dominant direction taken. Some see it as acceptable to encourage sacrifice and to cause pain for an end which is termed good such as this. But where to draw the limits? Was it Wayne Dyer who observed that only 15% of US service personnel fired their weapons from 1943 to '44 in the war? Anyway, this is an interesting insight. There is a clear conflict between empathy and revengeful desensitization. Could empathy be expected to remain fully in place in a war situation, despite so many painful and horrific experiences? It seems it can survive, just as the First World War Christmas soccer game between opposing sides in the trenches on the Western Front demonstrated.

Some say Jesus was just a man. Well if that were so, then how great was his sacrifice and his commitment to and for us all, showing what we each could achieve with firm resolve and iron strong faith? He did not undergo all that anguish, agony, and despair for his own benefit! His beliefs either as man or as God's appointed are both equally valid. His teachings are equally right. His work was just as blessed. So it is for all profits of love, kindness, and peace: by their works you will know them. Ghandi was not a blessing just for what he said but for his vision, his humanity, his love, and his caring - which inevitably produced action. Action was the inevitable outcome of his knowledge. The Buddha, Siddhartha Gautama, has given a great legacy of truth with ways to discover truth which have benefitted so very many. More than all that he led by example. From living a life of extreme luxury he chose poverty, a search for ultimate truth, and service. God's messengers love God's creations and so lead through their caring and certainly not through destruction.

There is an almost organic living process and strength which enables all and any to change for themselves for the better, within their mind, in the light of fact with reasoned ideas. Choice is such a powerful activity, as it is so full of positive implications. In contrast, a Right is promoted as being simply right and not subject to reason regarding a specific course of events. Rights should have a flexibility which allows for circumstance, situation, and responsibility. Rights need to be able to influence and thereby prevent, but not when thought and reason dictate harmfully otherwise. There is an apparent need for a framework for obligations and Responsibilities to be enabled from one community to the next through agreement. The list of Rights is a good aid to discussion: preferable and more effective over time than brute force. What happens when a Right conflicts with a responsibility? Which should have priority?

Some blame God for allowing the tragedies created by humanity's free will being exercised or else from chance outcomes. Existence is an interaction of different energies and forces with chance outcomes being inevitable. There is always variety and chance. Social manipulation through Rights is very different from teachings and internalization of our Responsibilities to ourselves and to others around us. The wearing of a 'sensibly'-sized crucifix by a Christian is hardly cause for concern any more than a football supporter's club badge or jersey. However, what does seem to stretch the bounds of reason is not allowing a crucifix but providing special 'modesty' sleeves for a few of many Muslim women to be worn during hospital operations and similarly some Sheikhs being permitted to wear bracelets on the *understanding* that they are pushed up beyond the elbow, possibly needing to be done repeatedly during the process of surgery. The sterile nature of the operating theatre is clearly the greater priority and a Health and Safety issue (April 2010 UK). Divisive allowances being made for some religious artefacts or customs while others less problematic are prohibited seem guaranteed to create offence and hostility. Could the hysteria produced by pressure groups rather than the opinions of the majority be the cause, one may reasonably ask? Religion informs; it promotes awareness of 'the better way'. By promoting understanding, co-operation is encouraged with allowance for individualism. Greater understanding through freer choice can be most constructive, with the individual even deciding freely to be religious or not but upholding the norms, decencies, and interests of the Social Family. Sensitive and *sense-able* behaviour is the outcome: using clear and sensible mind promotes balanced action.

Dream Spirits

The CNN Radio broadcast an interesting piece on Dream Spirits: the belief that in daydreaming we briefly enter another existence. This, we are told, although 'strange', is a valid experience which can inform and direct us. Strangeness does not define reality any more than writing down a concept of rights makes them right and consequently fixed under most or all circumstances. For many years of modern science, the speed of light - 186,282 miles per second - has been the measure, the fixed, and the undeniable fact to be applied. It is amazing even to think of being able to measure such a speed and to a millionth of a second. Relevance can and does change along with what is known and can be assumed. Quantum mechanics states that twin subatomic particles can be in two separate places acting the same way and at the same moment, and that their strength in this will increase with distance. This is an unknowable activity without the correct base principles to work from and powerful enough appropriate apparatus available for use. Scottish collaborative researchers from Glasgow and Heriot-Watt Universities, both members of the Scottish Universities Physics Alliance, have slowed light and returned the influenced photons to 'normal' surrounding conditions where they remained slowed, rather than returning to the speed of light as previously expected. This was proven (announced January 2015) despite all previous evidence to the contrary. One form of evidence may be one form of mistake due to event interpretation. To some extent our mind accepts an inner world of religion, following serious study; and research, also having followed sound principles of integrity and having avoided any form of indoctrination or coercion. This awareness informs and instructs. It generally leads to positive modification of behaviour once sensible understanding is in place. What may have seemed impossible might prove to be possible and real. The 'miracles' of modern discovery emphasize this conclusion. Examples such as the potency of new soil bacteria and antibiotics, Wi-Fi, lasers and CDs, the microchip, and nanotechnology exist. Further the recent use of pre-surgical operation, 3D printouts point to a whole new future also in medicine. What we already feel and know finds an organizing avenue of consciously arranged words and practices to work through and then act upon these hitherto hidden 'dream realities'. Some things can just feel right, and conversely others are or feel wrong. To accept and state a moral stance is commitment from experience and 'gut reaction'. Group commitment and acceptance enable greater group cohesion with so many forms of progress. Such requires the INVESTMENT of thought based upon a very real self-interest. Being such is no bad thing if it benefits the well-being of the Social Family. Sadly violence can be a part of self-interest which tears the unifying fabric of harmonious intent. Creative vision is real but fragile. There is no room here to waste on violence. Parts constructively working together produce positive progress.

It is observed and reported that Kurdish Muslims respect the 'God's House' of all peoples, including Christians. This is the expected view of right behaviour and I believe is the opinion of the majority: Godly Muslims, Hindus, Sheiks, Jains, Jews, Buddhists, Beihai, Christians, and others. This is illustrated also by some Muslims who donate in order to help Christians in areas of Iraq. Strong beliefs often require some forms of self-sacrifice to promote kindly good.

Personal and Social Growth

As one guest on CNN Radio suggested, we can identify a positive contribution for the group good via 'Religion as a moral standards enforcer'. It should also and equally be noted that these religious standards have been formalized in a way which is acceptable and constructive.

One may wonder what religion is for and where its value lies. Religion may be accused of being unscientific regarding sociology, geology, biology, psychology, and 'criminology'.

Broadcasters who suggest religion is anti-science or not scientific are arguing from the wrong perspective. Religion does not promote itself nor see itself in those terms or restrictions. Science is demonstrated through the scientific method and finds or works its way into religion due to fallible human involvement and supposition. For example, some proponents of the Green Planet Dogmas state that they are the Scientists in the know. Aspects of the Green message are undeniable, except to the most blinkered minds. While some suggestions are speculative, there are other equally probable explanations being ignored. Too often the 'you carry my bag' approach holds sway on the ground that I know, you don't, so follow me! This expert versus you the ignorant is a handy and too easy argument: a form of intellectual bullying. This approach is also evident in questions of Rights. Where understanding is lacking, education must begin. One major problem concerning the environment is its call to give up or change an existing benefit. This needs to be accompanied by an understandable explanation of how to achieve the goal and minimize the inconvenience or pain, balanced against the alternatives. There needs to be some generally agreed upon target with activities to win gains which are agreed upon, individually aimed for, and consequently more readily accepted. But how? Next up is the uncomfortable question as to who could or should pay for the changes. Would it be too trite to write that a problem shared is a problem halved? Within the equation there would possibly be a growing awareness of sustainability linked with tax incentives.

Information + Experience → Belief → = Action

Kevin Kahn

Islam

Ed. R. Pier Beaver et al. (1993) *The World's Religions*, Lion,

First some Information and Observations Regarding Islam and Christianity

JIHAD or Holy War against non Muslims first phase starting systematically from the Years 634 to 644, to expand Muslim territory. This was begun by Caliph Umar who conquered Jerusalem in 638. Spain was mostly conquered by 731. The word Jihad also means *"Struggle".*

CRUSADE: a medieval military action to recover control of the Holy Lands and remove the murder and abuse of Christian Pilgrims. The official First Crusade was in 1096 to stop the actions started by the Deldjuk Turks

MONGOLS (or Tartars) lead by Genghis Khan (1206-1227) devastated huge areas of the lands of Islam with lasting outcomes. Muslims and Christians fought against this threat

Muhammad's death has been recorded as in the year 632, when conditions clearly were very different from today. The Second Caliph, Umar ibn al-Khattab (634-644), promoted **"Holy War"** or Jihad to expand his Muslim realm. For him and his followers the world was divided into the *Muslim 'Sphere of Peace"* They labelled all non-Muslim lands as the *"Sphere of War."*

Shari'a Law evolved. It was strongly promoted by Abdalla Shafi (d.820) to control some of the extremes of the autocratic Caliph and others. This system also placed limits on corrupt practices. Shari'a is based upon the Qur'an, the Hadith, a consensus of Muslim legal practitioners and both the use of careful debate and reasoning.

Many Muslim women believe that their beauty is the Creator's gift to their husband, not to be defiled by any man's lustful glances in the streets, hence their deciding to wear the *Hijab* head scarf or the full veil *Niqab*. However, these ideas can become extreme and result in total segregation. Dogs can also be a problem for it is often accepted that "no angel will enter a house containing a picture or a dog." (Hadith)

There is room here for both misunderstanding and conflict.

These notes were composed referring to:-

Gaskell ,J.M (2003) *Explaining Islam*. CTS Explanations.

Notes of Michigan University upon *The Crusades*, available on the internet, also with other sources.

It is said that 30% of Islam's followers speak Arabic, which means that these 30% can read and interpret the Koran for themselves, if they are literate, should they wish. This situation is no different from the days of dominant Roman Catholicism where Latin was the language used and which nearly all could not translate into their native tongues. Under such circumstances people are almost totally dependent upon others for understanding the content. When another language is in use, potential dangers emerge of mistranslation, manipulation, and misinforming which can lead to an experience of differing levels of manipulation. Too cynical?

In the Islamic faith Mohamed is the last of its prophets from a line of prophets which include Abraham, Moses, and Jesus, for example. The faiths of "the Book" as they call it, refers to the Jewish Torah, the first five (Torat) books, the writings of David, the Psalms (Zabar), all in the Historical

Old Testament, and the Gospels (Injil). . So three religions share basic beliefs in common amongst which is a living God, a need to do good, and a commitment to personal spiritual growth. These connected faiths are Judaism, Christianity, and Islam. Good works and prayer help towards this end. That which goes against God is not of God. A study of the various prophets will show the difference.

Shad, in CBC's Studio Q (03/12/2015), conducted an admirable and enabling interview with Canadian Boonaa Mohammed, the maker of the film *Tug of War*. Boonaa is an eloquent and brave speaker and as a Muslim he is not representative of that vile terrorist minority. He renews an uncorrupted view of what is right in Islam as well as highlighting its distortion by such as ISIS. In one revealing moment he touches on his experience of arriving for his first day at his Toronto High School, daunting enough for most, but it happened to be 9/11. How well he communicates the despair and turgidly repetitious questioning from others with that unwanted role, thrust upon him unasked, as a speaker and authority on Islam, a role for which he felt totally inappropriate and unprepared. His interview is worth downloading and listening to.

Do these two examples, of very many more like them, read as if they relate to the same faith that ISIS and such terrorist follow and promote!

*"NO act is valid without good
intention and each being will be
judged according to intention"
(The Prophet answering a direct question).*

*"....seeking peace and harmony,
preaching justice among men and
showing tolerance for others are acts*

of faith." (For Muslims every act can lead towards good and faith or evil.)

True integration for many immigrants in foreign lands is prevented by the formation of language ghettos due to language barriers. Isolation grows. Unconnected migrants suffer a form of progressive shock. Combining aggressively brings a purpose and so a security. Avoidable misunderstanding and power struggles within take place with exploitation. In Turkey Imams must undergo both religious and secular training, a practice which is both unusual and commendable. In some places training of any kind is absent as self-appointment of Imams takes place. There should be no necessary conflict between the Muslim and the West. There need not be any. In fact there are millions of good Muslims who are part of that West. Those not wishing to be in Western Society have free choice. If a society is so appalling to someone, then why remain? If safety, comfort, and regular meals are the reason, then be grateful. Many Europeans emigrated to find a better way of life and their form of freedom to live as they wished, and they continue to do so. To live in a Muslim tradition-based country will mean Muslim ways of living. Conversely, to live in Western countries will mean Western ways of living: hopefully by avoiding the vices in both. If one is safe and enjoying the benefits of a Western or Muslim, or any world, then have the decency, respect, and sense to behave. If one is not wishing to do so then go to where those beliefs and feelings are the preferred norm. There is no benefit to a family demonstrating hostility towards local custom which has an understandable appearance of inviting - or causing - conflict. Add to that being isolated linguistically there can be no useful deepening of understanding or constructive compromise. Refugees given shelter and a safe place to live would vis-à-vis expect and respect difference - it would be hoped, and not unreasonably so. However, there is nothing wrong with or inevitable about gratitude. Resettlement does not come as a right but as a gift. If the new way of life does not appeal, then other choices are in abundance. If Westernization is a form of unacceptable secularisation, then so be it; it is not a fixed collection of religious doctrine, for the West has experienced and rejected that one. Rather, Western ways are much more adaptable, and because of this those used to and approving autocratic life will experience insecurity, alienation, and even loneliness. This Western style of adaptability is why it works so well, since it can more easily adopt and adapt. It is rather a matter of the people's open and respected choice.

In Canada it has been suggested that the Imams here should clearly state if they are actually properly and academically trained for their Responsibilities. This is not an unreasonable assumption for all religious leaders. The almost inevitable alternative is an 'anti-intellect.' Intellect and broad learning is not and never has been just the territory of the Christian West or the Jews. It is a reasonable prerequisite and expectation of a leader that they are as fully informed as possible, which includes awareness of argument, shades of meaning, definitions, point and counter, opposite positions, and so on.

Christianity

and God's given gifts

God allowed humanity awareness and understanding which they need. Coming with that awareness is an obligation to share with others so that they too can benefit. If one does not acknowledge a God, then the sharing is still pertinent. The *gifts of the spirit* (Galatians 5:22-23), being the work and desire of God and not man, demand that humanity uses these gifts.

"Oh, joy to those who … delight in doing everything the lord wants." (Psalms 1:1-3)

"When you follow the desires of your sinful nature, your lives will produce

…. Evil results… but when the Holy Spirit controls our lives, he will produce …. Fruit in us." (G a l a t i a n s 5:19, 22)

The Gifts of the Holy Spirit are love, joy, peace, patience, kindness, goodness, faithfulness, gentleness, and self-control.

"If we say we have no sin, we are only fooling ourselves and refusing to accept the truth. But if we confess our sins to him, he is faithful and just to forgive us and cleans us from every wrong." (1 John 1:8:9)

"I am the resurrection and the life. Those who believe in me, even though they die like everyone else, will live again." (John 11:25)

Each gifted person has their own responsibility to decide how to serve others, to establish who and what they are, and to identify what they have a responsibility to do and to be. While using the God-given gift of free will and free choice, each must freely decide just as Jesus did as a person and fully as a person: Jesus accepted an available choice with associated duties and Responsibilities. We are expected to ask, to question, to seek, and to be honest with ourselves. Only when this is successfully concluded may better understanding enable the freely given life to goodness. Giving to goodness is for God, in God's ways, and thus also shows these ways of being to fellow people. This better serves and is served by the creation of individuality and the individual spirit, which is infinitely more interesting and interested, bringing with it the extending bonuses of achievement, happiness, wonder, and above all sincere affection, care, and love. Tragically some use other free choice directions and take the other option towards evil, hate, manipulation, and thus despair.

As in nature, life develops itself using those aspects which may be called 'the world': complex, interesting, varied, and infinite in that variety. Life adapts, adopts, and fills the many potentials, discovering the relevant possible niches, ever evolving as God intended. In all this opportunity the births of Confucius, Buddha, Jesus, Mohammed, and other manifestations were not only inevitable but also intended and facilitated by God and through their goodness are the very nature of God's creations - and God made man - whom He did not then just leave but rather stayed like any good father would, not following the real option to leave. Through the Bible accounts it may be recognized that He helped, chastised, and encouraged but always with individuality being promoted. We are intended to vary which is for our individual good and that of those with whom we interact. The slide away from God cannot be personally resolved by a Christian. There is no Human Right there. Only Jesus is accepted as being able to secure that salvation, because nothing other than His sacrifice was adequate. However, like any gift, it has to be accepted first to become one's own.

Society can be seen as the acceptance of historical aspects of correct and exemplary behaviours and the outcome of a religious interpretation; this is what Nicholas Wade termed "The fourth instinct".

Emile Durkheim's Religion < = > Society

Durkheim is viewed as the father of sociology as an independent academic discipline. Society he saw as many parts working and evolving collaboratively in a Structural Functionalism in which those elemental forces within society produced a balancing social integration through a mechanism of free will.

Diagram 8: Personal And Social Growth

Personal and social growth

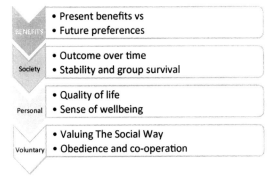

BENEFITS	• Present benefits vs • Future preferences
Society	• Outcome over time • Stability and group survival
Personal	• Quality of life • Sense of wellbeing
Voluntary	• Valuing The Social Way • Obedience and co-operation

Human Qualities and Democracy

Feelings joined with a wish to belong can easily be interpreted as very human qualities which are either developed from birth or blunted from that point. Further, control through the process of manipulation through raw emotion, hysteria, or pleasing acceptance have proven to be highly successful. Using emotion to bypass both reflection and 'balanced' thought is a well-established means used to raise sales, through silencing the expression of alternative avenues of thought and even matters of truth. Generated is a preference due to an emotional and not infrequently termed politically correct position. Racial hatred and the hatred of difference is nurtured through emotions such as 'scapegoating'. Child pressure is motivated without appeal to conscience in order to sway parental choice. For example, toys for fast food or sweets at the cash desk are payback for the shopping time boredom experienced by youngsters, used to far greater freedom, who have become thoroughly fed up with the restrictive shopping experience. There seems little pleasure for the young when adults shop: to play with the Claw Machine to win a small toy are little incentive to cooperate.

It would be interesting to know how many would support laws to ensure a commercially-free childhood. France again seems on the right track at Christmas time, with its continued ban on child-targeted advertising. No discussion of freedom or the need for information there. A universal condition of the responsible would be to remove this form of child exploitation by rendering it a potential crime whenever used: children should enjoy freedom from this dissonant sort of pressure, while parents need to also be protected as 'a right'. Such exploitation may be recognized as leading to a form of 'adult insanity' or pressure causing mental instability. One in five North Americans reportedly now have emotional problems. There can be no reasonable excuse to flood children with what is bad for them and for their parents. The outcome is higher sales for both the drug companies and toy producers, and these may be two of the causes for the freedom or rather licence captured through selling strategies!

There are food industry problems. One reason for this might be the legal cost of fighting international conglomerates. Big industry is not necessarily best. It is important to produce 'good' food. We are what we eat. One meat tenderizer is from the protective sap of a plant which if ingested by a feeding insect rots its innards, so the insect dies. The moral and responsible way forward is obviously not to find what an industry can 'get away with'. For example, by introducing synthetic colour, flavour, and texture produced using chemicals derived from petroleum oil to increase profit. Good quality should do that. If a product changes colour due to a process, then one assumes that is natural and acceptable. It is not an uncommon occurrence. Sad examples of irresponsible behaviour appeared in China regarding a baby food; then there is the Western World's use of 'scrapey' in animal feed; the bleaching of bread to ensure whiteness, or the dying of bread to achieve a better shade of brown; the watering down of milk; poisonous cooking oils; highly suspect sugar substitutes in diet drinks and foods; ice cream with no cream content; and so on. The public rather than the producers should decide without chemical manipulation hiding the fact with additives. The old saying when seeds were being planted was how nature and the ecology of ecosystems worked: "One to the frost, one for the mice or birds, and one for the crop". However, this ratio does not look good on a financial ledger, and so masses of poisons are sprayed each year over crop and soil. Do people really prefer that? Or maybe this is an indication of how powerful and successful lobbyists and advertisers are compared to our better interests. Then there are the hidden changes affecting specific groups and unappreciated by the rest. Changes have taken place in America's North which have reduced the number of caribou from 80,000+ to 14,000. Herds have been decimated which has resulted in the loss for many people living there of their main food source. They obviously had no say in the matter.

Worthwhile democracy exists in step with responsible choices based upon accepted responsibility. This requires high standards, decency, and participation with active consent. All else is false democracy, with the most pernicious being that self-centred anarchical individually-driven process which operates through power struggles - the outcome being to break others and take over their power. People have become simply a means to that end. For democracy to work well for all is almost an impossibility, especially once vast amounts of money, advertising companies, and pressure from big business are involved. The only greater power that could overcome these would be 'good education' and the united action and will of people. To achieve these very clear and simple objectives many forms of choices would be required since populations are so varied. How to find a unity in such diversity! It is clearly easier for the interest groups of money, industry, and politic power to select specific goals to advance their own best interests and will. The quality of democracy seems dependent upon group size. If a group is 'too large', then smaller individual contributions too easily become submerged. So this system works yet again for the strong rather than the weak. The centralization of government and power into ever larger units is one of the main threats to personal relevance and choice. Democracy would be better protected by decentralized government since this would encourage and support local activity and better protect relevant Human Rights in a more balanced way. Smaller units offer more at the personal level with less need to dig down, unearth, and collect information which then must be analyzed. An informational chaos results from the less 'human efficiency' caused by economies of size. However, with mass and efficient communication methods evolving such as social web use, there is a possibility of real transparency and democracy developing to replace our current 'partial democracy'. Equal access of information and the vote are now available to all, although human apathy is still a major hurdle. One 'dream' scenario would be a workable system of local political candidates who are locally focused, using local funds, and promoting local production made possible through less demands and waste: a Social Family collective view.

In life little matters more than that we are honest with ourselves and that we have honestly tried to do what is best within the conditions we find ourselves. Responsibilities are our personal challenges with problems further complicated by our own imperfections. We can do no more than honestly try to do our best to live our life properly, as a 'good' life, which includes care and consideration of others as well as care and consideration of our own. We each need to promote our own abilities to 'reasonably' fulfill ourselves. No one else is really in a position to know what that is, what that entails, and why. Free choice, respecting the points of view of others, and balanced discussion rather than confrontational argument each reflects a responsible and *reason-able*, sane, balanced approach. Once the emotive shouting starts, then balance is lost and a form of sword comes into play rather than sound sense and consensus. Privacy and respect for an individual's personal time to relax and socialize, as each individual sees fit and needs, will promote mental and physical health as well as a satisfying life. Such a way of life should reduce a tendency towards aggressive behaviour and a focus upon Rights due to personal insecurity and anger.

It would be easy to conclude that our individual rights disappear when aspects of the news media take it upon themselves to drag people into the public arena for theirs and the media's own gains. That it harms the focus seems unimportant beside viewer figures. These self-appointed guardians and unelected judges and juries of right and wrong turn a buck butchering people's peace, reputations, and lives. Real investigative journalists operate through balances of decency; a real and consistent moral position; and the exercise of appropriate good taste supported by their refined intellect. All good journalism is informed, balanced, and driven through sound morality and understanding of both right and wrong. They are brave, seemingly tireless, and honest. Another look at examples found in the book *Dial M for Murdock* illustrates too well the dangers of news media perversion. So many journalists can and do play the essential role of social heroes by defending the bedrock of our society and ensuring the strength of the boundaries of decency, honesty, and the proper use of power. These can and should be recognized as the modern 'chivalrous knights' prepared to put themselves at risk for the common and not so common good. Conversely, so many of the others are the filth of self-interest and greed, pretending to be part, but in reality choosing dishonour to exist in the shadows of the real journalists. They are the refuse on the information waters.

Intellect and integrity rest and are nested within a concept of freedom; they are a basic human need if 'peace' is to be achieved. We all fall short sometimes, but do the jackals have a 'right' to bite? Our freedom to live would include an acceptance that we all periodically make wrong decisions. At such times, assuming no intent of wrong, spite, or crime, a little understanding is called for. Unfortunate vulnerable individuals need the effective protection and support of responsible people due to the unforgiving and ambitious parasites. Likewise, if a family has a member dying of some genetic illness, they need support rather than the whole family being penalized through various insurance penalties. The purpose behind insurance is to spread risk for the benefits of its contributing members and the more vulnerable amongst them. The initial purpose behind insurance was not to make huge profits and administrator bonuses, which again can be seen as investor theft. Further, we do not have any right of information (whatever that is) to highlight and have reported in the newspapers or other media news of some poor soul going through the agonies of depression, divorce, illness, or loss just because they are well known. This misery has become such a money-making business that there are even gutter press which invent their "news" and sick-minded people who buy-in and so reward it. There are sad and sorry people who pay good money for this trash. University student stress is shown in suicide figures for first year students. Reportedly the change in marking levels from what they had previously experienced in high school is a primary cause of the shock and depression it can produce. One survey of students, reported by the CBC, showed over 50% of first year students polled were suffering serious stress. That should be something never considered as acceptable, yet earlier experiences of unrealistic inflated marking and grades are still being demanded by those in charge of many schools. Learning to cope with reality and finding workable remedies is an essential part of growing up. We all need to learn how to cope with pressure and "failure" and to be able to dust ourselves off and start afresh. Life is like that and we each need to be prepared by developing the necessary grit. We may learn this from participating in sports and games with others "doing better" than us and winning awards and in turn having their "off days". We also benefit from reasonable use of the word "no". Children need to hear "good try" or "well done" and "that is worthwhile", but I question the use of "brilliant", "you little genius", and "superb", etc. except for the very occasional fitting use. Children are even being robed and mortared for photographs of their "graduation" from kindergarten to Year 1: unbelievable! Parents comprehend the floor-show, but what is the effect on the children as adolescents with inflated egos and expectations!

Currently, for university students having built up substantial university debts or being in the process of accumulating debt, it seems reasonable to expect that they will be able to complete their course without it being shut down part of the way through. One of my grandchildren had this sorry experience without any loss or reduction of the debt but with loss of the course. Also, following successful completion, each university could have a register of willing potential employers, preferably greater than the total number of undergraduates, in each field. This does not seem to be an unreasonable responsibility for institutions, provincial, and federal governments to support and promote. After all, the taxation gained in the ensuing working life will far supersede the costs.

First Nations and Northern Canada have the highest suicide rates; they run into tens in each area. This cannot be because of the Human Rights agreed by Canada but rather the Human Responsibilities so neglected. Also, arguably living on the streets for some is a form of suicide, the last slide over life's wintery cliff. In contrast, how acceptable can it be to have Tracking Apps to keep a continual watch on our children? We fail to allow them freedom as they develop, as they are now always under surveillance. Is this an abuse of Human Rights? Further, it is not good for us as parents. These 'aids' are the product of the promoter of fear - and fear grows. As pain makes us more susceptible to pain, the same is true of fear. This fear for our children's safety needs to be firmly kept in balance if parent and child are not to suffer ever increasing insecurity and depression. We have to be able to depend upon ourselves; survive a few knocks; and explore with freedoms of choice to become confident and competent members of society. To keep our children and the vulnerable safe needs to be focused upon and achieved at an individual level. We all are responsible and we all have the responsibility to be so. Once a person chooses to step outside the reasonable and act in an antisocial manner, restraining action becomes necessary. At such times loss of specific associated so-called rights will have to be part of the outcome. Since she or he had freely chosen their path, they must suffer the consequences of that choice. Conversely, those aware and responsive to their Responsibilities deserve to be protected and supported by the law and its agents. If the violent thief is injured in being prevented from his or her miss-actions, then those acting on behalf of society need to be confident that their reasonable protective action will initiate reasonable support from the powers that be. Again this is a matter of finding a reasonable balance, whereas using the letter of the law in documents of Rights is full of pitfalls and traps exploited by the unscrupulous with a clear target to cause imbalance. Those who defend and thus promote the law breaker through technicalities and loopholes are like moths destroying the garment. Fair trial is another matter. Further, corrupted attorneys are a disgrace to their profession, though by their action it is clear they care little for that and so have chosen to become enemies of their social families. When victims choose suicide following rape and the 'free' display of the act via Wi-Fi wizards, the perpetrators need long prison sentences. Such displays via YouTube and others, though totally against the wishes and agreements made with YouTube, happen due to lack of learned inner moral checks by these sick infested forms and their search for some available unsuspecting victim. Disclosure leading to "discovery" should automatically result in photographs of the perpetrators being released to the media for the protection of other to encourage any other victims to come forward and as a warning to other socially sick minds.

There is nothing created that
cannot be manipulated.

Promoters of racial, political, and religious hatred are the spreaders of a mental disease. They infect people and whole regions. They choose to sow spite, fear, and criminality. They have made their decision to unjustly lead a war against the foundations of society. As such they freely choose to move beyond society's protection and so-called Rights. They only need the charges brought against them to be proved. That is The Primary, the first action, the crucial initial strike, the notice to others that they are not invulnerable. The courage and preparation to press charges supersede any secondary consideration. The benefits of living in a country which believes in the virtues and constructive nature of free speech need not be extended to abuse. To say in private to a few friends that this or that individual appears untrustworthy is totally different from standing outside shouting it to the world or outside a place of work. How much worse are the peddlers of hate and violence as they spread their poison? The proven importer of illicit drugs causes enough harm to the Social Family to be permanently removed once guilt is established. If not, they have the contacts and networks to continue their vile trade. It is interesting to consider the quality of life for convicted law-breakers and terrorists when compared with that of the far too many homeless, Native Americans, Métis, elderly, and infirmed. How they would like three meals a day, warmth, entertainment, care, and a clean bed? These resident groups receive less support and financing at this time (Jan. 2016) than our newly arrived immigrant 'instant' residents. Does our society not have a responsibility to *ensure* the wellbeing of both and all groups? One can understand the broadcaster who repeated the quote that 'The Indian Act is Canada's pseudo apartheid.'

So on to a constitutional right to carry a gun.

CONSTITUTION: "*The system of fundamental laws and principles of Government, state and society.*"*in* Collins Pocket Dictionary [CPD]

Out in the wilds of the out-back country the gun is needed to survive but there should be no such call in a city. That guns are felt to be needed shows a failure in national morality, law, and its administrators. It is sad to reflect on any society so devoid of decency and respect for fellow citizens to make toting a gun not just felt to be necessary protection but to be a necessary action to ensure survival. A similar case is found in the ghettos of South Africa, Brazil, and Nigeria. Guns are required in order to have a measure of self-defence against the threat of others. This is a very real threat, all made so much worse because they have that right and can carry a gun. What had been a product of history does not need to become modern reality as well: social maturity could see to that. The 'right' to carry a gun should solely be based upon need and danger. Danger from wild animal attack such as caused by rabies is one such example. Hunters need their weapon, but they do not need to be able to blow a hole through a truck or spray umpteen bullets in a second: skill, not brute force, should be the hunter's boast. Police and members of the armed forces will need guns sometimes, but hopefully not all the time. Their dedication and bravery on our behalf carries a duty of both respect and care, but for a very small number this seems to be a free licence to intimidate and dominate even in a 'peaceful' situation. It is a sad reality that some 'broadcast' their views of the shortcomings of others to hide from themselves their own. Cruel abuse of power is thankfully infrequently seen in Western communities and emphasizes the quality of almost all forces of law and order. What also needs to change is that not infrequent reality that armed forces abroad are the front line of trade.

· · · · · · · ·

CHAPTER 10:

The SOCIAL HUMAN QUALITIES
Caught and Taught

*Love does not end with death; we pass
it on generation to generation.*

Each Social Family member 'benefits' from different layers of experience through which each perception interprets within *its reality*. Everyone is different, everyone is unique, and everyone needs to find ways of 'blending' to achieve the Canadian W. Blatz's (1966) **"Independent Secure"** state. The process firstly is one of experiencing. Next comes recognition, then internal debate, and eventually one hopes a peaceful and co-operative acceptance. For this to take place, imposition will not work. It is through agreement that the soul may rest. Through agreement social units become the family. Respect and respecting are crucial to human harmony. Imposition is not harmonious: it is the clash between a lesser power with a greater one. An outcome may be achieved but probably only on a temporary basis. With the acceptance of Responsibilities there is a natural growth progression. Awareness grows with age, and we each learn to 'play our part'. Inclusivity is better and more effective than exclusivity. Empires and kingdoms come and go but the human race goes on: or rather it has up until now.

A Right is an expression or summary of a social goal. It is an aim: a target to be achieved through acceptance of both specifically spoken as well as undefined Responsibilities. If the *Responsibility Aspect* is neglected, then the goal will be temporary and insecure. The 'inner' Responsibility empowers the act: the external Right is a definition of accepted 'Inner Responsibilities'. The empowerment of the powerless could be seen as 'a rule of thumb' for the final test of any 'right', for when upheld it is seen as and acts as The Right Way, independent of power or influence. Such acceptance produces stability and has a greater chance of survival. Such a creation is a confirmation of established consistent behavioural practices which are accepted as social accepted norms and are thus part of *Social Family Traditions.* Their form and reason for being are listed below:

1. Physically

2. Socially aware/being recognized or reinforced

3. Taught - having been conditioned

4. Culturally experienced

5. Are imagined, developed, and practiced

What too often is a rare accomplishment of growing up is the creation of *Emotional Elegance:* that strong gentleness of spirit that is unassuming but honestly and actively concerned.

Some Scientific Advances

The wonders of DNA data are seemingly endless. Gene-based banks of information are being linked each day with regions and history. An increasing number of names, addresses, and personal details are also being collected at the same time which produces concerns. Interesting historical information emerges regarding our ancestors in the HAPLOW GROUPS. The National Geographic Geno Graphic Project is clarifying several of the tangles of human history. Meanwhile, at the other end of the scientific 'wonder-sphere', biogenetics increasingly offer early intervention to reduce the damage which aging would have brought to many. In 2008, for the price of $2500 a personal analysis was available. For a small governmental investment, how much less expensive could this become to the benefit of all through preventive proactive medicine? With whole nations being tested, the health bill could be greatly reduced and care for the elderly could be improved with care becoming less necessary. Consequently even the $2500 figure appears a small investment beside the benefits. The possible educational benefits from improved health suggests a very open opportunity here: experience with growth of knowledge. Further, with proof that 66% of ill health is caused directly by our specific behaviours, David Agus (co-founder of Navigenetics) argues for our own responsibility to and for ourselves with the medical 'business' becoming increasingly more an Art than a straight science. How many people suffer daily with the annoyance and embarrassment of HALITOSIS (bad smelling breath), unaware that it probably is food-choice initiated and there-fore totally 'curable'?

Human Potentials

Alistair Smith, *"Accelerated Learning in Practice"* Network *Educational Press,* (1998).*UK., ISBN: 1 855 39 048 5*

Michael Stubbs, *"Discourse Analysis"* (1983). *ISBN: 0 631 127631, Basil Blackwell*

'Potential', both in the scientific sense and in the human resources sense, is such a broad-ranging word. Its power is directly a function of possibility: no possibility = no potential. However, once into these realms of possibility the singular no longer applies. Potential here is in effect always potentials, in the plural. To suggest that it is possible to achieve a person's "Full Potential" is nonsense! There are not enough years or hours of life to do that, even if several lifetimes were available. The use of this phrase is another example of intentional dishonesty to achieve preconceived goals in a preconceived manner. It is such a neat phrase with quasi scientific overtones that it has been accepted by edu-cationalists and parents as a truth and a possibility. All sorts of emotional genies have been let out of the bottle rubbed by this word Potential. Cries of such and such action will be reducing their full potential, or such and such is sacrificing their full potential, or that action is ignoring their full poten-tial, some stifling effective change through experience, etc. these phrases are 'thrown about'. What crass nonsense! The human mind and body are capable of so many possibilities that it can truly be said, "as one door shuts another opens". The best person to judge which doors to open is the indi-vidual. This requires a certain maturity born of experience:

very much a moving target. It is nothing to do with reaching a specific age band. The greater concerns regarding Piaget's pronouncements demonstrate this. His theories and sometimes faulty research were once the 'Holy Writ' of a large chunk of educationalists, some of it justifiably so. However, sensible caution needs to be exercised when dealing with absolutist statements.

With the successful use of Vygotsky *scaffolding* (and the rest), and the winning of W. Blatz's (1966) *Secure Independence*, the focus of so many potentials happens. They become able to select on the grounds of experience, excited interest, and curiosity which potentials to pursue, for pursue he or she must if the selected potential potentials are to become actual fact, though almost inevitably modified in the process.

Humanity tends to form people-clusters. With clustering comes the bonus of security, and so clustering becomes firmly established: the levels of security vary from person to person but within this security are also potentials born because of that security. Clustering evolves into ever greater forms depending upon security levels, need for projection, and available ambitions (the nice sort), with positions of responsibility either implied or 'agreed'. Once agreement is made, then security is sealed.

From out of the strong, confident, and caring community well-balanced people emerge. These will happily fulfill civic duties and be active in fostering the benefits to both society's whole and single parts while also enjoying the journey.

GROUP GROWTH: one view

A. Family > clan/tribe > chieftain > nation or alliance > conqueror King/Emperor/President elect

B. Chieftain > authoritarian with undefined power > consensus leader with restricted and defined legal powers (constitutional King/President)

C. Law keepers versus big business and big money - corporation…..ambitious law changers – dominance

Diagram 9: Positive and Negative Empowerment

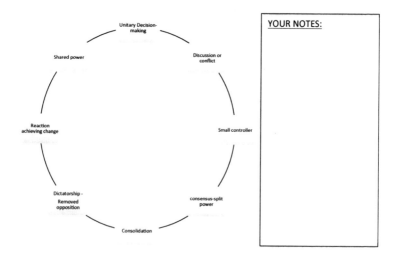

No person is capable of reaching their full potential since potential is not a single entity; rather, it is comprised of many very different possible outcomes. Hitler, Stalin, and Mother

Teresa all with their particular personalities, a full potential if you prefer, but no prizes for which was the most worthwhile 'potential' to achieve. The present legitimate Dalai Lama was revealed by the searching monks in a small village; if they had wrongly chosen another child the suggestion is that the Dalai Lama would never have become one of the great minds of our time but instead a rural lad growing up to be a rural adult who would have been quite ordinary rather than outstanding, inspirational, and unique. I disagree. This represents two potentials, both subject to redirection and evolving change. Rather than concerning ourselves with directing children towards achieving the impossible full potential, it would be far more constructive to *enable* them to find and value their own natural talents and to explore and find their preferred interests using these; to develop interests from exemplars of quality; to develop self-control with self-direction and self-respect; to choosy unity with and of their society (no need to encourage and promote the cult of some irresponsible and totally self-centred adolescents). Steep those in an exciting environment and remove the unhealthy and unconstructive temptations of the 'wrong' potentials. We need to become mature enough as a society, or as a society of societies, to decide what is to be excluded, removed, controlled, and yes, even suppressed. Some potentials harm, injure, fester, and corrupt: these must be opposed with the unswerving resolve of the caring whose duty it is to protect and lift the weak. For example, significantly growing signs of Nazi-style abuses would justifiably bring a swift, strong, remedial reaction.

It is both possible and advantageous to establish some of the beneficial traits of a personality with careful and caring observation and then specifically encourage their development. To 'bring out' is the essence of education rather than trying simplistically to pour information in. The process of learning is one of forming links within the individual's own and unique structure for understanding. Being able to identify what those lines were or where they lead is fraught with difficulties, it may be suggested, beyond assumption or the law courts. All people differ but there are generally proven approaches which work well to promote learning and mutual understanding. Fear is not a good tool for this. It has been long recognized that fear blocks any understanding while interest and excitement construct understanding. It is not certain how the latter works, but the brain clearly responds and organizes itself in *its own individual way*. The brain also appears to continue on its own account to sort and sift personally significant problems within our subconscious, eventually providing solutions months later or while we are at rest. By then we may have even forgotten that there was a problem. There is much yet to understand.

Dating agencies look for complementary and compatible tendencies. This often appears to be a successful approach: possibly educationalists have something to learn here. *Accelerated Learning in Practice* (1998) is one of a whole series of excellent publications produced by Alistair Smith and others which draws upon many threads of research from Nobel Prize winners to excellent effect. Tony P. Buzan (1984) has devised his Mind Map system to organize information visually and thereby show linkage and development. This approach encourages clarity and is a quick reviewing process, not dissimilar to earlier *concept mapping* but with different intent in processed linking. Such personal brainstorming gives a clearer understanding behind thought, just as the *Discourse Analysis* outlines by Michael Stubbs (1983) can provide better understanding of actual intent or meaning in group discussion. His *Sociolinguistic Analysis of Natural Language* demonstrates the danger of assuming that words necessarily indicate an intent. Simplistically, Stubbs looks at how to better appreciate the meaning behind the apparent meaning. We start from what we think we know, drawing upon experience. This will continue to dominate unless altered within ourselves, in our minds. It bears repeating that force is not the more efficient way to achieve this; rather, force will most probably achieve a form of opposite outcome.

Desperate WANT Versus REALITY:

Want can affect perceptions of reality, as can motive!

A Psychological View

DREAVER, J.(1952) Revised Wallerstein, H.(1965) A Dictionary of Psychology, Penguin Reference Books. Harmonsworth,UK.

A PATEN: *a metal plate, a solid fixed shape, a Di.*

A PATTERN: *1. A design.*

2. A model or pattern used in making things.

3. A regular way of acting, a behavioral pattern.

4. A person or thing worthy of imitation.

5. A simple GESTALT: A form, a pattern, structure or configuration; an integrated whole.

ATOMISM: *that the conscious state can be analyzed without loss into elemental states.*

GESTALT PERCEPTION: *"We perceive figures and forms as whole patterns that are different from the simple sum of individual sensations.*[For example, the wristwatch is composed of many different parts] *People organize sensations into whole patterns .These include figure and ground, perceptual groupings, and closure."*{The FIGURE is the focus while the GROUND is the background. These can interchange the relationship of each. PERCEPTUAL GROUPING is the arrangement of what has been sensed in one meaning while incomplete recognition may be *made* to fit to achieve CLOSURE} The integration of thoughts, feelings, and actions, for example: the parts of personality (**Frederick Peris**).

HUMANISTIC THERAPY for problems involves mostly 'the clients' being responsible for improvement supported by a therapist in the here and now (Also Ref: **Carl Rogers** 'personal centred therapy.')

As Sigmund Fraud showed, mental disorders can more than reasonably relate to *subconscious* conflict. From such a premise any intensifying of this subconscious conflict would logically seem to cause a deeper and more serious disorder. Application of what is seen as unjust 'force of law' will achieve this. Better to discover and agree. Fritz Peris, founder of the *Gestalt Therapy*, emphasized the enabling nature of recognition of a certain 'wholeness of personality' to replace a feeling that 'something was missing'. Our behaviour is the product of our total existence. Our emotional nuts and bolts rely upon past experiences, and use of law does not remove the problem. Rather, if the outcome is a seeming acceptance of an imposed position, without the necessary restructuring it merely resembles a behaviour-only cure rather than a full cure based in fact. The problem remains to re-emerge later. Disregard for a so-called Human Right needs inner adjustment and not outer force. The time to deal with this is best during the early years when it will be termed by some unfortunately with the emotive term 'indoctrination' which generally signals wrong intent, or a form of brain-washing contrary to the child's own Human Rights. The conflict of this position is obvious. The Gestalt system argues against being "someone else" to fit into others' preconceptions. Likewise, blaming others for our perceived or actual predicament is fallacious. It is far more constructive to decide for ourselves through a due process of honest self-analysis and inner awareness and therefore accepting our responsibility to be ourselves, able to live calmly in that state of illuminated awareness. Such balanced and empathetic awareness goes beyond legalistic rights to a deeper internalized awareness of human Responsibilities being exercised by each of us towards, as we see it, equally valuable other beings. Jean Paul Satre's focus upon individual existence respects the reality of an *"analysis of everyday life"*. We build our own reality and meaning through personal experience and decision making. One could say that beyond ourselves there is no other relevance since we create our meaning. Imposed standards remain outside until such time as we choose to accept them or any alternatives as chosen by ourselves. Little gain is achieved for civilization if it is seen as other than natural (R. D. Laing), and rather as a form of captivity. So saying, some of our assumptions, as argued here, are therefore those of mentally imposed upon captives. It has been suggested that the only value of ideas and objects of civilization are that they enable so many more to survive through their successful continuance. This being so, one may ask which is most important: to protect the state or to protect the individual? I suggest that the two are inseparable. As I understand, these were points made by Thomas Drake in Michael Enright's CBC show, and they seem undeniable. We establish strong beliefs through which we CREATE our security. That these will more than likely evolve and change is inevitable .... they must change, or else our lives will become a dead and boring experience.

How we experience life forms our life-view. The factors causing these views with their assumptions come from outside of us. We interpret these from within, using our experiences, while progressively each culture informs and thereby promotes specific experience and thought direction. A culture teaches and we learn. The Outside Conditions create the responses from inside. To relate in resonance with others deepens our being and our mental confidence while strengthening basic thought, assumption and response, community co-operation, and thus the Social Family. To alter successfully we generally need others. Security is crucial in this as both an enabler and a goal, achieving consistently clear outcomes. Imposing what seems entirely wrong and endangering to an individual will inevitably lead to dissonance which can lead to action that may be violent and permanent in its implications. The 'adjustment form' needs to be working willingly 'from within'. Thus, a new experience of 'the within' follows the achievement of understanding and balance, with the preceding unwanted situation discarded, therefore successfully enabling change to occur. Carl Roger worked towards this end via the group therapy of peers all striving to help each other. But the first step, it may be suggested, is that an acceptable evaluation precedes any readjustment to succeed. One questions if the law and Human Rights achieve this constructively or rather perceive this as force which will at best remain a temporary 'fix'. Free reappraisal following honest reflection is called for, unhindered by the wrong forms of emotional response generated by forms of external force. Eric Berne neatly identified three aspects of interpersonal interactions in which the self-image could be that of an autoreactive *Parent State*, the balanced and rational *Adult State*, or the self-centred and dependent *Child State*. Parent and Child make demands in contrast to the secure and much more flexible Adult. It can reasonably be suggested that for successful revision of 'prejudicial attitudes' a true adult state of mind is required with its constructive co-operative tendency rather than a somewhat destructive demanding, self-centred, or authoritarian one.

The stance or positioning of the mind will not be unrelated to physical experience. Thus, this also needs to be considered. Perceived injustice and unreasonable bias need to be resolved in a way no law can achieve for the individual. Complete disregard of one's own value systems by others is a breeding ground for reaction and conflict. More laws will not diminish this whereas reason and positive experiences can. Stress, anxiety, conflict, and confrontation lead to unhealthy conditions of imbalance. The calm and secure person is most unlikely to become violent and confrontational in a balanced day-to-day relationship. Emotional and conditional balance is such a valuable tool for achieving worthwhile goals that it should not be ignored. Pythagoras was well aware of the soothing and restorative power of music within the environment, so long ago. More recently, dairy cows have been shown to be more productive with the right music playing: mood leads to outcome. How we feel affects what we do and say. Can confrontation and the law be seriously considered a productive way to resolve anger? Visualization of success has been demonstrably beneficial to more than a few sportswomen and men with its adjustment to motivation and resulting achievement. A different attitude to others can equally be achieved through Visualization, but again a specific perception or desire requires a very sensitive balancing act.

Again and again culture returns to this discussion. Different systems include different values which will vary considerably. However, there is far more uniformity than some would care to accept: it is only the few who initially comprise much of any interpersonal problem. It is wiser to not grow any problem through perceived injustice and anger. Some of these few are self-interested people who, through continual repetition, force a pattern of thought 'into' a growing number of individuals' minds who then spread this 'new cultural virus' to an ever widening number as it also becomes incorporated as part of their 'perceived' culture. Difference becomes a danger, a growing threat. Stories of incidents ascribed to these deepen a developing rift and increase personal alarm with associated feelings of vulnerability. What was only an idiosyncratic or flamboyant way grows into a threat: a sign or a symbol of what lurks in the background of our minds. Possibly it also draws upon the effect of a 'collective memory' from past generations (Carl Jung) which may be built into our DNA.

There is a point at which what was feared and viewed as unacceptable can become an understood way and therefore be accepted by individuals. Instead, a constructive and positive position is a better way to build acceptance of difference. This desired change needs to be seen, experienced, and accepted as a reasonable balance, with reasonable levels of give and take. The long established majority's viewpoint which constitutes the status quo must always be kept in mind. However, some fine tuning and reasonable innovation is not only unavoidable but essential to progress. Should violent opposition be one party's only recourse, then and only then does the law *need* to step in. One of the most significant contributions to cause conflict is loss of trust, a loss which can be reduced through discussion and other forms of interaction. A community centre can be a great enabler for this if it has not been identified as existing for and used exclusively by one group: this would only cause further division.

World Responsibility: The Big Society Recognized

A person and a nation demonstrate caring concern by their reaction to internal and international poverty. These are two aspects and two priorities, but how a democratic nation acts on behalf of the poorer vulnerable people is so because it is what the majority of the people are prepared to accept and permit: thus representing a lack of empathy. This permitted distress is the result of poor emotional development, brutalising entertainment, or actual experiences with no shortage of dominating selfish priorities.

Problems regarding loss of both sympathy and empathy are an avoidable cause of the undesirable saturation of minds with violence, both from a young age with interactive computer slaughter and irresponsible road racing and then the lifelike films of violent gratification or sick minded disease portrayal. Emotionally appropriate responses are inevitably blunted and HUMANITY is weakened. Further disloyalty, self-interest, and dishonesty seem to be promoted by the same sources, not to mention an undue preoccupation with matters sexual. How can we balance such mind-deadening pollution with reality? The surgeon through experience and exposure is able to overcome human tendencies to avoid cutting open bodies, which they do, to achieve their wonderful results. They become - I use the word hardened - hardened against the action and emotions of the one to produce the benefits for the other. Loving grandchildren care for others such as grandparents, despite the misery for the elderly of weakness, incontinence, mental illness, and loss of memory and self-respect. How can they live most days in such sadness? They grow hardened against the condition and, please God, softened toward helping the person. More examples of life's angels are the efficient and kindly nurses, almost always (seemingly) happy and caring. How could they deal with the many things that are 'thrown' at them if they had not become hardened to the condition but also open and able to fully use their gifts, time, and energies in caring for others? So too with cleaners, builders, drivers, and soldiers. All find value in becoming hardened against the 'unpleasant'. We probably all have such occasions to deal with in life.

The media and computer game orgy of violence, misery, and stupidity (going for kicks) blunts our capacity to empathize; we lose our empowerment to effect change, to correct what is avoidable, or even to care enough in the first place. We are hardened and deadened by fatal and unreasoning violence. The remedy is to stop buying and thus supporting the deadening media stuff: computer madness with media self-interest pollutes the mind. Words have been invented to hide or soften reality in these games for the benefit of business and mindless eyes. Also, news is no longer news but is linguistically downgraded to 'stories', and we all know what a story is. Further depravity graphically displayed and filmed is called adult entertainment, action-packed, and exciting. How more appropriate it would be to call such material arrested adolescence. There can be no justification and we know it. Sexual responsibility is ignored. The semiotics of the advertising posters are too often basic pornography: if someone says so, then they are labelled with some mind filth, told that they need not look, or told to grow up! Yes, one does need to look and form a judgement. We all need to see and recognize what is being done in our names. The next positive step is to demand higher standards fit for our children, our adolescents, our newlyweds, our middle-aged, and our elderly people of what was once called decent society. You get what you pay for, so what should we be paying for? There seems to be a justification for 'a licence to practice' in order to make money. This licence needs to be reviewed and withdrawn. As the CBC reported (22:07:2011), seeing so experiencing visually sex, aggressive action, violence provides an appetite for it.

To find out how to live a full life is not to be found on the internet. Only the elderly have that sort of experience.

Constructive Publicity

Publicity has purpose: the publicist decides what that purpose will be, which may be for better or worse. Good quality requires and works with the intervention and involvement of the public. Our presently warped and warping news appetites need time, space, and direction if the abhorrent forms are to heal. Why, following an accident on the road, do people slow down the flow of traffic to "rubber neck"? What sickness is this with all the additional traffic problems it causes by hampering the Emergency Services? I doubt if people look to see if they can help or assist! One is tempted to ask where a proper respect for the victim(s) is?

A 'need to know' only applies to safeguarding and maintaining health and security, and it is linked with an ability to influence events and offer support or remedy. It should not be used to promote voyeurism. Its main significance is promoting that ability to take meaningful action. A main aim of publicity should be for the benefit and good of members of the Social Family and in helping them meet important needs. What, how, where, and why are central questions answered by publicity? It should mobilize public opinion to cause change for the better or deal with problems, as should religion. The touchstone for publicity is if it has benefitted or helped improve a situation or condition.

· · · · · · ·

CHAPTER 11:

LAWS, RIGHTS, and INTERACTION

The Law is devised, evolved, and reviewed by citizens for the protection and benefit of citizens. It is freely agreed upon, and it is recognized as being reasonable. Citizens agree to collectively make reasonable efforts to stay within these laws. To do otherwise is to choose to be an outlaw, functioning outside the law. Having chosen the outlaw path, the full weight and powers of the law will fully and properly be used to control and punish offending anti-social and anti-citizen elements: or so it is intended.

Tellingly, there is a difference between the *"letter of the law and the Spirit of the law~!"* as Greg Smith, once of Goldman Sax, observed in interview.

That seems to be axiomatic, but the implications are some-what disconcerting. It is necessary to promote a proportion-ate response to achieve prevention of wrong as well as the provision of any punishment. 'Proportionality' is a difficult process to achieve since it is time-based related to expecta-tions and current levels of morality and awareness.

The law becomes "injustice" through deliberate design and not accident. This occurs through misleading argument, omissions, misunderstanding cause of intent, perjury, and money's purchasing power of the corrupt and corruptible.

Why it is when so much in life has improved and progressed, there is an increase in murder figures and the number of prisoners? What has been taken out of society which can be seen as a probable cause, and what has been put into our life experiences to unsettle the decency and honesty of so many? There appears to be a serious fall in levels of self-control and empathy. There must be a cause or causes. Sky News AM. (20th April 2011) reporting on sex crime figures stated that these had risen 3%. Has sex education from film, television, and advertising images anything to do with the growing problem over the years? On the 31st of March 2015, the BBC (UK) reported that, following a survey of youngsters, over 11% of youngsters have experienced pornography and have taken part in its filming and broadcasting with many becoming traumatized generally through the use of cell phone photography and cell phone broadcasting! Through 'licence' and apathy, the 'Muck Medias' factions have become more emboldened, explicit, and violent: it is not any wonder that there are increases rather than cures. As belief systems are undermined and devalued, the breaks acting upon the movement of filth, violence, disrespect, and plain stupidity have become weakened and ineffective. We realize this 3% increase of personal misery and tragedy from the previous year is the tip of an assault pyramid. Numbers can be so tidy! Too tidy! The interviewed spokesperson said of this figure, in a encouraging tone of voice, that this "is better than the 7% [increase] of last year." 7% +3% makes over 10% in just two years (2011). One almost fears to ask what level it has reached now! What 'social glue' is now missing? What is there less of and what has been added to enter the minds as well as the digestive systems within our Social Family? How is it that we have reflectively become so much poorer when financially we are so much richer? No wonder the Western Way is being rejected in extremist forms, for it seems truly to have lost its way in too many key areas of life.

It is the responsibility of all in society, but particularly The Family, to care and raise our children to be response-able, honest, self-disciplined, and prepared to work hard. Further, there is an equal responsibility to care for the ill, infirmed, and elderly. Without these forms of care, society almost counts for nothing. Possibly the time has come to form elected Ethics Committees to refill the loss of local places of worship and ethical leadership. This also could assist migrant workers and immigrants to adjust, and promote aboriginal greater justice. This is not the end by far, for there are questions related to food and our water quality and beyond.

Some would laugh at a suggestion that a food(s), drink, or other substance could be part of the cause of *behavioural decay*. However, pupils arriving at school having enjoyed a 'good' breakfast have been found to generally be calmer and achieve better results than those without. Further, there is the question of the physical and behavioural detrimental effect due to chemical imbalances and allergens within food. Concern with harmful "Diet" sugar substitutes, flavourings, and colour additives in foods have been shown to be valid. Then again is the fact of seeing and experiencing vocal and visual violence and horror in the media, developing an 'appetite' for both while producing imitative behaviour or else traumas and fears. Surely the repetitive mass of sexual imagery and innuendo in advertising, film, and media 'tip the balance' of some individuals, with specific age groups being more susceptible than others. It is reasonable to suggest that some are actually intended to cause arousal of a violent or sexual nature. Repeated experience of these can lead to *Personal Displacement of self-identity* leading to a form of role playing - the so-called 'reality shows' and soap operas have a similar influence. Repetition is a useful and effective learning strategy. The repetitive natures of exposure to these forms of social violation are a learning process. The two outcomes are one. Showing murders, sexually explicit activity, brutality, coarseness, and gang films can and do influence and corrupt by producing copy-cat activity. This can produce a misguided form of security!

Social groups hold group-beliefs which enable the group to 'dance to the same tune'. The cost of not passing on these beliefs is the loss of that consistent accepted membership structure which holds the group together. Religions afford a considerable amount of 'social glue' to effectively teach and unite the group, with this even extending across countries and continents. The example in sports of 'fair play' and following rules can support and strengthen 'Social Glue'. The problem, as in all religions, is the prospect of power they can offer the inadequate and ambitious. In religions the ambitious may use superstitious fears with indoctrination to control others. This is cultivated and grown to form a social network in which the inadequate rise, multiply, and generate in themselves a feeling of unjustifiable worth. To boost themselves further they dress up in unnecessarily fancy costumes which further suggests both to them and the gullible their 'superior' status: too often 'greatness' is ascribed by inference rather than earned, but this is not inevitably so. Whitewashed grave stones! Sadly this flotsam can easily kill the original message and submerge kinder, gentler, and less powerful ambitious souls until the inspired original teaching has been defaced so much that original teachers would neither recognize nor wish to recognize the direction, characters, and many prominent individuals of the religions so preached in their names.

We cannot always be right just as we cannot be always wrong, but neither can we always be in a position to know which is which. However, we can always aspire to do what we honestly believe is right by following a set of affirmed beliefs, verified by experience and the outcomes produced. Obviously what harms is harmful; what is enabling enables; and what is good is right. We can do little more than what we *reflectively and honestly* believe to be right, which emphasizes the benefit of good, intelligent guidance. By following a course honestly we can never be entirely wrong. We may be mistaken, but since we were following our beliefs honestly the likelihood of doing harm is reduced. Such is the essential nature of setting aside time to reflect, ponder, and consider. The clear guidance of an established 'grounding' belief structure being taught to new members and aspiring members cannot be overstated. These beliefs are the skeleton of the body-social and their importance is central to a cohesive and confident society. A society which has been brought to doubt itself is in jeopardy, since in that insecurity reasoned self-examination with a reasonable measure of confident flexibility is abandoned to the destructive vagaries of mob-popularized inclination. Sometimes the luxury of time to ponder due to circumstance does not exist, at which point the honesty of beliefs takes over - or else there is chaos. So again the importance of early instruction with honest self-analysis of belief shown to match social action is so important. The youngster should not be expected to find these things out unaided. A society of mixed messages is such a horrific schizophrenic nightmare that the young will progress into chaos. In time, destruction of surviving values must occur to bring greater suffering. Our society is such that it could be idyllic but the wrong concepts of freedom have produced licence and perversion. Liberties have lost their Responsibilities while Human Rights have been used as the Trojan horse of destruction for some who have been in the way of ambition - all because they carry the force of laws rather than a flexible subjectivity of reason and responsibility. It would appear that these tools of Rights by becoming absolute are now sacrosanct - almost the rules of a new religion. With this a new excuse for inflexible authority has evolved. If this intransigence continues to deepen, then the confidence of a mixed humanity based upon intelligent reflection will be lost, as will a caring acceptance of Responsibilities beyond our individual selves. What harms is wrong. The lesser of two evils still wrongs. Often what harms others stems from selfishness, from manipulative ambition, from self-delusion, from stupidity and impatience, and thus from evil. A fabricated appearance of right is used to produce a self-deluding cloak to cover the wrongfulness as a power-backed argument replaces reflection. Multiculturalism is not a necessity for a democratic system to operate. Consensus, stability, and shared values are. Imposing and thus forcefully promoting multiculturalism too quickly only creates more instability and violence as one likely outcome. It is what is within people's minds that needs to accept such a social arrangement and that takes time with good experiences and therefore good memories.

Any person should have the right to enjoy the honest fruits of his or her honest labour. This cannot be any less true if applied to a group of people. Their rights can no more be diminished in any way than their obligations, but obligations there will be. The process of tax collection needs to be justified and justifiable, or else it is theft. However, successive governments have repeatedly over-stepped and abused their temporary powers which were loaned to them by the Social Family. Elections cannot redress wrongs done. True there is that problem when governments change and consequently have to face the inner debate regarding which promises made by previous governments to honour. These problems crop up despite the political manifesto. Times of crisis bring the need for special measures. World War I demanded the maximum support and sacrifice of its peoples. Shell-shocked soldiers were shot as they 'deserted' the front lines to escape their torment and as a result of Post-Traumatic Stress. Ostracised families and dependants failed to be properly supported while suffering their loss. War ship building demanded additional revenue found by taking 'surplus' resources from the wealthy as increased 'death duties': this could occur several times as one eldest son replaced the next killed in battle. This emergency measure was supposed to end with the end of the war. Enlarged Death Theft is still an accepted activity by government. As with all families, young men went to war to secure their nation's safety and prosperity. With a death, 'death theft' was levied on even the briefest wealthy inheritors of the family estates. The next eldest went to fight for his country and died and so within the same year or a few years death theft was again applied. This could and did reoccur, repeatedly impoverishing some and also resulting in staff being 'let go' with all its ramifications. Stable communities were destabilized and the world was even more changed for many, as it still is. Today income in the UK is taxed at the rate agreed upon correct at the time of payment. However, following that full payment of taxed income, if saved by someone who then dies the government now demands an additional tax on monies which through the estate is being passed on. Further this version of legal death theft demands penalties be paid for any late payment, on that amount, possibly due to awaiting income from any sale caused to settle this "debt" and monies - judiciously saved and having already been previously taxed, before death.

Elsewhere inventive, persistent visionary individuals search out and find valuable antiquities which would otherwise remain lost due to the course of history. These would have remained lost if it were not for their efforts. However, they know that they could lose the majority value of their efforts due to UK Treasure-trove Law. A registration of these artefacts and a nation's first offer to purchase seems reasonable, but should this extend any further? Where do rights fit in with these two examples, and how are these balanced with fulfilling Responsibilities to the Social Family?

There are many hidden and unintended beneficiaries of law and the 'rights hurdle race'. It is difficult to see if any mechanisms can be put in place to protect and ensure natural justice and fulfill obligations. Two of the purposes of law are to encourage a safe and secure society and to punish offenders, hopefully by improving their behaviour. However, if a violent person is given pretrial bail with court instructions not to approach the victim, then that person is enabled to decide to disregard the court and cause or threaten to cause harm to the victim and the victim's family. There is a greater right or an obligation here in terms of the state safeguarding the victim. One crime has already been committed but another needs to be prevented. Then there is the additional mental stress caused, for example, by the rapist through forcing explicit repetition of the event when cross examining the victim during the trial. This must be wrong, but it is the right of the accused and a difficult one to bypass. It is high time to rethink and improve this situation rather than just talk about it. The right of cross examination is central to law and Natural Justice, but there is also an obligation for the state to make a reasonable attempt not to further cause or permit distress to a victim at appeal. Historical influence of trial by one's peers is another problem. To better achieve fair trial there is trial by jury. This jury needs to be a jury with peers being "equal, of the same rank". Jury members come from the voters roll with a reasonable expectation that some would have experience of a similar background and so be able to judge fairly. Also, a properly qualified legal representation is made available. However, Aboriginals are generally neither afforded this prerequisite of jury justice nor afforded a legal representative of their choice and culture. So much for rights!

CAN THE LAW BE WRONG?

Ugandans suspected of mass murder in their own countries have successfully and legally gained political asylum elsewhere. The suffering Ugandans left behind remain our responsibility, being members of humanity, and this a responsibility to both those murdered and their survivors. Atrocities occurring daily in the Congo fail to make the news while a car accident, hit and run, or small town robbery do. Where is the balance? Yes, there is too much horror in the Congo, and no, the media cannot report it all! The barbarity continuing in that region is unimaginable. We are learning more of such barbaric brutality with the rise of ISIS - a far cry from the peaceful earlier spread of Islam into Asia via trade and scholarly pursuits. Islamic charities were closed in USA following 9/11. This murderous collection of events was not separated from the legitimate Islamic charitable works. Sometime in the future the background of this action will emerge to explain a seemingly vindictive act of reprisal. Questions keep arising regarding the practice of Shari 'a law based upon the *Qur'an* but more from the example of Mohammad (Born 570 A.D. in Mecca) and the collection of the *Hadith* or traditions, which could be termed precedence, taken from *stories of his deeds and sayings* (Ed. R. Pier Beaver et al., 1993, **The World's Religions.** P313Lion). Can every part and aspect of such law have been definitively demanded by the Prophet (as a sincere and God-directed man), or are some parts 'time bound' to a particular set of circumstances that do not or should no longer apply and which God and

Mohammad would now alter? Alms of 2.5% of one's cash balance need to be given by followers of Islam with a right quality and not ostentation. As with Christianity, the "inward attitude" is all important. As in periods of Christian, Hindu, Jewish, Islamic, or Buddhist history, it may be usefully asked if substantial details and legal points owe their existence to and from the very human minds and self-interested parties interpreting their ways and therefore promoting a particular self-advancing path for that individual or 'power block'. Were and are all parts morally right at the time of appearance? If so, then what authority do such sections of pronounced law or belief really have today, particularly so far beyond their inception and History? Do the reasons for so-called Christians burning heretics at the stake; and drowning, branding, or torturing suspected witches and Heretics (the infidels of their day) deserve respect today? Were the crusades against the 'Christian' Gnostic Churches and Cathars in France and beyond, which constituted the first real crusade, justifiable? Was the murder and burning alive, probably of hundreds of thousands of men, women, and children, justified because an aged papal and so called follower of Jesus, in a corrupt period of Christian History, said so? Should women still be considered less able second-class humans, with their word of little value and their being subject to the dictates of men for all their lifetimes? If it could be considered right once, then should it be considered right today? Is the practice of slavery in the Middle East, Africa, and beyond acceptable today? Should workers be vassals of a person, because of their debt (possibly a debt from funeral practices and traditions) owing everything to that person, effectively working for nothing or almost nothing in their master's field, houses, or factories: even if a debtor's relative (e.g. a niece) were put there as a 'substitute' slave? It seems all followers of major religions, if they have not done so already, should re-examine their background history and reasons for prohibitions and controls they support and promote. There is a worldwide cry for both help and change, but the more fortunate and self-interested seem too thick-skinned, bigoted, and deaf to hear. One may reasonably wonder why the laws of some nations still permit this to continue: this is despite lip service being paid to a so-called value system of Human Rights and a just God. Firmness cannot be compared with brutality aimed at a cowering opposition. Dictatorship is exactly that whether dressed up in religion, robes, or military uniform. As with past child labour in England, preventing such indefensible practices demands the action of people of 'sensibility', integrity, and religious fortitude to ensure and 'Give Teeth to the Law'. There are many who firmly believe that all prophets who taught and promoted goodness, kindness, honesty, and charity are God-inspired and God-sent, no matter which part of the world they may have lived in.

One of the greatest dangers is believing mere fantasies. All our beliefs would benefit from observable result and reasoned review, followed by the addition of faith.

Forms of Slavery

BK: Kevin Bales (2012), *Disposable People* and see **Jamain Bacaman** 'Anti slavery International'BK: *Journey of an Orphan*, discussed in **Michael Enright's** Sunday Broadcast

BK:: (Ed.Margery Ellen Thorp (1956), *Ladder of Bones*: A history of Nigeria, 1853-1953. With plates. Jonathan Cape

Dr. Kevin Bales-'Free the Slaves' Society [Modern day Slavery] Various books and videos

Few in the western world would argue that slavery is not wrong and is contrary to both natural justice and Human Rights, and yet we still have slavery. Elsewhere it is considered a right and right to keep slaves. This practice has been going on no doubt from the beginning of human existence. There are those reports from terrified south coast dwellers in England of whole villages being scooped up by Muslim slavers from Africa, over a thousand years ago. The conquering armies of early empires or tribes met some of the costs of war with the slaves they took as their right and might. But rights change.

SLAVE:

1. A human being who is **owned** by another

2. A person who is **dominated** by some <u>influence, habit,</u> etc. *(Collins Pocket Dictionary)*

1. A person **held in** servitude as the chattel of another

2. One that is **completely subservient** to a <u>dominant</u> influence

3. A device (electrical) that is directly **responsive to** another

CHATTEL:

1. An item of tangible or immovable property, except real estate (as buildings), and things rather it connected with real property

2. A slave or bondman *(11th. **Merriam-Webster's Collegiate Dictionary** .... in Franklin*

Maritime Nigeria particularly provided a vast number of slaves and has slaves still, with some figures for Total African slaves as high as 27 million. Slavery, which is still very much alive in SE Asia, is estimated as having twice the number of African slaves. In India and Pakistan hereditary debt is paid through a process of bondage - that lives are lost is seen as 'collateral damage', like war. Income today from slavery is valued at $32 billion which is a value twice that of <u>all</u> the slaves that were taken from Africa. These poor souls of all ages suffer torture and sexual abuse. In the United Kingdom some descendants of Navvies and Tinkers, often miscalled Gypsies, enslave homeless people, eventually sending them out to work in fields. Yes, they are cowered and abused. Carpet weavers, child soldiers, child prostitutes, and so very many more live a slave-like existence, though in theory they are free.

- More Dr. Kevin Bales and others (REF: *www.freetheslaves. net/*).also cites many examples in Europe.

In the past Serfs had to pay to the master a daughter's dowry for a daughter to be able to marry. Serfs were not allowed to leave a specific area without permission. They had to work and give up large amounts of their produce. They did not own their shacks nor the land they stood on, and if they were of age, then they would freely add to the chief/ lord's troops, as required. Serfs could not freely walk away: nor can they today!

There are the Pimps gaining income from 'their' prostitutes and operators distributing, pushing, delivering, and selling drugs - both equally 'un-free'. Koranic *interpretation* permits slavery in West Africa. Work at a strip joint bar requires tax payments which could well suggest that the government is Pimping. Casinos, with their 'peculiarities' in slot-machine displays, have enjoyed government involvement more than suggesting legal collusion which profits from the entangled unfortunate gambling- addicted clientele. There are strange historical practices in West Africa, with children sent to the local shrine for six years to atone for an adult's sin. They can then become a slave for life. There are slaves in Brazil and there are hidden slaves in USA. Because slavery is illegal does not mean it does not exist. There are also parents who live off their children's earnings or sale. The 'right' for freedom, which is opposed to slavery, needs to be within all if it is ever to be removed. Sadly the actual cost of slaves has fallen greatly, thus affecting the curse of slavery .... bargain selling!

> "Well-behaved people never make History." Sheila Rogers, speaking particularly of women.

It could be considered a Right to be allowed to work but it is not possible to have a right to be given work: one without the other makes both irrelevant. Should it be the people's will that their Government has an obligation to provide and safeguard conditions enabling work opportunities for all, or nearly all? Full work protection would be required with international trading consequences and a free choice of where to work and as what.

Governmental Bills, Rights, and the Canadian Way of Life

Constitutionally Canadians have a right to life, security, and liberty.

The rejected Bill C-30, known by some as *"the online surveillance or warrantless wire-tapping bill"*, was concerned with paedophile and possibly terrorist activity but was criticized on its threat of undue and unjustifiable intrusion and infringement to public liberty and privacy. It proposed to give police and other agencies, home and abroad, the potential ability to obtain cell phone and computer information *by all means*. This open access was without a need to obtain a warrant, as demanded for in Australia. The reason, one might assume, was to enable broad and swift action to protect both individuals and society while detaining those who threaten both. This bill, which was known as "the Protecting Children from Internet Predators Act", generated opposition in Parliament, the media, and the general public. However, if the government had remained fully united over this, it could have become law despite all objections! That could and would have superseded a number of rights and liberties as occurs with the successful Bill-51. Removal of Bill C-30 led Lindsey Pinto of OpenMedia.ca to state the following:

"..... the government has finally heard the voices of Canadians."

Yet this does not mean that government had to act in accordance with that "voice".

Another area of contention is concerned with the prostitution 'industry'. It should go without saying that those 'providers' should be equally protected from harm and exploitation, as with any child. Some would place the care of animals ahead supposedly because they, like children, cannot well protect themselves. It seems unreasonable to legislate in such a way as to place these people in a less safe working environment. They either have a right to direct their own lives in their own way or they do not. Hunting is a national pastime, which many a deep freezer attest to. Hunting for food is one thing while hunting for the fun of killing is not quite the same. Constitutionally Canadians may freely be armed; traditionally this enables both social and personal safety. One historical example is the ambitious, coveting military attacks from south of the border, the invasion by the USA, in 1812. However, the need for weapons in Toronto would seem somewhat unjustifiable now as it would for anyone who is not in a wild area or who is not a member of the forces. So, freely available weaponry is a potential threat to all if placed in an unprotected state.

Bill C-36 threatened this safer position for prostitutes while at the same time removing illegality from their 'industry', if freely chosen by them. Meanwhile those who assist with, offer genuine protection for, or avail themselves of these services permitted under the Bill would be criminalized for so doing, despite prostitution being legal and it being consensual sex between adults. Human Rights are such fun! Then again the sex worker could be subject to the law, when plying their trade, by *"communicating for the sale of sexual services"*. The question becomes if the use of consent is one's right or a crime. The approach here suggests it is a crime which in turn suggests other forms of consent could be viewed as a crime also. Consent becomes illegitimate by circumstance, which mischievously could suggest the likewise consideration of electoral consent, conferring powers on no one. Since many individuals become disappointed with the result, does this invalidate them? Madness!

> *"We know all too well from two decades of missing and murdered women in Canada and extensive research by our team and other, criminalizing any aspects of sex work has devastating impacts on sex workers' safety, health, and human rights."*
>
> **Dr. Kate Shannon,** Director of the Gender and Sexual Health Initiative

Government spokespersons on the matter have said that it is the intention of the Bill to do away with prostitution and that the workers right to safety and free choice are *irrelevant* to this.

•

However, the exploitation, dangers, abuses, harm, and trafficking of prostitutes remain a horrific reality for many workers. The associated stereotyping, perpetuation, and victimization remove from many workers safety, hope, self-respect, health, and happiness. Forced prostitution remains a reality.

The loss of safety, health, and ownership - all "Human Rights" - are to be replaced by insecurity and danger to life, limb, and property due to crime and terrorism produced in Bill C-51. This was summarized by Public Safety Minister Steve Blaney that the then government was demonstrating a "firm commitment" to protect Canadians, with their values, from jihadist terrorists:

> *"The international jihadist movement has declared war on Canada and our allies....... they despise our society and the values it represents."*

It was judged necessary to increase policing powers to better enable police to tackle any activity they saw as endangering or undermining Canadian life. Powers would include information sharing, detention increasing from three to seven days, legally reducing the travel of suspects, and using action on suspicion. All aspects needed to be monitored to catch and discourage any abuses and to protect the innocent when inevitably mistakes are made. Further freedom of speech and conscience could be seriously affected.

What the above clearly demonstrates is that Human Rights are adaptable and subjective and that conditions surrounding them can be crucial in judgements.

United Nations 242 states:

> *"Land may not be acquired through war."*

This relates to all nations, including Israel and others: the colonial days SEEM at an end but are not.

BODY ENERGY and Growing Up

Goldman, D. (1995). Emotional intelligence. *Why it can matter more than IQ.*
ISBN: 0-7475-2830-6

Marlene Caroselli, Ed.D , (1996). P.E.R.S.U.A.D.E., *Communications Strategies That Move People To Action .*
ISBN: 1-57294-053-0

We may ask why we help others. Interacting with other people through interpersonal behaviour brings us answers we probably seek. Also, we discover how we can treat each other to better promote the personal development of all. It is how humans act towards each other which creates our concept of our environment. The trick of life is finding happiness and general contentment. Many personal answers come via interacting well with other people. To help this process we can project our appreciation of THE GOOD in people and our environment, including its loveliness and our feelings towards it. We can help others appreciate what we experience, and then help others 'see', recognize, and know which enables the unity and the truth to grow. This unity is not the same as blind infatuation, for anything which actually removes or lessens that freedom of logical constructive thought is probably wrong: 'addiction' is a form of slavery and some believe that "merchants" use and promote this path.

The Interpersonal Ethic is how we relate to each other, especially children. Adults should try to avoid taking responsibility for more children than they can give shared attention to.

By achieving a good emotional balance, parents or guardians remove a 'survival need' for siblings to aggressively compete for attention, seen in selfish and destructive rivalry. Too frequent distress and worry further leads to ill health. We need to learn how we can best keep the positive bodily energy level up.

LOW BODY OF ENERGY ~ caused by STRESS → mental and physical ill health

One proven way to reduce stress is to share it with a caring person or group. To do this there needs to be a respect for confidentiality. Children need to be included in conversation but not to continually dominate it. They need to learn to listen and contribute effectively. This will help to enable them to work out sensibly their fears and problems and then find answers and actions for themselves: a mature skill. They need to be given unconditional love to develop self-discipline through secure confidence and friendship. Continual nagging and shouting while correcting them drains their energy while also teaching a wrong and counterproductive pattern of response. Children need to learn the world from adults and each other, not through games of culture. Disciplinary matters need to be clearly understood, consistently applied, and such that the child believes them to be fair. The adult can vary responses to better meet the child's need and at an appropriate level: cultural traditions tend to be somewhat unforgiving. All the energy does not have to come from parents alone and it is good if it does not: Discipline needs one-to-one attention of the clear, firm and fair kind in differing situations. Children need to be told the truth but at their level of understanding and emotional development - it just takes some thought. There comes a time when they should be able to work out and know when fantasy is fantasy as well as when we are being sincere: shattering ideals and dreams comes with a price to pay.

In addition, unthinking emotion to a person, persons, or things is a wrongful flow-of-energy and is wrong-mindedness. A reasonable 'give and take' approach produces buoyant action rather than the sort that drowns. By contributing successfully in group situations, a child and adult experiences acceptance and builds reasoned confidence. Enfeebling dependence excludes development of independent energy from outside us. Sensible guidelines, however, prepare for this process. These may be found in traditions and religion, but not exclusively so.

When we feel a loss of *personal energy*, this may be resulting from others' emotional drama and manipulative control which is used by another party to force their own energy flow to supersede ours: to manipulate our emotions and weaken our resistance. Paedophiles and bullies know all about this force as do the shouters and screamers and parents trying to dominate and control. Often they believe they are not in the wrong which can make matters more difficult to overcome. Constructive confidence needs to be based upon reason and reality, as quoted in the Dalai Lama's and Goleman's (1995) *Destructive Intelligence*. These despicable characters will often portray themselves as deeply feeling and caring. This is also the tactic used to ensnare women by many a pimp, as attested by over-used prostitutes.

Brazelton's *Emotional Intelligence* speaks of confident optimistic development, as opposed to a failure-expectation resulting from loss of reasonable approval and encouragement. Confident optimism is thanks to parents who:

> *".....understand how their actions can help generate the confidence, curiosity, the pleasure of learning and the understanding of limits." (p. 192-3)*

This improves the prospect of a child achieving a success-ful life.

There is a reserve of energy we amass within us. This mental and so physical *force within* may be dependent on a 'co-rela-tionship' when each wishes to be in control. Conflict inevita-bly results in what has been called *"an illusion of completeness"*. This state sadly but too easily becomes a power struggle, as within partnerships.

It is best for romance to follow BOTH people in a close relationship to having completed their initial personal inner growth, be it sexual or beyond, in their own way and so establishing for themselves just how to stabilize and usefully use that inner energy. With successful independence we may freely achieve a 'higher and deeper' agreed upon relationship to evolve into what some have termed a super person. We all must grow out of and away from `our co-dependency` to become ourselves, achieving total self-revelation as to how and why we act as we do. Outcome is a form of peace within.

Whenever we meet other people there is always "a message for us." Each time how we all chose to respond is both crucial and valuable for and to us. A person cannot play a `control drama` if the other does not play a matching drama. All such response plays are generally hidden strategies: they contain personal reasons which are probably based upon experiences. Consequently, bringing these 'reasons' out into the open removes their hidden nature which in turn can promote reality and therefore a greater honesty or confidence. With honesty and openness we overflow to give others energy, which within we all are working for. This sensitivity and sen-sible-giving reduces another person's need to manipulate, for it encourages balance, calm, and acceptance: surely a better way to be! One needs a very effective memory to maintain an existence of constant fabrication, as this is so tiring, so debilitating, so destructive, so stupefying, and so negative.

One sign of a need to communicate is spontaneous eye contact which is said to suggest it is time to talk. It is reasonable to assume that this recognition, with or without individuals having met before, could be a meeting of minds, by recognition of a same thought group. One person can uplift another through sensible honest interaction. This uplifting, which is most probably beneficial and energizing, seems to be recognized through eye contact.

Fair Trial, Leadership, and Stability

Questioning brings more confusion or greater understanding. Is fair trial guaranteed? Can it be? Is a trial desirable, and if so, for whom? Trial is only fair if it is guaranteed to be and is consistently so over a broad range. If the law is an ass, then it need not be so. Variety may be the spice of life, but not in law. Variety needs and is needed to be dealt with! "The person who pays the piper selects the tune" is not too far from the truth. So over and above knowledge qualification is a question of afforded quality and qualities. There is the primary responsibility to the Social Family to ensure justice following due diligence. Those who 'provide' the vehicle of the law are leaders by their actions and through their Responsibilities; their quality relates directly to their attitude, aptitude, fortitude, and qualities of leadership. Leaders have to make decisions and direct the passage of events. Their lives should reflect an exemplary character. Yes, we can all make mistaken choices, even those within the legal system, but there must be that line. Lawyers supporting crime, political crime, and criminals need to be removed. Who guards against the law makers is always a knotty problem, one which certainly cannot be left to an indulged and indulgent press with baron ownership and big business priorities, nor left to political whim.

There is a conflict of interests in a trial being acted out on both sides. Both interests will be valid in their own ways. Not infrequently these are different 'justice' sets and the nature of each is the result of circumstance and not necessarily evil intent. The impoverished hungry person knows that the wealthy supermarket won't really feel the loss of a few articles while the honestly trading supermarket expects to be protected by law. One set of 'justice' is wrong and the opposition of this set is enshrined in laws following careful analysis and reference to precedent: a choice is then made following an adversarial trial approach. Two aspects of the debate look at the question of a jury system being more likely to achieve a fair trial or else three or five judges supposedly knowledgeable and most experienced in the 'rule books' of laws with their active enforcement. If the letter of the law is paramount the judges must win, but if flexibility is required then the jury and the leadership of that jury would appear to be crucial due to their collective broader experience rather than the enclosed alternative academic form. However, use of a more private and less adversarial approach with three judges could be more acceptable and encouraging for rape victims. Use of jargon and strange strings of words brings back the discussion of language, its use, and the meaning being conveyed. Without clarity and achieving full understanding by all parties, a fair trial seems in jeopardy. The accused needs to understand fully what is being said to provide appropriate responses - hence the attorney, lawyers, and barristers. So again the availability of finance comes into play. There is a demand for a written and defined set of national values. However, if these are fixed then the vitality and adaptability of an unwritten constitution, such as for the United Kingdom, is lost. Awareness and provision for the individual and individuality - which is a part of achieving a happy and rewarding/fulfilling life - has its place central to the concept of justice.

Society is a continuous and continuing series of group photographs. Each face is a story. One photograph is made from many stories becoming the picture which represents and speaks of the Social Family. Each member has particular skills and experiences which are part of the whole picture: each is important and a living 'input' point. The law is there to protect this marriage, this relationship of infinite possibilities and variety. This necessary variety should neither be likened to rail tracks nor the 'sleepers' holding constant their distance, thus enabling a safe journey. However, the law might.

WHY PUNISHMENT?

Research shows that acceptable punishment is more constructive if and when it swiftly follows the act. Being able to repeatedly go to appeals followed by repeated appeals denied is unhelpful. A victim recalled to the appeals hearing again suffers and so in effect is being punished by the perpetrator of the crime. Most prisoners are released after serving some of their time. While 'inside', loss of liberty and choice coupled with effective treatment and support are supposed to render each captive safe, no longer a threat, having paid their debt to society. How that can be done has always seemed a mystery as it probably does to many of the victims, assuming they survived. As this hope for end too frequently does not work, the question arises as to what practical alternatives there are. Since the days of punitive punishment even for minor 'crimes' there has been much change. The improvements of prison conditions, resulting from the work of the Scot Jonathan Howard and others in the mid to late 1700s, continue up to the present. However the improved condition is not matched by an equivalent proportionate fall in the number of re-offenders. Something more is needed to change the mindset caused by nature or nurture or both. Even with conversion to a more social, honest life, crime being a supply and demand system swiftly and automatically finds replacements for certain kinds of crime, when one expert is caught and removed. Life-sentence comes with hope of earlier release with "good behaviour", after the suggested corrective sentence seeming to succeed, which makes nonsense of the term "life". Why use it! Evil men and women, once identified through their choices, need to be isolated for the sake of the majority. That majority community is both good and the source of what we use and need.

JUST AS THE LAW CAN BE PROVED WRONG, SO CAN CONCEPTS OF RIGHTS.

SELF DEFENCE

A problematic area.

Gun laws of Arizona stem from a historically essential need to hunt and be able to defend oneself and one's family. Does this still apply? Weapon rights may reflect a general disbelief that the forces of law and order are both willing and able to adequately protect citizens. Restricting availability fails to prevent weapons arriving from another country, for example high capacity ammunition magazines from Mexico entering the USA. These have a far greater killing potential due to the vastly higher capacity of the ammunition carrier. More people can be slaughtered in confined areas when an insane individual goes berserk: like a fox in a field of lambs or in a chicken run. However, restrictions in availability and permitted use do reduce gun crime. For a citizen to go about their lives without the fear or possibility of gun crimes should be a Right. This would be better achieved by all being prevented from carrying guns or buying any without special known and agreed upon reasons. One would expect this restriction to be in place in any civilized and law-abiding society. If gun crime is a problem, then that speaks for itself.

How Valid is What We Observe?

Ref: Classics in the History of Psychology. Festinger and Carlsmith (1959) Published first in *Journal of Abnormal and Social Psychology*, 58, 203-210, observing 71 male Stanford University students in their 1954 Cognitive Dissonance Study.

Leon Festinger and James Carlsmith (1959) proposed the term *cognitive dissonance* which can be recognized in every individual since each has their own way of evaluating themselves. This self-evaluation usually occurs by comparing themselves with other people. In this way we can design our own truths. The authors concluded that people, when persuaded to lie and so holding opposing points of view without being given enough justification, will perform a task by convincing themselves of the falsehood's correctness rather than as actually telling a lie. This cognitive dissonance is a state in which an individual holds two perceptions, judgements, or memories. Conversely, Behaviourists (Ref Daryl Bem) have a different view of *self-perception theory* which simply states that an individual's outlook, pose, or disposition is a reflection of their behaviour, and there is no need to assume any motivational drive to reduce a mental clash, disagreement, or battle within. The "SPT" theory suggests that people 'bring on' or conclude attitudes without first considering factors that might influence or cause the concluded surrounding, either supporting judgements or memories and states of mood. It declares that when there is no previous attitude, for example due to a lack of experience, then by observing their personal behaviour they develop their attitudes towards others and conclude what attitudes must have been the cause. More recently, Fazio, Zanna, and Cooper (1977) suggested that both have a part to play. Assumption rather than reality can play a large part, as evidenced with regard to facial expressions and how we see them altering the response of others. (See also James Laird's [1974] and Tiffany's [2006] work on association.)

BULLYING via the 'Law'

The CBC reported research which found that 10% to 12% of people have been involved in bullying. However this is just a fraction of the problem. I have found that when informally asked most people have responded that they have experienced bullying in school or at work or both. This spite-filled infantile bullying behaviour by an inadequate personality, at its most simplistic, is a working out of aggression rather than the mature process of reflective learning HOW to cope with conflict. Acceptable failure experiences can help with a progressive broadening growth of maturing personality through development of this life skill. Team sports are just one good way to learn grace in success, determination in all circumstances, and the value of working together. Also, as a team member we experience, see, and learn that we all make mistakes and can overcome them. We learn to appreciate there is a benefit as well as a group need to follow rules. The brother or sister intent upon causing trouble and punishment for their siblings gains a warped form of security through the distress of others. They may never lose this sorry skill. This problem causing can be a diversionary tactic in an erratic household and later develop into bullying.

In Canada there are restrictions on election spending to balance the activity of the powerful and wealthy, which includes the unions and the corporations. Such capping is right and responsible if democracy is to be a believable and achievable goal. The drowning of opposition with a flood of cash is not the norm this side of the border; consequently, our politicians have had to prioritize more as to their messages. These priorities will reflect more their guiding attitudes. Should they decide to follow the route of indoctrination, then their advertising machines or hatred will show their lack of worth to a goodly number of thinking voters. Bullying with so-called "funding" is less likely to be a major factor as a result of limits supported through the law.

Human Rights regarding sex, race, and age may be used by a self-interested and an ambitious few to further their self-interest: rights used simply as one road to fame. Others ignore them. In the UK and with coming elections in West Africa (2015) there are reports of children abducted, mutilated, and sacrificed to give wealth and power to their captors and in some cases this is believed to have brought political success. Far less evil but very distressing is the case when striking refuse/trash workers fail to accept the Responsibilities associated with their work, particularly where community health is involved, let alone the stinking piles such forms. Strike action in the current Western world seems unjustifiable when we have so many benefits with good arbitration also available. However, some people justify their position and achieve a perception of power, thereby advancing themselves through causing confrontation to the inconvenience and harm of others. Having forced themselves into the public view they are better placed to promote their political ambition. Unfortunately, misplaced support or subjugation can both be the outcome. Equally, company policy can and does get used to coerce sets of employees and fellow employees. The powerful take over: as occurs in most conflicts or war. Positions are adopted and hardened. Those in responsible positions need to be beyond this state; they need to be able to exercise flexible judgement which is one of their more difficult Responsibilities. The last thing we need is the bully or bigot making use of well-intentioned legal 'shells' to justify their worker-management prejudices or to provide some gratification of a power urge, be it physical, mental, or political.

Remember the misery of UK in December 2010 and January 2011? Human Rights begat Health and Safety and both were confounded by a right to that outdated strike 'action'. We have a greater right to health and safety, but the strike went on and on. Striking against whom? It was the people of the 'Social Family' who were hurt by this sustained physical act of social violence. It seems that the first to exercise a 'right' believe that theirs is the dominant right. Remember that both beliefs were prominently used in the refuse workers strike: their action caused misery to many, many more people. It caused potential disease outbreaks from rat and mice infestation - there was a real danger of the rats causing the spreading disease and endangering small babies in their cots. So, what happened to responsibility? The Responsibilities were accepted by those workers with their employment; they began when they accepted funding through wages paid. They had chosen to work on behalf of the far greater number of homes which later became badly affected. How did their striking vote count for more than the far greater number of people affected? Did their co-workers, responsible for organization and administration and which some like to label 'the bosses' or 'management', have an equal responsibility to keep things running? Did the duty and responsibility of both parts of this <u>single</u> workforce have a higher responsibility to their paying 'customers' than one mere right? More thought was needed by both regarding the unity and oneness of the 'Social Family'. With the research of Leon Festinger and James Carlsmith (1959) in mind, it can be seen how those on strike would need to persuade themselves of their action's apparent rightness due to this action producing "Cognitive Dissonance" from which there would not be relief without their rationalizing the justice of their action. Two consequences collide: the need to strike conflicting with the outcome to cause harm. So through a devaluation of their strike action's affect upon the public enabled and in place, the now "justified" strike action went ahead, with all the misery and danger involved acceptable to the strikers. .

Refuse Services administration is no more important than the 'field workers': both are needed. Administrators would look rather stupid administering no people. Likewise, the 'field workers' would need to form a body of administrators to organize the logistics of this 'public service', for it is a 'service' which accepted refuse collection and other associated Responsibilities. The same is true of workers at airports providing services for travelers and holiday makers. We all provide for each other; we are networked, linked like cogs in a clock. One need not wonder how these same people would respond if a member of their family needed a medical operation, or a doctor's prescription, or a rotten tooth extraction, or to take an academic examination, only to be told they would have to wait till after some strike action had been resolved! I believe the same argument would not be acceptable nor accepted by them. The long past history of gross exploitation and workforce needs speaks for itself, but surely we have socially evolved far enough to find a suitable effective alternative. Sense seems forgotten. After all, the name 'strike pay' can be a contradiction in terms with any consequential outsourcing always benefitting others.

The repackaging of old ways into New Age quickly erodes centuries of emergence from paganism and fear-led beliefs. That living beings on a big rock (Earth) can be so strongly affected by other lumps (planets and stars) so far away in space bends credulity to the limits. That ritualistic recitation, other forms of mysticism, and even sacrificing are re-emerging is frightening. We generally accept that there are those with specifically developed abilities well beyond the norm, but so what! See the pentathlon competitor, the theoretical mathematician, or portrait painter at work benefitting from special and 'unusual' abilities. There are many more abilities which harness attributes of the human being which do not relate to planets, stars, spells, potions, or strange sounding utterances. I have personally experienced the mind reading ability of a youngster, seen haloes of energy around people, and even healing by touch. There is a lot yet to be discovered and teleportation of information using 'entangled particles' (Anton Zeilinger's University of Vienna Tea is just one). Meanwhile, the media continue to promote, advertise, and indoctrinate for the money it promises, all to cultist advantage. They too frequently prostitute their art. They are well prepared to betray those to whom they owe a duty of due care but poison their viewers' minds, perverting and confusing their perceptive abilities. Reality battles with Perception: what is perceived can too easily become a personal reality. Infants integrate more or less without analysis or thought, soaking it in via the senses. Their growth is a social conditioning surrounded and orchestrated by their genetic biases, a build-up which is providing additional interpretations of sensory data via their receptors - mainly eyes and ears. Personal beliefs inform the perception, not necessarily reality. Perceptions are integrated and assimilated to inform future perceptions. It grows from its roots but how it grows is dependent upon how it is fed. Pollution of the mind is exactly that. The infant, however, does not start with these problems which they must later cope with.

The use of the terms like Kraut, Jock, Nigger, Paddy, White Nigger, red-neck, Taffy, Newfee, Grockle, and Eskimo can cause offence to one recipient, a smart response from another, and total indifference from yet another. I had a West Indian friend who jokingly called me Snowflake: a funny term borrowed from a TV series. No problem! That a name is used can be less troublesome than a punch and certainly a knife or bullet. Both ignorant and arrogant people will always find ways to be unpleasant and invent new ways as required. Further, they shout down the words of those they are opposed to. The perception and pain of inequality really are both subjective. That is the way life is, and so we need to be strong enough to cope. Words alone cannot harm; but reactive interpretation can.

CHAPTER 12:

THE FUTURE AND SOCIETY:
BOTH SOCIAL AND POLITICAL

Why is there a structure we call society? It is the successful interaction of very many potentials and preferences.

Human potential is plural since it comes in many forms. The suggestion here is that it functions somewhat like a family. Within there are several parts. Each brings its own unique qualities to the total group, within which there needs to be organization. In turn the total group operates best with clear levels of authority, accepted rules, and traditions. The strength of family is when its parts work together for the common good, aware of what each can do in a constructive structure. Families come in various forms, but if they are caring and organized, respectful and aware, they should prove to be strong, confident, resilient, and more open. Family takes many forms and no one form is absolutely right. However, there are similarities to be found just as facial expressions (Facial Action Coding System – FACS) are duplicated through nations, cultures, and races (Ekman's Universal Emotions). Conditions change and so must the family. Adapting through a consensus makes sense and raises the probability of success through willing and constructive cooperation. There is this need to "work together" regarding the vagaries of life to achieve group goals. Reading facial expression is one avenue in the successful transmission and reading of ideas. When this understanding is reduced, as with some illnesses or handicap, security and belonging are weakened or lost.

In togetherness lies strength.

An outcome's responsibility needs rest with and within the active group: so *my cause produces my effect*. A social structure modifies what action will be taken due to a broadening use of reason brought to a situation because there are a greater number of thinking and contributing members. By forming together into an effective Social Family, we become safer and more 'broadly visioned'. Through the fact of greater numbers more may be attempted through co-operation. Greater co-operation leads to greater security which enhances confidence. This enables more trials, some error, and attempts at benefitting from learning which lead to more likely success. A dysfunctional society is divisive, divided, and self-destroying: *my cause producing my effect and others be damned!*

At various points in time arrives the 'spontaneous impulsive society,' as now. Values are dimmed by the demands for quick gratification; self-indulgences are preached from all sides. "Me first" is the call and "You owe it to yourself". Me first becoming all that matters for far too many that the social glue weakens or even disappears: people become rudderless, a mess of free-floating flotsam. So many objects are promoted with no real worth or value, just flash-in-the-pan gratifications fulfilling some phoney dreams, promoted and engineered by unprincipled, irresponsible advertising. Too many members of the press seem to go for quick and easy rather than responsible reporting and balanced debate. A few descend into downright lying. There is no true nourishment of the spirit then. Those higher ambitions, which may not be achievable, often achieve other lesser goals on life's journey full of so many choices and opportunities. Current shops changing one's "gold for cash" can too easily 'unlock' their true value for someone else. Quality needs time. The loss of will and ability to reflect and consider, with infrequent time set aside for this, has reduced the quality of life throughout. However, we do see hope in the warmth of ordinary people welcoming and supporting refugees from the horrors of dictatorship and a propagandist-corrupting caliphate.

Social Theft is a disease which also needs to be remedied, for it is contagious and destructive. Our future and security are destroyed by street gangs; airport strikes ruining the worked-for and needed holiday; teacher strikes corroding pupils' social development, respect for authority, and individual examination hopes; the very teachers society depends on trying to cope with appalling child indiscipline without being adequately supported; junk food creating junk bodies; and media excesses focusing upon fear, sex, and violence devastating innocence and the lovely through brutalization leading to instability and more antisocial activities. This is not Democracy; it is rather mad self-destruction and the erosion of the good society with its strength of vision only to leave a chaotic vacuum.

Amongst all this confusion and engineering of social messages, the people become confused and lost as to who are the worthwhile role models to follow: who, why, and more problematically when? The glossy magazine and other media with their shallow images, designed to promote 'outside' and unreal objectives, become the touchstones of judgement used; promotion through hysteria, envy, and greed replace reflective appraisal and judgement. Screaming audiences at live TV shows illuminate the sheer stupefying aimlessness which abounds within those vacant heads. Both recorded laughter and audience applause replace spontaneity and deserved response. Soap operas replace family reality and unity. Little space and thought are permitted for the gentle shades of positive values. Here it seems it is both 'being in' and 'the cool thing' now, or it is to be placed outside. The outcome is the affliction of others, the rewards of free ranging greed and anger, a brand-new nature that is continually being wrongly fed. No longer is the way we live centred upon quality, trying to be constructive, doing good, living with honour, and giving kindnesses for others. So much has been lost, become accepted, and rejected without adequate thought, testing, or debate.

We garden and plant trees for the future and for others to enjoy:

customs of good behaviour and good manners are much like that.

Every individual
needs to ask: *What are my priorities?*

Why ?

Where did they come from?

What benefits do they bring?

What have they become?

Are they still valid?

Appearances **Versus** Achievement and Quality

Shallow impressions	Versus	Outcomes of value and consequence
Surface Value	Versus	Constructed
Passing/short term	Versus	Researched and developed

Repeated Costs and limited Versus	Product of work and commitment
Emotive rather than reasoned Versus	Seriously committed due to knowledge and reason (quality)

Write in the table below what you consider good, constructive customs or habits followed by writing lesser substitute choices you have seen in the second column.

LIST: Good Customs or habits	LIST: Shallow options or alternative choices

Power increasingly resides with those who have greatest control over technology and therefore so many stored potentials. Such power has control of cash, consensus, opinion, and inventive 'insight'. Insightful mutualism using a planned future outweighs, but not necessarily 'out-guns', the oft-practiced 'technology ricochet responses' of cash, cash flow, and the social repercussions resulting from the egocentric and selfish governing bodies of today. But can they be anything other?

Social Experimentation

Experiments, not to be confused with demonstrations, generally start from known specifics generating an idea, concept, or belief and beliefs remain just beliefs unless tested/checked. There is also the exciting prospect of acquiring new knowledge and new understanding through reason and planning with applied concepts supporting action. Studying others' publications produces a tendency towards more rigorous thought and better avoidance of mistaken conclusions. A workable experiment results from due care being taken in planning on the basis of knowledge and following academic discipline.

Much more care is needed for experimenting with the dynamics of society simply because social change generally is progressive and may well remain hidden for some time: it can be a walk in the fog. Rushing into ill prepared and poorly planned innovation may make for powerful political coin but produces unwelcome outcomes with time. Major mistakes sadly often first affect silently the defenceless members of society. Should the innovation be built on emotion or a form of hysteria rather than clear thought, the outcome too easily may become a misery extending for generations. By its actions and outcomes what is caused is known, but it may be too late for remedy. There has been much wonderful research regarding society and interaction of its members but with plenty of contradiction and poorly understood processes. Theories rise and are superseded because previous knowledge later proves to be faulty and "falsifiable". One example of human developmental theory changes is behaviour due to 'nature' becoming due to 'nurture', then morphing into various combinations of both. To place an experimental social preference into law is unwise: the imagined outcome may well prove elusive. Placing Human Rights into the category of Law is premature if they do not stem from established norms of accepted responsible action. The use of law is necessary for the very occasional antisocial dangerous person. Enabling society to be protected through legal action produces the positive change or else removal of that person from mainstream life. Too many details and knowledge gaps exist, especially when the condition is pretty much a new one.

The arrival of numbers of people from different cultures who must settle in a culture which is alien to them is fraught with potential problems: a generous host does not necessarily produce gratitude nor successful assimilation. Assimilation is an unhelpful word with poor dictionary input. This arrival situation is made so much worse with a refusal to learn the local language which leads to increased anxiety, mistrust, confusion, misunderstanding, avoidable mistakes, and worst of all a feeling of isolation which generates deep anger. The philosopher Thomas Hobbes suggested, over three hundred years ago, that without *social controls and restraints* people would in all probability attack each other. These constraints are the local culture, not the newly arrived one. It seems sensible and easier for the new arrivals to 'fit in' rather than to attempt to force the considerably more numerous to change, but they both need to understand, accept and agree how. Social *systems* develop over long periods of time during which fine tuning (*adaptations*) continue to occur. These systems work towards specific *preferred outcome* becoming a major part of the established group's *identity* which they will actively need to support and *perpetuate*. Talcott Parsons collected and organized the Functionalist approach not surprisingly called "Functionalism", which indicated that within society all its social institutions had active purpose. While he and others concentrated upon organized groups such as the forces, government, and social class there is a clear dynamic of tradition and group identity for the individual members of the Social Family. Functionalism ignores the individual in favour of concentrating upon social systems. However, it is those very social individuals who stand to lose most by forced change. This change at a lower level causes a loss of balance or "Equilibrium", termed by Talcott Parsons, which produces counter-change in another until a new balance is achieved. It would seem to be easier to introduce the new to organized groups rather than to a massive number of individuals. This will extend well beyond the nuclear family of about four people and the centrality of successful reproduction in groups and on into full socialization and social membership. William Beveridge's concept of the *welfare state* places on society's members the remit and Responsibilities of citizenship accepting and supporting fundamental base of health care, employment, education, food, and housing. Responsibilities and rights have little to do with the free play of market forces with fuller individual freedoms. It is more the duty of citizens to ensure availability of the fundamentals for living: achieving a reasonable life even at the expense of some free choices. Our Responsibilities to each other come first. The debate includes how best to interact to achieve this goal.

The opposite of interaction is the avoidance of contact with others, also termed isolationism. The avoidance of involuntary interaction has to occur through organization and so it could be seen as one of the causes of the development of towns and cities. Anyone living in a small village will know how little remains private. In these larger town-city structures, people search out and find ways to limit or control this interaction while variously being herded together to travel, gain provisions, or escape through sport or entertainment. Television has changed the rules. Today group membership is often maintained through the cell (mobile) phone or internet. One way to remove the unavoidable interaction of street and public transport has been the ever growing use of headsets and iPod type gadgets. Empathy and suppositions about others are neither experienced nor tested; instead, guessing and the acceptance of stereotypes predominate. As a result we have evolved into a *fantasizing society of stereotypes.*

Changes Caused

Social strengthening and rebuilding may simply start with nurturing a 'local people's newspaper', like *The Sun* in Canada, or through informative media such as CNN. These started out as the vision of an enthusiastic socially-minded politician and were originally aimed at what was termed "ordinary people," presumably referring to small business owners and the workforce: a vision to benefit other people. Too frequently there is simply a passive acceptance of the existence of an "underclass" of enfeebled people who are in that state due to the existing circumstances of their births - nature or nurture. They do not have the security nor dignity of secure employment, the advantage of recognized skills, nor any ownership of things to buffer them in time of acute distress: they have "fallen through the cracks" and beyond society. This cannot be right. This despoils a belief in human dignity and rights due to its very existence and experiences, for ghastly experience is what it is for their whole lifetime. The title of freeloaders and idle leaches are applied to these helpless and hopeless members of our Social Family. But we fail to also address the problem of how they can or could be otherwise. Cultures change but can maintain a conservative tradition or fundamental package of beliefs: responsible behaviours and obligations remain. These beliefs and aspirations are almost religious as a constant essence of that group's life. Knowing is membership. Ownership of this awareness is membership within the group, a fitting in which enables security and, I would suggest, happiness. There is value in the uniform way for the right reasons, a non-competitiveness, a group identity and identification, and a real feeling of connection.

The cell phone revolution, started by the Canadian inventor Martin Cooper as reported by CBC's *Ripple Effect*, is already immeasurable - let alone in years to come. It's enabling a power benefitting, for example, the establishment of new businesses in third world countries: the spinoff is immense. Instant communications and data interrogation with the photographing of incidents linked with worldwide publication are being strongly exploited. Where it all will lead is impossible to predict any more than Queens University's William Leech science-based and original description of the possibility of space flight, in that vacuum, which probably led to Jules Verne and other writers, with research into jet engine flight. These are the vast consequences of seemingly small developments which of their nature were obscure.

Activities obviously involve our 'being busy'. How much broader the personal experience if that activity is group-benefit related. What adds to the group's resources strengthens the group. Hold actions up to the light and check them out with the Rule of Two: Does the action result in good or not? If not, then responsibility demands abstinence. Too frequently a denial appears using mockery and disrespect. It seems that if one can laugh at something, then these empty-headed fools feel they have won an argument through their vacuous noise rather than understanding that they were unable to summon the necessary thought and language to achieve that end. Unquestioning traditions can pave the road to social insanity. WE have a brain and we need to exercise it. Unreasonable protection of the so-called family name or honour, especially when doing so breaks the basic beliefs of reasonability, justice, and decency and in so doing ignores Responsibilities to others, shows it for the *mental excrement* it is. Such is the self-defence of the coward trying to justify ignoble action with the title of dignity and honour.

There is no sure way of knowing how to achieve a better society other than by experimental *adaptive consensus*. Insisting upon legalized Human Rights is not achievement: Look at ISIS and the Congo! Education must play an essential role which starts with the experienced leading the very young. This needs to consider an allowance for different base-line positions. These different *starting points* need to appreciate a common *arrival point* which they believe right. This will not be the end but rather a point upon the time-line of existence. Wrongs will not be changed; they are experiences and they are the business of the future. Clear discipline and regulation enables the young to live and explore safely. Such structures a security. Security leads to independence (W. Blatz, 1966). A tragic fact of life is the appalling reality of child abuse by the sick minded. This is in no way to be linked with those members of our Social Family afflicted and in some cases overcoming various handicaps, mental or otherwise. Sometimes strict adherence to a path of considered behaviour will lead to a better life. Paedophilia can be, we are told, the result of learned behaviour with victims becoming exploiters. Proven or not it would seem to suggest that children's role play on this theme is totally inappropriate. There must be better ways to reduce child abuse: a situation unaffected by children's rights which hold so little relevance for those 'animals' practicing abuse or 'bug-eyeing' computer films of children and their being abused. Such people give up their PERSONAL rights by choosing primary or secondary abuse to and of the Social Family which through their own free will and choice they have left. You shoot mad dogs, don't you? How do vile human animals fit into this frame of Human Rights protection when they have effectively chosen war with the Social Family denying their humanity?

Constantly being promoted and renewed is the Culture of Character – VALUES Versus CULTURE OF PERSONALITY Versus ACTUAL PERSONALITY. We need to ask what was lost and what can be gained by following cultures of personality. There is a current battle between *Values and the visually exciting*. It may be asked if we still know or have human characteristics expressed as values or even know why they exist or care! Advertising is 'buying the vision of a person' first, rather than the actual product. It covers and soaks the mind in 'ideas-soup'. Endless repetitive media exposure with self-promoting role model forms hogging the limelight encourages others to follow suit. The alternatives to instruction being humorous product promotion would be so much more creative, enjoyable, and satisfying than current attempts at 'brainwashing'.

It is easily understood that people enjoy stability and the excitement of free choice. Rollercoaster fairground rides, hang gliding, vehicle racing, and mountain climbing are some examples of these. However, our daily preference seems to be safety and security surrounded by the familiar. Probably one of the most frequent comments upon returning home from a holiday is, "it is so nice to be back." Interpersonal activity needs this security which if lost repeatedly can lead to ill health and mental problems. Antisocial behaviour can easily result, for there is little reason to value a social system which appears hostile and intent on your harm, imagined or not. Open-plan offices reduce privacy but can improve interaction, group identity, and cohesion. Such togetherness can prove extremely beneficial, especially when the group size is not too broad. Large impersonal groups tend to break up into smaller more personal forms with "their place or area": as soccer and ice hockey supporters will recognize. Collaborative work can promote constructive group-creativity, since it more easily promotes cooperative thought, initiative, innovation, and confidence; yet it leads to exclusion for some.

In school, class group-work rather than individual learning is being seen as cooperative exploration of ideas and processes. It can produce the opposite. For the shy it can be not a short moment to deal with but rather a nightmare. Regular and familiar 'reading round the class', with all taking part, can greatly help the shy to learn alternative strategies. The value of independence can blossom through variety and peer support. That one can rise to the occasion, despite a potentially viewed situation of threat and anxiety, is to discover that one is on the march to mature strength. Our problem moments generally need to be faced and to be successfully dealt with. If such no longer are felt to be problem, then they would not be a problem anymore. We extend ourselves through recognizing that we can and do win with the right learned approach. Problem solving experience is important for developing that nebulous quality called maturity. Then there is the extravert versus introvert approach. We need to understand that both behaviours have time and place value: again a maturity skill. Joking around appropriately is one example, while being able to give and take leg-pulling is another. Success with these helps consolidate the group but more significantly the individual.

Social Manipulation and the Positive Censorship Debate

Censorship is often seen as a road to dictatorship and loss of reasonable freedom. Yet Santa Claus is removed with nativity plays from schools by the politically correct mash-heads, as are assemblies with a religious and moral teaching content. Gone the same way are many children's stories which have become victims of the madness of the *thought police* bully groups. These try to force a sanitized and bland educational experience on all because of their personal preferences: another form of dictatorship. Folks, we are all different and we need to learn how to cope with this. The world is not always nice. The price paid for freedom is bought by 'freedom martyrs'. These freedoms are not to be swept aside by the bullies of thought with their brand of madness be it religious, financial, or social. So why not have that very clever but dangerous black knight which some like to link somehow with race! It is what is inside the can that matters. One crass director of BBC Television saw fault in Father Christmas and he banned it as sexist! So much for tradition and that freedom to continue with fondly remembered and harmless traditions. This sort of stupidity is the meat and power of the arrogant and irresponsible. One wonders if he felt that women were so immature and helpless that they had to be protected so much by HIM, which suggests that he felt foolishly that they are inadequate and unable to look after themselves. Do women really give a damn? If he needed to impose his mindset, then he must have a very poor opinion of most women's very real ability to both think for themselves and act on their own behalf. Lateral thinking and multi-tasking is not just a male thing! Remember those wonderful moms in Northern Ireland who stood between the troops from one side and those from the other? Also there is the great work achieved through the MADD (Mothers Against

Drunk Driving) campaign. So many people's way of behaving has been modified due to the thought, inventiveness, and strength of these two groups, and there are many, many more. They fulfill Responsibilities first rather than rights. No, we do not have the Right to drink alcohol where, how, and whenever we like. With it goes certain Responsibilities. Such wrong actions need to be personally and socially censored. Purposeful constructive and purposeful censorship is necessary. The question of the reopening of UK pubs all day seems more a matter of tax gathering than of what is best for the public. What appeared to be advantageous regarding the work force during war time seems still equally applicable after. Contrast this with the prohibition of those wishing to smoke in a special smoking-room in a pub or on a patio...... why not, for heaven sake! If the law makers feel so strongly about such matters, then they can and should make all smoking illegal and imprison those benefitting from tobacco sales, whether we call it tax or business. What is wrong is wrong, so they need to sort out this pressure group's bullying ways and their own double standards as they count the taxes gathered.

Peter Buffett's Dec 26, 2013 discussion on CBCs Q was a breath of fresh air with his dad`s phenomenal financial success in no way diminishing the man. In fact, it raised him to the place of visionary, guru, and exemplar. All of his dad's honestly accumulated wealth is now being redistributed through charitable organizations. This financial expert has the humility and sense to leave this gifting to the charity experts. How refreshingly honest and sensible! Peter Buffet, a musician and now a charitable director, has explored the dangers of what he referred to as 'Charitable Colonialism`, no matter how well meaning. How often is there an implication and expectation to 'do as the giver does' required of the recipient, who may believe in all honesty that there has to be a better way? Humanity can be both ethical and achieve self-fulfilment irrespective of any concept of God. This could and should be the goal of all to promote the welfare of all as best can be. Humanism is more easily practiced at the individual rather than corporate level. This vision of life better enables a shifting 'of the weight on the see saw of life'. It is difficult to imagine how to be efficient and competent and to achieve knowable goals other than by grass roots experience and imagination. 'Charitable Industrial complexes' have evolved by more efficient individually developed means. There is a clear need within poorer society to get rid of loans and consequential condition-clause linked debt with the work and untried new ideas of imaginative people, thereby leaving such "complexes" as the UN out of the equation. Currently these 'aided' people need institutional support to survive, but by use of their own experience, local knowledge, and intellect it would be more beneficial and productive for them to be freed from 'charitable complexes' and thus enable each to be truly "creative", locally responsive, and effective.

Peter Buffet, a modest and eloquent speaker put forward many clearly thought out conclusions. He spoke from personal research and experience. The `Novo Foundation` is in safe hands, I believe, with his creative gift to the future through this Foundation`s aim to produce the most efficient and "people relevant projects" they could reasonably sustain. Peter is the son of a billionaire, and he seems to have achieved an admirable balance and set of values. Buffet amassed a fortune which is now directed towards constructive aid by his musician son.

> **"Our mission is to foster a transformation from a world of domination and exploitation to one of collaboration and partnership."**
>
> *(Novo Foundation's mission statement)*

Charity too frequently is a socially prescribed and directed activity. It reflects what is already present "within" each active group, either directly or indirectly. What *that something is* may not be easily understood "outside". This "within" force or influence is the driving force of each group. Whether or not to help others is not a question for aid workers. However, for many others it is not even a consideration. Some even oppose it. The sociologist, Charles Murray, suggested that welfare benefits made the poor *"dependent"* and lazy. To ensure this would change those having been identified as in such great need producing welfare support should have this welfare removed. I imagine the 50% of Greek youth in Greece (2015) would have something to say about this concept, as would many in the historical UK Poor Houses. That welfare is properly regulated and monitored is simply a responsibility of good governance. Meanwhile, for others of an unwary group, poverty directs their footsteps towards a dangerous temporary avenue of comparative wealth, `ratified` through loans and future intimidating debt collection and charging huge interest rates: such so called help is taking second place to their lender's money "pig trough" which they feed from. Making inflated amounts of money from other`s difficulties is clearly wrong. Too frequently lack of 'voice' enables this financial abuse and can even be responsible for creating this position for those in the social downward spiral of despair. Few Rights pundits try to address this plundering of the impoverished nor the associated intimidation which is quite common. Petty officialdom, with their suggested 'greater knowledge' and gate-keeper function linked with some power-projection of themselves, enables injustice, despite the fine words of government and the laws.

Peter Buffet's interview seems to focus upon changing an "industrial charities complex" of self-benefit rather into one more recognizable as philanthropy. He is in the extraordinary position to understand and experience the "giving" world.

His background of selflessness highlights the actions of others which may be unintentional but sadly are no less real in negative outcomes. "Philanthropic Colonialism" may be well-meaning, but the attitude is to 'do as I do' which may not be appropriate. Too much charity has "strings attached" and international requirements. Buffet intentionally avoids this.

> HUMANISM: 1. *A rationalist movement that holds that man [people] can be ethical, find self-fulfillment, etc., without recourse to supernaturalism.* 2. *The study of humanities [language and literature, human thought, history, philosophy, the fine arts etc.]* 3. *The movement that stemmed from the study of classical Greek and Roman culture and helped give rise to the Renaissance.*

Humanism exists and acts at the individual level. This is the starting point. This is also the level at which help and support are needed and given. It rests and depends upon clarity of mind, direction, and accurate perception. Freely given, under no condition should charity be considered misdirected and ill advised. To 'freely' provide support demonstrates the action of a concerned benefactor. The giver is outside the condition and experiences of the recipient and probably cannot adequately envision their lives. To donate or give away income or cash in the pursuit of promoting the well-being of others is distinctly Human; it demonstrates a right behaviour. This can also be seen in the care and treatment of children and animals by most of us. Interestingly, this generosity is to be found sometimes in animals: a number of animals exhibit the same 'morality'! This genuine concern for individuals, born from both sympathy and empathy, is an ultimate indication of civil and social maturity. This concern is subjective and intellectual in which social objectives matter greatly. What deserves and can be, should be. This is a Humanistic position. Deserving and needing seem to be parallel demands.

It is necessary to stop tinkering but rather to commit to shift the weights of the see saw of life of the unfortunate: uplift the destitute. Waltons of WalMart were worth over $42.3 billion when I checked. Rockefeller when asked long ago what he would wish for if he could have one wish granted reportedly did not select peace, healing of illness, or removal of starvation but rather one dollar more. Possibly this was a very sorry attempt at humour. Though to see the many endowments he made shows that he had these problems very much in mind. The majority of the world's wealth rests in under 10% of the world's population. The average Canadian would probably be surprised to learn that they are extremely wealthy when compared with the world's majority of people. What are the rights of the majority, and equally pertinent, what are our Responsibilities in this regard? Interestingly nearly all cacao pod cutters (for chocolate) have never tasted a cube of chocolate and do not even know what their crop is used for. The question remains of how to efficiently and competently meet the needs of those unable to do so themselves? How can we socially and internationally achieve such goals? Concerned imagination is needed, but not frequently demonstrated. The giving-reflex to establish 'Industrial Complex' charity and to support the outpouring of non-governmental 'political' aid requires a more discerning side to its application. Well-meaning giving may not bring the benefits hoped for if delivered in the wrong form for a misguided goal. One form of help may produce changes which produce social loss. Because it is good for us, does not mean it is good for 'them'! A well-meaning missionary working in northeast Australia experienced the annual 'carnival' and ceremony of stone hand axe trade. Aborigines had travelled great distances to attend. The missionary perceiving a great need generously acquired a large number of long lasting metal hand axes, which he distributed. Now there was no need to meet. This implied that there would be no meeting in following years, no new relationships for the young men and women to enjoy, and a substantial fall in the number of Aborigines in time. This is an example of a kindly act which through ignorance went badly wrong.

· · · · · · ·

The personal wealth data listed below was accessed on January 21st, 2015. It relates also to stock market values. Of these members of Forbes top ten wealthiest people, four are mentioned below.

> 1st. Bill Gates at $81.2 Billion 3rd. Warren Buffett at $73 Billion
>
> 5th. Larry Ellison at $54.2 Billion 6th. Christy Walton and family at $42.3 Billion
>
> In 2014 there were 1,645 Billionaires worth collectively $46.4 Trillion, a X3 growth in 10 years.

Some loans arise from serious need while others from a qualifying demand; however, misinformation, loan sharks, and changes in personal circumstances can too easily sow the seeds of destruction and social loss. That very need to repay a loan can remove the imaginative creativity that generates innovation and effective change. In this way success becomes fear and caution takes hold. It can too easily become a 'millstone' around the neck of those very young and creative innovators almost guaranteeing their inability to innovate due to the burden and fear of debt. There appears to be little that can be done to remedy the situation. One either summons up the courage or stupidity to try, or one does not. Charities and Foundations have been established by individuals such as Prince Charles with great success to help younger people follow their skill sets and plans. Wealth generously given can both support the innovator as well as our quality of life. Some of the works Prince Charles raises funds for include Romania; Rainforest Protection; Organic

Farming; Foundation for Building the Community (England, Scotland, Wales, Canada, etc.); Traditional Art School; Regeneration; Cambridge University Business Studies; and many more: over £100 million a year.

To maximize a world embracing innovative approaches the young need to be free from crippling debt. Good education and planning remain central. Debilitating debt, worry, and health issues are destructive, yet the bright who attend university too often are creatively crippled through student loans and expenses and demanding outside work needed during study to inadequately help meet the bills. Let them live in the light of learning, acquiring the wisdom and thought of others, able to accept challenge and responsibility. Creativity needs support to grow, at all levels. The young need to experience a certain generosity to encourage them each in their turn to actually wish to give back to society. Experience demonstrates that rather too easily there comes a grinding down and loss of vision due to the reality which has been caused by their aspirations and vision suffocating under the weight of long term debt due to student loans. Preoccupation with personal survival does not generally produce widespread benefit, but simply a localized outcome or two. These students are an investment in the future, and if loans are seen as necessary and a way to educate them in the way of the world, then let the cost be more appropriate and lessened greatly.

PREDATORY PEOPLE are a curse and strategies need to be devised to deal with them. Likewise there are no "easy ways" to gain finance, just crooks and loan sharks. A cancerous dynamic of our world is 'Predatory Industrialism' and 'Predatory Economics' responsible for so much waste, loss of work, and even gaining governmental power through sponsorship. Industry's own perceived needs are overriding slowly but surely as the democratic ideal. This will be replaced by the autocracy of dead finance. Power is returning to the selfish and self-centred replacing of the philanthropic, supportive, and caring society with an internationalist corporate hammer. The social porcelain is being systematically smashed by these dinosaurs as they frantically tear at each other in financial and real wars to take hold of even more commercial meat. In one to one disagreement, the NEED to shout down demonstrates a feeble point of view. This is where reason and thought are unvalued and vacant noise takes their place. Brute force from loud noise is as destructive as loud money. These Tyrannosaurs quietly plan, hunt, and grow. The silent corporate movement is less easily detected or understood.

. . . .

POLITICS and OFFICE

A deceitful man or woman in office is neither worthy of respect nor office and should be removed. These 'sub social' people can however prove highly effective negotiators, gaining power from purely (or rather impure) lies, pretence, besmirching of others, bribery, threat, and bullying to satisfy selfish greed for a short time before moving on.

Nation of Influence

The New England Transcendentalists.... Ellen Hansem
ISBN 1 878668 6

One can only have a great deal of respect for what is understood as the 'ideals' of the USA with the hope they could bring. However, what is seen - sadly and too often - is not what is suggested or expected. This wonderful dream remains just that: a dream for far too many unhappy souls. They are born. They live. They suffer. They die. They are forgotten. What sort of dream is that!

This condition seems unimaginable when placed beside the kindness, openness, and generosity of the Americans I have met in the USA. The reality seems at first to differ little from its main source, namely the United Kingdom. Both have an 'elite of wealth'; some are socially active while others simply live off their good fortune. Both nations believe in basic freedoms and personal Responsibilities. In both lands anyone could, in essence, become either President or Prime Minister or the head of state's spouse. In the UK the traditional 'holders of power', the Lords, are prevented from becoming Prime Minister: not so in the States. Further, leaders of industry and the product of corporate power rise to 'grandeur' and with these go the national ebb and flow of beliefs and understandings of 'bottom line' Responsibilities. One could easily gain the impression that the presidency is paid for and so excludes almost everyone. And yes, the exception proves the rule.

I believe it was Alex de Tocqueville who said that it is *"better to count heads than crack them."*

However, there are other ways of causing great harm and continued social inequality must be one of the biggest. We as individuals are not the same and never will be, thank God, but that should not be an excuse for permitting misery especially where there are great surpluses of wealth. It is a self-evident truth that all people are not created equal. Some are born healthy, some are born to wealth, while others are born to despair and pain. What is a self-evident truth is that this sorry condition can be much improved upon. New England Transcendentalists Margaret Fuller and Bronson Alcott believed in a sound education:

"*society's progress depends upon the improvement of its individual members.*" (p. 28)

"There is hope in the words of the erudite." **Henry David Thoreau**

"*For it matters not how small the beginning may seem to be: what is once well done is done for ever.*" and then sadly he adds "*We love better to talk about it...*" (p. 38) and "*if a plan cannot live according to its nature, it dies; and so a man....*"(p. 40 in the above).

In The New England Transcendentalists... Ellen Hansem

CHAPTER 13:

MEDIA, ADVERTISING, and FREEDOMS

Well yes. We all believe in no censorship, don't we just? Sarcasm can be the sword of truth. Those wonderful electronic games teach us that cars are for racing and police cars explode and the policeman walks away alive. Those 'wonderfully creative war games' linking like-minded creative people across the continents who then battle it out as 'mates': so cozy, so constructive, so social, so safe. Then there are those wonderfully educational films which instruct in the gentle arts of robbery, mugging, rape, seduction, sadism, spite, effective deceit, lying, explosive murder, or subtly undetectable murder. What great arguments are these against censorship, 'cos it might remove these very creative works of art. How about the vital skills of bomb building? Now there is a useful social skill... Oh yes, it is on the internet!

Advertising means, "Because of the money spent we can affect the behaviour of the consumer." So very, very much cash is spent or 'invested' in it. The cash comes from the customer who would have to pay less if there were far less advertising. For so much money to be thrown at advertising it must prove to be a successful financial investment for the sellers, while being less so for the purchaser. Its underlying purpose is the manipulation of behaviour. The outcome is supposed to be to inform and benefit, but does it? Affordability of these products is questionable since so many people may run into financial trouble, overextending themselves with close to or 0% financing, till the reckoning date that includes the percentage hike upwards. There is a tiptoeing toward bankruptcy, just like the spiteful hand of loan sharks with their very temporary fix and long term anxiety. Medicines do not necessarily spread due to their benefits but a perceived need promoted by advertising. They have well-motivated and articulate sales persons 'doing the rounds'. On the CBC they quoted that 75% of doctors often prescribe new drugs, unaware of some side effects which become a major concern. These are often more expensive but fail to offer much in the way of extra benefits. With the use of the word "NEW" they create a perception of greater value, forgetting that new may carry some unforeseen problems: possibly Less Well Tested would be more informative than New and consequently more appropriate.

QUESTION: When is porn not porn? When is envy not envy? When is self-worship not self-worship? When is doing your best in your world not good enough? When is greed the way to live? Should advertisements have to portray a 'good' way of life or support a 'good' way to live? Should it inform or tell? Should it direct or dictate? Should it make money or inform and help make a better world?

ANSWER: When it is advertising. It should not be necessary to use the turn off switch to get away from watching the trash.

Marketing forces are used to profitably chip away at moral values. These forces make money using statements such as "No, censorship is bad: we should be free to exercise our art...."; "Oh, let them do what they feel is best for them"; or "You owe it to yourself"... if one is not able to resist the repetitive suggestion, then the advertisers win! That is life, but is it right? Or is it considered our Rights? Can Rights defend us, or does a social conscience and a full appreciation of our Responsibilities offer a better and more dependable deeper way and future? A friend of mine took out a copyright for a specific use of the word RESPECT because he so rightly saw it as a key component in a mature society. People recognize and wish to be clearly identified with what they see as right. Such perceptions appear on t-shirts and goods, and then go on to become a money spinner. What mom or dad would not like this RESPECT concept to soak into the psyche of their children: good business and good citizenship linked? Making a stand is important. For example, some will never enter or buy a product from a Benetton Store due to their past advertising choices. One crazy comment in the media was that watching a specific sport was a "privilege". What a nonsense that to watch a team would be to gain privilege. The cost-inflated ticket was for sale and so becomes a form of adaptable value in the form of money: exchange is what it is for. No privilege there, rather another example of the power of misused language which has been suggested through both advertising and confused current thinking. Also, it has been suggested that some injustice has been committed when hockey parents are asked to pay for seats to watch organized matches their protégées are in. It is difficult to see how! Inflating the price would be unfair, or is that another example of "professionalism"? After all, professional players "soak" the fans! These parents are happy enough to give their children an edge over others by paying their way to get them the necessary training and experience. Is that not seemingly their reason and the point? How can it be wrong to pay for a seat that needs paying for unless it is a free seat with no costs attached? That is not reality. Though we pay our television bills, much of our time is wasted watching unwanted inane advertisements. Further, the broadcaster permits these advertisements to interrupt and ruin a good show, and it comes out of our pockets as viewers. It feels much like paying a "con-merchant" to trick us.

Whole swathes of the media seem intent upon the progressive de-sensitizing of our youth through violent and horrific TV, film, and advertisements. The 'bad' behaviour in many advertisements could easily be remedied: it is not funny nor clever. Sadly in advertising there is a tension between a purely informative format versus indoctrination which takes place through subliminal conditioning or rather being influenced unaware. There is a need for stronger guidelines, controls, and censorship, but by and from whom? Cigarette advertising has been censored. Censorship exists because of human nature, and so it is necessary. It could always be said that we don't have to do this or that or to watch this or that, but people will and do. If censorship were not necessary, then there would be little need for law, which is censorship with teeth. If it were not necessary then there would be no addicts, no violence, and no theft. Society censors these actions, but these actions (and worse) continue. Without restrictions, which is after all another form of censorship, far more harm would daily and hourly occur.

ART and Existence

ART:

1. Human creativity

2. Skill

3. Any specific skill and its application

4. Any craft or profession or its principles

5. The making of things that have form and beauty

ARTISAN: A skilled workman: craftsman

An ARTIST:

1. A person skilled in the fine arts

2. A person who does anything very well

ARTLESS:

1. Without guile or deceit; ingenuous [deceitful. stratagem, trick] (MWCD)

2. Simple; natural

3. Lacking skill or art

4. Uncultured, ignorant

(Collins Pocket English Dictionary: CPED)

The Arts have been the way to interrogate and display elements of our ideas, beliefs, meanings, and very existence: art is creativity, has purpose, and is not destructive. Art is the product of our mind using awareness and physical skills at their peak, rather than sinking to depths of randomness. Art is comprised of activities the products of which bring insight, deeper awareness, understanding, and even enlightenment. Art can bring relief and happiness to people and so assist not just society in general. It can add 'colour' and open awareness. Art promotes 'good'. Conversely, that which is designed to bring destructive grief, fear, and a feeling of loss is the product of intentional mind deformity, and so is destructive and bad. Such deformity of what potentially could be beneficial is similar to the religious perversion practiced by terrorists. Worthwhile creative activities (admittedly a subjective condition) may be promoted through the focused with established or adapted media practices and processes, use of demonstrable skill and interpretation through a purpose-filled rational activity. Concepts develop from experience which encourage belief or visualised hope of achieving a subsequent now known predictable outcome by using a process that is known or discovered in that media. High standards and skills are demanded. This outcome may not be achievable by some, but so much greater are the successful. Each successful artist is successful because the vision and skills demonstrated are both frequently demonstrated and is appreciated by the observers. Because of this their creative outcomes are accepted, discussed and understood by most. One may assume the artist has produced a fine product valued due to thought, care, and skill each consciously or subconsciously specific goals:another form of success comes from base cash investment. Furthermore, the outcome of completing a good painting tends to provide emotional information rather than having its 'value' in mechanical application. Rules may or may not seem 'no-brainers', while a system of graded response is adaptive. Skills evolve and adapt to novel situations with a skill base to make fuller use of such *opportunities*. This is one reason why I believe that the Arts and Art are close to and a part of the scientific mind with its elements reorganized and used in new and appropriate ways to both discover and reveal.

> *"The mystery of human existence*
> *lies not in just staying alive, but*
> *finding something to live for."*
>
> *F. Dostoyevsky*

Similarly this mystery lies in the quality of Art rather than its mere existence. The philosopher John Locke was sure that the human mind started out like a blank sheet of white paper and was written upon by our experiences through the senses. I would add that these experiences then inform, respond, and add to each other. One assumes this would hold for all newborns, yet birds are not taught how to build their nests. Nest-building is a highly complex task, a skill that seems to be the result of knowledge internally passed on and added to with experience during the building. It is improbable that observing from within the nest teaches the fledgling. However, internal knowledge presupposes a starting point of organized awareness which has patterns or rules. J. P. Satre believed that how we respond is what builds our 'character' beyond just knowledge gained. Modern Existentialists see people as continually analyzing and updating themselves due to how each acts. The artist will be well aware of this concept. This self is what orchestrates and builds the products of our art. It draws upon and modifies our experiences which are stored within our minds. Just 'doing it differently' fails to be Art. It is the reasoning act, the product, the reception, and the demonstrated skills which justifies such recognition. Research shows clearly the different response zones of our minds depending upon the need or task involved: that is how we are 'hotwired'. Creativity is a product of that just as is recognition: while being largely experience, it is not entirely dependent upon it.

We change with time, as does our thinking. Each age, decade, or period places different emphasis on aspects of interpersonal behaviour(s) and these are expressed, evidenced, and mirrored in the different media and arts as well as behaviour patterns. They are an integral part of time and history. They bring a fuller understanding of what motivated and drove that age. We can learn of both mistakes and successes, the dynamics of the time. We make informed judgements with the benefit of the past Vinaigrettes of behaviour traits that emerged due to their period-based reality.

Bad Role-Models and Opportunity

Behaviour is an adopted and adaptable response pattern. The sports' world sadly produces too many bad role models and too few fine role models in an environment where such could easily not be the case. We need also to see others constructively succeeding in making good come out of something which had all the potential for being bad. This appreciation of a determination to survive and battle onwards is a jewel of human character. How much better when polished! How quickly can the kind act or act of bravery change prejudice to respect? Racism initially operates at the personal level and so needs to be resolved there. It comes from direct or reported experience further complicated on both sides by poor understanding. Force is not the way to resolve this. Others 'like us' are considered positive, while 'just like them' tends to be a negative statement. The sound of the word 'them' is outgoing and separate while 'us' is incoming and unifying. Further, 'them' is often associated with 'not us'. To impose a position using the law as the 'heavy' enforcer is depends upon dictate rather than acceptance, and so is less than positive creative thinking. In this situation administrative bullying creates the environment to promote and deepen racism with and because of growing resentment. Role models can achieve so much more without the handicap of pain or fear.

The Western World stems from aristocratic ways and is very much the product of its past. An appetite for the finer things of life has generated inventions, innovation, and a legacy of buildings and beautiful gardens which many can enjoy. Both luxuries and practical aids to life were devised to later benefit larger numbers and then almost all. One modern example is the unseen benefits of the mobile phone. Their positive impact upon poorer nations through improved communications is creating great opportunities and in consequence accelerating the rate of social change and mobility. Historical problems are those influences that extend well beyond their own time. The world of disorder, anarchy, wars, and robber bands of killers leave their mark on society. A system of Human Rights has been invented to address many historically-generated problems. In North America wild animals are no longer the potential threat they were and humanity has generally calmed down. However, the anachronistic right to carry arms remains. It is hard to see how something so clearly producing abuses and wrong can be called a right. Living in cougar and bear country makes the point for defensive arming, but hopefully only following relevant training and certification. It is far too easy to find a location where for only $400 one can buy an automatic weapon, the use of which the more insane members of the Film Industry glorify. Both are social madness. A high capacity bullet magazine can be added to the 'cult weapon', a Glock, which can then spray 30 rounds with one pull of the trigger. At Tuscon 31 rounds were fired with the inevitable result. This mechanical obscenity, along with others which are even worse, is available and - it could be suggested - promoted by hip hop and television. Weapons appeal to personal insecurity generated by movies. The police have weapons to 'protect and serve', but would these weapons be as needed, for example, in the USA if they were not so easily available? Their availability may be a right, but is it a responsible right?

Absolute Laws

Once one resorts to law, matters will plough ever on with little prospect of turning back. Rather, legal processes are almost mechanical, robotic, and will probably run their course to the end decision like a social, national, and international bulldozer.

As a central stabilizing force within Western society, the rule of law has been exported around the world. So far so good. Around it and with it all life turns. The purpose of law is safety, good order, and security. It is a conduit of real force expressing and protecting a person or a group against the excess, reaction, temper, spite, or hatred of others. Those 'others' may use words or actions which flow contrary to the will or perceived accepted way of doing things by the society in which it exists and consequently are *punished* by way of that society's legal system. The law could be likened to an orderly teaching tool which rewards right doers with protection while punishing wrong doers in a fair, accountable, and almost impartial way. Is it immutable, the final line in the soil, the absolute truth never to be added to without careful consideration and judgement: an entity to be protected, with its own version of high priests as protectors, guardians, and promoters? The system has almost the last word within a process which can and does respond slowly and deliberately to changing times and conditions. However, since there is the safeguard of appeal, it is absolutely clear that mistakes are EXPECTED to occur and a clarification process has been provided. Parliament has powers to make and change laws simply because this is so. It is clear that The Law is recognized as having within IT the seeds of fault: it is not expected to be perfect, hence its adversarial nature of opposing sides. Further, local bylaws are not universal so some areas of law need to exercise discretionary interpretation dependent upon specific circumstances. Like the American constitution with its many amendments, the law is not the end of the argument; the argument is how permanent and right each law is until the time of any change or amendment. It is a mature system intended to be conducted in a mature way. It can be fallible and so changes are made: hopefully for the better. Human Rights are now part of all our lives in 'the West' but they are just as fallible. They have been made for the politicians and the people. If they were so Right, then there would be no more starving children or adults; there would be no homeless; the sick and elderly would be always well cared for; all children would leave school able to read and write and do their own accounts; all would have work; and there would be no advantage or point in exercising prejudice. In our now perfect world the unity of agreement would ensure that all people would respect the preferred way to live to 'benefit' all peoples. These imagined pipedreams appear right for individuals or for the promoters of their own perception of an overall way of existence. The rights of a poor homeless man trying to sleep in the freezing cold, beside a Tim Horton's air vent, did not deserve public disgust and anger when water was deliberately poured over the man, his dog, and his cold night-time bedding. The action itself generated the public reaction. Rights had not protected him. One could ponder if politicians generally and genuinely even care about individual justice other than in photo-opportunities and sounding 'good'. Further, there is the question of individuals protected versus protecting the best interests of the corporations and their labour preferences. Human rights or individuals wronged. Further, it seems unimaginable that a homeless person trying to be able to sleep on the streets of a wealthy British city - simply because of the slightly warmer climate - can be officially set a fine of £1000. What idiocy!

To have clearly understood guidelines is essential for the growing child in the form of child-sized Law. Most adults are aware of the basics: it is the specifics which may need sorting out. Yes, we all need guiding law and order. This Human Rights trick is a child: it is long overdue that she gets out of her nappies and grows up. It screams its way, abusing the will of whole communities; it emboldens the bullying self-interested exploiters of the moment; it neglects those suffering genocide, starvation, epidemics, and ignorance while standing aside as billions of dollars are miraculously found to shore up the corporate wealth and individual fortunes of those corporations and the banks. It shoots toys into space and denies medical researchers the essentials to succeed. It is fortunate and confident in the current state of health insurance (wealth enabled insurance) and survival chances of its corporate overlords and their beneficiaries. Such concerned care is equally evident in communist overlords of previous communist regimes. For whom are these Human Rights honestly intended? One may have far greater faith in the individual acting fairly to support the individual working appropriately, within the ramifications of very different situations, than a blanket covering the same. Local is lovely, small is strong, and community is essential, as is being able to speak to each other. To empower small communities, good education is needed for all - not day-long prison camps for children. Small well-funded and caring schooling is the key. Sharing community mealtime builds on this as do team sports. Well-intentioned, well-supported, well-resourced, well-disciplined, clear-minded, and fair-minded teaching is not preferred but essential. This will promote the responsible societies, which will in turn promote the responsive local leadership, which by progression will promote responsive world governance action operating through well-established Responsibilities, one to each other. Proof of any corruption needs to be politically terminal. There needs to be realistic respect and confidence in those accepting and using our individual powers on our behalf. The fact of being responsible and honest needs to be both demanded and clearly demonstrated. Education, education, education, does not need to be a cynical call aimed seemingly to gain power, but rather the dreams of so many being fulfilled rather than becoming sad memories of crushed hopes and personal failure. Education needs to be the reality. To achieve this requires the exercising of self-discipline, respect for those who teach, and respect for each other with accepted Responsibilities. Yes, everyone needs these standards. In addition we are all responsible for the protection of our community. The need for our own individual courage comes initially by enabling the agents of the community to arrest, remove, and punish all forms of serious offenders: this means fully supporting those agents. Members of the public who know wrong is being done must exercise their Responsibilities by speaking out. Many offenders are highly educated but sadly use this ability to take advantage of others. It would be almost impossible for many or most criminals to operate if we all co-operated in disclosing and removing offenders. Lord Salisbury was so perceptive when long ago he stated:

"Education without religion
simply creates clever devils."

The educated need to have firm moral principles. If not taught at home, they will need to be taught, caught, and reinforced in schools. Exploiters have no trouble using the feeble naivety of a system of absolute Human Rights seemingly set in concrete for their benefit. Others, while having done similarly, take the short cut later to sort out their opponents with the gun. The spray of bullets is self-evident: a disregard for those key and deep-seated understandings of the important place of life. No consideration of Human Rights is to be found there because there is no empathetic impulse or ability. They have not lost, not gained, and not learned to appreciate what civility, care, resolve, kindness, and strength of character could and do outflow. Civility and civilisation are grown and are not simply joined.

So in this immature world of a near human-rights-dictatorship and political correctness, the highly adaptable avowed enemy of both a state and every citizen can safely grow within and even blow us up! It can be and is protected by the rights dictatorship on a technicality, providing "it" can find or invent one, then to continue on its anti-Social ranting or activities. The exercise of the Right to free speech in *Finsbury Park* in the UK, London, with its Mr. Hook, was just one such theatre which proved to be grooming Islamic terrorists. What kind of madness is that! Their attitude and ambitions were known: they shouted them out. The police prevented members of the public from objecting. Using the statements 'we have to be fair' or 'it is my religious right' is the sort of argument kids sometimes try to get away with. If you know you are doing wrong, you know you are doing wrong! Deal with that first. This blind following of slavish Human Rights and PC politically correct ways are so open to abuse that they demonstrate extremes of stupidity personified in their abuse of decency. It cannot be justified. It seems it can be on the grounds of 'rights' of those being protected that others with assumed lesser rights are undermined and fall. How can this be when such an action defies sense, natural justice, the will of the people, and plain common sense? The law may be an ass but that is because asses administer and make the law.

Amateurism

Building from a strong experience and thoughtful base has and will continue to produce people with considerable gifts and skills which benefit both themselves and the Social Family. Apprenticeships are an excellent road when properly run, making enthusiasts aglow with vision-producing masters. Each amateur is a potential master. So much in life follows the rule of two: either it is yes or it is no. It is good practice to ensure evidence and information are collected before a decision is made, or else it is not. The development of a knowledge-base to effectively enable valid observation and interrogation of the evidence should lead to sound conclusions demanded by a situation, and thus effectively informing the development of sound and perceptive decision-making skills. This takes time to grow with focus and support from those with plenty of experience to pass on. This generally calls upon the older and longer participating members. Within our Social Family the elderly are essential to continuity of fact, with their accounts of actual experience. However, analysis and passing-on needs to be carefully organized and not simply left to chance. Here a lifetime of moral, logical, and philosophical learning can result in an army of granddads and grandmas strengthened and strengthening the value structures of our young and the Social Family. Too often the elderly are and have been *pushed* into the role of useless decrepit person, elderly servant as a child-minder, money-tree, or an annoying responsibility. They are not amateurs of life; these elderly are tried and well-tested in this respect: neglect their experience and advice at your social peril. This old age is not the realm of amateurism but rather the realm of the knowing.

We have the gifts of reason and discernment and it is a Responsibility of ours to use them. Their use better ensures that constructive change will occur. That successful circle of life in which the new are cared for and nurtured by the young, benefitting from the experience of ages passed on by the elderly, adds a vital reflective balance. The elders of tribal society are shown respect and their experience and advice are valued. This has a personal benefit of promoting dignity to those who are past their physical prime but who are enriched in experience. This is opposite to the brain-drain from loss of elderly knowledge and insight disparaged and unvalued - 'a Tsunami of Grey' (Dr. Benett).

Far too frequently the brash noisy young gain an audience. Their disrespect unforgivably gains them a media-based importance. Shout loudest and you will be heard. So now shouting loud is believed by many to be important, to be empowered, to be worthwhile, and to be strong. Most of all the payoff is a person being noticed: noticed not for worth but rather worthlessness. They use established "burp words and phrases" established by and through the shortcomings of too much of the media. News reality becomes and is called "a story"...... gross; criminality becomes "master minding": the world's gone mad! What response actually lies at the door of both parents and single parents needing to be out at work to make ends meet? Latch-key children of child neglect leading almost inevitably to adults shouting, "Notice me!"

Some of these noisy irrationals rationalize their antisocial behaviour by playacting a so-called activist role. These are a noisy, impatient, prejudiced, and an intolerant few. They fail to see the advantage in gradual persuasion, instead prefer-ring the bullying `mallet on the head` approach. In animal rights some see a justification even in murdering people or the freeing of dangerous animals, thus enabling these to wreak havoc amongst indigenous wildlife - so much for a love of animals! There is the real need for a less amateurish approach to information giving. Sources need to be depend-able, credible, balanced, and accurate: in short, trustworthy. It is necessary to be able to access good positive and nega-tive arguments. These require a use of meaningful depths of experience, hopefully a lifetime's work, with intellectual development and reading.

Our social responsibility is to 'counter corruption' which includes corruption of information. In this it is particularly necessary to exercise due caution and sometimes safe conceal-ment: the opposition may well be both ruthless and uncaring.

We have a duty of care regarding our culture, for this is our very foundation; this is what we are formed from. To people joining our culture, our culture is not negotiable: accept it or move on. Yes, it is not perfect but it is up to us to make any fine tuning which YOU, coming from a different perspective, could outline/explain a different but most alternative to consider. Our ways could intermix happily and grow but that needs to be through mutual respect, agreement, and time, with the growth of friendships. No culture is a single entity but rather an accumulation, a conglomerate. Learning is what we do all the time. Adding to a culture is the result of living. Things educational, along with the realities of political life, need not be separate from everyday people. To shape and to run society demands a *collaboration of specialist professionals'* times of inspiration which are best achieved with a public of the well-informed. Here lies a deeper good than what could be offered by television and cinema: the power of the visual to promote sound rational standards and social behaviours. Compare this almost instant response with the slower 'growth' through the printed word beside thought-filled reflection. Development of 'ideas' experienced through sound, action, comic strip, and drama are too frequently underestimated, misinterpreted, and viewed blindly. Too frequently entertainment fails the 'quality test' for it is focused on insult, it is unthinkingly shallow, and it promotes the antisocial while providing gratification for baser instincts which include 'bad behaviour'. Again the vacuous trite comment, "well you don't have to watch, etc." is too easily accepted as sound reason just because it is so frequently said. Racism operates on a similar platform as "There is no smoke without fire!" How wrong can a statement's logic be! This is foolishness in the extreme. The authors still get paid for their corrupt thinking and work upon repeats, if we chose to watch or not: some people chose to watch. If we fail to watch, they still are shown: within these products there is social-family power here which may be negative or positive. If we the public fail to watch this garbage, then this garbage will go. The support staff do likewise if their program(s) are ignored: sadly some could and would start their own perverse organizations. Advertisers see advantage in juxtaposing their wares or, for example in Canada TV, running their advertisements into the perverted feature, without a pause or space or warning. Too often is another programme advertised with the 'good bits', seemingly as bait, loosed suddenly and unexpectedly upon the unwelcoming viewers! Such introduction could well lead to some beginning to dabble in, seriously consider, remember, or re-enact in their minds the corrupting thoughts and ideas portrayed. This cannot be good. So tragically February 2015 in Halifax could be one response to the violent gratification provided by the media. A balance of consideration and argument becomes replaced by a form of easy and instant emotional awareness and gratification unhampered by critical activity: either in the mind or in the action.

Equally dangerous can be explosive "moral panic" which generates forms of unacceptable extremism. The women's rights movement is credited for advancing that cause rather than the millions of wonderful women achieving almost miraculous industrial production, social strength, and nursing in response to the WWI war effort: so many women responded magnificently to all the various involved national needs. This occurred as a direct result of so many of the male workforce being away, fighting for their country. Those held back from miners to "canaries" more than proved their courage and worth. The proof of women's abilities could not be denied after that and life for women quite rightly would not return to the old situation. Whose was the greater role, those smashing windows, chaining themselves to fences, and starving themselves or those getting on with the work and doing a great job at a time of international horror? Women have always stood firm with their men, freely together when needed.

Down the ages misinformation has ill-served humanity from attacking herbalist 'witches' and Protestants so 'madly' persecuted. This then extends to other reactionary social groupings such as those producing the UK mods and rockers, motorbike gangs, on to the concept and misnomer 'dark humour' without the humour, ever on downwards to the rotting and decay being provided with low animal level gratification.... However, this proclaimed "adult content" is a triumph for the advertising 'reflux'! Wrong mindedness is what it is and it is sad. The slide into these areas by members of the public cannot generally be by design but more misfortune. Sympathy is called for. There is a real need to recognize and identify exploitation by groups who titillate and distort the extent of benefit or threat, and who learn to manipulate and generate 'misrecognition' simply to provide a personal advantage as a result: cash and not freedom. Their goal is enslavement..... Go buy a LOTTO ticket ... or other because 'someone has to win': their organizers win every single week.

Any thinking person knows that all of a group cannot be bad, not even most, especially with regard to a random viewpoint as a result of race, colour, faith, or orientation. Human DNA has been shown not to work that way. And unless it were to be so then there can be no grounds for such prejudice. Fortunately a majority of people know enough of other persuasions and orientations to recognize and appreciate the generality of goodness in people. The kindness of some prostitutes to the destitute is well-documented. Here is suggested that in the thinking of a professional there needs to be an avoidance of the pitfalls of stereotyping, stage setting, inadequate research, and emotionalism, as all are the hallmarks of a certain type of amateurs. Recognition and amplification of the good in life using sound logic, ethics, praise, positive reinforcement, and emphasis of their broader social consequences are all the duty of the professional. The fuelling of fear, anger, and associated concepts through sensationalism used to create a 'market' or extend one is clear sign of the inadequate. That object of manipulation is to gain power. This cannot be allowed and so must be resisted with the "professionals" of the media and information sources forcefully at the forefront. How wrong and potentially evil to blame all followers of Islam for 9/11. What a revelation to the confusion of Mullahs visiting the UK from Afghanistan when they experienced the UK reality. The forces of misinformation had achieved much. They were astonished to find Muslims able to worship in roomy and well-kept places of free worship, walking the streets openly and unoppressed, healthy, educated, and cared for as they should all be in contradiction of the lies of extremist so called faithful followers of Islam. The Mullahs rightly corrected the propaganda of the Taliban and did so from a position of strength due to their studies, learning, and religious experience; yes, professionalism.

· · · · · · · ·

CHAPTER 14:

THE MEDIA

JOURNALISM: The work of gathering, writing, and publishing news through newspapers, etc.

NEWSWORTHY: Timely and important

NEWS: 1. Reports of recent happenings, especially those broadcast, printed in a newspaper, etc.

2. New information, information previously unknown...

JOURNELESE: A superficial style of newspaper writing with many clichés (**Collins Pocket English Dictionary**)

Quips about the word <u>News:</u>

> *It's true that an echo is quite accurate, but it doesn't contribute much that's new.*

> *Not all the news that is fit to print is fit to read.*

Current events are so grim that we can't decide whether to watch the six o'clock news and not be able to eat, or the ten o'clock news and not be able to sleep.

Bad news travels fast. In many instances it concerns people who did the same.

Most of today's news is too true to be good.

There are TV anchormen who receive twice as much money to read the news as the President gets to make the news. **(E. C. McKenzie, 14,000 *Quips & Quotes*. - Wings Bks., ISBN: 9 780517 427125)**

Journalism

The News Hack-Definition or impression: To manipulate rather than present and inform.

Responsible Journalism in general is one of presenting balanced information impartiality with, where appropriate, a balanced argument or presentation of fact-led opinions.

Each argument or point of view receives an equal amount of exposure.

Also, in a written debate, the reader/viewer looks to ensure clear intelligent impartiality regarding the topic-focus, taken by a journalist, followed by any conclusions being stated clearly as such.

Further, there are clear grounds to consider some things best left unreported, but then the question arises: who ultimately decides? A guiding factor here could become the information appetites of people rather than what is better. In the battle for sales, media seems to rush headlong towards sensationalizing, silly sound effects, causing shock, fear, and to titillate. The Law should provide adequate safeguards against exploitation, exaggeration, and sensationalism, but that could be considered censorship of a free media. The point is what benefits the Social Family? Open debate could establish acceptable outcomes of market forces, media sales, and acceptable influence extending to greater self-control and more constructive and usefully disciplined thought with a better informed public.

The significance of journalists and reporters cannot be understated, just as the potential harm of lazy, self-interested, and manipulated journalism cannot be promoted. We have neither the time nor resources to research the many aspects of society which affect us as worker and family member and thus our democratic vote. Further, we do not have the necessary network of links. Honesty is essential to reporting, as in life. Open reporting enables uncluttered transparent reflection and at times a necessary period for opinion adjustment too, thereby both defending and correcting our social perceptions. No one should be beyond <u>a constructive information network,</u> least of all the researchers and journalists themselves. Language as a transmitter of ideas has been fraught with influencing problems, and so skilled journalists are necessary if the pitfalls are to be avoided. Those unable to speak the dominant local language suffer many forms of information deprivation and run a greater risk of isolation, misunderstanding, insecurity, and manipulation. Inevitably disconnect, disillusionment, and isolation follow. It is the clear responsibility of each to learn that language of their new community via an empowered structure built to enable this. The journalist is a purveyor of primary experience and information, presenting any resulting concerns with balanced conclusions. They can also transmit community thoughts and culture. Their character and moral 'metal' is almost more crucial than that of political leadership and government. Just as open debate is essential to a parliament, this is also so in journalism. However, although the structure of government is designed as confrontational and of conflict, journalism is "gifting": it freely provides information while suggesting options where needed and prepared to suffer so many challenges to do so. Journalism is best when it is unbiased and apolitical.

Achieving a balanced debate within the media requires a certain 'genius' for which not all people are suited. Opposing sides of an argument need to be presented "fairly", although they are probably not equally strong debaters, nor as viable or 'worthy' of presentation. Giving equal time is a double-edged sword. Yes, it can demonstrate the weaknesses of one point of view, but it can also give the appearance of another point of view being more important than it is. Anarchical factions, one could conclude, would not be able to recruit so many destructive, cowardly, and pathetic people without the exposure of their ideas and the pictures of their sick activities via the media. The sad sight of Chelsea Soccer Supporters activities on the Paris Metro (The week of Feb.15th, 2015) in their arrogant racist activity as guests in another country no doubt will encourage more recruits to join them as they now know where to go. Meanwhile, the poor soul who is insulted and bullied because of his unmovable but equally valuable skin will sadly and justifiably feel more anger and isolation as a result of media exposure. We are promoting the growing numbers of despoilers. Of note is how their sick, childish actions have grown in destructive force and pathetic intent with publicity - a sociology project there! The rioter will not listen and seemingly cannot comprehend. One wonders if this downward spiral has gone beyond a point at which it can be checked. One past example of such destructive build-up was the reporting of shop windows being smashed by the brain empty fringe. Every day in the UK a tally count of window destruction for the previous day was printed in The

News'. The tally grew and grew. When a decision was finally made to no longer print the numbers, this in fact resolved the growing problem: yes, it went away. There are many Responsibilities with regard to reporting, and these are not always obvious. One does not need to be a super brain to know what blood on a pavement-sidewalk means, so why is it necessary to show film footage of such blood from several angles repeatedly? Are several pictures essential? No more is it necessary to show the remains of victims and the wounds of the unfortunate to inform news reports. If events call for graphic proof later, maybe, but this is not necessary for every unconnected occasion, sometimes set to crass added sound effect, or believe it or not: even music. How sick is that! It may come as a surprise to the media that most 'normal' members of the Social Family dislike these photographs. Being human they find them distressing. What 'value' does such sick sensationalism provide! Creating and feeding a ghoulish appetite is not good journalism; in fact, it is close to being evil.

Again, the fact that so many reporters refer to news incidents as STORIES seems to indicate a certain loss of reality in such matters, as well as poor English use. Possibly reporters become brutalised and therefore detached from reality. These happenings are either story inventions or actual incidents; likewise, society either views criminals as anti-social deviants or applauds them as 'masterminds'. One could also wonder why drums and rhythm generators are believed to add to the information provided by the poorer quality, less professional news stations. They must be well aware of their inferiority to others and therefore conclude that they are in need of something else to bolster their sound effects. Theirs seemingly is mere work, rather than a profession: a form of international soap opera designed to entertain rather than inform. That seems an easier audience route to take. Further, there is little point in showing the same old film footage over and over in the same report and sometimes over several days. The facts alone, when well-balanced and expressed with relevant observations, would be sufficient as news, typified by most reporters being actually present in the field of conflict. Obviously this is not so for the disconnected directors and department heads, nor the others who are comfortable and safe in studios.

To help and inform the public, journalists usefully need to be fully committed to objectivity. They must review the positive and negative aspects of any position or argument as well as the advantages of any 'middle route', this with a mind to clearly present the pros and cons. This is balanced information presented fairly. The choices are presented to the viewer via a presenter or expert analyst. There is room for more inspiration and less distraction. Newscasts carry a greater duty, responsibility, and obligation to the public not to simply be led by 'need to feed' sensationalism and to protect that money invested by the shareholders. Many act on this with great bravery and integrity: others need to be relocated. True and responsible journalism is a calling as sacred as any and sometimes more dangerous than most. They weed out corruption and the violent, protect the home from anti-social infections entering from outside, and defend against corruption of wealth. This is totally unlike the corrupted media and overly powerful vested interest. How easily some media descends into mob evil because it pays, and it pays a lot! The price is the long-term cost to the Social Family: loss of reasonable privacy and peace of mind. One can only guess how frequently evidence was clearly visible but intentionally ignored or glossed over for the sake of the 'story' because to do so 'would be unpopular and not sell well'. 'Popular' has too frequently meant 'of the mob' rather than of the mind. If what appears to be the will of the people is so sacred then there is a strong argument against so much news embellishment accompanied by intrusive and repetitive advertising. More of that elsewhere.

Responsible Reporting is a Decision

Let us agree that the public does not need to know everything, nor can they do so. With good checks and balances in place, emphasis can be re-established to inform and educate responsibly what is needed rather than the less 'exciting' news being displaced or reduced. Why is deserved coverage being replaced by some explosive, brash event? There is also a clear difference between a need to know and intrusion. Crimes are an offence against society, meaning us, and those antisocial people need and deserve to be known. Hence, there must be press coverage. Private matters affecting two people or a few but having no clear detrimental effect on society need not be reported. Someone's success is not a reason for exposure when things go wrong for that person. The argument can follow the line that the public makes people famous, and so they have a "right" to know about private failings or indiscretions - that word yet again. Not so. The famous bring something to the public which is valued - the famous give and the public receive. When things go wrong, trial by the public and press goes against natural justice and what a mentally-balanced society knows to be right. Sure enough, public figures have the same Responsibilities as the rest of us, but that is where it lies. Again, think about the messages provided by media's use of the phrase 'criminal mastermind'. How easily this can conjure up and send the entirely wrong message to our young and not so young. It is irresponsible use of language. A criminal is a criminal. Media centring upon good news seldom fares well. However, we need good news to stimulate and act as an example for others. It seems unlikely that a public appreciation for good news could not be developed by our ingenious media, just as has been done for violence, misery, and sexual matters.

Responsible Interviewing

From time to time a person is heard complaining of their television interview having the order of their comments and responses rearranged, cut, or qualifying statements left out, therefore altering the intended meaning. So much for those all-important media supporting rights and standards of professionalism. Should this travesty become the standard, there would be no reason to listen to any interviews other than as a collage of moments put together to entertain. Too frequently interviewers do not seem to respect the impartial position which was once assumed important. Some give lists of their question in advance, with those in opposition not having that advantage. There is a perception that the questions responded to are on the spot questions, but they may in fact be orchestrated. A prepared answer can prove to be a fuller answer but could well be less revealing, since advance notice can more easily be tailored: further questions from the interview can be added later, after the fact. If differing sides of a discussion are involved, then both should have the same opportunity to prepare or not. Edited interviews and rearranged sections of "clips" have been constructed to produce, emphasize, and support a broadcaster's point. If this became the norm it would be unprofessional and contrary to both public need and balanced arguments - a 'professional foul' endangering all. Such editing destroys or seriously calls into question the prize of freedom of speech, seemingly supported by our media, for some only when it suits.

*It is not so much money but rather
seeing the affordable opportunities
and then troubling to act wisely.*

The TV Infection

In Canada there was an advertisement illustrating an unintended message, an "un-message". It shows an ideal life, years
ago in the Maritimes, with smiling content people and a
cyclist joking with a pedestrian. Contentment and good
humour call out from this first half of the ad. Suddenly it all
ends as in rushes the alternative to real happiness: owning
things. We see exploited modern greed and envy with the
focus becoming ownership and driving a new car. How
well it advertises what has been lost and why. This is what
we have become. The new role models on the screen are
being carved into our collective psyche. One may ask if this
blind response really matters. I remember leaving London
and the UK to live in an environment free of burglary and
daily violence, within an interdependent community with
no police or ambulance sirens frequently sounding. In too
many cities, and Barnet UK is an example, ten minutes do
not go by without the sound of screeching sirens: they could
nearly drive one mad. But what do we see on TV (Tedious
Vision): police out of control, sex mad and manic nurses and
doctors, barmy vicars and priests, pre-recorded people laughing at "unfunny" jokes, screaming audiences seemingly with
little vestige of self-respect left, and so on. These are the role
models, so it is hardly surprising that courteous policeman
and citizens are becoming harder to find. For those police
driving cars in London it seems that any excuse causes them
to sound the siren shouting "I'm here, look at me, I'm important, I'm hard and dangerous!" - as seen on television. The

public responds likewise, following the script. School children often with minimal real family life become what they watch and play. Anger and violence soak into them through their enlarged eyes and diminished minds. Education, with its record spending and its real cost to the needy, is despised by many as are those children demonstrating the will to learn and displaying interest, respect, and intellect. This rejection of 'quality' - the nerds - is even to be seen in some teachers. Lack of an ability to maintain a constructive educational environment, disillusionment, and paperwork-fatigue cause many needed dedicated and capable teachers to give up and leave the profession, thus leaving in 'the job' increasing numbers of what appear to be blunted, self-satisfied, arrogant, and even greedy buffoons just there for the 'perks'. Who do they blame for educational shortcomings, one may ask? Certainly not themselves; rather what has become known quaintly as 'The Management' which fits nicely an industrial rather than a professional model. Educating our young is not an industry, though it supports several. No wonder that reading and math abilities have fallen through the floor. No wonder schools are becoming more like detention centres and homes for rude disregard and sloth. Centres for the promotion of excellence - don't be silly. Political pundits talk of a goal to develop student independence, their full potential, their expressiveness, and their creativity. Once our educational system demanded respect, discipline, real craftsmen and women, and plenty of intellectual stimulation. Because of these they therefore were able to initiate the awakening of understanding and associated enjoyment of real achievement. There was no pretence of ever believing any individual could ever reach their full potential in its many, many forms, even if what were our potentials within a system of so many influences and varieties of knowledge. To achieve our potential is a stupefying abstract absurdity. Searching for moments of personal excellence through high standards and effort was the goal of the sane majority. To be happy and feel fulfilled is achievable.

So What Do We Too Frequently Observe?

Oversized and harmful school environments have taken on the presence and form of child factories of a new kind which are both dehumanizing and unsocial. In these dumping grounds of humanity, children learn to bully and to be bullied; they learn to swear, obstruct, be idle, and avoid the worthwhile; they learn to use newspeak, to play truant either for self-protection or for petty crime; and they learn to look at striking screaming role models as the norm else ineffectual buffoons. The public expects their teachers to be superhuman and therefore able to cope, but too often fail to provide that early years training of their own children which would enable teachers to achieve what they could well and dearly wish for if properly and responsibly supported. There should be no need to compromise. Too often teachers' hopes, ideals, meticulous planning, respect, and authority are undermined. Sadly and avoidably they become too aware of the real dangers of both violence and misuse of the law. Those majority of school teachers who feel they should look after their charges are forced to leave wage negotiation and work conditions to others, these are most willing to prepare and adapt their work properly believing that it is their professional responsibility; they once regularly and willingly supervised playtime, mealtimes, clubs, and sports to enable a fuller understanding of their charges with their support and a more fruitful relationship, thus producing valuable added experience and feedback for their students. These teachers are too often overlooked and forgotten. They are the social language that has been created and maintained by our society. They are the golden opportunity lost. Once they enjoyed well-earned respect from both parents and friends. They were trusted to run their schools efficiently without a committee of outsiders ever interfering. For too many fine teachers, we need not worry about the changes in their condition for too long. All but the most determined will probably soon leave the profession.

The economy of economising is the leprosy of our society. Some things are just not economic but are so necessary they MUST be paid for socially and in trust. Further, some gifts are priceless but cost nothing, like good manners. Many administrators are uneconomic and unnecessary, but appear to be glued to the fabric of their essential services. They rupture the finances by existing in too great a number, by being too highly paid, and with expenses to match their oversized remits. They disturb good organization in order to justify their unjustifiable positions and somehow manage to reproduce more of themselves. They are like the sample of Literature Doctorates who gained by detracting from the greats of literature rather than by producing something worthwhile themselves. So fortunate are those who were of the times when they were certain to read and study great poetry with Shakespeare, Ibsen, Shaw, Dickens, Samuel Johnson, and the like at school as part of their education. They know how they benefitted from A SERIOUS AWAKENING OF THE MENTAL EYES to the colours and magnificence of our language. Subcultural language cannot hold a candle to such, which is why it is so easily passed on as inferior and is rightly called a SUB language.

Media, Advertising, and Freedoms Small and Large

Some form of local district councils are essential in a true democracy. Small can be beautiful. Further, the training-ground of locally elected councillors with voters who know them launches those who have proven themselves. Beyond enabling them to demonstrate their honesty and integrity via their track record in office they learn the political game and pitfalls. They rise through these political testing grounds to provincial and national government, having begun where a bad apple cannot do as much harm. This way they will have proven their commitment and ability earlier, at the local level, and should they wish they have the opportunity to choose whether to move on or stay. Democracy is worth little if not based upon honour! Without honour, dishonesty, opportunism, and shortcutting will flourish and life will become fraught with the dangers of hidden agenda. The power of advisers to influence the election of the President of the USA and world leaders is required to get them to these lofty positions and as such is concerning. We need the selection of those with proven integrity. Lobbyists are potentially very dangerous to the wellbeing of all since they generally represent the interest of the few: a minority with too much power.

Ask what that honour actually is with regard to both self and others. The two, self and others, are part of the one. The one is fully aware of the other. One chooses and the other receives and experiences. Honour envisages a right way, a better way, a valuable way. Honour focuses upon our effect upon others. Honour is social and civil. When we recognize an honourable act as such, we value it for its added value and thought rather than selfish opportunism, for example. Honour is fully focused in time and it is condition-specific; it cannot go beyond and dishonour others.

Invasion of Iraq

That Saddam Hussein was a brutal autocrat intent on invasion, this is a matter of fact, as Kuwait demonstrated. That
he needed to be stopped remains open. How he would have
best or better been stopped remains the big question and the
answer is unknowable. President Bush was in a tight spot.
Intelligence of a vast threat appeared to have arrived from
both Italy and the UK administrations, thereby suggesting
that uranium had in all probability been shipped to Iraq. The
British administration's link is emphasized and important.
An extremely respected, long serving US official, who had
also held various African Ambassadorial posts and others,
was asked to investigate. Ambassador Wilson reportedly
discounted any such sales of uranium from Nigeria following
his investigative meetings in Africa. His findings appear to
have been misinterpreted or misapplied. The invasion took
place and the rest is still unravelling and will continue to
do so long into the future. Where do honour, integrity, and
guarding rights enter this sad passage of history? Apparently
Wilson had key official roles under Presidents Clinton and
G. W. Bush: he was clearly considered a trustworthy person
with proven integrity that was beneficial to the military. It
was stated that he was critical of George W. Bush regarding the Iraq invasion and he tried to correct the impression
of his role in the matter. A smear campaign seems to have
followed. His wife's name reached the papers, perhaps as
payback. This was more significant since his wife, *née* Valerie
Plame, as a high ranking CIA Operative with overseas experience, she should never have had her name revealed as she
was serving for the CIA. This effectively ended her service
career! Her name was released as the CIA operative who had
put forward Wilson's name for consideration to 'help' in that
matter. This suggested a self-interested nepotistic act rather
than one of good judgement. Wilson being considered seems

a perfectly reasonable suggestion, bearing in mind his long service and experience. The suggestion was that presidential and vice-presidential powers were used to end the matter. The Wilsons took various members of the government to court and lost. However, several of the appeal findings were far from complimentary to those in power. Presidential abuse of power was much under scrutiny. The one person who was "nailed" for lying to investigators, 'Scooter' Lewis Libby (legally trained and the Vice-President's Chief of Staff), had his prison sentence commuted by the President removing his thirty-month sentence, but not his US$250,000 fine, with supervision. Possibly the financial implication would prove less of a problem for one who was at his level of public service. Seeing this level of concern at this level of government suggests there is much for investigative journalism to uncover. Those with power need to demonstrate the responsible use of those powers to fulfill their obligations.

So back to the elderly after a lifetime of serving the community. Having lived an honest, hardworking, and honourable life, elderly people deserve security and respect. The media often depict the elderly in a less than flattering form, thereby foisting the prejudices of the writers, director, and producer upon the audience. Elderly people have suffered repeatedly from this discrimination without a fraction of the reaction screamed out as from and on behalf of racial stereotyping and sexual orientation differences, but then again, some might say the elderly are almost dead! Such are the realities of Human Rights. The fit and active men and women, without the problems and fears of our elderly, bring lucrative legal cases against others for some act or prejudicial comment, be they people of the same background or not. These legal actions are valuable in that they are showing the different interpretations of both law and law associated practices as an insight into the mental processes, prejudices, and legal machinations present. People devoutly Christian can also suffer from a similar branch of spite which teaches that Christian ways are humorous (at their more benign form of discrimination). The insulting of Christian beliefs is not seen as bad taste and degrading as in the case of another race or belief. The teaching that Jesus is there for everyone who wishes is trodden underfoot. Not being protected by the law shows a certain bias against this right to worship. The list goes on to add stay-at-home mothers, 'nerds', nuns, and too many more. When people have lived responsible lives, there generally comes a time when they need support for their bodies and reasonable respect for their mental health. Fear is no way to exist. The elderly, who are the previous world builders and maintainers, deserve to be recognized and respected as such by the young, yet the 'street level mind of the time' denies this. What a wasted resource! When the body is less powerful, call upon the mind: great experience and well-honed powers of thought are there to benefit society and any enthusiastic and interested youngsters, no charge! Each individual elderly citizen on their own may be physically small, but together they could and do exert a massive positive social contribution at a very cost-effective and attractive rate. Not all can be this constructive, but neither can the members of any other age level. If ever there was a sign of social decay it can be identified through its lack of care for both those dependant and at risk of all ages and those who have given their life's effort. The elderly have sensibly had to hand on the *torch of progress* to younger citizens, some somewhat reluctantly at times, but that's life. If there is no respect for the achievements of the elderly, then that torch of progress and font of information is in danger of being extinguished!

Onward to Mind Numbing TV

Another touchstone of society is the emotional state of the *secure but vulnerable*. For example, volunteers and nurses experience grateful love and hopeless despair on a daily basis. They manage wonderfully, or crash out. They should be treated and viewed with the respect they merit and be given high social position, good pay, and essential rest time. Too often they are not. As often as they deal with the pain and fear around them, their own trials go unnoticed, as do their extra kindnesses. They continue in their VOCATION because they know and have freely chosen their Responsibilities: bless them! This is irrespective of dissatisfaction with work conditions, lack of support, poverty, administration demands, personal exhaustion, and anxiety. Nurses are the bringers of relief and peace and deserve to be able to enjoy reasonable security and comfort when not on duty and particularly when they become elderly.

Good entertainment can bring relief and help 'recharge the batteries'. *Love Actually* is a notably beautiful and mainly happy film which periodically appears on BBC TV. One sits and watches *Love Actually* -cringing at each brain-dead interruption courtesy of the advertisers. I recall those idyllic days when there were no interruptions from advertisements and later to advertisements only before and after the show had finished which left the paid for enjoyment unadulterated, the blessed norm. What went wrong? Without advertisers' rude interruptions the progression of the storyline would remain intact and unspoiled. Even better were the days when no advertisements appeared at all and one could watch the same length of film starting at the same time but ending maybe as much as an hour and a half earlier than with advertisements. PVRs and Netflix are two ways of reducing this annoyance if affordable and available. No wonder people lack sleep, thanks to popular films being more frequently interrupted. World War II psychological studies by Edwards demonstrated the significant loss of concentration and skills due to shortened sleep periods. Now the ad-mad media has spawned a new art form, the 'desiccated storyline'. In this the viewer hops about like some demented flea on the red hot stove, back and forth in time and over and around the different cast members: I suspect purposely designed and good for squirting in ads, but bad for the story; bad for relaxation; bad for continuity; bad for concentration; and bad for the mind. Add periodic bouts of filth, violence, cruelty, and vile illness with just a shred of humanity, all part of the program, and any advertisement subtracts little from the mashed up story .... if there really is one sane appearance of an uninterrupted 'plot' it will be hard to find... Changes to viewer behaviour and electrical equipment will and has produced changes in advertising. Company paid for 'placement advertising' is now common with strategically placed product labels and use within films and programs. Current pulsating images on our e-mail page or web pages will spawn far more obnoxious forms of data-analysed unsolicited advertising.

· · · · · · · ·

Life

Life is that *extra consciousness* in which we are searching for meaning, the meaning behind experience and existence. There often 'appears' to be no meaning, for life is about simple living, survival, more efficient provision, and our growing abilities. If life were about an already specified meaning, then there would be little point in such a life, for it would quite simply echo its reply. Questions without clear answers make life a journey of discovery. Yet we have choices, which makes it an active experience of participation with revealed meaning. My mother said of life, "you may choose to either laugh or cry, so make up your mind which you prefer to do!" Thanks Mom! This choice extends to how we are prepared to see others. Perception can often be about choice, and choice is about grades of preferred outcome. Life is basically about *doing*, but every action comes from an open-ended situation and the outcome is the result of one choice. It is worth remembering that even reflexes do not always reflex. Life can be of enhanced value when we go beyond ourselves, what we were, and what was rationally attainable. Life can be about leading each of us to identify our point of balance, thereby enabling us to become an integral part subscribe to, and voluntarily fit into a perceived worthwhile way of being. In this, as they say, time is of the essence, for time we have but only an unknown measure. Heaven is not the essential; there too often lies self-interest, though it is for me a nice probability. Life matters regarding a heaven, but if there were no heaven, then life would still matter. What matters, what inspires, what focuses, and what succeeds is our constructive focus and our effect on others who are all in the same boat. My successes are their successes. Their successes are mine. Their anguish and despair are mine also, just as mine are theirs. It is not if we have time and resources to succeed but rather if we care enough to make the necessary first step that will lead to success.

I bless my Canada that she has enabled me both time and space to think about, reflect upon, and experience the realities of nature and thus life. I worry for my Canada that she has started to throw it all away. The boundaries are being shifted by the noisy mind-bullies I experienced in the UK for many sad years. Those exploiters, believing themselves to be new thinkers and so more right than the established ways, move from the reality, from order, and from experience and once established in firm territory they spread their mind pollution: uncaring self-interest and so on to despair. Oh

Canada! Our responsibility calls us, for we are needed always to stand on guard for thee. This means to act, to be active, and to be focused, for at no time is one fully safe and at no time can we be fully secure. Life is insecurity, so learn to live with it constructively. Play an active role to strengthen and defend both Canada and ourselves.

I and millions of others live fortunately in a wealthy and welcoming country. To provide luxury one has to have a view and experience of it: this is the same with justice. Life is not just; it is just life: we make life just or not.

CHAPTER 15:

DEMOCRATIC FREEDOMS and MANUFACTURING

GOVERNMENT

*There is no glory in wars, just the
tragedy of lost humanity. (R)*

Courtney B. Cazden's *Social "Context of learning to
Read"*, Language and Literacy, Volume 2, OU-Mercer,
Pgs. 150- 153, ISBN: 0 335 15558 8

In L. B. Resnick and P. A. Weaver, Eds. (1981), *Theory
and Practice of Early Reading* Lawrence Erlbaum Associates, INC

. . . .

GOVERNMENT:

1. The exercise of authority over state, district, group, etc.; control; rule

2. An established system of political administration by which a nation, state, etc. is governed.

3. All the people that administer the affairs of a nation....... **(Collins Pocket E Dictionary)**

Governments exist due to design. It seems reasonable to suppose that a governing body has been agreed upon by some; however, in a Democracy it can supposedly be voted for by all casting a personal choice -selection vote and therefore order and government exists through agreement. Electoral candidates have previously been chosen by the vested interests of finance and power. In Canada the strict regulations regarding funding try to regulate the power of finance on a realistic and workable basis, recognizing their dangerous intent. Money generally promotes and wins nomination to candidacy, but not always.

AUTOCRACY: A government in which one person has extreme power

ÉLITE: The group or part of a group selected or regarded as the best, most powerful, etc.

ÉLITIST: Government or control by an élite

INTRIGUE:

2. To get by secret plotting
    1. Secret or underhanded plotting

    2. A secret plot or scheme

INTRINSIC: Belonging to the real nature of things: inherent...

> LOBBYIST: A person who tries to influence the voting on legislation [RH. This is often a paid for service by big business, power blocks, and organizations. The lobbyist may also have something to offer in return.]

> LOBBY: To frequent the lobby, as of the House of Commons [UK.], is to influence [parliamentary] members-else to try to get legislators to vote for or against (a measure) by lobbying.

VESTED INTEREST:

1: An established right, as to some future benefit

2: A strong personal concern in a state of affairs, system, etc.

3. A person or group that has such an interest

JUNTA: A group of political intriguers, esp. military men in power after a coup d'état [take over]

(Collins PED.)

The people who have chosen to enshrine their ideas in Human Rights Legislation are vested interests who have intrigued and lobbied to achieve their life preferences for us all, through law. This is not through understanding and acceptance being relied upon to add emphasis to aspects of personal responsibility. Rather, this is <u>enforced</u> general acceptance. Governments need to be strong enough or chaos ensues, but there are obviously different ways to be strong.

People forming into groups
have responsibilities which are
internalized or innately felt.

Basic Social Standards versus Élitism
- and their attributed benefits

The established upper power groups within society will dictate standards. Some standards can well be designed to filter out and exclude others, whether called a democracy or not. One could argue this approach is present in an international context. Examples of power clubs are G8 or then G7, manipulating trade, etc.; Warsaw Pact was created to protect communist countries and to hold onto power, a reaction to NATO being formed. NATO was set up as a military mutual protection club; UN arrived at the end of the first World War to provide better world security and descended into jobs for the boys and girls; EU appointee system of ministers follows the same corrupt path; etc. Alternatively, minority groups can hijack well-meaning legislation to manipulate the direction of change more to their liking. The people's taxes paid for trials with umpteen appeals, abuses of welfare and healthcare, *out of context* charges of racism, and the 'disrespecting' and breaching of dogmatic rights and so on. Often one hears the erroneous charge of "you are a racist" or "you are a bigot" from some extremist trying to shore up their shaky and ill-thought position. It is quite legitimate and natural not to want or join in or accept certain customs. Should this equally apply to genital mutilation of women, especially when one realizes that secondary infections frequently set in and sometimes infertility or even death results? However, an unfortunately buried up to the elbows issue of being stoned to death is another matter, since the intent is to terrify others, cause terrible pain, and then almost thankfully achieve release through death. There is not any phrase or concept deep-gutted or shaming enough which is sufficient to fit these ungodly stone throwing cowards. When it is suggested that a tradition is uncivilised and unnecessary, the racial Rights card may be played.

To comment on Rap-singing as 'West Indian monotony' may lead to the bigot card being used. My brother rightly says that when force is used in a discussion you are aware the user knows that they are losing the argument: their blows can then ensue. The importance of standards is that they are there to guide. However, context may be overlooked and those with power can exert greater 'leverage'. If those with power share the standards of those without, then Responsibilities and obligations have a good chance of being effective. It has been pointed out: "If it works, don't change it", which in turn comes down to....*good change versus unnecessary change.*

Dave Salbulki, a Canadian Cabinet Minister whose Japanese parents were internees in World War II could well be expected to be a tad anti-Canadian. I believe that all his parents had worked for was also confiscated. However, Salbulki shows the strength of intellect by looking beyond anger and rather the context of a situation, which in this case showed great injustice, to become a valued social and community leader. He may have drawn from Native American experiences. Fixed laws have a way of causing injustice. Salbulki and his parents both succeeded in overcoming this aberration due to intellect and logic: something a number of these rabid Rightists seem deficient in.

Centralization of all the individual political units promises greater cooperation and the efficient spread of information, experience, and skills within: "good" data collection and analysis also follow centralization. It is also seen to empower better business planning and investment. Such 'improvement' better ensures more profitable marketing, shareholders' payments, and expansion. However, investing in self-interest can increase ignorance and isolation, make it harder for those wishing and needing support to obtain it, and enable raw self-interest and selfishness to take over. Ample example is shown in the infamous self-awarded bonus payments for overpaid Directors, instead of reinvestment in jobs, pay, and plant.

The élite of India speak fluent English, which is a skill less often available moving down the social scale. The English language then becomes a 'gatekeeper' keeping others out. Anti-language is never intended as the 'main-speak' of standard language; it is intended as a safeguard to a group, a code, and a way to foil general 'outside' understanding and even directly the powers that be: it is not the property of only the least financially strong. Such use of language may convey one clearly understood meaning while sending a very different message. It also extends to show belonging, a form of bonding, to mark the 'tribe members', the peer group with those who do and do not belong, just as a uniform will: such constructs are also used to exclude, "Hey, what's up?" Language message-form builds and changes within a group situation. There would be no need for language if we were all isolated and entirely on our own. Babies unfortunate enough to find themselves in this sort of situation lose several capabilities and emotional traits, as demonstrated in Nazi Arian breeding houses: being on lay line nodes failed to bring any benefits. Language develops and grows, its details are not innate whereas its structure seems to be (Chomsky and others). In peer groups beliefs are woven through their language use. Those with higher standing within influence the most and the rest adapt generally to these language leaders. What is considered "good" and "right" is created there in language and through language. Broadcasts and other media bring ideas to us in a solitary way which we process ourselves. There is less peer interaction and less peer influence, though what we choose to look at and see may be directly influenced by our peers.

Regarding teaching reading, study **PIERSTRUP'S** (1973) research (in **Courtney B. Cazden's** *Social Context of Learning to Read*: Language and Literacy, Volume 2, Pgs.

150- 153, OU-Mercer, **ISBN: 0 335 15558 8.**, in **Resnick, B.** and **Weaver, P.** Eds. (1981). *"Theory and Practice of Early Reading".*

Lawrence Erlbaum Associates, Inc., in a study of Black children, found an "interference" and thus a disconnect between the language used by teachers and that used by their pupils.

The interference was either:

1. Structural; or

2. Functional.

Either could be a misunderstanding, either a *temporary* or else a more *serious barrier*, depending upon what activity took place next. ***Outcome became dependent upon the attitude and approach of those involved.*** Understanding and interpretation is also about relationships between the text or words presented and personal interpretational experience. This is also true well beyond the classroom in respect, for example, of governing groups and the Law.

Equally questionable is overly pretentious or conversely relaxed English: these are conscious statements of identity. The additions of Latin, German, Dutch, Danish, and French to the English *language-stew* all focus on identity with a beneficial variety, though some would argue against the benefits of spelling consequences! The use of language requires objectivity and discipline. Application of rules and norms is the same in games, in life, and in speech. Grammar and sentence structure matter. The functionality is a heightened unity enabling ideas to be transmitted via the group's acceptance of norms which support the accepted form that follows. Language is a main blood of the group and its personality. Certain spoken conventions are demanded as 'good practice', similar to good manners. Following conventions demonstrates acceptance and sensitivity regarding the group as well as towards individuals. As a "social marker" conventions are useful and transmit clear unambiguous meaning. There is an integrity in the flow of meaning-form, a reasonable expectation of understanding with an avoidance of misunderstanding and possible conflict or insecurity resulting. NB: Our individual control of personal resources is limited, so we share. What each has is shared to some extent. Use of language is an imperfect sharing of minds. Life is too complex to KNOW all, so security needs to come from within a group structure. The group recognizes its members through behaviours and speech. People clearly need security forms.

Belief in what can be right is far too extensive. Limits are created forming clear boundaries which can more easily be followed: they "fence around the law". The concept of right varies individually. Further there is the philosophical question if right actually exists at all. An important life-skill is being able to live with failure and with hope. Failure can mean wrong and success can mean right. This hope with an associated positive outcome may well depend upon a group conforming identity. It is constructive and useful to accept that all of us are linked in many ways which once accepted form a structure of mutual support. Government is best when it enables successful unity. Governments, administrators, voters, and workforce linguistically can travel onto separate paths within a common world of language. This could threaten the unity. Useful to both understanding and agreements would be starting from a similar point in language-use: assumed understanding is the 'nerve way' of politics; later, variety may usefully enter.

Government personnel should be of exemplary character in promoting and demonstrating honesty, responsible conduct, and confidence. Then the question becomes how long lasting is government, and what actually IS THE Government? It may reasonably be suggested that THE elected Government is a continuum irrespective of which political entity or party holds The Power. The Power Holding is it! In the West the state continues, during elections. The civil services and the armed forces continue, education and health services continue, the Acts of Parliament continue, the law continues, taxation continues (especially during elections), so it is reasonable to suggest that the placement and process of Government continues in an unbroken chain: a chain with many varied links. By its nature certain aspects of national policy established by one period of government need to continue unless directly offered to The People for change through national elections or referenda. This is a central concept.

For example, our pensions are contributed to over significant time spans and are clearly part of each individual's planning for their future. It is the Responsibility of any government to maintain and protect our pensions. This is a legal entity. This goes beyond a governing body's particular political lifespan. The pension is a trust placed in Government and a condition of their authority. Brake or ignore such remits and authority lent evaporated, so enter autocracy or chaos. Our society has accepted the primacy of such forward planning, so it needs to act through a policy for all shades of government to pool resources for the benefit and stability of this fund. The pension never relates to the lifespan of a particular party's time in power. It is the government's Responsibility, remit, and duty to maintain and promote.

Each individual should contribute towards the Social Family's well-being and, when the time comes, draw upon the resources to prepare for and live out those sunset years. Clearly there are basic commitments and processes that MUST be present in all political shades of Democratic Governments.

Significant laws are born from experience and precedent. The courts and Government decide, but laws reflect the will of the people. In this 800th year since the Magna Carta, guaranteeing certain liberties-rights to the Lords, its effects have very slowly "trickled down" and are still strong while being a foundation of the USA constitution. So the leaders of our Social Family point to - or rather should point to - how we need to behave, and if this direction is severely enough ignored then it becomes a matter for well-established and argued legal action. Dutch William III (UK) upon arriving in the UK. reaffirmed Magna Carta principles which interestingly had a great influence upon the formulation of The 1689 Charter of Rights and Freedoms (CND). Their decisions and laws agreed that due processes of Parliament must be demonstrably just, right, and proper with clear goals in mind to be acceptable. For example, the collecting of revenue to enable government to function needs to be equally circumspect, reviewing all relevant circumstances. Taxation should never be a form of legalized theft, such as the perpetuation of forms of Governmental Death Theft. If a person honourably pays their social dues (taxes) throughout their life, saves, works, and builds wisely, then how can taking a gigantic bite out of what would otherwise be passed on to the family, in the form preferred by the deceased and written in a will, be right and proper? There is no Right to control one's own product of frugality! How can this be honourable and right? Such is wrong and is legalized theft. That an extra portion of a person's resources be <u>siphoned off</u> by government upon a person's death can have no moral base. How can this be just and commensurate with Human Rights? This rights thing is too often shown to be a farce and a convenience that is used as a tool to take or gain more from others.

Furthermore, why does the British Government pay less in pensions to Britain pensioners living abroad in some countries than in others? How can that be right and fair and just? Why have Britons living, for example, in Southern Spain, France, or Italy been paid a winter fuel allowance of £200 and those living in Canada with six months of real winter cold have not been paid one single penny? People keeping the countryside alive and worth visiting, while supplying food and resources for the cities, receive less from society than those in the cities. In addition, rural residents have their way of life and their community traditions attacked from all sides. There needs to be a more even spread based on a recognition that we do not live in a 'one size fits all society': we differ! Let us individually be more in charge of our own space, more responsible, and more self-accountable. Society is like a machine in which we all are the cogs. This litigious society, created for us, may be long overdue for a change: it is offensive, aggressive, divisive, greedy, socio-destructive, and has to go. Or do we like living in fear of the courts of law? Do we, like small children, need to be cared for by a suffocating nanny state?

US courts award custody and visitation rights to the children who suffered from violent abuse. It seems unbelievable that the abuser can have such 'rights'. Those unfortunate violated mothers or fathers need fullest protection by not being reminded and recharged with fear by his or her actions and choice, that 'unreasonably' violent father or mother should be removed from any such right.

Through participation, initiative, and overcoming difficulties we grow. Loss of community affects our finances, our social existence, our security, our family, and our self-image. We benefit when we become more fully involved in community: ownership leads generally to a more careful, secure, and happy existence. In both rural and urban centres this 'communal spirit within' needs to be nurtured if it is to grow. Reading a local newspaper is an aid to community. It informs, suggests, acknowledges, and rewards active members. Reading local news brings both community and family closer, as we share. However, one first needs to be able to read. For some this is not easy, despite the expense of national education.

A sample of 'byword' characteristics needed socially include *inclusion, awareness, care,* and *friendship.* Each needs to be nurtured specifically as a matter of policy. Clearly all is not well in the body social as we move towards ever greater units of ever lonelier people. Regarding social and family problems, we can individually be the medicine: all of us - every single one. The few weary souls attempting to keep things going need our support and thus our active time which is a sure way to offer encouragement. These hard working minorities are 'killing themselves or rather burning themselves out' with their involvement, yet they are sadly aware that they can't do it all despite fantastic efforts. They work on, but for how much longer and .... what comes after?

Individually we own our own time and should be able to direct its use. Ownership demands and develops personal judgement but conflicts with the excessive imposition of controlling procedures from "life". Blindly accepting such control leads to a passivity with loss of identity, which in turn leads to our being collectively manipulated. Multiple/repetitious taxation is one example. Procedures have been built up over time to entrap, hold, and manipulate the citizen. This is an autocratic form, unlike the natural Social Family Model. Autocratic forms of so called democracy dictates and disciplines through a culture of almost indestructible bureaucracy with their recorded data collected on forms and now computers. Papers have become more important than individuals. Information and data access facilitates the power for gaining control: we no longer own our own space.

What the forms and documents give, the forms and documents can take away.

We can and do say that a situation is "my cause and my effect", when in fact it has become "They demand and I do." Furthermore, the promises made should prove to be the outcome: the outcome or product is the test of any promise with the making of it. Democracy enables us, the people, to replace the promise breakers, but we may just get more of the same! It is less easy to focus on political failure with a Hung Parliament of inter-party compromise.

Good democratic government gathers together a consensus and then acts upon it, instead of relying upon the use of raw autocratic power following some personal preference. This sharing of commitments strengthens the Social Family with its united collective vision of our future, while at the same time laying the ground for later generations to flourish. Since we cannot know all things, we depend upon the honesty of Government to inform truthfully. Unfortunately self-interest will play its inevitable role: again, this is another reason why electing persons of proven integrity is so important. They each need to arrive with a known background of the same: tried and tested morality displayed in previous community service. One wonders how the payment of vast amounts of taxes to federal, provincial, and local governments has been permitted to enable them to grow so burdensome and to ride rough-shod over those who 'pay the piper'. One of these days people on mass will 'vote' not to give their hard-earned income in this way and Democracy will have to change from a 'submerged dictatorship' to become an open autocracy - or become truly democratic.

POLITICS and Office

Sadly, followers of **Karl Marx** and **Freidrich Engels** fail to appreciate the tunnel vision of their mentors in *The Communist Manifesto*. *Political Power, properly so called, is merely the organized power of one class for oppressing another (Pg. 71, Arcturus, 2010).*

The Party hierarchy versus the rest, this has been repeatedly proven inadequate as a too limited and simplistic statement. Rather, the quote above builds a grandiose statement which through impact is designed to be more likely to be taken seriously - too seriously. Some aspects of this stationary viewpoint position are useful, while others are clearly not. Their 'snapshot moment' has been repeatedly just that. No doubt Marx's wife could have made a point in this regard concerning family life. Since the earlier argument is about upwardly mobile groups being unsuccessfully blocked by those above, the political 'arena' would contain at least two power blocks, not one. True, they would probably be largely in opposition, but they would have common ground as well as what might be expected from members of opposite camps. That individuals would and still do care deeply to move away from their "roots", for want of a better expression. People do care deeply and recognize their Responsibilities. This mindset empowers them to see beyond time-fixed group accepted norms. The research and outcomes which centred on the book *Darkest England* is one case. Philanthropists continually show this, as do daily donations from everyday people in the form of voluntary work and regular giving to charities. The work of the Webbs and The Fabian Society in the UK with countless other groups all demonstrate aspects of working 'political power' - not to oppress but rather to raise people up. That there is no magic wand which may be waved to right all problems comes as no surprise. Progress takes time, planning, and damned hard work - something Marx might have pursued to the advantage of those close to him. Oppression comes in many forms.

Paul Martin, Canadian Prime Minister, said this following years of government and the exercise of power:

> *"In Government you see the world from thirty thousand feet, but when you are out of Government you see it from the ground."*

This perception of advantage of position and broader view, or divorce from reality, explains a few things. The purpose of elections is to select our representatives and to transfer our individual power collectively to those elected, as well as the removal of the powerful and abusive from office. Elections should proceed after candidates have made clear what they promise to do with this collective power (e.g. The Manifesto). For the voters to be fully franchised, all adults must be represented and meaningful information must be readily available. The voting process is the democratic process, often termed a right. It is the essential part built into the process of handing over power. It cannot be omitted. It is therefore not a right but more the essential part by definition. One approach is that representation is arranged in a process that is proportionate to the votes gained by each group. Minorities have fewer representatives as a result. This should mean that their power is proportionate to their percentage of votes. They become able to speak, but unless they are significantly influential and persuasive, they are unable to change much. In a Hung Parliament there is no clear winner; thus, bargaining, Manifesto compromises, and alliances form. Combinations of groups occur with compromises which may differ greatly from already announced policy. What was voted for is changed, but not with a new vote of public ascent being required. In this situation a tiny group can disproportionately gain access to power and influence well beyond their voting support since their vote holds the balance of power: a form of legal blackmail takes place. This situation, until it was changed to first past the post, used to be the fate of ungovernable Italy and has also been seen with extreme Right Wing faction in Israel. These two positions produced Mafia growth in the one and further Palestinian hardship in the other. Neither was the will of the majority of the people, and so the democratic principle was violated. But what else could be done? The Right dictates an exact proportionate power regarding the vote, but there is a Responsibility to the nation to form a workable government and avoid chaos. A compromise results via a coalition: it does not ensure policy balance. Therefore, a minority has the power to withhold its support and when doing so can precipitate a new election. It is able to wield a disproportionate amount of influence and power. In this situation a convention accepting a perception of the 'greater benefit' supersedes the right. Government by election on clear principles and policies is changed into another form based on minority control and rule.

In Canada there are large numbers of people who entered the country through the right channels, who are permanent home owning residents paying full Canadian taxes, and who pay municipal taxes. Yet they are told that like an illegal immigrant or prisoner they do not have and by suggestion do not deserve a vote at election times. They may conceivably even have Canadian children and grandchildren. This fails to reflect 'democratic rights'. It seems that those with power over these good disenfranchised neighbours do not even bother to care, or else this stipulation would have been changed. It is clear where responsibility lies here: in government. Emergency immigration now confers residency on people present in Canada for just a few minutes following under a year of processing their application. For others who are less in the news but no less desperate it takes years. One case I am very familiar with is a couple who applied for entry in 1987 to finally gain residency in 2002, despite the intervention of the Member of Parliament for that Canadian Municipality and despite having sponsorship.

A deceitful man or woman is neither worthy of respect nor office and therefore should be removed from any position of trust or better still not gain such a position in the first place. In New York a Rabbi had installed a video camera in a digital clock in an orthodox ladies ablutions at the synagogue. One hundred and fifty people were reported as being compromised (mid-Feb 2015). The right action of expulsion was taken. Society cannot prevent intentional wrong any more than accidental wrong. Abusing the privacy of 150 women in this obviously premeditated way was an absolute betrayal by an individual who was expected to know and be better. This was not the fault of the synagogue. Perverse and confused PEOPLE, found in all faiths, can however prove to be highly effective negotiators. They are devious and cunning. They are prepared and able to manipulate and lie to gain power and advantage. They plan and they "groom". They are found in governments, in the legal system, and in charities. Their actions are purely (or rather impurely) worked through lies, pretence, besmirching others, bullying, and selfish greed. Practice makes a formidable social enemy of this form of social virus! There appears to exist a law of undisclosed self-interest and self-protection in their world.

We have the choice to co-exist or to withdraw. The choice favours acting in harmony or contradiction of an accepted way and does not suggest a better approach. Contradiction and opposition are not the same thing. Opposition tends to have clearer ideas, goals, and outcomes; it is not unusual in life nor in physics; and it is a reactionary force. In parliamentary terms opposition is a form of co-existence. When accepted, respecting and respected form the basis of democratic societies and their law courts. Opposition searches out and exposes weaknesses and hopefully strengthens the whole. However, contradiction does not care if it fits in or not. It can so easily become that 'loose cannon' bringing conflict. Some 'hunt' people: trampling their beliefs, self-respect, and very stability by constant contradiction. Contradiction appears in families, club meetings, staff meetings, politics, and planning. If contradictories find they have gained real power, then they unashamedly use it, even amorally. They contradict and argue at every turn, frequently in a self-indulgent battering of verbiage. By shouting louder, interrupting, and ignoring any 'right' of reply, they take over political space. Due to the gullible and the fearful, they grow in power. These sadly are present in every theatre of life, but they are all from the same self-centred spiteful mould. They poison the 'well water' which results in others being unable to drink. Responsible political opposition tries to constructively search out defects and thus improve the outcome. One may ask if the shouters and screamers should have the same rights as the more thoughtful, calm thinking members of honest opposition. I think not. They failed to live up to their Responsibilities to the Social Family. They clearly have a long way to go before they wish to listen, learn, and discuss. They do not deserve the same rights, privileges, position, respect, and opportunity properly enjoyed by more mature and trustworthy members. Abusive arrogance needs to be seen as unrewarded to clearly send a better message.

How can a government have any credibility, self-respect, or expectation of support if working outside the Social Family - for example, when cutting the medical provisions for those who are dependent upon them? Likewise with educational cuts, made to save cash for speculative developments, this weakening education weakens the Social Family's future. These attacks upon the vulnerable and are the act of a bully, an unenlightened autocrat, and not a true representative of the people. This hopefully would be less evident with a more balanced representation. It is understandable that more elected women in Canada's Parliament, though highly desirable, won't greatly change Canada. However, just, honest, constructive, and responsible policies will. Such policies are not the sole preserve of women, as that strange feminist minority would like us to believe, any more than the virtues of kindness, caring, gentleness, love, empathy, artistic creativity, and the family are. Different people have different experiences, gifts, and visions. The male and female 'sides' of personality are a fun idea, but they are just that: someone's idea, a successful public relations exercise. The most vitriolic and vicious interpersonal activities I have witnessed have been between women and homosexuals, BUT some of the greatest kindnesses and exemplary self-sacrifices have been the same. Sweep away generalizations and prejudices. What a person does is what a person is. To see and observe the essential benefits from this sex difference is to lay oneself open to abuse, but cannot change the fact that they still exist. Yes, we are different, but in smaller significant ways. These are levels of an attribute which again vary from person to person and across sexes: unconfined to a sex. Much of today's certainties of character are well "advertised", but are actually accepted myths. Difference with a broader vision may well promote a more constructive progress. Our very variety is what has moved humanity forward and still does. It is one of the strongest arguments for a free, accepting, and responsive society, with that essential sense of humour and responsible self-discipline. Sharing our world is the reality. Absolute power should not be in the hands of any one man or woman. Absolutism has proven too often blind to all but its own wants, and so should not exist.

Is the following example of humour simple fun, or a sexist attack?

"If I said you have a beautiful body, would you hold it against me?"

Within democracies there are certain and clear variations. It would be interesting to establish if democracies enable greater diversity of all forms. There appears to be essential, accepted, and consistent practices with inclusion of minorities. Recognized political continuity leads to promised support and confident decision making which produces and enables accepted attainable progress. Logic and empathy applied to identifiable needs are far more productive than rigid law and dictatorial demands from an unyielding and maladaptive status-quo battling the odds. Such intransigence is convinced of its own unassailable rightness. Such self-assurance is an irresponsible recourse and undue focus upon perceptions of fixed rights to the detriment of adaptive responsible behaviour and Responsibilities. Complaining whingers need to accept that "things happen", so count your blessings and wise up! We need non-surface thinking, or rather deeper thought to evaluate several of the 'fathomable' contexts and outcomes before deciding to act..........as they say, 'please first engage the brain before activating the mouth'. The concept of Human Rights has a plural remit: it should concern itself, for example, with the defence of the endangered many rather than brief unessential singular encounters. None of us are perfect; all will have moments they will later regret. Displaying anger can be a bad thing but a resulting over reactive injustice is equally wrong, if not far worse. In democracies differences are the accepted reality. People will differ as to likes, dislikes, fears, and security. Rigid social law, unconcerned with human realities and flexibility, is more the stuff of communism or the organization of a robot society.

Rules, customs, traditions, and laws need a developing Middle Logic between conception and activation. This is the region of *adaptive thinking*. At this stage more input could well benefit reflection and resulting reasonable changes could be made. Here *Induction* and *Inclusion* are parts of the reasoning processes along with generalization and validation, which proceed from the collection of facts to a process and then conclusion. These interact with *deductive* processes to remove irrelevance and focus upon the specific: the essential factor or factors to be considered for action. These become identifiably part of the same 'conglomeration' and facilitate decision making.

An APHORISM is a concise statement of principle [CPED].

Achieving such clarity better identifies limits or limitations. We need to ask, "What if any are the REASONABLE limitations that can be placed on law? What can identify and define legal injustice?" It is highly questionable that the extended 'trials', in and because of recurring appeals procedure, are the right way to go. Is it better to enable the raising up of standards rather than to 'legally' knock them down? Must we must question whose standards and whose concept of right should prevail when the bounds have already been established?

The greatest glory in this life is not in never failing but in rising every time we fall."

Nelson Mandela

The Energy Question

How to approach this big business and finance question without considering the effects of cash flow, dividends, share prices, bribery, corruption, and causing individual harm? Each needs proper consideration. So much goes on within this waterfall of mega bucks that understanding seems almost impossible. The science of global warming is compelling but uncertain with many alternative focuses suggested including the earth's rotational wobble as another factor. From so much evidence, one cannot reasonably deny that warming is taking place, but the reasons are still being debated. From my point of view it is essential to take all into account but act now upon the leading identifiable culprits: there will be no second chance. Further debate and fine tuning can take place later, but start now. We are going to have to change the ways we live. Better to be in a position to choose and select than have to act by plugging or rebuilding the dam that holds back the flood of world disasters. History does not help with its periods of atmospheric revolt: there just is not enough causal data available. Theories abound but we just do not know the full details. Ideas, plans, and experimental results exist that can honestly and clearly show a possible positive outcome is still possible, but there is considerable doubt.

We all know that humanity and greed are out of control. We all expect and demand far too much. We blame the livestock and crops which feed us, even the trees. We blame our industries and their produce for providing for us, but we fail to accept fully that we are the problem. Want less, take less, produce less, and our lump of universal rock can sustain us. Arrogant belief in human mastery and our greed will, if unchecked, be the end of us. There is no energy question because no one is asking The Question. It does not exist. What exists is a pattern of detrimental behaviours raping our planet. These behaviours must stop if we are to survive: the factual evidence shows this. We need not find more but rather need to learn how to individually do with far less. Moderation and sustainability seem to be a safer way forward. We may yet even find we actually do have a future as a race, as a Social Family, from introducing a far more responsible present. Only by agreement and working together will this be possible through cooperative discussion.

QUESTION

Is a case still true when reduced to its smallest whole form or parts? Such a whole form would be recognizable as being complete though not as extensive. When it has been proven to be complete it may be enlarged by multiplying to greater numbers and still be true. If only two people remained in this world, they would reflect actions initiated by many couples: they would still have Responsibilities. These Responsibilities being shared by them would be for the benefit of their partnership. These Responsibilities would be acted upon since they had and have personal value. Interestingly with the two there would be no one outside or beyond to insist or enforce these concepts as rights. I suggest that Rights are the invention of people drawing upon existing form and feelings which promote <u>accepting Responsibilities</u>. Moreover, these higher feelings do not come from nor depend upon enforcement; they come from accepting specific significant and thus emotive actions or activities. They are the product of what I would term the human soul, which recognizes Responsibilities to and the need to share with others: exercising empathy required for fuller awareness.

Another Question: Whose world is it?

Is it your world or the politicians, the oxygen producing and carbon digesting plants, animals, the industrialists, the financiers or the military, or the yet unborn: whose world is it? Who or what are in control?

Who or what makes the greatest contribution to our lives: us, plants, animals, climate, farmers, energy, or what?

There is a powerful minority who freely exploit and despoil our planet. Would it be better to promote local food production and industry? Such would provide work, reduce appalling waste, and reduce use of distance transportation thanks to known demand informing production. This would reduce fuel demands and promote local food crops in favour of cash crops which are generally bulk transported elsewhere, like flowers in airplanes from Africa, while this process degrades the fertility of the soil and dries up natural water! Local production encourages and strengthens community and reduces the carbon footprint. How can it truly be cheaper to mass produce with so much waste, unemployment, and underemployment? Many are undervalued, unhappy, and unhealthy while others starve in 'successful' industrial lands.

Being powerless, should we care?

FREEDOM OF SPEECH

In 'democracy', there is a right to speak and express one's point of view. Since democracy allows for a broader picture, our knowledge benefits. These are ways of expressing our freedoms to choose for ourselves, not imposed on, rather chosen. Responsible freedom comes with free choice, but with accepted obligations. To do harm or cause harm to others due to their appearance, social preference, originality of thought, or otherwise is unacceptable to most. Democracy allows for difference: it exactly why it came to exist. Dislike, anger, and harm happen. Our social organization has developed to reduce these. As a result of demonstrably pernicious prejudice or other forms of abuse, this may well remove the obligation of group 'protection' of miscreant abusers. We learn of examples of such abuse perpetrated over Europe by some of the worst from Asia, Arabia, and Africa upon and with those from Europe. Correction or rather punishment occurs through the democratic system's agreed legal body. In fact, when meeting extremes the law has a duty to react and defend. To deal with uncivilized anti-social behaviour, officials have to become involved. It is difficult to appreciate how this protective role is to work within the mob mentality infiltrating migrant minorities when they only become identifiable after committing illegal activities. This is a political situation with varied accesses to real power complicated by Human Rights and extended subversions of personal interest: nightmare situations. Intelligence agencies, by operating reasonable monitored surveillance of both innocent and guilty parties, go against generally agreed upon Human Rights of privacy and information but not governmental responsibility. Such activity is a response to special cases having become established such as constant safety concern. This shows that Human Rights are not absolute and <u>are</u> 'negotiable' under the right set of circumstances. Agents take action to fulfill their Responsibilities to and for the Social Family, just as the police break speed restrictions in a chase. Each Member of Parliament (MP) is elected to represent all, irrespective of who their constituents voted for.

The electorate are all politically equal. They make their electoral choice based upon what is explained and promised to them. A Member of Parliament speaks not on behalf of just himself or herself but for their many constituents for whom he or she is responsible - in line with the MP's base beliefs outlined during the election campaign. Any democratic constitution, if it is truly democratic, facilitates and protects this "right and these obligations". MPs will act responsibly and responsively and enable their constituents" concerns to be heard. This principle of freedom of speech goes well beyond parliament but carries with it the restraints of responsibility and respect, though only up to a point and that point is often personal. Freedom is not one sided.

Centred in Finsbury Park UK was a refugee "spiritual" Muslim leader, Mr. Hook. On the days of "worship" HE chose hate. In many other areas of Britain there are other imams desiring to preach similarly some form of negative creative-bitterness, recruiting the devout Muslims to their Hell and their Abyss. Fridays, for them, do not become days of fatherliness, friendship, fostering love and kindnesses, faithfulness....but rather frustration, fantasies, fear, fabrication with created insecurity, and hate. The ravings of maddened, corrupt, arrogant, and violent cells, migrant guests of Europe, WILL lead to horrendous conflicts unless swiftly and fully dealt with. This will entail use of armed forces. Putin's activities at various points of the globe, such as Scandinavia, Ukraine, Syria, Iran, and recently liberated

Soviet states, may well be opportunist, if one is being chari-table, but are definitely beyond dangerous.

SOCIAL TRAINING and A Work Model

Antisocial people appear unable to understand fully enough the important roles of developed self-control nor the need and advantages for having democratic leadership and leaders. Currently schools and police have their work made so much harder by a too permissive attitude. Our region of the world has chosen to become "too permissive". When social solidar-ity decays, self-harm increases (e.g., drugs, theft, rape); the young are prevented from an efficient and rewarding educa-tion; abuse and discord increase; and the safe use of peaceful public spaces even for children are no longer safe nor peace-ful. The list goes on. An insistence upon self-discipline by a mentor provides guiding experience while extending aware-ness and knowledge. This creates a base for positive and interactive social behaviour, a conformity which has been both agreed upon and internalized by most.

The usual models used for society and the workplace are hierarchical: a pyramid with most people being near the base and a pinnacle at the top, which is extremely flattering for the one finding him or herself placed there. This is also used to show the position with regard to power: the workforce comprises the basal section. Now, if we were to place produc-tion first, the pyramid would be upside-down and balancing on a point. This does not provide a satisfying image or semi-otic for the few now at the bottom. However, the precari-ous nature of being in charge is closer to reality. The 'Point People' are only too aware of their precarious position at the sharp end, especially since so many are somewhat greedy. Thus, pyramid after pyramid needs to be placed next to each other for balance in order to stay up. Social training with successful hierarchical models has perpetuated the 'them or us' expectation rather than the reality of 'them with us'.

1. There are two main inputs: of the mind: ideas, work, and then comes organization (people)

2. The changing processed material (raw materials to be worked on) THEN -

3. The makers and the product, a combined joint output. Beyond that is a totally separate dynamic of income and skills brought into and during the process.

4. Distribution

Diagram 10. A More Realistic Model Of Industry And Production

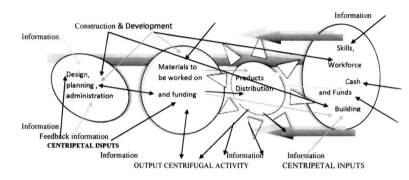

Remove any one of the industrial process spheres and the whole thing ceases to function. Here, shown above, is an alternative model. Industry is linear and as such a pattern is a more real model than the pyramidal over simplistic form. The power pyramid model is inaccurate and fails to show the real picture. The 'Administrators' directing efficiency are as important, no more and no less, than the Producers. So all are on the same level. Finally, without efficient 'centrifugal' distribution, it will all fail. The Japanese financial and industrial worker-caring modern and far more informal Zaibastsu (evolved industrial conglomerate) is closer to this.

We NEED each other and ALL are essential. Carl Marx did a great disservice to the world by focusing on a first revolution of overturning power without looking beyond what could occur if it had not been autocratic but rather leading on to a *second 'revolution' of co-operation and community*. But there again he disparaged the "lower class" as lumpenproletariat or "miscreant rags"! This disorganized group of criminals, vagrants, tramps, and the unemployed to him lacked any idea of their collective interest. They themselves (and not poverty) caused themselves to become an oppressed class, an underclass.

The Communist Manifesto states:

"generally applicable ....in most advanced countries.."

"8. *Equal obligation of all to work. Establishment of industrial armies, especially in agriculture.*"(Pg 69, Ed. 2010)

I imagine that prediction would get a few laughs in the countryside. The 'revolution' has moved on, as did agricultural mechanisation which was needed partly due to free decisions by individuals to move on to towns and cities. However, it is probably true that no matter where they are, responsible citizens have an equal obligation to work. This is one outcome of social training. What will happen when the thinking robots take over is too uncertain and different to tell: paradise or catastrophic conflict! Insight, forethought, and action will be swiftly required. Robots fighting Jihadists is already a fact.

There is that element and quality which make the great sportsman, team, speaker, scientist, or artist. Seizing the moments offered by chance takes confidence as well as skill. Enabling a sensitive confidence is a human duty of social training. It is the BUILDING of patterns of thought and ways of being until they become, in time, the natural way, but through social training always for the common good ... a different part of that being a development with a clear aim or goal in mind for personal and <u>deserved</u> advancement: the European ideal.

It is reasonable and sensible to affirm that this social training begins somewhere.

Not surprisingly and quite naturally as a baby is born there is a new start with so many opportunities within the community. The baby is like a board covered with colourful oil paints. It could become an abstract, a Picasso, a Mona Lisa, a Laughing Chevalier, a Cezanne, a Vasarely, or a muddy-coloured mess. However, development begins with those people and things which surround the newborn. With all of these are the child's own built in and developing nerve 'developmental-and reaction affinities', dominated by the senses and organs. A child who is taught reason and firm discipline will most probably exercise the same: the opposite is our alarm-call.

Some thing or some things make all the difference.

The individual is like a game with many rules for play. The greater meaning comes in keeping and RESPECTING the restrictions imposed by the rules by maturely accepting them. Then, recognizable success can be achieved within the boundaries of that game. If it is a team game, as in life, the game is best served by cooperation: conscious decisions to work together and thereby achieve a positive result. Within this agreed upon cooperation, each part will view options differently and consider the options present from their own position while calling upon their own life experiences to inform both consciously. Memory is crucial. In soccer, for example, a defender will record the action of the game differently from the striker's very different view and also from the midfield player's perspectives: the same activity is viewed differently by each. Each will have to operate 'give and take' for the good of the team. Selflessness serves all. Sooner or later some will put personal glory first in a selfish way. Some success will be achieved, but at what cost to the team?

The baby learns to walk somehow.

How can that happen? But we expect it to happen. Such learning/values are in learning to talk - another miracle. With talking we are sharing cultural messages which develop into ways of seeing, thinking, understanding, interpreting, and responding. These influxes of images may easily override other earlier thoughts, feelings, and intellectual responses. Any one of these could become dominant, especially if apparent and supported amongst a group. If this focusing upon specifics and symbols were not effective, then there would be little point in advertising nor any point in providing symbols such as flags and uniforms. An often repeated idea seems to become assimilated: if not as fact, then as having value in its own existence. Depending upon its direct relevance or relevance to other ideas and experiences, this idea if once accepted will become fully active or else otherwise 'switched out' under the process of the economy of memory. As the thinking mind recognizes a reality moment through its role as a caretaker of the total mind, it directs and indicates a specific path, generally a 'right path' to either follow or reject. The baby learns to walk, to go its own way, and to discover its own things. It moves beyond a controlled and outside focused awareness. Fascination and enquiry step in, but the security of conformity will periodically return.

Learning to go further.

A common 'national faith' can help in promoting a collection of universal norms for the communal good: ones seen and expected in most religions. Acceptance of a 'right path', however, can be confused by background, peer group, and events. Naturist native groups provide social pressure to reinforce and generally produce acceptance of their naturist practices and forms. Such acceptance is through tactical management, where they take control of a process or event specifically to highlight their position which through this acceptance by most can usefully be the way to go. Breaking with the usual is far more noticeable than following a predictable path. In his gang study, Thrasher (1925, 2013) shows the world of gangland in which the evil and poverty of such areas do not necessarily cause evil people. He provides examples of "The Angels" who organize and appear in such places: groups of local people, generally young, who go out and about offering kindness and supporting the endangered. This shows the unpredictable nature of social training or possibly an innate constructive awareness at work: nature rather than nurture. These groups are credible, neutral organizers who "interrupt" what otherwise would seem inevitable. St Paul might well have met and encouraged such groups of volunteers who operate self-denial and abstinence for the benefit of others. In play we learn to be supportive, to operate self-control, and to share. These are attributes of the good citizen. To encourage these and so much more, children need to experiment and take risks clear of parental 'interference'. This is just one reason why we must again fill our parks and open spaces with children safely at play, not just organized games, though these as an addition are excellent. Recent events in Germany including child rape work against child freedom. This is also true of the work by an English Judge at Law who is supporting efforts of paedophiles 'campaign' to permit child sex as a child's human right. I believe it would be better to lock the whole lot up for a long, long time. One primary role of childhood is the safe development of self-motivation leading to experience, while also learning to reject other options which may seem fun but are unsafe or wrong. Also, learning that all 'failure' brings knowledge that can well be useful later . If we do not fail occasionally it is difficult to see how we can learn when or what to avoid. Developing a process of thought without panic is evidently preferable to learning under duress: panic produces rushed rash remedies and decisions both inevitably leading to more of the same. It seems a thing of wonder that any child should be able to emerge from our massive Factory Blocks of School as a balanced individual. How often for some is the school that 'bridge too far, beyond hope of safely crossing'!

DEMOCRACIES and EDUCATION

With so much current discussion of freedoms, it is a bit surprising that we still have compulsory education as it is experienced in its main forms. This means, unlike adults, some children are forced to continue education very much against their will and even at personal risk. Too many are unwillingly "imprisoned" in a hostile and hateful environment, for no crime other than being born. If this is seen as necessary for the greater good which also results in the harming of a few innocent children, then corporal punishment could well fit under the same umbrella of logic. After all, if corporal punishment is administered with care and restraint it might enable better learning, a calmer environment, less bullying, and a happier school experience for far more students and encourage the recipient towards a happier life overall: a whole crop of greater goods. I imagine suicides are not often the outcome for the unruly and vicious pupil, but more the gentle, sensitive, bullied, frustrated, and hopeless victim. With stronger focused discipline, bullies and disruptive people might even learn to behave at school, at home, and in our communities. This might occur if greater resolve and social good were a more active concern of those in the fantasy land of authority. With less disruption, more could be taught with fewer children having their learning experience harmed. A happier end with greater pupil success could well be two justifications. If improvements are not forthcoming, then the separate systems will grow and grow, or is that the intention of the "powers that be": a huge new market with so many external productive links? As a sideline, more expensively trained teachers might remain teaching with lower training costs resulting in more parentally trained and motivated children. The saved funds from being able to keep good teachers could be better invested in the elderly, sick, handicapped, and better, kinder, smaller populated schools and classrooms. If a teacher is a danger to the development of his/her charges through laziness, spite, or other, replace! Their colleagues know only too well who would fit this description. There is a vast pool of replacements for several years awaiting their first full-time teaching post. Many newly qualified teachers have seven years of being "on call", as fill-in staff, before being offered a permanent position at a single place of work. The dross could be removed in one go! Yes, those who work each day in the schools do know best, but are seemingly not well supported in this. The more teachers there are, the more goes into the pension fund with its administrators. Further, all principals should have times regularly timetabled for teaching. If they prove ineffective, then they should be replaced. How often do parents have to resort to expensive fee-paying institutions or extra tuition? The argument for state-funded 'secure' special education is clear and just and for many on the "back boiler". Civilized Societies are about looking after those most in need as well as other day-to-day provisions. Bullies are also suffering from their own emotional handicap and need both controlling and special focused help. All children need.

Political stupidity is never politically correct.

Any student ending schooling early clearly could later be given the opportunity to return to the learning process, probably with a clearer view of an appropriate career and options they prefer to pursue. If suffering from some educational difficulty, then the time 'outside' may prove a boon and an avenue into a training scheme that works well for them within a discovered ability range. Such a situation can produce above average ability in their specific areas of interest. Richard Branson does very well, and he is even a role model. Plenty in the entertainment industry may have not been best suited to schooling but succeeded elsewhere. Why force them to stay? If all left school at 16 with the offer and assurance of two or more years of study free of charge at a later date should they need, then one could reason that there would be less waste and unhappiness in school and college. Less costly truancy, reduced indiscipline, damage reduction, and more value could be the outcome with fewer good teaching staff leaving that profession. Just imagine attorneys having to exist similarly unprotected. It is better to be and have a motivated returnee than a miserable and boring inmate of the school. Apprenticeships and junior assistant learning posts would probably be preferred by many youngsters. Welcomed and relevant community hours in Canada demonstrate this with staggering success. Students are finding out how the real world functions, and when these findings are both honestly and successfully used the start of many a business and stellar rise in industry has been the outcome. Also, there is a strong argument that overcrowding, indiscipline, and forced attendance results in the incarceration of some youngsters in a special isolation school room. This is not far off child abuse. Sometimes it is child abuse! Such lengthy 'disciplinary methods' are perpetrated due to the individual's lack of child power or effective rights. Try to do the same with an adult! It seems foolish to spare the rod and spoil the child's future. A meaningful format for the child is 'carrot and stick approach' which can and generally does work: the form this approach takes is the difficult part, but nothing succeeds like success. The "stick" part generally does not need to be used. Successful social and skills/knowledge learning should not be merely the educational achieved aim but the *recognizable outcome* for and by all student individuals, including an awareness and support of their discovered main interest.

Unfortunately there are a lot of misunderstandings pro-moted within education. 'Confusers' of thought and theory can achieve significant fame and rewards by succeeding in disestablishing the established. This is not necessarily because they are right, but rather that they were more able, especially when dealing with the dead, and so they 'did it better'. New is often considered good while 'tried and tested' can be viewed as old and 'past it'. However, nothing succeeds like success and that is the major teaching goal: enabling others to legitimately succeed. Some learning is easy while other demands commitment, determination, and effort. Self-disciplined study is a learned behaviour. It, like most things in this area, may be either caught or taught. Good background experience assists easier and deeper learning: this is a consequence of planned involved parenting. The outcome does need to be knowledge enjoyed. Sometimes one method is more efficient and successful than the others for different students, and so teachers need to be adaptable. Children respond differently to their different teachers. A child who is at odds with their single classroom teacher is doomed to at least a year of misery, and if this conflict is not sorted out then this misery will spread through the entire schooling experience. My own position is that a variety of specialist teachers is and would be more beneficial to the students if this practice was adopted in all our schools at all age levels. This would give all involved parties a break from each other and a richer deeper learning approach. While this would also give the principal a lot of organizing to do, this is, one assumes, what the principal is paid to do. I remember it well, but it works! They say variety is the spice of life and lesson time may well be a case in point.

Teaching to facilitate learning, at its simplest of interpretations, is comprised of directed activities to master words placed with ideas, links, and progressions. The performance of feats of memory is not the same as mastering processes of thought. Thought processing is more about bits of knowledge, like building bricks, which have value in a process of their assembly into meaningful structures. *Use-full* education promotes an interest in exactly how ideas are placed together as well as why and where there are other possible combinations this may lead to. Again, competence is confidence and *secure independence* of thought should be the goal of teaching [see William BLATZ, 1966]. Confidence comes from frequently walking the ideas-path and arriving successfully. Yes, there is repetition. This journey takes imagination, focused effort, and self-discipline. The whole process becomes easier and more fun as we learn to 'PLAY' with appropriate learning and enjoyment at an emotional level. The learner needs to be able to recognize regular progress as a direct result of personal action and therefore experience recognizable success that is earned and achieved. This success when related to life skills is best associated with and derived from people-experience. With this there is a socially active ingredient for a learner experience. Impersonal machines can send an entirely different and unhelpful message. What is more, teachers need to have small enough classes to frequently review, mark, and notate children's work providing useful revisable feedback for the students. Teachers need to know all their students' names quickly along with their respective characters; to have and be themselves confident in their specialist knowledge; to expect and achieve social order in the group of youngsters; and to be able to rely on a system with teeth regarding bullies, the aggressive, the abused, the disruptive, the dishonest, and those at risk. Teaching is a craft, an art, and an instinct. Teachers need to be idealists and well-motivated specifically for the benefit of those being taught. They need to be unafraid of longer working hours, constructive frequent marking, adaptive to situations, and quick to praise at an *appropriate* level. Dedicated servants of the Social Family who achieve pleasure in their charges' learning ↔ speed ↔ confidence and a useful creative memory. Only so much can be taught to would-be teachers, and only so much needs to be usefully mastered by them. But it is clear that too many should not be allowed to remain in the profession due to their laziness, ignorance, political ambition, greed, spitefulness, and simple but corrosive apathy. How often could we rephrase the car sticker to, for example, If *you can read this it is despite your teacher*! Thank God for the majority who consequently have to carry a heavier load caused by colleague indolence.

Subject teachers see their pupils over a number of years. They are better able to provide expert subject teaching, useful digressions, and continuity as the pupil moves up through the years. Furthermore, a good teacher keeps the class entertained. This stems from experience, confidence, and personal method. Students have good reason to laugh and know they are free to quip and joke *at appropriate times*, and so they are happy pupils. These have learned a vital positive life skill that they will happily use till the day they die: knowing is fun. The continual loss of that experience with teacher resignations is due to indiscipline and disillusionment. This loss is tragic for the children. Clearly, positive motivation is key to success and success is key to motivation. Lesson planning targets success and motivation. However, achieving success and feeling successful are subjective: too easy work is no success at all, and unrealistic praise mars motivation. So, the trick is enabling success by personally overcoming - or rather mastering - the challenges. Repetition proceeds to familiarity and that in turn produces calm thought. Fight or flight is not a problem here. Useful repetitive learning obviously has a substantial place. This repetition can be done in various fashions to be effective; therefore, this repetition needs to take the appropriate form. Sometimes it is only necessary to know the how and not the why. Fullest understanding of the why may grow later with specialization and an academic need for more knowledge to draw upon.

Our appraisals of our children, when linked with our beliefs about them, need to be thoroughly honest. Indulging in both fantasy and 'ambition displacement' does not serve them well. Yes, love them, but conditions do and must apply. Love is a strong force which all parties must be worthy of: love needs to work both ways. Clear ***ground rules*** (basics) are needed in all families and groups from the very start. Clear in this case means discussed, understood, and agreed by all. If rules are permitted to morph, wax, and wane, then instability ensues. Simple and clear is one way to go. Firm but fair is the other. One reason why the Biblical Ten Commandments were so effective is their simplicity, and this simplicity comes through agreement.

The Cub Scout Guides movement demonstrates the huge benefits of consensus functioning freely with and through good discipline. Its members consequently advance both in knowledge and personally. The members promise to do their best, follow the agreed upon rules, and help someone else each day. This is constructive and successful.

Learning particular ways of talking to present our personality demonstrates our self-identity, but this way of talking needs to be fit for purpose and so achieve what it is supposed to achieve. We try to achieve this appropriateness in most areas of our life. Fit for purpose is our goal, so why on earth do some 'academics' suggest that otherwise is just as suitable! Effective language form is no different in that it must achieve its objective. I remember using British Rail on many occasions, as it was, and neither being able to understand the announced train arrivals nor their platforms due to an Indian sub-continent accent. This was inappropriate use of manpower and an unkindness. My dad, a Scots Glaswegian, learned to use two ways of speaking to fit the occasion. Further, it seems somewhat foolish to take the trouble to learn Dockland Marseilles French unless one is going to live and work there!

There is a limiting value for an unsuitable way of doing something. Writing neatly and being aware of effective grammar use for educational and business purposes is a bit like putting petrol in your car as instructed, rather than diesel. Both have their time and place.

· · · · · · ·

CHAPTER 16:

RIGHTS WITH RESPONSIBILITIES

THOMAS PAYNE "Fathered Human Rights ..."

> "A Declaration of Rights is, by reciprocity, a declaration of duties also.
>
> Whatever is my right as a [person] is also the right of another, and it becomes a duty to guarantee as well as to possess".....(p. 76)

> "It is for the good of nations and not for the emolument of aggrandisement of particular individuals, that Government ought to be established, and that [people] are at the expense of supporting it. ......Government and Constitution, both as to principle and form, must in parity of reasoning, be as open to discussion as the defects of a law, and its duty which ever [person] owes to society to point them out ...... and consequently those subjects, as subjects of investigations, are always before a country **as a matter of right**, and cannot, without invading the general

rights of that country, be made subjects for prosecution..."
.......................(p. 114)

Rights of man evaporated during World War I and II. The conditions shattered so-called deserters who had no human right to protect and save themselves, for that is a reality of war. The individual had been replaced by the war commu- nity-machine with its expendable exchangeable parts: if a weak link is identified, it goes. Clearly a terrified part can still march forward with an advance to boost the appearance of active number irrespective of any ability to fight effectively. No Human Rights there.

> *"Monarchy, Aristocracy, and Democracy, are but creatures of imagination; and a thousand such may be contrived as well as three."* .... (p. 104)

The so much promoted democratic state of easy rights, with their sadly forgotten obligations, is a central cause promoting conflict as well as a tool to manipulate for the cowering parts of the population. An ill-judged moment of name-calling can bring prison sentences, loss of pension, and loss of employ- ment. Distinguished police officers have had their careers terminated by 'unwise' responses to criminality with that obligation to be honest having been ignored. In the same way there is too little leeway for the sick, young, and elderly in such matters. Cracking the nut with a mallet comes to mind. When put to the test, too frequently Rights are being used as a convenient creature of imagination and a contrivance to force a benefit.

> *"The right of Parliament is only a right in trust, a right by delegation......Government with insolence is despotism; but when contempt is added it becomes worse; and to pay for contempt is the excess of slavery."* ....
> (p. 82)

> "A Declaration of Rights is, reciprocity, a declaration of
> duties also. Whatever is my right as a man is also the right
> of another; and it becomes my duty to guarantee as well as
> posess....." (Page 76)

The simple acceptance of rights is too easily done; it seems
to create a freedom from the process of reason and thought.
Members of Britain and members of many other nations in
their own lands are *and*......

> "have been imposed upon by parties and by men assuming
> the character of leaders." (p. 115)

..... for wherein lies the great national benefit of blind acceptance! We are cogent, thoughtful creatures and as such have
a responsibility to ourselves to resolve the questions of our
day rather than abdicate. At all times there is variation and
variety: final and inarguable rights are inappropriate to
the changing conditions and demands of both society and
history. The argument regarding historical precedent and
therefore a binding assumption versus that of putting certain
powers of decision into the hands of elected delegates is well
argued. There is credit on both sides. However, despite the
fragility of a *precedent* being empowered 'to the ends of time'
I suggest here that some Responsibilities do remain constant
no matter what the regime, propaganda, or power structure
of the moment. That an isolated and intimidated farmer
should be gaoled as a result of self-defence against very real
personal danger and an elderly lady should be gaoled for
refusing to pay local rates for something she totally rejected
are just two instances signalling that something has gone
very wrong. Further, a dictatorial sweeping aside of British
long established and more democratic local councils (municipalities); selling off of school playing fields for development;
and allowing the opening of the way towards greater abuse/
temptation/desperation through excessive alcohol licens-
ing hours and gambling demonstrate the faulty nature of

our decision makers. Basic decency seems to be forgotten if higher income, an eye-catching advertisement, or a form of entertainment will bring financial gain. Sadly the list seems endless.

Along with Thomas Paine, one can sympathize in regard to the conditions leading to the French Revolution about which Paine wrote. Equally we can more recently sympathise with those abused peoples of the Middle East. No wonder they revolted, took up arms, and aspired to form a state based upon their take on decency and security. Sadly, as with the French Revolution, the viler forms of humanity moved in to dominate the positions of power through their inhuman brutality. Imitators then arrived, seeing the opportunities in their own lands. They could steal while the peoples of North Africa, for example, lost ground from genuine self-defence to factions of opportunist banditry and greed. It is equally easily understood why endangered people from those regions would wish to escape, but by entering other countries and accepting safety there comes a commitment to local language, traditions, Responsibilities, and obligations which are common to those homelands. If such reasonable respect for the existing "rights" of the local hosting people are ignored and even disrespected, then it is time for them to be moved on to find where they can truly be and feel at home: forcibly if necessary. Unpopular compromises or confrontation will otherwise inevitably and understandably result. If violence is their avenue of persuasion, then superior violent power is demanded.

Being an individual is demanding, but that is what we are. Why should we all conform? Why should we all be forced inside some social strait-jacket by strangers' ideas of what is right? What is right for us can only be what we individually decide is agreeable and acceptable. We can learn responsibility or irresponsibility. Every man, woman, and child should have these Responsibilities and options presented to them.

Displacement action - doing other than our reason demands
- is not a sane way to go. Individually we need to follow our
own lines of considered actions and our chosen compromises.
Life-balancing, which

> "...amounts to the combination of persons in one
> common interest"

......was used to argue against a House of Landed Lords, by
Paine, regarding the Parliament of the United Kingdom, but
it is also a neat way to be used to describe Community. If
we do not act in harmony, then the option becomes discord
and strife. To avoid this it is perfectly reasonable to expect
'newcomers' to wish to fit in. By making an effort to do so,
their unique contributions have a good chance of reciprocal
respect.

There were Rights in the past to own slaves and even to
'viciously' beat one's wife and children. Hopefully we can now
all agree to view these once rights as definitely wrongs. Some
present cultures would disagree and do even worse with children open to sexual abuse as child brides. These differences
cannot be negotiable. If one way of life promotes these crimes
against the person, then they have to be dealt with, changed,
or removed. There is no room here for uncivilised domination, cruelty, and even dishonourable honour - murder. This
is not a matter of individualism versus conformity; rather, it
is a matter of our responsibility to protect those unable to
adequately protect themselves from harm.

The presentation, demonstration, and teaching 'ways for life'
are first established in the home where two additional guests
generally reside, namely television and computer technology.
They both teach and influence. It is society's responsibility to
enable this home nurturing to be the best it can: why else
empower individuals to represent our interests, through
a pseudo democratic system, other than to better support

this goal with others? The child has a right to be prepared for the society in which that child exists: schooling and belief teaching fulfill a vital role here. To have to deal with strongly opposing societies rather than accepted co-existence offers confusion and promotes conflict. Parents cannot know everything nor cope with so vast a spread of difference. This knowledge gap can easily breed insecurity and again conflict. Parents start out with inadequate experience, great hope, and love - if they have been well supported in their own development, this is reflected here. They need support, information, the experience of others, and the ability to proceed rationally in their own particular ways. These once fully dependent children, having found their natural gifts, have been successfully nurtured in their family, schools, and social environments. They have become the people who make society work by administering and defending it. Also, they care for their parents as well as their other dependents, and then in their turn they receive care and support themselves. Such can be generally the case. Responsibilities are varied, changing, and many. If a society is or becomes dictatorial, autocratic, unresponsive, confused, and unfeeling, then there can be little reason for accepting it as it is simply not up to the task. The ruler will have lost the right to rule due to abusing the power given. That power had been allowed by the population in the expectation of a set of Responsibilities being followed and fulfilled in a particular manner, on behalf of the many and varied individuals. In democracies a number of those Responsibilities are reemphasized or redefined at election times: a standardization for a more harmonious existence. That some things will cost more in terms of effort and money is axiomatic: the balance of these changes chosen and agreed is crucial. We are a most varied group in which we accept conformities which form as a consequence a stable society. There is the dichotomy personal choice versus group generalities......

· · · · · · ·

With our differences - our individuality - we chose to go beyond some minor boundaries. We break away from some norms. This makes life more personal, liveable, enjoyable, and progressive for us. Eccentrics were once readily accepted and not infrequently enjoyed. Some rules may be imposed upon us, such as codes of dress, while others spring from within. It could be questioned if we actually could continue to exist if we were to keep all the rules and conventions. Since there is this choice in reality, rules could be viewed as real and/or imaginary. Real if we comply and only imaginary if we don't. Somewhere there is a form of conscience in this with the whys and becauses. A world full of so many 'people-units', with such a variety of choices experienced by each, that 'The Whole' must specifically impose some common restrictions to maintain an orderly and productive community. It becomes advantageous to remove much of the potential randomness to ensure stability and quality to life. Interestingly this Whole seems to take on a personality of its own.

Our 'modern world' 'jitters' in its confusions. We suffer from insecurity and lack of focus, which in its turn undermines and contaminates our reason, reasons, contentment, and entire lives. As through history, some achieve what they feel strongly about by manoeuvring themselves into positions of power and impose these ideas upon us all in ways so diverse as to achieve a catch-all outcome: or nearly all. Further, we seem to have been indoctrinated or cowered into believing or feeling that to disagree with the mass is to commit a 'thought crime'. In consequence, thinking can descend to mere repetition of sound bites and mantras, following the perceived group, herd-like actions, and the abdication of what should be at the core of our community. We have become so brainwashed that we seem to decide, "I know different so I must forget." Too many are torn between self-flagellating of the mind as a result of a sickening submission to the tension of an inappropriate surrealist social vision. Also, social advance seems held back by certain dual tensions created by Marxism and Freudian thought with anti-labour structure, wealth creation, and confusion regarding friendship and family love being viewed as something sinister.

· · · · · · ·

Our differences are what make our individuality. Individuals differently recognize opportunity, press forward, and produce change. Change brings evaluation, re-evaluation, revision, and hopefully positive progress, but not necessarily so. We have a duty therefore to go fittingly exercise our differences. It is our responsibility to do so for our friends, our community, our present, and our future. Our children and we, from our different experiences in life, interpret the relevance of what occurs, what to accept, what to adapt, what to change, and what to reject. Generally there are many choice options. This is a personal responsibility if we believe our lives have purpose: Responsibilities are more important for their inborn structure than the imposition of invented, impersonal, verbose expressions of rights.

Within this context the finality of both documented and perceived rights is a far more serious issue since Rights achieve harm when they fail to deliver. This is true of vast swathes of the world and its population. Expectation demands fulfilment. By their nature and title, as Rights they are permitted to wear an axiomatic mantle as statements of fact, an entity, a reality, and not suggestion nor guideline. Often they form a 'stand-alone' proclamation, which fails to sufficiently coalesce within a 'community of central ideas'. These rights also would and should of their very nature be open to debate, re-examination, and reaffirmation or else be subject to appropriate change. However, they seem to have an unassailable protection. So, who or what is to be the regulatory instruments for those processes, and what is to be the balance of forces in such a debate? How should the tensions be balanced within when free debate is denied and those who would debate are shouted down?

In reality our responsiveness is to and through our needs. Decency next expands this concern of need to the needs of others in widening circles of neighbourly concern. Central to this is the acceptance of Responsibilities: some are stated, others are felt, and yet still others are facets intellectually processed and then internalized. Responsibilities are an awakening: a realization to take action. Rights sit and wait on paper. The complexity of our shared existence and the complexities of the parts (people) demand that our society ensures two very important - no rather crucial - interrelated activity interventions:

1. The priority of good education meeting 'life's needs'; and

2. The debate and establishment of social understanding and reason based upon Responsibilities.

Rights are not sacred; they are an invention. Some no doubt would see them as an expression of a one world belief system. They can be dangerous and cause misery both through action, later action followed as a result of confirmed belief, and inaction. They should not be unchanging in our ever-changing world. New conditions, outcomes, or circumstances can devalue or invalidate a previous aspiration expressed as a *Formalized Right*. Interpretation continues to be at the heart of appropriate application. Rights are a summary of ideas penned under a certain set of circumstances in a particular historical context. The French Revolution, so admired by Thomas Paine for a time, is an example of Rights existing in order to meet a need of the times and of necessity are formulated by specific imperfect humans following their own very personal experiences, preferences, and environmental influences. More particularly, they are penned a certain way simply because other things were in place. They follow assumptions of a specific time and eventually become 'old fashioned'. Rights are indicators out to promote a way of collective existence: rights for one individual, living in an existence all alone, would be somewhat meaningless. They currently advertise, coerce as needed, and dictate. They are a preference, or an option accepted by one group of people - if other things are in place. They have a theme which is again dependent upon a block of people and those people's time-based interests: our society. When a right endangers or spoils the quality of society's life, they are no longer rights but are rather imposed edicts of an authoritarian or negligent government. However, emerging from all of this is the very real question: does our global society now have to take precedence over our local or national ones? If so, then why are so many innocent people permitted to starve, to suffer, to die, to be oppressed, and to be exploited? Why is war declared to defend one group but not the rest? Inaction shows the hypocrisy of our concept of a Global Society while conveniently forgetting our Responsibilities and obligations. Inaction, just like apathy, is not a governmental option in a global society. A government's reason for being and so having accepted various Responsibilities includes to respond. Government and the elected should not permit harm to be allowed to flourish. However, members of government are right to decide for themselves as elected representatives but at all times bearing in mind the wellbeing of their electorate. As one would appreciate, the electorate sometimes cannot be privy to the information available to governmental personnel and mostly have neither the inclination nor time to approach being so. This is why we accept Government. Governmental personnel, like teaching staff, are the operating decision makers encompassing their duties. Public pressure by too audible and visible pressure groups can be less than constructive. Let the locomotive driver drive the train. Rights can be wrongs, and as Rousseau would have it:

.....to yield to force is the act of necessity, not of will....(ch3 p8) and 'as such', I would add, is to lose.

One starting point is Thomas Paine's *Rights of Man* which clearly argues against a certain immortality for such matters. Each generation must decide its own priorities: they will change, as will the surrounding conditions. These are often powers expressed as rights. Assuming a belief in an elected government, the people have the power to choose, to remove, and to agree how such a government is to be organized and what direction of "rightness" they will be permitted to take, all through the electoral processes.

. . . .

Of the Past

Fables, history, literature, and religions can each prepare and inform us. One aspect taught/revealed by the Adam and Eve account is the double-edged reality of free will. Free will is a blessing which we may turn into a curse. It can uplift, or when abused, it can destroy. Free will, willingly self-controlled for a common good, is truly a blessing, while the free choice taken at the expense of the community and the common good - so easily done - is a curse, as are its proponents. Such abusers, including shoplifters, bullies, pedophiles, and drug dealers became emboldened by escaping the consequences of earlier smaller matters. These people extend and grow in their sickness: they descend beyond. The only remedy for the community is to turf them out 'of the garden' of free choice and into the wilderness of separation and despair.

Prisons are the outward sign of a community's civil sicknesses and failure, as is war: its response to loss of reason or hope. The community promotes its right to both, but like taxation there is no such right. These are violent acts depriving citizens of freedom, life, or the product of their labour. There can be no confusion here about an individual's rights, for it seems each has none since the State can disregard each. So to have a State with a government is to give away all rights and privileges to a form of committee without clearly stated safeguards and laws, written down and protected. Again, it is Responsibilities that precede any right. If Responsibilities are ignored, then our preferred existence, encapsulated in the artificial form of 'rights', means nothing. There may be a decision made by the people to empower such things, but there is no right. Without universal acceptance of agreed upon Responsibilities of each, there is no community or civilisation. Weaken responsibility and the whole edifice of the community is weakened, decay sets in with greed, and destruction becomes the end result. Thus laws cannot prevent the inner voice of each individual nor force the restraint and self-control of the civil being - but a law does warn. A 'civil being' is an existence sharing reason, respect, common beliefs, and accepted Responsibilities as the norm: agreed rather than dictated. Such peoples prosper and find contentment in this security of mutual respect, shared values, and concerns in common.

With the above in mind, it seems incredible that cities and citizens displaying so much surplus wealth seemingly ignore the very visible destitute within. How can one group of people waste so much, when others die for lack of just a fraction of that waste? Equally unbelievable is the illogicality that instruments of war are introduced and dispersed by the wealthy and afforded through expensive loans to the politicians of the impoverished, all at the expense of their despairing communities. How can we look on and let it continue? Absent is our reason, absent is our justice, and absent is our humanity when we well know our Responsibilities to our fellow peoples of our Earth. Yet we do nothing at all, and all in the name of a nation's rights! What a convenience. What an excuse. Meanwhile the wealthy arms producers and dealers get wealthier as people cry out for peace, and as they die in their hundreds of thousands starved, wounded, and murdered. What rights? What a sad indictment of community, the state, and so-called civilization, flowing from faulty values, reason, and lack of sound questioning of reality.

deBono and Essential Open Constructive Discussion

Edward deBono, *Six thinking Hats*, Revised 1999, ISBN 0 14 029666

Conflict regarding energy supply and technology's needs is very real, as are the questions surrounding pollution, chemical poisoning, and global warming. These are not specifically tied into a question of Human Rights, but the right to a future is very relevant for us all and our descendants. In a world increasingly returning to the days of Princely States, Lords and Barons, now called the conglomerates and super rich, the way ahead seems even more dangerous. This outlook promises growing conflict. Sensible discussion is needed to provide sensible decisions and direction. Parallel thinking as opposed to the adversarial is needed.

Better promotion of constructive discussion requires placing oneself entirely in the separate aspects of that discussion. This is a cooperative approach rather than an adversarial one. Different viewpoints need to be given a balanced and thoughtful role. The rules are simple. Keep to the format under review. deBono identified six key approaches to information and planning. He gave each a distinguishing colour. Discussion was then restricted to those properties. Following is a very simplified version of my understanding of his recommendations. GREEN came first and is identified with growth potential. It is exploratory and imaginative and it employs lateral thinking. Having established some possibilities, organization and management come into play. BLUE is a time of calm with exploring alternative methods and their organizational feasibility. Negative aspects are noted for later. The discussion could move on to WHITE, which is specifically concerned with the facts and actual available information: belief or supposition do not feature. RED is the area for this and each member takes it in turn to out their feelings and hunches with any emotional implications, thereby ridding discussion of acrimony. YELLOW sunshine thoughts come next with implementation and benefits to the fore. Reasoned value and seeking support from the team members are the aim. BLACK comes either before yellow or follows it with its critical functions and calls for caution. It is a time to weed out the inappropriate, wrong, or weak ideas. Then finally back to WHITE with its facts and information and BLUE focusing upon organization and management. In this way a meeting focuses specifically, separately, and wholly on six focus aspects of discussion. Each aspect is separate.

If the planet becomes poisoned, we all suffer and die. Clearly there is currently a diminishing return in technology's ever accelerating spread. For example, massive use of truck transportation needs to be reappraised with farms bankrupted and dying daily due to imports which so easily could supply locally but such products are being transported from afar. Local output reduces road maintenance and polluting fuel used. Cheap goods come with an expensive community cost. It seems a no brainer that it is in the best interest for our children and descendants to maintain and encourage strong community with local community production wherever possible. Our nations are tipping into the sea with international trade and shrinking productive countryside. If extra fuel is to be used transporting food, then why not create cities and towns on poorly producing land rather, with any greater travel distance, using production from that prime farming soil. Loss of good finite renewable land seems more the current norm. There is a need to encourage and support these surviving farms and fertile soil to employ and feed the local people into the future. We need to join together and stop behaving as if we are indestructible. Edward de Bono puts forward the very workable process of collective parallel thinking. The successes this approach has had worldwide due to its increased adoption illustrated this better way of planning for future change. One listens to the screaming and shouting in governmental debate, infantile posturing in the United Nations, conflict and threat between North and South Korea, and the anger and hopelessness that spawned ISIS, and it is clear that a better way is needed. Technology rolls onwards but it is time to call a halt to a seemingly total focus upon the sciences and mechanised cash-pumping production. Now is the time to emphasize the importance of introducing sensible effective controls. Proper consideration of all shades of opinions of those involved is required without caving in completely to conglomerates of production and their bankers.

Higher performance levels through the advance of technologies can, due to the novelty of a situation, leave people vulnerable. New advances may precipitate a conflict between established processes and accepted rights because of new possibilities. The touchstone of responsible agreed upon behaviour should settle the matter but may not enjoy sufficient power to achieve this end. Parallel discussion seems a way to better achieve this, without tears. From the early days of the internet, harassment of others has grown exponentially. With the invention of inexpensive cell phones, filmed abuses of others are instantly sent to feed a growing appetite and audience. Big sound systems in cars pollute the peace. Genetic modification to suit chemical crop spraying may well be poisoning us. Schooling seems less able to help our children towards a happy and fulfilling future. Text messaging abuses have become a nightmare for both adults and children. Advertisers and media producers seem able to get away with almost anything. There must be better ways. Strong, effective training is needed to provide processes which establish community-friendly results. Internalized standards of accepted Responsibilities with self-control are a centrally accepted social benefit, achieved through parallel discussion. Accepted norms of behaviour with agreed upon limits, rather than those fixed in imposed forms, could greatly reduce such problems for all but the socially insane.

In committees and meetings we have a habit of trying to think about and raise too many alternatives and separate issues at once. Using the word "But" can be poisonous when progress seems just around the corner.

> As deBono points out, "*Confusion is the biggest enemy of good thinking.*" (p. 11)

Focus is the way forward and requires shelving some aspects of the discussion for later. deBono offers a simple way to achieve this. *Appropriate input timing* seems a satisfactory way to describe his approach. In addition, it may be suggested that Rights are an attempt to safely 'fence in' our social and personal needs, but they also appear to keep out parallel discussion in which different approaches can be drawn together to achieve a better mutual understanding of possible outcomes. The legalistic Rights Autocracy ensures conflict through adversarial action. One would not wish to argue with their concepts but rather the manner of enforcement - often by self-appointed 'champions of justice'. But how then can a wide spreading plurality of personalities with such differing needs effectively be protected? What are our needs and what are our limits, especially in an ever faster chang-ing world full of diverse evolving characters and conditions? What role must media awareness play; who is to decide and when? Any single decision maker can readily attract distrust and the claim of representing factional interests. In business, networking is generally considered a valuable exercise prom-ising a 'win win' outcome, but to make it work allowance for different viewpoints is necessary: this is true in life. We rationalize, adapt, and adopt aspects of those with whom we interact. Sometimes we may produce a discordant and totally opposite viewpoint rather than adopting a more harmonious approach, but conferencing the deBono way has proved very effective at considerably reducing the conflict risk at board level, jury service, planning committees, etc. Uses of the internet almost instantly highlight this very human condi-tion as experienced on "My Space" W3. it seems to be the practical people within our Social Family who enable the whole thing to work. These adapt as needs arise. Theirs is a gift of perception and adaptation which shows that 'common sense' is not so common. Isolated input can cause horrendous complications, as most will have experienced via Facebook, e-mailing, and others. Like scientific discovery, agreement flourishes under certain conditions and shrivels under others. The generator of science is unrestricted and analytical in thought: not to be confused with undisciplined varieties. The practical nature of the scientist enables cause discovery, adaptation, and change. We do not think of science as fixed, I hope. Everything is up for review and verification. Equally so should be debate and those invited to take part. So frequently what is taken as truth is found to work, but for other reasons be only partly true or plain wrong. Assumptions tend to go in that direction. Similarly fixed rigid rights depend upon assumptions. Change is the state common to humanity: with time comes change and in all things both imagined and real. The ultimate primacy of Responsibilities precedes and informs rights. Where this does not follow, there is a serious error. Consequences of Responsibilities, due to the variety of lives and living, also change while legal rights are un-adaptive to change because they are fixed.

Too frequently one hears of a legal case in which the Responsibilities to a victim suppressing the 'rights' of the perpetrator are overturned. So the rapist can cross-examine the victim, in detail. The deportee, already proven guilty, stays the day of deportation by repeated appeals paid for by the public: not once but several times. In December 2010 in the UK, a hit and run criminal continued to break English law and drive. An illegal immigrant was allowed to remain in the UK. Having successfully twice impregnated his partner, the illegal immigrant now had two UK children born in England, paid for courtesy of British taxpayers. Meanwhile in Wales a young man escaping from Afghanistan and fostered for years is to be repatriated, despite his wishes, all because he reached his 18th year! No rights nor decency there (2014/5). There is a responsibility that administrators fully review relevant options, but this will not happen with stifled debate. Being politically correct is seriously dangerous for full discussion. What is present around us needs to be fully open to scrutiny and relevant appraisal.

In CBC's *White Coat Black Art* (12/11/12), Brian Goldman stated regarding health care that 'free will is not absolute'. But it is clear that in some cases it is. However, the permitted 'free will moments' are politically decided while others are frequently swept aside. There is a convenience factor at work. A reasoned and agreed upon balance needs to be maintained with due consideration of surrounding circumstances, just as there needs to be for the application of so-called rights.

Opportunism

It requires little imagination to appreciate that 'can do' does not make it right nor does 'getting away with it'. Only the crass and immature will see acceptance or long-term advantage in such a state of affairs. We see this destructive attitude in activities of the workplace-bully or school bully; the person who shouts down the views of others and believes it has 'won the day'; the use of game rules foul to gain an advantage to win the sporting championship (Argentinean Soccer); the smear-campaigner, be it in or outside the media; and also the cost of political correctness. All these have bypassed what is reasonable and respect for the other person or persons involved. We do have every right to hold a different point of view. Of course we do. Others who disagree should be able and expected to express their own position and generally would have a responsibility to do so. Silence will not bring understanding nor reconciliation where needed. To be able to disagree is a full blown Right if Rights exist. Maybe when reasonable consideration of and use of restraint regarding the other's point of view is used, useful progress will result. Too often the primacy and strength of a cherished view or strong wish (ambition) or a preferred way are taken as proof that that is the way forward, on the grounds of its emotional input or magnitude. With 'emotion' comprehensive education was advanced, slavery was supported, and Death Taxes (theft) are permitted. When Prime Minister Harper appealed against facial cover being allowed at the citizen swearing-in ceremony, upheld by the courts, one commentator (Enright's show CBC 2nd. March 2015) stated that most Canadians would disagree with Harper. Yet research found very much the opposite. Too easily our own view can seem justifiable because we believe in them so fully, only to be proved entirely wrong: a case again for deBono's parallel discussion, maybe.

Facilitated by deBono's Red Hat period set for emotionally-based input, a 'space' is provided for this aspect of a debate which achieves greater understanding and more constructive behaviour affecting the discussion in a safe way. This enables a *"switch in and out of emotional mode in a matter of moments"* [which proves to be] *"most advantageous"* rather than experiencing resentment, sulking, and taking offence with all the bother and argument of time consuming confrontation and conflict (p. 62). Political Correctness denies discussion in its unthinking knee jerk reflex. Despite its appearance to the contrary, political correctness is not and never has been The Law. That is why it is so dangerous, for its very real victims have no constitutional protection. Anything so steeped in social relevance needs the deBono's approach foremost and not dishing out retribution., (Ref: *The same man in Love and War*, Page 129 Ln 20 by David Lebedoff)

> *"At all times the emphasis is on*
> *designing a way forward." (p. 4)*

If a situation is not constructive, it is then in all probability destructive, neutrally unfinished, or unimportant. People who follow along with some process are actually agreeing to that process: the opposite is rejection. As he goes on to clarify,

> *"we are very quick to make ..... snap-*
> *judgements and to become locked in*
> *to the emotions they release." (p. 54)*

We need to be able to examine suggestions, salient points, outcomes, and especially 'suppose-itions' in a dispassionate way.

The very nature of argument is conflict. How much better and potentially more rewarding would be achieving agreement: parallel thinking alone will not produce this, but with mutual respect and orderliness it can. Emotions of confusion need to be identified and neutralized. Out of respect and by recognizing key facts with accepted Responsibilities a self-regulating set of norms or self-laws evolve: policed from within. It can be useful to approach some questions from a different direction than the one being expressed. For example,

QU: What is the great value of democratic systems?

Possible answer....Agreement, peace, stability, the exercise of a rational way for the benefit of all.

QU: What major contributor within democracy makes it adaptable and workable?

Possible answer ...... More ideas, debate, consensus, and respect for others. There is an essential place for each of these if democracy is to be strong and adaptable to a world of changing needs.

QU: What reduces the value of our Democracy regarding the poor, those at risk, and the disadvantaged?

POSSIBLE ANSWER: Your turn !

When a minority number of people have been elected into power, it is due to that power handed to them that they become 'the majority'. (R)

That Internet

Internet and privacy seem to potentially go hand in hand. Messaging is instantaneous and direct. Families and friends thousands of miles apart are reunited while purchases, photograph development, and sharing have become secure to an extent unimagined. Secure conferencing is worldwide with news and weather at one's fingertips. All this takes place beyond prying eyes and with no body contact required. Yet it is not always so. The *thought police* grow in legal powers. Criminals and some new organizations break the laws of respect, decency, and freedom. Political units gain entry, our bank accounts are invaded, and some can even know when our homes are empty of people. Yet our Human Rights in these matters remain at risk while squabbles over less harmful rights issues remain at the forefront. Our world's clean water supply is diminishing fast, as is the moisture in the atmosphere; our food is being poisoned and animals are being tortured when alternative methods of science are available; the homeless remain homeless and the unemployed thank their schooling. Yet our society can still get hung up on colour, race, sexual orientation, gun ownership, and stupid insensitive name calling to the exclusion of these 'equally important' matters such as starvation, homelessness, death, and injury which could include so many more unlisted here.

With the internet it is a matter of choice how we use it. Lack of full censorship enables all sorts of activities and discussions previously made almost impossible in the person-to-person interactive world with its many lookers-on. Within the internet-worlds there have grown codes of accepted use and a sort of internet national conformity. It is redefining both what is acceptable as well as how business is conducted. A person with or without justifiable prejudices can, if due care is exercised, proceed privately outside the reach of Law, hyper sensitive rights groups, ISIS, and political correctness storm troopers. Only the truly dangerous and deadly practices are attacked: there simply are not enough operatives to do more than prioritize what to search for and deal with. As the public become more concerned and aware of the ramifications of this shortfall of people, they will increasingly take action through forming organizations and informing official agencies. Hopefully sensibility and the more 'beautiful' ways to live life will be clear, generally approved, and dictated and imposed by no outside agency other than ourselves.

As always, adequately broad education at home or in institutions is the more constructive way towards a better informed future of high standards. Learning from television/ internet could produce a golden age of choice and aware- ness rather than from the too frequently misinformed and ignorant. Teaching geography with fuller information, local history, and cultural content in movies would dispel much misinformation and Chinese whispers type 'facts'. Fear of Human Rights questions, accusations of racism, and politi- cal correctness pitfalls put so much useful education beyond reach and so the whole educational process of knowledgeable critical thinking in jeopardy. Let the young face reality in a safe environment and they will get it! Religion seemingly can't be taught in government schools while unnecessary animal dissection can be, which could be better studied on a DVD recording of one experienced researcher's dissection practices. World studies using film and personal accounts need to show both the good, the strange, and the bad: all these are largely subjective. Yorkshire Television (UK) was excellent at this. One Peruvian boy was filmed in his moun- tainous home village and then filmed during his visit to the UK. His interview was both fun and informative. He was also able to ask questions about the unfamiliar and strange English way of life. One example was his question about our dogs as pets. He noted Peruvian dogs played freely and ran with their owners. He could not understand why it was that English dogs took their owners for walks, leading the way. It is so easy to misunderstand others' ways. If we are to become truly multiracial, then there needs to be better Geographical knowledge and understanding, with cultural, social, and historical information included. This would teach a better awareness of society`s need-to-know values, norms, and con- ventions. Simply saying this or that is how things should be is never enough: <u>why</u> also needs to be understood and this often requires knowing when, where, and how things went humanly wrong: an opening here for the effect of prevailing philosophy and beliefs of each time.

In film we see common social goals portrayed while in sports we experience games rules which show expectations of good in-game behaviour and fair play. These ideas and ideals clearly can and do spill over into individual behaviours, just as examples of anti-social behaviour and fouling can. These are lessons for living decently. Songs, stories, and the law all pass on ideas, ideals, and standards. Blacks sitting at the back of the bus were socially reinforcing. Ideas and standards can be essential statements of what should be. Strong cultures last more than a few festive days - Chinese society's wish for honour, without the killings, is an example. However, one way personal individuality may be demonstrated is by 'kicking' against the conventions. A person's ``anti`` behaviour may simply be more an expression of self and only vaguely related to the act. Personal growth is arguably more prevalent in the successful as they appreciate, accept, and use the current values and then go on to grow within the majority of these values. So often social growth is achieved by finding and defining the strong boundaries, but the trick is how that is done. Being able to do so assists the development of character, social understanding, personal agreement, and social membership. For development to take place, the young personality kicks against a few of these boundaries, tests and `proves` them, and finds that the outcome is having to give way. This facilitates the growth of respect without harming anyone. So-called silly rules are the pennies enabling the pounds to look after themselves: "a fence around the law."

CHAPTER 17:

ON POLITICS

When does Democracy become an Autocracy or Tyranny?

Since democracy is a governmental system devised to follow the will of the people, when government will not listen nor act upon the will of the people and when respect is denied to those without the same level of power, it has moved towards the realms of tyranny. Self-interested use of superior funding, manipulating elements of power, and the use of force to gain advantage all decay democracy. Loss of democracy results when the financially able buy influence using subtle and less subtle forms of bribery to gain position and contracts; they can find, fund, and foist their preferred political candidates upon society. They clearly feel confident, secure, and certain of their trained (indoctrinated) sponsored candidates' support. These power brokers can and have toppled govern-ments down the ages. There is little to do with rights here and all to do with might. Through apathy and short sighted-ness, we ordinary majority empower these powerful people who control and influence our lives. We let them do so. It is the responsibility of all of us to unseat these undemo-cratic manipulators by rejecting their political puppets and not buying their products. The sad fact that party politics have taken over from personality politics further feeds this situation. Cross-national conglomerates, corporations, trade unions, and organized crime are just some of the culprits.

One may ask how and when democracy is at its greatest. Is it when democracy peacefully agrees to put aside a portion of the preferred way of the majority to protect a preferred way of a minority? Successful compromise, as we see in constitu-tional monarchy, is the outward evidence of true greatness. It simply comes down to discussion and respect. Such political discussion aims to find and firm a political consensus which probably needs changes in perceptions replacing belief with broader verifiable fact: actions to promote recognizable good outcomes being the objective. Such matters will vary in scale and breadth. Calm ordered discussion is better able to facili-tate the amalgamation of groups, factions, or otherwise for a common good by achieving peaceful broad consensus rather than creating some future 'flash point' as the imposition of one viewpoint is almost sure to do. We all recognize that the screamers and shouters in debate are aware of their weakness which is why they use force and intimidation: they aim to subdue the opposing idea, and they are bullies. Why do we allow this to continue? The first victims of the prison camps, later to evolve into concentration camps, were Germans opposed to the Nazi regime and concept of a new German way of life. Power, tyranny, and fear stifled the opposition and prevented it from successfully organizing itself while cowered lookers-on knew too well that they would join the imprisoned dissidents if they dared to openly disagree with the regime. Only politically correct thinking was permitted at that time, and so it seems now. In our time, there grows the one new tyranny: that of certain members of big business who wipe out the 'small person' at the expense of community and more local producers in order to better safeguard their growing monopolies. For greater power and security they burrow into the political system like Green Bottle larvae burrow into the brains of un-medicated moorland sheep and deer. Madness ensues.

Which Political 'Medicine' could Better Protect Us?

Such protection stems from free speech, removal of political correctness, respect for others and their points of view, and enabling the voice of local people to be regularly heard and once more empowered. The return in England of their local governments would also revitalize that democracy. The trade-off between freedom and efficient administration can probably never be finalized. However, locally there is a stock of experienced people known by far more local people throughout the constituency than a parliamentarian can hope for. Self-respect and respect for others should flourish within our political system, but there are too many strangers and variations which have to be organized: an impossible task it would seem without the local government format. As the breadth of different people within local communities demonstrates, it is encouraging that so many show their commitment to the community, their community: their care through considerable local action, and their selfless work, respect, and resulting community growth. More concerned and committed 'community spirits' are always needed. Despite this great effort and expended energy, communities do become disrupted. Within some new communities in Britain, women are prevented from learning their new home tongue of English. Male self-interest, insecurity, and lack of trust and respect for women make integration and inclusion almost impossible. This is unacceptable manipulation and dictatorship within the home: hardly fertile ground for assimilation and calm entry into the broader community. If these people do not wish to assimilate and join the people, then their decision removes the community's Responsibilities and for the community's sake as well as their own they should go to a better suited community where they can happily become fully respected and live at peace. I use 'they' because their action is a rejection of us, in this context, and as such are not of us through both choice and actions. Their choices are freely made and taken. Others from similar backgrounds chose to be extremely constructive members of the community and will already have proven invaluable because of their constructive and creative attitude and behaviour. As has been said, 'Those who help row the boat seldom rock it.' Communities and nations need to self-evaluate what is past and consider what may result, but mostly develop ideas of improved ways and then as many constructive ideas as possible as to how to achieve the worthwhile and desirable goals. Negativity produces either the negative or can proceed to a re-evaluation while positivity promotes the positive. These growth perspectives need to be effective and get the project finished. The positive approach, as deBono points out, brings with it value and a sense of achievement which are good and motivational. This strengthening of `vision` can be the very reason outcomes once viewed as impractical or unattainable become the very opposite. Multiracialism and multiculturalism bring risk, but so does life. Another way of viewing that risk is "opportunity". If the very group in question refuses to take the risk, explore the opportunities and become a co-operating part then there seems that nothing further can be done: a negative mindset on either side wastes and defeats opportunity.

The Self

What are we? What should we believe? What should we do? The auxiliary word of obligations "should" appears in two of the preceding questions. They relate to outside ourselves. What we consider we are goes far deeper. This is our essence and our being. All our cherished and hidden beliefs are part of that identity. Most of it we did not ask for but most of it is essential to US. To use law and force, rather than accepted reason to make adjustments to that self, will produce a visible or submerged reaction of anger and opposition to the original proposition. Using unwelcome force produces a forceful response. With acceptance of our condition comes respect for the freedoms we enjoy which we certainly do not wish to give away. In agreement there is a self-control and so a dignity. This constructive agreement stems partly from our previous 'failure learning' from which realism is awakened and provides moral strength. How sad is the result of over-protection of children and adults so they are denied the valuable learning of constructive adaptive behaviour. Helicopter parents and over-protective society damage or even destroy the essentially needed realism and understanding, which can be nasty but necessary. If aspects of our world or that beyond survival demand awareness, then so be it. If the danger is small and can be coped with, then that small harm can lead to successful self-protection and support also for others. The unpleasantness of removing a rotten tooth never negated the need for the removal. However, the following relief makes it all worthwhile.

The Caring Society

So much is said of Human Rights, but there are many examples of its failures with non-existent application. Further, our quality of life too frequently may be attacked with impunity. Considering there is reasonable variety and different ways preferred by others, this perfectly reasonable reality should not go beyond the comprehension of most. Such things benefit from a balance. For example there should be a fundamental human right to peace and calm without the excesses of sound from house or car radios and players; similarly the spoiling of expensive TV relaxation due to unwanted and intrusive constant interruptions with 'badly timed' advertising; also it is wrong to be able to promote concepts and views of evil, sadism, violence, and sexual gratification freely as producers injecting their unwelcome 'products' inappropriately in totally unconnected entertainment forms and genres. If such simple matters can escape sanctions, then no wonder they grow and spread into larger and more complex ones which too frequently develop since these practices are ignored. We need to concern ourselves first not with what is demonstrably wrong, but rather with what might be detrimental.

The Blind

In our world so much more can be done for those with sight problems; for example, bank statements could be supplied in Braille and sent directly to a blind account owner. Visual and Braille information could be easily set up for the printing of envelopes. Graham McCree, in an interview on CBC radio (2010), focuses on how a support group being awarded charity status can ensure a less encouraging and active expectation being there to move the blind forward. Thinking that a job is done is not necessarily the same as it being fully completed! He suggested as examples the CNIB and CCB as "abusing their position acting like a corporation" which means the profit motive is an essential goal of the administration. Further, the act of classifying a support agency as a charity moves it away from a national Responsibility of Government to that of voluntary agencies and volunteers: a choice, not a governmental obligation. The blind need 'Blindness Allowances' as direct 'help' rather than a system of concessions. As in any human condition the questions need answering of what can and can't a blind person do: the cans leading to avenues of education and training even at special training centres similar to special focus Sports Academies. The blind generally have wonderful senses of hearing, touch, and taste; surely it is not a leap of imagination to predict wonderful musicians, physiotherapists, and blenders of wines and foods just to name three of many opportunities.

WITH A KNOWLEDGE OF FREEDOMS COMES THE REALITY OF RESTRICTIONS.

Parents *having to go* out to work and economically having to put their very young children into day care in order to pay the housing bills is another example of social failure and mistaken thinking. If it is a choice because to remain 'home' would cause emotional harm, for example, then what must be must be. But that keeping a roof over one's head and providing food require unnatural sacrifices is political and social failure. That children benefit from the secure and encouraging presence of a parent is good for both and for the Social Family. Having to unwillingly leave or place a child with carers is an example of social dislocation which could be avoidable but which has sadly been built into the system. Costs for housing are far too high. Further, the working mother can too easily be the product and victim of propaganda, unless not wishing to remain at home. That mother wishing to remain with and care for her child, and able to do so, is right. After about nine months of doing so already, this choice is obviously a no brainer. It cannot be right to force the two to part through inflated pricing. There is strong evidence that in some this day care may produce shyness, fear, and neglect which if necessary is unavoidable though not the preferred option, like a tooth extraction.

Choice also plays a part in pension provision. One can choose to enjoy a greater proportion of income up to retirement, when fit and able to make the most of it relying upon an adequate but not over generous state pension for later; or one can subscribe to a top up fund, so called 'private' - this a personal choice. However, the Golden Handshakes for already overpaid 'workers' for doing the job they were paid to do becomes more objectionable and dishonourable with fixed salaries and 'laying off' further 'down' the scale.

With Knowledge there is
THE WORLD BEYOND

It is worth thinking through how our world could become truly "interdependent" or even if it should do so! There has been a massive reduction and squandering of cultures, traditions, quality of life, and resources to achieve this so called "interdependence": for some it has been annihilation. The implications of this are approaching a tragedy for humanity. What was and still would be right ways for a minority, which is in effect numbered in millions of people, is ignored in favour of the perceived advantages of what may well turn out to be a fatal mistake called industrial progress. The engine of this process follows a parasitical form called 'demand': demand, not 'need'. Both are manipulated and promoted too largely by financially bloated carcases for their own ends. With available use of their vast accumulations of wealth and resources, many of the world's worst problems and issues of suffering people could be resolved. Divide and conquer seems to be the strategy. Citizens add to this by entering into conflict regarding political correctness, religion, sexism, investment, and wasteful purchases - and those same carcases prosper. Amazonian Indians are dispossessed; denuded hillsides flow down to destroy homes and lives; good farmland becomes building sites; rivers and lakes are polluted as is the air we breathe; over fishing is matched by quota licence waste; living units become smaller; foods become more unsafe; education is dictated by industry and financial institutions; smaller hospitals, care centres, libraries, and schools are shut down to economize and rationalize while their chief administrators are enriched by bonuses for so-called 'efficiency and cost cutting'. Entertainment appears to continue in a downward spiral of lower forms of gratification with unedifying and brutalizing obscenities interspersed by promotion of unwanted and certainly unessential products. The depiction of community and family is increasingly soured. Can this really be progress? Further, does it need to continue?

The euthanasia debate is fierce. Dogmatism replaces reasoned concern and rational reflection comes under fire with many opposing arguments: some rational and others illogical. I, like others, would not willingly permit the continuance of unending pain and chronic suffering for one of our animals when avoidable, yet by law we must allow this inhuman disregard for suffering to continue in unwilling human beings. Recently Quebec won its case for compassion. Safeguards can and will be put in place. Our society will not allow a right to die while permitting a street dweller to do so prematurely. How can this be justified! We are constantly reminded of costs and values. How much of our resources are used to house rapists, drug dealers, child molesters, dissident immigrants, and murderers while so many others are forced to continue living on the streets with most not wishing to be there? One is too many of these street people to be allowed to freeze to death in winter - there are far more who suffer terribly. Next we could consider the elderly, the unemployed, the sick, the handicapped .... Too many need a place to live to receive adequate health care and especially to have an address in order to achieve offers of acceptable forms of employment. Too many of the elderly lack sufficient funds for food, home repairs, and heating. Can this be progress? Sadly the list seems almost endless, while money is readily found for other things, and is even sent abroad.

· · · · · · ·

CHAPTER 18:

THE CITIZEN and NEW CITIZEN

Definition: *CITIZEN: Member of a state or nation* **(OPED)**

"A native or naturalized person who owes allegiance to a government and is entitled to protection from it" (**11**[th] **Collegiate Dictionary**)

A member of a community by birth or choice who accepts the community's laws, traditions and responsibilities. (R)

If one were to assume a citizen becomes a citizen on the basis of their residing in a specific city and later becomes aware of the broader Nation State, then immigrants would become citizens of the state after some passage of time. However, they have been a part of the Social Family from birth. By living in a community, having been "allowed" to do so, that community has accepted certain obligations towards the immigrant and vice versa. Just as the newborn baby is given protection, so should the newborn citizen. With time, both will be able to demonstrate that each accepts citizen obligations, duties, and Responsibilities.

Born members may prove to be willing or unwilling citizens. These unwilling able bodied are the apathetic and idle since they fail to take on certain obligations expected of the citizen. They may hide their opposition with a cloak of inaction and this unproductive behaviour indicates their chosen separation and disconnect from the precepts and demands of citizenship. If obligations are ignored, then the "city" or state has far fewer reciprocal obligations towards them, other than those of humanity.

Citizens have a 'right' or reasonable expectation to a life free of the fear of being attached, to a secure life in which each can enjoy the benefits of liberties typical of the better Western forms of societies. There should be no opportunity for arbitrary arrest or imprisonment. Fair trial should be available to all as required. It is the duty of politicians, administrators, and representatives of the law to protect this expectation. Citizens in their turn are obliged to respect others and to keep the law and customs of behaviour. In times of shortage or for victims of crime, resources should be transferred from any additional provisions provided to those who have repeatedly and willfully broken the law. There is an obligation of care for the involved participating citizen which does not apply to the same degree for those who chose to be 'outside'. A prisoner receiving better care than the elderly, young, or unwell is an affront to the agreement between the state and the compliant citizen. Under circumstances permitting such neglect, the relevant administrators of the state have failed their remit; having proven their inability and unworthiness to serve the community they should be replaced. The community needs to have a safeguarded avenue to ensure the removal of such unfit persons to a place which will safeguard the community from their 'disregard': these places would take appropriate forms. There is a primary responsibility to care for those at risk and in need.

An essential aspect of civil liberty are our obligations, examples of which are the honest payment of tax with a respect for both the letter and spirit of the law. One benefit of chosen compliance is a sense of belonging and security: it is emotional. With the availability and speed of travel there are many who migrate from place to place for economic reasons without a bonding of the spirit to a state. This is different from immigrating to a specific selected state, as a single change, resulting from a sincere belief in a new way of life, thereby carrying with it the will to comply to and with a local 'citizen code' of behaviour. Benefits are accepted with their associated debts of obligation. Thus, the act of arriving in a state and accepting a refuge carries with it certain understandings and obligations. These should be made clear with any questions being answered so that the traveller may accept or look elsewhere before the move. These same fundamentals are the ones which need to be taught by parents and passed on from generation to generation of citizens. Some will be fundamental to the group and others will adapt and change with time and circumstances. Where the community 'draws the line' is what that community is. For example, communities founded upon a religious philosophical base find that once they start denying that belief system, its structure breaks down, and inevitably the group changes into something different.

There needs to be agreement. This is an understanding as to the expected patterns of behaviour which are important to the group. These are the same for all no matter what age or sex or race. When viewed from afar, such as when travelling, these patterns can become more obvious and not just an accepted norm.

Canadians have a respect for honesty, effort, and tolerance: there is now a certain permissiveness or leeway. It is a useful exercise to establish what distinguishes a citizen of any group. An undefined belief system leads to lack of identity and direction. Realization of this would probably lead to a dependant state of insecurity and produce a vulnerable identity as the outcome of all this doubt. Conversely, following an established set of beliefs releases a citizen from many forms of worry and brings fuller secure freedom: a conformity.

Defining what makes a good citizen and identifying customary motivations produces generalizations. Outcome behaviours are a good indication, though still only supposition. Having a sense of identity is a form of belonging which calls on loyalty. This loyalty could even mean that one is prepared to go without and sacrifice for group ideas; it promotes co-operation. These are strong indicators of shared ownership. Citizenship entails group empathy. It is what unifies us rather than some appeal to diversity. It is what comes naturally. Having been understood and agreed, it is instant with awareness. It is also accepted by minorities and visible minorities. It can become apparent accidentally through an experience or by witnessing something which is contrary to our group beliefs and social norms, thus defining or making the norm clearer. It is what remains true for us after other things have been dismissed. It forms the essence of community. 'Accidentally discovered' truth can become a watershed moment in our lives, changing our future direction or affirming it. What is common to all, what is respected, what is agreed to be fundamental, what links are seen as a universal truth form what we are as citizens: break those truths and we are in danger of becoming dis-unified and citizens no longer.

It can surely come as no surprise to the thinking empathetic person that a number of immigrants from war zones could be so angry and destructive. These poor souls are the survivors of untold horror. They have lost homes and loved ones and suffered hardships in their travels in their attempt to escape the evils which have permeated their homelands. Please imagine their joy at arriving in a seemingly "sane and safe world" only to find themselves the prey of evil bullies like those which they had thought they had left thousands of miles away: such a betrayal of hope! No wonder so many of their children disbelieve their parents' dream and join the demonstrably more cunning and stronger enemy. We need to face up to the fact that we in the fortunate parts of the world have failed these people. Their troubles are the result of interference, promises broken, our inner ambitions, and their situation. Yes, we and our leadership let them down. Some escape to arrive living with us. Since they are vulnerable, they need support and protection. One form of protection is the ownership of knowledge requiring an unfettered communications ability. They need to speak the new language so that they can interact better with official supporting bodies, and in doing so essentially gain better control and confidence. This linguistic ability is not generally demanded and ensured, and so again we have let them down through lack of a guidance and care. This bridge of language is necessary, preferably well before arrival.

There are opportunists in all groups. Some are for good and some are not. The criminals within these groups appear to be protected by our laws because they can find lawyers to work for them by tipping the scales. This can be at no personal cost with appeal after appeal slowing the process of law, meanwhile continuing with state support and benefits. What are frightened new immigrants to think! We have let them down since it appears the 'thugs' have the upper hand - and maybe they do. These vulnerable new arrivals see and learn that they need to beware! Comments are made about strange clothing, which is their comfortable normal. I always pack my travel bag with things from home as I assume do they. Rather than some of the other benefits, or perhaps along with them, local western costume could be provided to help these new arrivals to feel more a part of their chosen new community. A 'little' thoughtful help could greatly help. On special occasions different costumes have become a key component, like the Scots kilt, sporran, and plaid. Immigrant traditional costume could lead to a special celebration which all could enjoy. The ghetto phenomena should be avoided with all its pitfalls.

Jesus suffered anguish, despair, betrayal, mockery, and extreme brutality. Mohammed suffered ridicule, spite, viciousness, some persecution, and periodic despair. Both of these caring, creative, and imaginative people, despite being so mistreated, did not give up their gift of care for others. They <u>knew</u> their great God was leading them and instructing them. They made such a positive difference in the world, even with abuses of their teachings, as have other God-inspired followers of the Buddha, Brahmin, Zoroaster, Abraham, and so many other God-sent saints. There is great difference in the trappings of various beliefs but also great goodness and care common to all.

Then there are the Extremists!

By their works you will understand them.

Down the ages they hack the heads from the bodies of living people with the more evil using, by choice, a short knife. Sick! These less than animals recently sacrificed medical aid workers, peace workers, and reporters to die in their degenerate devil-spawned madhouse. In comparatively well-to-do Edmonton, London, UK, a black rioter hacked the head off an elderly Police Schools Liaison Officer in the Broad Water Estate Riots with its lucrative shop looting. God hates this evil! How to imagine the response to 'cooking' a Jordanian pilot in a wire grid structure! It goes beyond Sick! So far worse they are damned. No doubt. The eyes of pain and terror focused on their tormentors will have SEEN to that as they penetrated their sick and sickening minds, and since "the evil eye" carries such power for them, they will experience its fullest fury and revenge! These murderers are not followers of God, for they glory in their own evil. Anyone who rapes, tortures, or harms the young and kills has no place with a concept of God and justice.

OUR HISTORY

We are all aware of from USA filmmakers' weaknesses too often trying to change a historical fact to better suit their own prejudices. They frequently bend truth to fit their beliefs rather than fact: these show an arrogant view of the box office clients. This is not an uncommon practice. Such interference and intellectual dishonesty needs to be both resisted and confronted by or on behalf of the affected group if their own identity is not to be compromised and misinformed history is not allowed to take hold. Often I have heard the pained comments from adults watching an USA WW II film: 'They were not even there at the time'; or 'They arrived later'; or 'They got into difficulty and needed help' - help which was not acknowledged in the film. There were remarkable USA successes, as with the exceptional "The Battle of the Bulge". History provides examples of avoidable stupidity, incredible evil, and spite as well as honour, bravery, and foresight: it is an important teacher. We need to know history and not some half-baked box office product. Cowboy films suggest that this period was a major section of US history, whereas the long cow trails only lasted for about 36 years. Enter the rail barons.

The perfect children portrayed in Elstree Studio films and others were promoting an image of what was believed we should aspire towards in a Social Family context. It was less real in life. Federico Fellini's film *8½* is very much the product of a time of change as well as a significant cause of cinema progress. It focuses upon a troubled filmmaker at war with himself. There is the search for true personal happiness taking place in a modern fragmented and difficult world. *8½* is also about the loneliness and disconnect caused by the pressures of a modern changing world. Fellini pushed the realms of imagination by breaking with film conventions and inventing new ones, thereby extending the 'Art' further. Most film buffs have a particular soft spot for this work in addition to a whole raft of French black and white films with their surprises and new perspectives of life. Our life is subject to constant shifts and changes. Needless to say, if fixed rules were being applied none of these would have probably appeared. The changes encouraged will turn out to be a mixture of good and bad and all those shades in between. The misuse of systems of Human Rights is destructive to effective necessary adaptation and change. It is a bit like driving a car with the brakes on: something will break and end the journey. However, there needs to be an accurate and agreed upon awareness of what is good, with an honest recognition of what is bad and needs changing: both can usefully draw upon a full and honest appraisal of our varied histories which inform us for our present. So, the media's responsibility to us regarding history is that the program content they broadcast must be factual, honest, and reliable.

Exercising the influence of the media is clearly full of obligations to make clear the message and not to confuse. The unpleasant is part of the knowledge balance that is needed to inform decisions, having broadened the possibilities, corrected faults, strengthened chosen good practice with an honest view of emotions, and avoided inaccuracies and any avoidable unconstructive risks. This re-evaluation process is long overdue for serious debate. That racial tension can be caused by the arrival of unfamiliar cultures is inevitable and made worse by externally imposing seemingly unreasonable restrictions and prohibitions. How useful it would be to have an induction-mentored period for all in the group. This should last for several weeks to iron out the worries and explain the culture they are being submerged in. It works in business and could well benefit immigration. Who pays for it? An imaginative and caring society should make provision, otherwise both will "pay for it" periodically in a negative context of isolation, anger, and disillusionment. Sadly the cause of supporting those fleeing atrocious conditions abroad is undermined by the arrival of criminal opportunists. That legitimate refugees have every good reason to flee is highlighted by the barbarity and unholy viciousness of those carving out what they hope is a prosperous and secure future on all sides. Marines returning from Syria have reported nurses nailed onto tables in hospitals and repeatedly raped with patients lying dead around them all caused by the sickest of Saddam's troops. Equally horrific the murders, rapes, use children and women as human shields and far more. Crucifixion was a barbarity of the past but the past has resurfaced in full force, if it ever left.

The Daily Mail (UK) on Saturday 19th of March 2015, Ps 28/9, expands on one immigrant's successful exploitation of chronic weaknesses within the British system. No wonder there are shortages leading to difficulties for those legitimately in need of support. The following is not a lone case and nothing to do with current entries due to warfare and is an example of good journalism informing the public. In summary, a French National seemingly legitimately comes to Britain to work. Entry is by Eurostar but with faked papers. A bribed booking clerk of Eurostar, in London, originally from Benin, French West Africa, arranged for reduced early booking ticket a scam which cost the company an estimated one million and fifty-five thousand pounds or more, for over 6800 fares. Interviews conducted by the Department of Works and Pensions were attended with their own well briefed gang interpreter. These documents were later proved to be 'stolen' from persons who would then apply for replacements. An alibi is set in place. The result was payments of many different varieties of benefits to this gang, organised by an African from the Ivory Coast. This gang it seems had successfully set up a minimum of 225 convenience marriages facilitating non-EU people to become secure residents. Neither bride nor groom apparently needed to be present. The cost was reportedly several thousand pounds but enabled benefits to be claimed. This benefits' fraud brought in well over two million pounds, accounted for, to which could be later added a car export business which appears to have yielded unusually high income. The Gang leader had two children, he had been in operation for over seven years. His operation took a hundred officers of HM Revenue and Customs and the Metropolitan Police four years of investigation: a considerable expense. Earlier, in 2005, the leader was sentenced to jail following which he was to be deported. This did not take place because of his 'right to family life' under Article 8 of the European Convention of Human Rights.

Factual information seeds intelligent development and growth. An accepted reliable history helps the community avoid confusion. Similarly, certain so-called freedoms can be and are manipulated for financial and personal gain: this is an undesirable outcome. Both litigation and governmental involvement needs to be focused upon and provide communal benefit while of necessity being monitored, with safeguards fully in place. Implementation should achieve predicted outcomes. An accepted history provides the medium to explain what we do and believe and why we can usefully ask if the conflict with the Nazis in WW II can clarify what we stand for today. Accurate, honest information explains the past and indicates the future.

That Freedom Identity

In discussing 'free', it increasingly becomes clear how subjective it is. Personal freedom can be ascribed or an identity. Freedom can be gained or lost. It can be achieved by 'fitting in', being assimilated, or following patterns of behaviour. Rights are similarly nebulous, as each relates to a focused concept or condition. A leads to B and then there is also C. An identity when changed from one of dependence to a state of insecurity and independence will hopefully gain intellectual and spiritual freedom sooner or later. Social independence implies the emergence of a strong wish to follow obligations which is enabled through confidence. Obligations follow both mature empathy and sympathy: socially and financially supported and supporting. However, some self-identifying groups, thrown up in social conflict, become obsessed with their own identities. Their descriptors become longer and more tangled. They demonstrate their insecurity and confusion through excesses, anger, and even violence. They are not free, but rather the captives of their mental disarray. Extremism of any form is such.

Jeremy Clarkson, a much admired and extremely skilled BBC broadcaster, appears to have overstepped the line: we probably will never fully learn what additionally occurred 'behind closed doors'. To punch a fellow broadcaster, whether it relates to cars, boxing, soccer, warfare, or cooking is wrong and is known by all parties to be so. We all make mistakes, but one could be forgiven for assuming the gravity of the outcome came from more than one situation. However, for life threats to be levelled at the chief administrator for doing his job and in such circumstances is a responsibility he probably least enjoyed. Such a reflex reaction from a stranger demonstrates one can be so vulnerable due to the lunatic, undisciplined, confused, and probably dysfunctional members of society. I believe Clarkson would have little positive to say about the unrequested threats made to his Boss from an outsider disassociated from reality, despite Clarkson's own probable disappointment and personal losses.

A sense of involvement and belonging encourages feelings of fulfilment opening the way to greater freedoms, despite and because of the accepted commitments. To better belong to our democracy, a tax-paying non-citizen needs to feel that they have 'full social membership', they are involved and they are accepted: they also need to have some vote. Having not yet qualifying for taking full part in the national election, by swearing the oath of allegiance to Canada and the Queen, a tangible step of working towards this could be municipal enfranchisement. This is not a problem in the Royal Canadian Legion where the oath is taken upon joining. This government levels the payment of taxes without any vote for some new and not so new arrivals to Canada. This does not fit in with the concept of a Human Rights but more importantly fails acceptance within a modern democracy. To be denied participation in the administration selection process (voting) for where one lives continues, despite having to pay taxes nationally, locally, and with any Capital Gains is not Democracy! It nullifies the term Democracy since it creates at least two levels of social membership for residents.

One of our basic needs and possibly Rights is for adequate health care. Health questions and problems abound for non-nationals including residents. One appreciates there are limited resources, and that leads to the question as to who is seen to first. However, some form of insurance and or prepayment could be arranged. The full cost of medication comes as a heavy blow when trying to settle into a new country. This is the lot of many new arrivals as we found out. When my wife and I first arrived in Canada we had three months to wait before we could have health care, despite financial stability. Having to prove our health was good and safe regarding sexually transmitted illnesses, tuberculosis, and general body health via an expensive pre-arrival health check, we then had to pay for another separate police check before being granted entry. We were later informed, by the way, that the costly UK police check was not transferable and invalid once we were now in Canada! We settled in the countryside where we could not gain MD Doctor support for many years (not unusual for some 'full' Canadians either). Consequently, we had to go to Emergency if there was a need. Getting to the hospital was another problem due to not having a 'line of credit' to buy a car despite having bought a small farm. To hire a car we had to pay top insurance since our decades of clean UK driving licences were irrelevant to the insurance companies. Further, if we had not been able to speak French and English, we would probably not know of 911 emergency call number nor have been able to answer questions and give directions on the telephone. If we had been able to reach a hospital, without language we would have been unable to answer triage questions. Yes, European immigrants do suffer from immigration problems and identity prejudice. My wife and I have even been told we should go back to where we came from (London UK). Our `funny accents` are frequently referred to both positively and negatively. All this does not add up to an image of freedom nor has it welcomed newcomers previous to the end of 2015. As citizens, most such problems have ceased for us. However, there were other amazing freedoms to enjoy with national and community security.

NEGATIVE RIGHTS - so things won`t happen to you (e.g. you won't be imprisoned without trial)

POSITIVE RIGHTS - provisions that do happen (e.g. education, right to vote, eventual health care, and hospital access)

For new arrivals there is much petty officialdom to understand and overcome which too easily can led to misunderstandings. Tension happens. It is to be expected periodically due to limited resources and conflicting cultural ideals: a further need to achieve accepted assimilation. Affordability and availability battle with limitations of resources and fulfillment of Responsibilities. Further, there is that "bureaucratic" (Ref: Émile Durkheim) danger of blind unthinking rule - following officials with mechanistic robot-like acceptance of certain outcomes by following an arbitrary mindset, seemingly fixed and rigid: same with RIGHTS. Social Facts and their variations have to be recognized and allowed for when necessary. Creating a system of Rights can and will not remove wrong, but only tend to some `discovered wrong after the fact`.

The careful study of sociology injects research findings into what was previously purely subjective thoughts. Durkheim placed sociology in its impressive place as the social science it has become. However it is not nearly as scientific as had been envisaged. Considerable valuable research has been accomplished and some working formulae produced, but there it ends for the moment with far still to go.

"The totality of beliefs and sentiments common to the average members of society form a determinate existence with a life of its own." Durkheim

An unpredictable Emotional Override remains despite the threat of law. This can also provoke law-breaking.

Keeping 'worthwhile' things going generates happiness, going beyond the words and focusing upon personal subjective values.

Responsive and imaginative organization are essential to a happy society.

> *"What is or should be common for the benefit of all is the work of administrators and governmental agencies. Within this social family humans are meeting human needs and all play a role. By doing so each earns and deserves to be valued. Changes are caused because of increased and changed needs and we need to recognize the need to change. This is not freedom, but it enables other freedoms...."* **Auguste F. X. Comte** *(father of sociology, social evolution, and positivism)*

Our internal self-discussions are very much a part of our very being and travel beyond and dig into our perceptions.

> *"This Metaphysical stage involved the justification of universal rights as being on a vauntedly higher plane than the authority of any human ruler to countermand, although said rights were not referenced to the sacred beyond mere metaphor. This stage is known as the stage of investigation, because people started reasoning and questioning although no solid evidence was laid."* in **Wikipedia**

When dealing with the mind the only current certainty is its uncertainty.

> *"How the sciences... must stand, irrespective of the wishes of any one 'positivity'..[it].. is simply the degree to which the phenomena can be exactly determined....exactness or positivity...."* **Lester F. Ward**

THE SANCTITY OF MEMORIES

Reportedly much of the direction of current thinking leans heavily upon Sören Kirkegaard's works and the Existentialist approach to life's meaning or purpose, or rather lack of it. For life to have meaning, there needs to be purpose guiding it and behind existence so causing existence, otherwise it has no purpose and is rather absurd and meaningless. Setting aside the discussion on the existence of a Supreme Being, life without purpose has no rights or wrongs. In the absence of these it is for every individual to select their direction, thus providing for themselves their purpose and chosen Responsibilities. We are utterly alone and isolated. We are separated under these conditions. If we accept this position, then it is wise to find purpose which is to our liking in order to avoid insanity. To break the loneliness and pointlessness of existence, the selection of others as *significant to ourselves* is essential. These selections give our life and existence personal meaning and depth of experience. These social links, for that is what they are, have an emotional responsive source which becomes shared and strengthened through our memories. When such links are formed, these links arrive with binding obligations and Responsibilities special to us, individually. In time we discover many of these are shared by our "significant others" and the linkage expands and grows. Memories become the meaning behind our existence and the pursuit of "good" memories special to us as individuals. They become a prime goal for existence. This goodness and interpersonal support lead to the growth of reason and meaning along with the concept of the Supreme Being, free will, and purpose.

· · · · · · ·

CHAPTER 19:

LAW

INTERNAL Personal =>Acceptance
Versus *EXTERNAL => Imposed – Law*

JUSTICE: 1. Being righteous 2. Fairness 3. Rightfulness 4. Reward or penalty as deserved

5. The use of authority to uphold what is just 6. The administration of the law

Bring to JUSTICE: to cause (a wrongdoer) to be tried in a court and duly be punished.

JUSTIFIABLE: That which can be justified or defended as correct...................... **(OPED)**

In only one of the above definitions justice is *fairly and rightly rewarded, earned, and* NOT a central necessity. The only measure for such a subjective concept can be the accepted standards of the relevant society. Its members are the justice, for it is upon them and from them that the powers of law are loaned by a democratic society to those entrusted with its powers. When most of the people believe one thing and those given power for a period act in contradiction of that general will, then through their contradiction they become autocrats and dictators.

Law should lead to justice and not depend upon 'performance'. The "ADVERSERIAL" approach appears mostly concerned with 'winning' the argument rather than winning for society and Right. As an adversarial consequence, true justice may not prevail. Law is like that. Could a way be found to remove the competitive lean in favour of increased cooperation? More thought is needed regarding Adversarial versus Civil systems of trial. A failure to disclose information in order to win the case is a clear danger to justice. Such failings are also seen in so-called television reports (stories rather than accounts) and biased quasi factual/historical films. Too often misinformation does the public a disservice. Lady Truth is set in form, and is not a malleable semisolid shaped at will. One suggestion is that in trials expert teams could give independent evidence totally separate from prosecution and defence. This could result in more probable collaboration which would work towards finding and revealing the truth, rather than winning points (Ref: Alan Young Co-Founder and Director of 'Osgoode's Innocence Project'). Barry C. Scheck and Peter J. Neufeld founded **The Innocence Project** in 1992 at the Benjamin N. Cardozo School of Law. Students with faculty volunteered their time with the Innocence Project and have literally changed lives in the pursuit of justice for the wrongfully convicted. For example, Romeo Phillion was released after 31 years of imprisonment, in March 2009, when the Innocence Project helped him by bringing new evidence forward which they had uncovered.

We are told it is our responsibility to know what the law is: ignorance is no excuse. If so, then who has the power and authority to teach every citizen, especially those who do not care? Neither parent nor school can discipline and instruct. This responsibility to know makes legal expert representation essential for most. Further there are the innocent victims of the lawbreaker who suffer no matter how good a law-abiding citizen they are. They suffer and so society itself suffers. Also, retribution for PC (Politically Correct) rights infringements can be disproportionate to the act. An individual complaining about a racial group as being a constant problem can be suspended and investigated while the "white trash" referred to leaves laughing. Similarly, a person writing on their Facebook page that he or she hopes those black .... bullies seen beating up a white boy, caught on film, have their families treated the same way, can lose their job. I would like to believe no sane individual would ascribe the behaviour of a few rotten apples to a whole religious or racial group. By their works you will know them. All groups sadly have their over-publicized sad excuses of humanity while their far greater number of "saints and Angels" (Thrasher) are seldom reported upon.

Reports state brutality resulting from alcohol, anger from childhood abuse, drug-related incidents, and being over-tired and edgy, but heaven forbid blame would be accepted as stemming from lack of self-control. Lack of early years thoughtful, balanced, concerned, and proportionate family discipline, with a family lacking in 'moral fibre' and other forms of self-control, can brutalize their young! Beating up children and extended bouts of hysterical screaming do not often promote rational beings. Something good schooling, brimming over with creativity and activities for all, can much improve are the habits of a difficult child replacing those negative personality traits with worthwhile, goal-orientated persistence. Consistent and clearly understood firm but fair discipline can promote and provide security .

The question arises if decency and moral behaviour CAN still be adequately encouraged and taught in many current schools. Of course, if it is then that is thanks to the dedicated versions of teachers! Sadly and too frequently it is an uphill battle for them with some stupid over indulgent and complaining parents to deal with as well as the eternal tinkering of changing governments, chancellors and career curriculum builders. There is also the threat of children's lies about teachers, resulting litigation, and the threat of suspension. Since one cannot sue a lying child there is no legal redress; no right to justice for the teacher "set up" or wrongly accused because the suspension comes first. With suspension arrives plenty of reflective time, followed by long periods of worry and doubts and then hopefully final vindication. There is, however, the lasting affects upon the unfortunate teacher. Trying to work with nothing much to seemingly build upon makes the task worse. Child Rights are ever present which can be misinterpreted and misapplied. If this is not so, then what major moral approaches have superseded the previous behavioural-basics in preference for other newer forms? A child's natural ignorance is no excuse for adult stupidity. It appears that when a certain prevalent anti-culture and lack of discipline predominate, this produces a certain power structure which far better ensures a "good grounding" in antisocial and sometimes illegal behaviour. It is difficult to understand these interpersonal relationships or even know where to look for what should be promoted and how. Thus, highly expensive trained guides are required to explain how our 'rights' are to be fully considered. In large part this Rights patchwork is set on precedent, which could have been 'last week' or even four hundred years ago or more. Their meanings, use, and importance depend upon our finances, our state of mind, our age, and our will. It needs to be remembered that broad change depends upon political will and not necessarily a Democratic will of the majority. Determined minorities can effect change to better reflect their concerns and advancement. This can be achieved before the majority are aware of any change happening. It can differ in different areas of a nation or union due to local bylaws or national boundaries. A system of 'local laws' is common. Differences are apparent between Canadian Provinces. The letter of the law may well take precedence over common sense and natural justice. An offence may be added to due to our disagreement, anger, or sheer terror of the potential outcome, and in some cases is termed 'contempt of court'. No wonder the saying is that 'the law is an ass' and 'the law is blind': too readily it can seem to be 'non-understandable' and non-understanding. However, it remains our responsibility to know, for 'ignorance is no defence'! What of our rights then! Consequently it must be clarified which Responsibilities the state, politicians, and education have in this, especially regarding changes in the law, and our having an equal access to the law with its implications regarding race, beliefs, wealth, and power. Equality 'under the law' needs to be more than just fine words. This equality can be elusive, as Native American Indians, Inuit, and Métis will explain.

Over 80% of English potential legal cases are decided by (lay) Magistrates. These are people, deemed suitable of character, who are not primarily of the legal professions. They, however, are rendered competent enough to decide in most cases, dispense fines, and send people for trial in higher courts: the doorway to jail. Our educational system could prepare these lay judges and all members of the public better by introducing all to basic law as part of schooling. A far greater understanding of the law could and should be provided in our educational institution enhanced by and with a background in The Constitution and in Logic. At the very least it would benefit future Magistrates and those in authority as union representatives, employers, and those presiding at tribunals. A larger pool of competence should be the product with a general greater appreciation and respect for the complexities of the law itself, including fuller awareness of its broader implications throughout the community.

Of the criminal, the antisocial, the racist, or whatever falls foul of the law, it appears the unknowable is considered equal with an intent or intention. There is no way a person can know what they do not know, so there should be 'reasonable ignorance'. An occurrence can become a case in law with one part not knowing what the problem is; how an action, phrase, or word is relevant; and if for what reason. Too quickly a badge can be pinned to a situation simply because it had been a frequent previous occurrence somewhere or a method used to avoid exploring further since it would take too much time, thought, and energy. Parliamentary will or "interference" may not be the better way. A system of legal precedent may prove unjust due to the new conditions applying. Excess can throw out the 'baby of justice with the bathwater of law': it may be too "thorough". Clear Legal Code restriction does exactly that. There needs to be some reasoned give-and-take which is outside adversarial Law. There would be less call for changes or revision should this be so. Some trials lasting months suggest either extremes of complexity or a process problem needing to be resolved.

One could be forgiven for thinking assault required evidence of harm being done to body or mind - evidence supported by a medical certificate. That being poked by a finger can be considered assault is too silly for words. Surely the definition of assault needs to better protect a person from damage and not a small pricking of their pride. Tasering is bodily harm, punching causes bruising and bodily harm, and shooting causes bodily harm. The purpose of each law needs to be credible, proportionate, and therefore acceptable.

Offense Against the Persons Act 1861 (UK) still has areas
of confusion which need interpretation: there are contradic-
tions in places. A trial situation can occur in which there is
a question if it is the law or not. Remember, ignorance is
no excuse!

Those taking part in a trial need clear understandable and
accessible information. The client and Attorney- Lawyer
will generally have little appreciation of each other's experiences in life relevant to the case to enable better and deeper
co-operation. The legal representative has to be the client's
avenue to justice, particularly as the law offers too many
difficulties for the uninitiated. Much costly time is used in
identifying and explaining relevant legal niceties and relevant
strands. A better personal legal base from which the client
may begin would be of help and would also enable better
exchange of relevant details. There are such a variety of spe-
cialties in law that to adequately provide a usable layman base
seems impossible. However, if experienced retired members
of the legal profession were to work on this, assisted by
"Crystal Clear" language use along with experienced constitutional specialists, a series of informative and useful context-
centred booklets could be produced, as a start, to help those
caught up in legal action and educationalists. Could this
be termed now as 'Legalosity'? Possibly a simpler system
could evolve enabling a single reference book to be available. In turn, this would enable cases to be executed more
speedily due to better meeting of minds during the process.
Schools could make use of these to teach their own basic
law courses, given to all students over the course of many
years. This would enable each individual to better respect
and make use of law appropriately, if and when required.
Ignorance seems the obvious outcome of our current pattern
of legal education, with an exception of good television
programmes. The powers-that-be are the ones with the
excuses and lucrative employment. Affordable and available

is a copy of the Canadian Criminal Code for $25, apparently heavy enough to keep a door open but available if needed. Judges do come in for some very pointed criticism, but as usual this is a small minority. One wonders what the state of a legal system without them would be like. Judges have an interpretational role and provide legal detail as well as safe-guards. They are the guardians of legal accuracy, continuity, and fairness. The judge is referee, coach, and reporter whose responsibility is ensuring that legal rights are protected and a uniformity of outcome, relating to previous similar cases, is achieved by maintaining comparable uniform outcome and fair law. Common sense and concepts of Natural Justice must also be present to follow the letter of the law with its intentions to be appropriate for the victim(s) and all those affected. Governments and Law bodies review legal ramifica-tions of cases which have been submitted and offer sugges-tion. However, constant changes and additions, as occurred under the UK Blair Government, have been cited as causing anomalies, imbalance, and unnecessary complications in far too many areas. These issues have been detailed concerning Tony Blair's time as Prime Minister in Philip Johnston's 2010 book, *Bad Laws- Imposed by the Nanny State* (UK, Constable, London).

> **Statement of criminal law:** A statement, systemized into a Legal Code, for example in France or Canada. ***Warwick University, Comparative Law***

Legal Instruments are used to operate the law - the updated code in 1989 with its Tribal implications for those in Continental Africa, also The Children's Act (UK) regarding parental Responsibilities is not law yet. Why not? Can it be due to the cost to the public? Surely not. So what could be wrong? Have heads rolled of those responsible? Could it be political lack of will? Maybe there is a problem as to what to leave out and who must decide: those in the know, or those wishing to know! Many parliamentary members have legal backgrounds, so it is reasonable to wonder if that could be a reason as vested interests in a status quo.

Prison can never be the prisoner's 'payment to Society', nor can prison wash away a wrongdoing. If a crime is committed, it is an attack on society and us all. Prison must be punishment within which ethical care, help, and support may be introduced: beneficial intervention aimed at helping the criminal change for the better. Prison is used for separating those law breakers who have demonstrated such disregard of their social Responsibilities that they have caused their own removal to a secure location away from society. This removal prevents them from being able to further practice anti-social activities for a time but with the opportunity to change for the better. Removal is exactly that. Protection is exactly that. Prison is also for our protection. The fact that such removal may be in the prisoner's better interest - more attune to society - and prevent prisoners from indulging themselves in worse and worse acts requiring harsher regimes of punishment is obvious, but it is punishment, and not a debt. As a child, for a school punishment I received the customary 'packets' of learning work - useful passages from my school texts had to be memorized. This provided confident knowledge, usefully improved learning strategies, and a good non-violent correctional message. The urgent need to develop strategies to assist the learning process resulted in a better understanding of how I managed to learn. The benefits were there with 'the lessons of punishment'. My punishment was neither too harsh nor too soft! The prisoner has a time to reflect upon the loss of honour and social freedom and decide upon a practical better way forward. Not all will rise to the challenge, but the opportunity to constructively forward plan can strongly be supported in prison: the prisoner's future wellbeing is important. Much of the USA prison system is reportedly owned and run by offshore companies. They are paid by the numbers they have incarcerated in their prisons it seems: more prisoners means more income. Naturally they have strong lobbyists speaking on their behalf regarding and promoting changes to USA laws and their enforcement.

Appeals, a provision to question a judicial decision, are apparently essential to any concept of civilized justice, but there needs to be limits. The provision of legal representation for those unable to pay is likewise. That having enough cash can enable a considerable prolonging of a case seems less than just or fair. This tactic is used to stall deportation, promote a settlement, stave off a prison term, and so on. Additional costs are too frequently courtesy of the taxpayers and can add up to millions of dollars. A revised code for appeal seems called for, again via retired and experienced servants of the law: an age benefit again.

As an interesting exercise, try to define what law is in the reality of its applications and identify what it actually leads to and achieves. Having established aim and outcome these may be better researched to then establish the actual value of our legal system to the citizen, to the law breaker, to its administration, and to its practitioners such as law firms.

> TRIAL: Process of activating CODES of negative conduct defined with exemplars of good behaviours + that WILL to seek a right way + Acceptance of COST of the processes required + POLITICAL STAMINA to both defend and see through discovered necessary reforms + Providing TIME limits and meeting each + Summoning MORE WILL to REVIEW and act swiftly on advice + LAWs → a FUTURE embracing necessary changes to maintain and provide justice.

A system which is too complex is set to lead to misdirection, an undesired outcome leading to injustice. When reviewing the concept of rights it is impractical to have a mass of messy complexity built in. Language use needs to be clear and simple. The required goal must be explicit and not needing undue interpretation. It is the Responsibility of Government to be linguistically transparent and also to keep their actions clear and available to their masters, the electorate. For this to be achieved, there needs to be "Crystal Clear" wording and clarity. Those voting for change need to be confident regarding what they are voting for: a Second House enables extra scrutiny. Further, a citizen needs to be able to understand what the law demands. These goals of enabling fuller awareness are the duties of the law profession and of education. Where clarity is missing, there is opportunity for abuse which inevitably produces the abuser of THE SYSTEM.

Unsuspected use of unreliable evidence is a further problem. People lie, remember wrongly, imagine in line with expectations, have physical or mental problems, and have various ulterior motives. One person's view of a violation of Human Rights will not necessarily be another's. One may state such was an inexcusable breach, another may believe it was the product of anger, while another may say it was an annoyance but nothing more. What is currently pressing in politics or socially will probably carry the day. This may be wrong but is predictable.

To implement Law requires establishing proof. Opinion is not proof, though too easily it may be seen as such if forcefully enough presented. This is not justice. Giving evidence for the prosecution is reporting important information concerning an offence. This paints a picture of guilt: that is what it is for. Guilt by implication and argument works hand in hand with guilt by association. Unfortunately "offenders" then find themselves seemingly unable to have adequate protection. In ignorance of the niceties of the law, a situation could spin out of control. Such a situation calls for clarity of thought and calmness in the judge. The hysteria which can easily surround Human Rights is its own worst enemy, as are those who act hysterically in defending those rights. Rights relate to ethics and ethics relate to argument and discussion: these perform best in a climate of deep, calm reason.

Society aims for a peaceful co-existence. This peace may be too easily upset by local yobs and gangs. These antisocial people have rights also, but if they behave in an irresponsible manner, aspects of those rights and those of many others may well be put at risk. The results of antisocial actions can remain hidden until later: when these can produce danger for the less careful. Most actions can produce some form of unpredicted outcome which reinforces the value of exercising judgement and self-discipline. The sudden increase in aggressive use of hoodies to taunt and threaten was partly due to the interest shown by the media. Irresponsible media involvement is clearly a significant promoter of new forms of 'street cred' and in-your-face yobbery. Some skateboarders, radio carriers, and those deafening noise-machines in cars are just a few of the examples. Add graffiti on newly redecorated house walls, trains, and buses; and concrete blocks placed or thrown on rail lines (UK) and from motorway bridges (UK), and the human cost rises. It seems to be believed by a minority that they have a right to upset society and that this is acceptable as long as 'they are doing their thing' … cool …. Lol. What it clearly shows is further evidence of a disconnect between these social insects and the society which clothes, feeds, and protects them.

Sound ethical values proceed from sound logic but may also need to be defended or lost. Some encourage that loss. Rights embrace ethical values which are needed, but they can emerge from very different packages. Their emergence should follow general agreement with specified limitations. They are based upon an ability to choose and support liberties. Liberties may be considered frozen absolutes or a matter of and for reasonable balances.

Equal Access to Justice

Active Rights depend generally upon Law and lawyers, with the vagaries of Government, public boycotts, and financial support playing their parts. Too frequent abuses of the so-called 'rights' of the vulnerable and disadvantaged occur. Responsibilities on a one-to-one basis are closely generated by an individual's own experience and conscious decision. Legal aid costs $98 per hour versus wealthier expenditure of well over $300 per/hr. This can greatly affect outcome: the result is predictably that often the less experienced generally defend the less well off. With more cash comes the Legal Team approach, making the buying of extra research personnel, legal experience power, and so legal power to affect outcomes. This frequently demonstrated advantage is brought to the trial by stronger purchasing power which buys deeper resources and greater experience. As discussed by Frank Adrio, EXPERIENCE enables more successful focus upon relevant essentials ….. so well described on Radio CBC .

'Task capping' alternatives limit what may later be added to a task or resources, unlike being able to make or ask for full payment for more resources and time later. Such capping levels the wealth playing field for it reduces what a wealthier participant may command or add. Such a precaution is said to be a PRO BONO (for the public good) case – So a total acceptable expenditure possible is agreed from the start.

Clients of LEGAL AID versus Board Membership of conglomerates or associations do not produce financial and legal parity - those at the chalk face of industry and finance are very well protected. Some have funds set aside specifically, to the tune of hundreds of millions of dollars!

JURIES

The purpose of powers and instruments of instruction need periodic review to examine and establish their actual consequences with time. So what are the purposes for appointing a jury? Why does society and its members entertain the huge jury expenditure with its demand on members' personal time, energy, and resources? The reason must be worthwhile, and is namely to better protect and exhibit common-sense, impartiality, and 'natural-justice'. However, one is tempted to ask, "Impartial as to what?" when those trying to be impartial and just are dictated to and directed in a situation in which oratory 'powers' play such a key role!

The jury, specifically a guardian to consider both variety of view and experiences and enable fuller reflections, may be established and considered so that an accused person's action can be justifiable in certain circumstances. With so many opinions floating about and reflecting variables related to coping with life, concepts of 'natural' justice are introduced rather than just the cold letter of the law. All have prompted the system of trial by jury. Justice must be 'seen to be done', but that decision must be both according to law and based on a responsibility to fully consider the conditions surrounding the 'event'. These then become relevant to the experiences of those directly involved, as seen in the balancing force of a jury system. So, there is a benefit of using legally neutral, randomly selected citizen jurors in preference to legally trained 'committee' of citizens, somewhat along the lines of Justices of the Peace. This more everyday group is able to recognize and add factors relevant to their world experiences. Thus, 'natural justice' is promoted by providing a varied collection of 'worthy citizens' to offer a group-attitude which is hopefully more truly reflective of life. The fact that juries are considered so necessary attests to an agreed safeguard against a cold, dogmatic, inflexibility or bias influencing the outcome.

Lawmakers

An interesting conflict arises in the hypothetical case of a dangerous rise in extremism within society and its many negative effects on a current social community group. If an existing criminal organization were the only 'force' capable of standing up to a threat to the community, in doing so would this organization have become acceptable or even essential? Despite The West's imperfect political system, it still has Responsibilities beyond the limits of boundaries or shores. There will inevitably come a time soon when this will be fully put to the test. Members will need to decide what action would be right and finally demonstrate a determination and will to commit. This is being tested by ISIS and other Terrorists, which inevitably will result in 'boots on the ground' yet again. In life we all have to deal with crises and unwelcome eventualities. There may be no clear guidelines or else those which do exist may appear not to apply to the current circumstances. In reaction to this unsatisfactory condition, a new right way or law emerges which may or may not be acted upon at once - but the decision will have to be made.

The precision of the law, the spirit of a law, and the Responsibilities of the servants of that law require:

a.) interpretation;

b.) enforcement with confidence; and

c.) adaptation to meet new conditions.

So who decides? It is the role of politics and politicians in a Democracy to ACT ON BEHALF OF ALL its electorate and their dependants. No more and no less. There is a fundamental right to be heard which goes hand in hand with the right to reply. These demand a balanced argument with the presence of those who are directly involved. There can be no justice without legal respect being shown to both sides. Just because one point of view is not currently deemed politically correct does not mean it has no value or reality. However, when dealing with terrorists, it simply becomes a matter of survival.

In an efficient and relevant theory and practice of Law, there should be no need for an additional list of Rights to achieve individual, civil, and social justice. New laws are created to meet new situations and to change conditions. Law should support right action, right argument, right intent, and right outcome, irrespective if a majority or a minority is involved. Common law is the pursuit and protection of natural justice and fairness, and it is either a natural or an arranged acceptable balance. A question of whether to apply limits and if so how is equally valid with regard to Human Rights and Responsibilities. Resolving these thoughts enables society and its courts to justify being able to act and decide. The extension of powers regarding rights, like the Law, calls for extended resources which when in short supply will affect the quality and justification of and for the proceedings. There is the Responsibility of the judicial system to defend citizens and society, but to do so it must break with certain Human Rights through punishment and incarceration. Balanced with that are attempts at restorative justice with care offering victim-support as well as 're-education' for prisoners. Demoting certain Human Rights is unavoidable. Some must supersede others. Such adjustment is subjective and can therefore be challenged in court. However the promotion of one or more Rights over others is essential as a consequence to permit the enactment of the others as a priority. That is in order to protect or achieve an agreed interpretation of justice: a purposeful balance rather than the use of circumstantially disconnected absolutes: the individual Human Rights as written.

The old and infirm have a right to their dignity, to security, and to life. This may well depend upon availability of medicines, doctors, nurses, and even protected housing. Then differences of wealth lead to very different choices being available. It seems ludicrously wrong that an elderly person has to spend many times more finance on a tiny room, restricted access, and uninteresting and even nutritionally poor meals in a care home rather than in a very pleasant open hotel. Then compare a U.K. National Health Service provision with those which are privately funded. The lot of the penniless elderly is being reduced to relying on Social Welfare who in turn are subject to Governmental policy. Yes, we should all prepare for our autumnal years, but we need honest support, good advice, and decent wages to do so. Pension funds should not be touched by any organization for any other purpose than to provide pensions: they are not there to 'balance the books' and be rifled by company or Government - but they are. Baby Boomers were the workforce paying an increased total of taxes and pension fees, a goodly number of these sadly never survived to get any of their pensions back. Therefore there should be an even greater surplus. However, we are informed that the funds will prove inadequate due to those same numbers. It does not add up. There are no such shortages for politicians' pensions and they do not have to wait so long. These are all elderly people who are all needing care, but they are receiving very different qualities of life: from extreme luxury to bullying and malnutrition. This incompatibility is in sharp conflict with concepts of Human Rights. Call someone a nasty ethnic name and land in court, even prison, but the elderly can do nothing except cry, 'be medicated', and eventually die - often alone. Legal argument is needed. Conditions and benefits should be compared with those who are powerful socially or politically, thus informing a debate which should be a vibrant agent for change. There is a confusion of priorities here. The aim is the avoidance of abuse or neglect through, amongst other things, a duty of care. The State is that individual who exercises Responsibilities through Government and Law and who controls our available tax income for all our good as a society.

Retrospective Legislation is contrary to practice in most civilized states. A law may not be added in order to change what was not considered a crime or debt into a crime or debt weeks or years after. Such a prosecution under a new law regarding a previous condition is morally wrong. Rights and crimes created and enforced retrospectively are an anathema to concepts of justice and what is fair and right. An honest, hardworking, thrifty tax payer upon departing this life can be subject to Governmental Death Theft (Death Duties or Inheritance Tax) with forced sale of house and contents the frequent outcome. This clearly goes against both natural justice and Human Rights. The taxes of the deceased had been fully paid at the time, and what was left over was available to be used at that worker's discretion. Furthermore, this governmental theft and the distress it causes has criminal implications even when a government has made it part of taxation: and even worse is how they threaten to charge interest on that amount. In fact, it was reported last week that the UK took £4 billion from mainly middle class taxpayers this year! Upper bracket earners have escape routes...for their savings. War atrocities were similarly pronounced the right thing to do and 'enshrined' in law with regard to confiscation of Japanese properties with imprisonment (internment) in Canada, and Jewish belongings and businesses in Nazi Germany with forced deportation and execution as the same period of history testifies. To steal from the dead and their relatives falls into a similar category.

There can be two rules regarding the same activity. One may have significantly different implications than the other, with both being possible choices. Having sold a car in Canada, the seller will apparently still have responsibility for any accident until the sale has been processed by the DVLA (which can take four weeks). If the DVLA is informed ahead of time and in good time that a clear, agreed upon sale, within the family for instance, is to take place on an agreed upon future date (moving abroad for example), then the DVLA marks the change of ownership from the day of the receipt of the notifying document. Strange? Even worse, in terms of liability an uninformed seller's insurance would be compromised by the purchaser's accident!

The NatWest Three and Enron

Rights are enforced via a collection of arbitrary mental gymnastics processes. Those who have hold of the process of reaction and force choose the Rights with power and those which are pushed out of the picture. Precedent seems less relevant than in the 'real' legal system, possibly due to their shrapnel like splintering tendencies. That Human Rights can vary so much between nations is a concern but reflective of the 'conversation' surrounding them.

Convenient disregard of rights - the Nat West 3.

Following the 9/11 Terrorist attack in New York City, Tony Blair's government revised Extradition Procedures between the UK and the USA, and the USA and the UK. The arrangement was unequally advantageous to the USA. These increased powers were promised in the UK to be only used regarding terrorists. Three bankers from Greenwich Nat West saw an opportunity for Enron regarding Nat West Holdings in Enron investments which they explained to the Enron's chief financial officer. After a period of time the Enron chief financial officer acted upon that advice and brought the three into the financially lucrative transaction.

Enron's reputation has shattered with considerable criticism regarding how it conducted its affair.

The whole affair became one of law. All witnesses, reference materials, and information was in the UK. The USA would succeed in having the three extradited despite earlier assurances regarding terrorists being the target. At the same time, all relevant defending witnesses and information were in Britain, so not the USA. Further, these witnesses being within the financial world, felt it more expedient to remain there, in Britain. Some report they were contacted to this effect. The accused could not persuade the many potential witnesses on their behalf to come to the USA to testify. A frequent reason given was US agents' aggressive activities. One suicide was blamed on FBI pressure by his family in the USA. The accused three had to raise considerable funds for their defence with limited travel permitted. They received work permits for one year. They could only meet collectively with lawyers present. *The Daily Telegraph* had taken up their case and in the British Parliament the inequality and use of the revised Extradition Process was challenged by Nick Clegg.

The three were convicted with no consideration of their two years of pre-conviction confinement. They were separated and sent to different prisons. They were only able to return to Britain, where all aspects of the so called crime had taken place, by signing an admission of guilt. Upon arriving in Britain they were again close to their friends and families. How many rights were disregarded ..... and the rest! It will remain a matter of debate if this was fair and just, but seemingly it was legal.

CHAPTER 20:

SOCIETY and EDUCATION

Parents have both a right and responsibility to protect and care for their children with the administration of clear and fair proportionate discipline.

Society

1. *Civil society-* Has laws and is protected, a cul de sac where these are internal.

2. *Enterprise society-* The state resources all, so used for social outcome. Ranging from democracy to totalitarian.

3. *Connected Society* of respect with community links - central liberties serve the public well-being.

Ref. Michael Oakshott- politicophilosopher

Society is similar to a functioning living body which is composed of many interactive parts. These vary in size and complexity. Society is a social ecology of interpersonal activities meeting needs. As with the brain, it is built from almost imperceptible structures in a conglomeration of interrelating 'patterns' - some of which extend beyond the main 'structure'. They operate in a fine balance within an environment we may call the body. Upset the balance and environment sufficiently, and they die.

How we 'read' and respond to situations depends upon a collection of memories, sights, sounds, and emotions brought together to form our belief patterns and our reality. What existed and exists for us leads to what we choose to do: our responses. Reading a book uses the established sensory skill of sight supported by memory and is achieved through a building process. Written words are stored sounds in a pictorial form and perform similarly as hearing through recognition. Our life is a single long story full of remembered changes caused by new influences interacting with previous ones, which are probably almost forgotten. The sensory information enhances a building process with relevant external feedback which supports or modifies the structure. This building process uses similar inherent skills to initiate speech. Society hears and sees; speaks and feels. It recognizes tone, colour value, and contrast along with many other influences and additions. Society is affected by how its 'mind' is directed to a recognition of priorities, processes, causes, and effects. Responsibilities are the culmination of a vast collection of conditions and interwoven experiences which have coalesced over time. Imagine what all the insignificantly small bubbles of a dissolving Vitamin C effervescent tablet would sound like if all were brought together at one moment to form a single sound. The codes developed within the Social Family seem to be similar with each contribution affecting the final outcome: that beating of Lorenz's butterfly's wing (Chaos Theory) in which some small occurrence can lead to a significant change or consequence. We are certainly seeing the outcome of Toffler's 'Throw-away Society' in *The Third Wave* and *Future Shock*.

Choices and the actions of each part or structure, through its responses, demonstrate the nature and (where relevant) the mind of the beast. How our Social Family operates, the choices it takes, and the directions it chooses show the makeup of its interactive population. What the empowered are most concerned about they will act upon to provide the energy and resources needed to achieve their goals. If its goal is a just and kindly society, then that will be what it probably will become - assuming the self-discipline and resolve are in place already. As Greg Mordistone pointed out, we 'Fight through fear, build through hope'. The outcome is a product of the peoples' will or lack of it. To construct or build physically, socially, or mentally takes time, effort, and vision. The concept of POSITIVE CONSTRUCTION will do that. For example, what children experience and learn from schooling society becomes decision's data, goals, and outcomes.

Political precedent need not dictate the future. There might well be a better democratic alternative to having a Prime Minister or President who personally suffers so much worry and responsibility. One could be excused for wondering about the mental state of anyone seeking such a position. One wonders what in their background led them to wish upon themselves so much pressure and misery. Maybe the advantages after the job has been passed onto another make it all worthwhile. It seems unlikely that they believe they will be able to achieve most of their goals with so many other powers acting against them. A clinical unfeeling data collecting machine might enable fuller interrogation and provision of people's actual wants and needs regionally. Next the machine may be given powers to enable it to act on its emotionless findings following its own analysis of the data collected. Be careful what you wish for!

Fortunately there are many who think beyond now. These natural planners are both positive and creative. Their mind-sets lead to activism in the Social Family, which in turn can lead to contention, but they press on. There is concern but also a resolve. What to do socially regarding those people at risk? Clearly within a fully responsible and responsive society there would be far fewer risks and associated costs to concern one since obligations and Responsibilities are respected: a product of mind. However, we are not yet that enlightened nor caring. Those at risk include the hungry, the blind, the deaf, the elderly, the sick, orphans, the unemployed, the shift workers, the pedestrians, the handicapped, the very young, those who are unhappy at school, and the overworked. This is our world and it needs to be made better. Happiness leads to better health, while unhappiness leads to sickness, depression, dependence, and or exploitation. Further, realistically knowing our limitations is helpful. We need to be prepared to control what we can sensitively, to do it well, and to leave the rest to the future and planning. We should be happy with doing our best: simply just doing what we can. The worship of extremism is unhealthy both in work and exercise: few can fully survive its 'side effects'. We need to appreciate that what is preventable and what is harmful must be avoided both individually and socially, which includes unrealistic ambition whether this be personal or from our peers, spouse, or parents. That culture of blame needs to go. The question of Equal Opportunities is difficult except in clear situations of unsuitability for the task: though these are hard to find. Wishing for a family member to participate in one's life's work is also completely understandable. It seem unreasonable to view it as wrong, as nepotism, or as racism. One may joke that in the 'mafias' this is common practice, but it does not lead to their being sued! Litigation is another tool of the strong and wealthy to be used against the weak, but with the proper knowledge it can also be used to protect the weak against any uncaring strong and wealthy.

The Other Education: A Sampling

Every child should be able to spend a long period of time of secure innocence enabling their minds and bodies to develop 'gently'. This should be called a Right. Child soldiers, child brides, rape, prostitution, and human sacrifice are just a sample of the horrors some children have to find a way to survive. Children are exploited as 'slave labour', they are repeatedly beaten and terrified. All of this is a form of sad education in the brutalities of existence. Westerners tend to have a kinder start in life, but there are too many exceptions even when incarcerated in some school with the chronic problem of antisocial deviants: an emasculated system which provides little chance of protection or escape for some. Still, most Western children do not have to fear as others do, that is unless they have access to endangering technologies. Further learning and too early experimenting with 'those facts of life' can result in repulsion or confusion with all the misunderstanding, mental intrusion, exploitation, and por-nography which can leave its mark for years or for life due to confusion, a foolish moment, or another's hatred. No child needs a cell phone for daily life or schooling. The potential dangers are just not worth the risk. A parent who gives their young child a small sip of an alcoholic drink could find them-selves experiencing the full power of the law. To say ,"no you are too young for alcohol" could immediately prepare this drinking of alcohol as a "right-of-passage" since the prospect of drinking alcohol has potentially become a symbol of 'being old enough', a symbol of maturity through use of those words. It is arguably better to taste a nip of rough rye and be put off the stuff for life. The cell phone lasts and grows in its potential intrusions, abuses, and new dangers for children, yet children are given cell phones by their parents. We do not need to tell them how to be 'bad', but need rather through example and other's directions to learn how to be good. It would be encouraging to see more youngsters and adults without the cell phone seemingly attached to their ears, fingers, and eyes.

Role and Some Role Model Implications

Barbara Taylor, *The Last Asylum: A Memoir Of Madness In Our Time.* Penguin. Book, London, UK.

RESPECT is a valued behavioural outcome of experience embraced by reason, and respect is seen in others. Since it is valued, this respect often leads to imitation which is why socially agreed upon good role models are so productive. Role models are an educational instrument, for better or worse, and are therefore socially significant. Positive roles require positive support. Role play can be an investment in emotion. From what has been written before, the importance of change and progress is agreed, I trust. If the role model is bad, it will prove to be harmful and socially negative. Such role models need to be countered or made unavailable, especially to the impressionable young. As these negative influences appear, full use of social powers should be deployed to limit their harm. There are many changers of the world who have benefited huge numbers of others and thus our way of life (REF: Page 150). Respect unifies people, whereas the danger of legalistic rights is that they may also be used as a tool to gain advancement and therefore divide. Adopt, yes; adapt, yes, probably; but most of all ..... improve.

We learn from example, from the role models we admire and try to emulate. We also learn otherwise and negatively from those we distrust and fear. The outcome and value of gender roles can be a contentious issue, but it is important to sort this out for ourselves. Roles `pass on preconceptions of behaviour,` which are preferably beneficial and good. 1998 Gender Neutral Values Concept says `Let them grow free`, but how free? We all need to see what outcomes result, how positive it is or conversely if negative. Freedom can become a two edged sword. How far this freedom should usefully go and with what consequences will continue to be debated: it depends upon the qualities of what is gained or lost. If we accept that men can be gynecologists and nurses and that women can be soldiers and heavy truck drivers in this time of our Queen, Women Prime Ministers, women company directors, and soon possibly a President of the USA., then very few boundaries can be logically defended.

In Sweden, I understand, this focus on the neutral is to be found in rights, obligations, and even in toy design and selection. The word HEN is used to mean both him and her, a sort of he/she.

So, what traditional role models are relevant as a function of "good"? Hopefully aspects of character and morality are now foremost. This extension has greater potential for teaching opportunities rather than teaching failures. Improved self-confidence should be one valid outcome. Now to move onto a new focus on prejudice and introvert and extrovert personalities.

There is an alarming statistic of increased depression among the young. It could usefully be researched whether such unhappy victims of their own thinking would be less unhappy with a simpler system of clear role models. Such clarity may result in their being less victims of distress due to emotionally coping better through meeting more easily identified skill sets and behavioural patterns. No single system is good for all. As for early sex education, if some of the media could control themselves and get back into their pants and stay there, then there would be less need and cause for concern. Computers in children's bedrooms are ill-advised: better in the centre of the house where everyone continually passes by. Advertisements and computer games are just two culprits of corruption, another is irresponsible government and educational agencies which instead of attacking and controlling the providers of mind pollution try to salve their consciences with unsuccessful attempts to 'prepare' children for an ever worsening situation. Improve the situation by removing it. Don't try to prepare them like celebration turkeys. Get rid of the problem: do what you are paid for, take action ….. and succeed!

House Team System

Breadth of education could be usefully broadened to better enable so very many different pupil-student potentials. I was fortunate to start school at 8:30 AM with a teacher supervising outside play. At 9:00 AM we had a religious assembly with examples of socially secure people benefitting their society. They came from different races, faiths, economic groups, and nations. Some were in industry, some the arts, some were religious, some were children, and so on. Our schooling continued until just after 4:00 PM. when we could stay for tea and homework, drama, clubs, musical instrument classes, and various sports training. We left school at 6:00 PM. Students were divided into four teams called

Houses. These teams competed in several sports; for school work results; for acts of kindness, good conduct, and care; in music competitions; and in debating. Points were won which went towards the House Team total for the end of year's Best House Award. Houses took it in turns cleaning the play area and clearing the lunch area following hot meals which all attended, even the teachers with one at the end of each table. They could be very funny: we had a good time. Pupils had turns sitting with the Principal during meals and ideas were exchanged. We had afternoon games twice a week, and when we were older there was Saturday Morning School. Special work awards and certificates were awarded periodically. Each class planned and produced one morning assembly each semester. There was a school play for three nights at Christmas, a carol service, and an all school Art Show. Good House Team sports players or chess players were recruited for the school teams - Junior or Senior - who played many matches against other schools. We had computers, a whiteboard, pottery, and extensive ART (including History of Western Art) and Music with lessons twice weekly. The annual teacher show was a highlight. Comparative Religion was studied by all. Yes, I was indeed fortunate.

ARTS

Arts help develop empathy, creativity, idea-transferral, and adaptability with the bonus of deepening thought. Reflection is central to the Arts which are associated with an appreciation of skills and experimentation. Confidence is boosted as techniques and skills are mastered. Realistic feedback from teachers is valued, being genuine, not excessive, and more personal.

There is a strong case for separate health and education bodies with total financial control of these areas. They need to extend beyond party politics with their swings and round-abouts of policy. Such separate bodies could be truly committed to following their own published plans in a consistent manner over many well-planned years - uninterrupted by municipal, provincial, federal, national, or parliamentary elections and electioneering. The same could easily be said of environmental questions.

Ecological studies have taught and demonstrated that it is indeed necessary to appreciate how nature and we are one. To separate ourselves from nature is the road to disaster. Survival relies upon a balance within the "Web of Life". Is education any different? Society being based upon coopera-tion is "A Web of Shared Interpersonal Experience". Since we interact to continue our daily existence, what one does has an effect upon the others. Collectively our actions add up to a pattern of behaviours which promote our survival or oth-erwise. Our children grow into these patterns and become a part of them, and so learning matters hugely. Awareness and understanding arrive in moments of inspiration, our very personal linking of knowledge-units with sensory discov-ery or otherwise: knowledge awakened, passed on, thereby taught by others. This implies a caught not taught - better knowing which comes from within - as a recognition process, an experience, a momentary opening of "trap-doors of the mind", and a fitting together of jigsaw puzzle pieces suc-cessfully. This learning is primarily developed in the home experience, in a 'family' context. Its manner will affect future learning because of and as a result of our interpretation of that learning. This is the foundation of the knowledge-building process but it also organically grows within the new awareness structures. The home environment is therefore key to future mental and interpersonal social development and manner of response.

There follows a question as to what each individual NEEDS to obtain from an education system and why. Each of us has been born without our asking. Each lives because that is what we do for a time. Each has an emotional structure which directly relates to likes and dislikes, and these are directly a result of experiences. Unhappy experiences result in unhappy people and unhappiness. Unhappiness breeds potential forces of destruction. Destruction results in more unhappiness. With so much unhappiness in this world one could question the value of life and living, as some despairing souls do. It is reasonable to conclude that we live to be happy. In that context is laughter, contentment, friendships, good memories, food, and comfortable shelter. With all these in place, one assumes that safety has been taken care of and good health is the usual state. Since there are many of us we need to promote general comradeship, happiness, and wellbeing. It becomes the Responsibility of every person within the Social Family to accept full responsibility for their actions. In none of this can be seen that we have to work in order to live, but there is a responsibility to each other and so work can be a constructive and fulfilling experience. Yes, work can be and often is enjoyed. Bringing division into the workplace is an attack upon our happiness. Since we live and wish to be happy, any division and conflict are wrong: a direct attack upon our wellbeing. Some organizations and people only 'thrive' because of the divisions and conflict they invent, find, or promote. We have a responsibility to each other to work for collective wellbeing and happiness. The workplace is rather like a well of water. The well becomes a part of survival. What we can all do without is the well-poisoner. Unfortunately, we have probably all met examples of well-poisoners at work. Frequently these lessened people justify their actions through self-delusionary processes of thought. Some honestly and sadly believe that it is to the benefit of their colleagues for discontent and upset to be injected, maybe in the name of Rights or rather their

interpretation of Rights. The fact that discord was not originally there shows the point. There are so many better routes
than divisions and so many things more important than
money. In our monetarist worlds we need enough money to
provide the essentials first, hopefully with enough left for a
few indulgences. Living is essential and work comes later as a
means to living well: work is the servant of life. We therefore
have a responsibility to each other to facilitate the conditions
which have the best chance to promote a good life filled with
happiness and kindness.

Education, with the educational experience, figures here
yet again. Social development should build both a respect
and sensitivity for each other as well as our being exposed
to and appreciating 'things' of quality, which make the 'fuller
person'. Things of quality may include written work, thought
processes, games, discoveries in the Arts, and scientific
processes. Raw Rights do not fit well a school room of reasonable free debate. Forty years of teaching showed clearly
that mutual respect, friendship, fair balanced discipline,
good humour, and acceptance of Responsibilities are crucial
there. Further, how strange that we believe in the values of
one-to-one learning, only to cram as many youngsters as
we can into an oversized building complex like 'schooling
factories'! Also, size is not so beautiful, for example, when
a classroom or entire school is out of date and the upgrade
will probably be very expensive. Huge masses of resources
are thrown at the wrong places. When children are learning
how to be 'social', the last thing they need is to be swamped
by a mass of other children which makes the whole task self-
defeating for most and crowd control for the teacher. There
is a certain abuse of the child's Human Rights or right to
be human in the vast and often spiteful 'factory schools'. Get
the number thing right! Thirty to forty pupils in one class is
totally unacceptable and a crippling burden on the teacher.
Downsize schools to mentally upsize kids! Mere 'child units'

are pushed through a process irrespective of any pressing personal needs. The essential needs of the individual are under-resourced when over-crowded. New form professionals have been created to work in the 'factory school': only possible to resource due to the herding principle for the mass of human stock there. These new professionals are too often swamped and unable to do what they wish. They are unable to do what is needed by and for some of the individuals in their care - Loco Parentis! Some even add to the torture of an unfortunate child who has learned to expect daily grief, due to shyness, for example. Sometimes suicide is the only perceived way out due to the bullying from other children and occasionally the very staff themselves. If children could justly sue their schools and the bullies, I wonder what the outcome would be. For the unhappy there is seemingly no such resolution to their problem. All this is further complicated through oversized and unreasonable administration demands which are mainly caused by the size problems. This results in too much administrative paperwork and not enough meaningful class paperwork; classes and teachers out of control due to the factory school size, indiscipline, and classroom number problems. Social and medical professional findings and 'statementing' being ignored; adequate specialist structures or provisions neglected and difficult children sent out of class, electing to roam at will, or being placed in isolation rooms with little 'stimulation'. This dumping of children is an offence against decency, but the teachers have too few options or powers. Successive governments and administrators are no better than each individual. Remember that hollow "Education, Education, Education"! Their primary purpose within a democratic society is to serve the needs of the learner-individual. By so doing the teacher is attempting to enable a sound or even better quality of life for that child. The parents' obligation is to prepare their children for school and a cooperative acceptance of a disciplined organised world. Administrators choose their work as carers and servants and should not be allowed to change that role into something else. They use our effort, work, and money for the good of the 'Social Family'. The Social Family is the sum of its members. The politician and administrator is of that 'Social Family' and is not an emperor, king, or queen. They are not there to get wealthy, or rather shouldn't be so. Adult over-accumulation of wealth is a product of either forming a defence against the world due to insecurity or of promoting a greatly beneficial idea. Wealth achieved needs to be a proper reward from us all (small contributions collectively do add up to a huge outcome). A producer of something which maintains and improves the wellbeing and happiness of the 'Social Family' deserves no less. Sometimes termed feeding from the money-pot, the activity of a social parasite operates through a form of legal theft. Such activity is definitely contrary to a value of Responsibilities towards the 'Social Family'.

With sufficient funding, due care, and 'due diligence', people with special needs, from young to old, could be properly provided for. Some people need special provisions because of their mental state, hyper emotional volatility, or deep depression. This is a social responsibility. What some would call segregation others would call time apart, or special conditions to meet special needs. Barbara Taylor, in *The Last Asylum: A Memoir Of Madness In Our Time*, wrote about her personal experiences as an inmate of Friern Hospital for the mentally ill, Colney Hatch, Barnet, London, UK. Taylor is a supporter of the humane asylum system from firsthand experience.

With so much of our national resources and wealth being used for education it seems impossible that so many children appear to be learning less, are increasingly apathetic, are less socially aware or socially caring, and are more frequently out of control irrespective of the huge resources which have been created for them. There are also very many great and caring kids out there who work at and achieve amazing results.

These children prove to be honest and polite. Dedication in a number of teachers needs to be considerably greater to overcome the misery for many of their daily experience and lives; those interest groups referred to as School Clubs are run by generous time-giving and caring volunteer teachers - but these are sadly becoming fewer and fewer. Jamie Oliver (UK Chef, author, and TV Star) researched and showed that many school canteens were providing children with poor quality food which others have proved to negatively influence child stamina, performance, and conduct. On top of that, most children set off for home long before working parents can be there to receive them. Those bussing from the furthest distance often are first collected and last dropped off. These children have an even longer day with more time being restrained by their environments. Too often some arrive home before their parents finish work so requiring others to be there to meet them. Any consequential behavioral changes appear unstudied so unknown. These situations are unacceptable.

Scholarly articles for poor nutrition in schools (Google)

The role of schools in obesity prevention - *Kaphingst* - Cited by 435

Fast food: Oppression through poor nutrition - *Freeman* - Cited by 52

intake and risk factors for poor diet quality for children... - *Veugelers* - Cited by 110

The bus is the most exhausting part of school | Penelope Trunk. *education.penelopetrunk.com/.../t*Jan 14, 2013 - It's too long – for anyone. Not just kids. The average commute for adults is 25 minutes. The average school bus ride is longer than that. (Research shows that after 10 miles adult health is being affected. Penelope lives on a farm and decided to home school her son: others are unable to make this choice.

'Time-out Cards' were issued in some UK state schools following a parent's request since they 'fear' their child was suffering from classroom stress. By showing the card, a child could leave the room unaccompanied. This enables that child to wander out of class on a whim and often results in other classes being disrupted. This operates in Canada too. The staff member/class teacher seems to have no control over this practice. Teachers and other staff are insulted, sworn at, abused, pushed, and ignored. This is not a good socializing educational experience. One also wonders how and why teachers choose to stay put and take it. The fact is that many expensively trained teachers do not: they leave the profession. Again one could enquire what this has to do with Rights .... It certainly has lots to do with Responsibilities.

The cruelty of a single educational system filled with far too many pupils being pushed into the schools and overcrowded classrooms generates a stressful environment for many. This causes a multiplicity of insecurities while enabling bullies of all sorts to flourish unhindered. The problems generated for staff and pupils cannot be overemphasized. That these 'factory schools' are inherently wrong for many children is apparent: the lucky ones get homeschooling instead. Adolescent reaction is not just hormonal. Look into these mammoth establishments: they are controlled by people who don't even know all their staff - let alone the pupils. The staff don't know all of their colleagues. The exchange of feedback information is poor. Personal teacher time with each pupil is limited. The subject specialist teacher system provides a focused adult role model, subject specialization, and breadth with interesting variety in teaching techniques being experienced. Break-time interaction is often lost to staff as is an in-school group lunchtime period. With school lunches no longer provided, children walk the streets unattended and often buy junk food at stores. Student work is increasingly marked by computer, if at all, and so results are over-simplistic and lacking in advice and extension of ideas. Monitoring learning-progress with supportive data is increasingly no longer the job of the teacher who provides the lesson plans and direction of experience for each individual. Further, school policy on providing full, factual, unadjusted information regarding each student's TOTAL output and quality of work urgently requires scrutiny. One suspects some school inspectors exercise their own political agenda, lack sufficient teaching experience, and create negative pressure and outcomes: especially in England. A school's population can be greater than many villages with all that entails and without the age balance. Many children are uprooted every day, crammed into the dreaded buses, and arrive at an establishment to be poured into an educational block. Then they have their day extended due to travel time, so actual 'learning time' is reduced. Like some old Communist Russian shoe manufacturers, only left shoes are repeatedly produced - this is missed by quality control and remains uncorrected. The need for real choice and freedom is not practical due to the unit size generating the problem, while the learning progress is dominated by the creation of an expendable workforce for ever growing corporations rather than an intellectual force willing and wishing to work with job security.

Different children learn in different ways. How can this be adequately addressed by the use of a single class teacher all day long for whom some will not have or feel any affinity? And what happens at the end of the year? They all have to get used to a new adult's funny ways and preferences: better the variety of specialist subject teachers providing varied interaction, interpersonal relationships, and a broader choice of role models with deeper subject content understanding. What is more, changing classes gives the teacher a break and a broader experience and role.

Smaller schools in which all the pupils are known by all the staff are more conducive to a family environment and are less like an impersonal factory. Problems can be nipped in the bud and praise with other forms of encouragement more frequently and meaningfully applied. Smaller is beautiful, kinder, and more educationally efficient. Technical expensive equipment is nice but not essential; additionally, it is probably useless without the student being focused due to behavioural distractions. Good teachers are happy teachers in the right conditions. They respond to the potential opportunities and novelty of equipment and other resource changes. Using well these additions promotes valuable changes in students' educational experiences. In the right setting with business-like conditions teachers are happier, well-valued, confident, and imaginative and this passes on to the students. What a joy is the teacher with a good sense of humour and good 'class control' of their children. Such teachers are a delight to see and listen to, as is their laughter. No wonder that a total of 15 children in such a class all learn to read, write, do maths, belong to school clubs (real ones, that is), and become fulfilled and fulfilling adults. Their teachers also benefit much, as they deserve. After all, our teachers are the vital link between the Social Family and the small units of which it is composed. Quality teaching through gifted teachers is essential: forget the inspectors who too often are escapees from the chaos of too many in classrooms. One can't really blame them. Too few can take such daily abuse as the pupils fight back against their daily inhuman incarceration and emotional incineration.

Disruption

1.Leaving compulsory education without qualifications can easily result in little work-choice, too low pay, multiple jobs, scrounging or crime.

2. *To be cool within a culture of fear and intimidation is to be bad.*

3. *Joining a gang provides identity, protection, and opportunity within a small group.*

Many schools have become too vast to be socially and educationally efficient and positively effective for far too many youngsters. Crowd control was never good education. Maintaining a general truce between pupils and adults is not a way to promote respect and prove appropriate effectiveness. Adding parent councils in conflict with teacher aims and experience was never the way to achieve constructive co-operation. Let the blacksmith pound and shape the metal; let the chemist manipulate chemicals; let the factory worker complete those tasks; and let the teachers administer their schools. However, any establishment must be able to achieve its aims. It may be suggested that if these cannot be achieved DESPITE the adopted advised forms of organization, then there is a hidden agenda somewhere. It could be a political agenda or one relating to the products and labour needs of several mega-corporations and companies. There is no possible reason why a chef with vision, amongst others, should seriously choose to be called into question regarding the nutritional value of school or hospital meals. That educationalists working with 'their client students' see faults and weaknesses in the system is a real warning. Downsizing many of our school class sizes to provide a manageable and successful `product` outcome should be a matter of national priority. Proper socialization with planned development of co-operative self-controlled pupils should be first achieved while they are small in infant and primary schools where it is simpler to achieve and reinforce this positive behaviour. The key values and Responsibilities of students should be in place, not knowledge of sexual activities and difference of sexual orientation. The priority should be respect for each other with an open and understanding outlook, not these other extreme early instructions at the infant level. It is also suggested here that if we did not have such dehumanizing-sized schools, built for crowded isolation, all would benefit: the community, the staff, the child, and our future. Huge schools are ones in which the staff don`t know all their colleagues, office staff have little parent contact, and Head Teachers (hopefully first chosen for their exemplary teaching) are lost as teachers in the classroom to concentrate on dead papers, forms, administration, and career prospects. One could wonder if many principals work hard to ensure they can get out of the classroom to the comparative peace and safety of Senior Administration. One cannot be an interacting part of the school by remaining aloof and outside the working body: it is unfair on the pupils and possibly encourages negligence. Certainly for most the position is contact free of students, as they generally are 'protected' from actually having to teach in class due to the administrative demands of 'factory schools'. Student competence, confidence, and social development need to matter more than sticking out a job for its healthcare, days off, longer holidays, and pension: all possibly viewed as compensation for an unrewarding form of employment. Fortunately there continues to be for a time more exemplary teachers whose dedication and concern for their pupils is without question.

Back for the Future

In the past, social standards were promoted and Responsibilities were exemplified with the group `bonding` at daily assemblies. There were exemplar awards, visiting speakers, and stories from positive people who were all good examples of role models. School teams, house competitions, inter-school competitions, and open field sport permitted all to play a constructive part while enabling the able in wide and varied activities to shine. These activities helped create confidence, provided good pupil role models, and promoted co-operative activities. It all worked so well, so why change it! If ain`t broke, don`t fix it! And what about those great clubs and societies started by teachers who had special interests and gifts beyond the classroom such as photography, chess, public speaking, folk music, computer skills, electronics, geology, and so on and on and on: goodwill well displayed. Smaller schools were beautiful. We could afford them by the re-establishment of a proper level of concern regarding the child's position and feelings, also a rethink and appreciation of our obligations and Responsibilities, with a resolve to encourage teacher personal initiative while clearly valuing the same. The temporary unemployed and vulnerable justify support, but the idle do not. Remove all support and rewards from the ASOCIAL PARASITES with their 'street cred' for not joining our present work-ethic society. These people have learned how to go 'pimping' off others' work: they waste valuable resources which can and should be used better. How can anyone justify the reduction of care, special activities and support of the ill, handicapped or elderly and still pay vast amounts to those happily finding ways of exploiting our Social Family? All this despite their mostly having been educated in the current system! What went wrong, and how? Only with the necessary support and funding in place will those with special problems be better off having been returned to the community. People at risk need and generally appreciate a calm, protective, but well-disciplined environment within the mainstream: probably this is also true of and for most. You cannot make someone learn, but you can create the conditions and suitable environment where learning is viewed as a worthwhile end result.

Teaching Aids and System Base Aids

No constructive social and educational system will work constructively without cooperative "proper" respect and self-discipline of parent, pupil/client, and staff. There seems little in life that does not require some form of discipline, respect, and accepting sensitized forms of agreed upon compromise.

<u>Point 1.</u> The starting point is accepting the fact that The Social Basics <u>need to be</u> taught at the family level first as a parental Responsibility. Consequently funding, help, and support are needed at this level.

Social Basics: sharing and promoting acceptance that there is value regarding ability and benefits to being positive; encouraging positive emotional awareness; promoting REALISTIC confidence, understanding the benefits of deferring gratification; understanding the meaning of sensibility and the practice of self-discipline; encouraging emotional and reasoned respect for others; practicing social honesty; empowering recognition of the real, personal realism, and honesty; explaining and pro-moting objectivity; clarifying the personal implications of subjective; and promoting awareness and acceptance of responsibility with a rejection of apathy. Please do not blame the teachers for the absence of Social Basics: their calling is to build on basics and reinforce present 'stan-dards' due to home upbringing, to extend existing aware-ness, factual knowledge, and effective thought processes: all value added. The term Value Added is the term used in education to label in school and of school activities which provide extra learning advantages, possibly social, and so value has been added to the educational experience. It generally relates to additional factors or activities which are regularly put in place to benefit the student experi-ence. If all teachers have to do this with undisciplined 'mud', then there is little hope of succeeding. Firm and clear behavioural patterns are demanded, which could be termed social self-discipline. The family is the first society in which a child experiences life. These *protosocieties*, being the infant's beginning of social membership, differ as will the parenting, which can be a great advantage in producing interest and constructive variety. However, when it is chaotic, undisciplined, or of an aggressive form, every single aspect of future development will be affected and generally not for the better.

Point 2. The child is responsible for his or her actions and needs to recognize this. Children exercise choice. Choice expectations relate to age developmental levels.

Point 3. Schools and 'schooling' are an extension of the family and are supportive and encouraging of both social and personal development. The family needs our support with clear aims and objectives to *work* with. Both schools and the family consider advice and exemplars where proven beneficial.

Point 4. Society will encourage both school and home in their collective Responsibilities by providing security, clear child demands, and duties with protection, encouragement, and support.

Point 5. Authorities and governments accept that they act on behalf of the well-being of its social membership and that of all society. Processes of advising, financing, education, health, support, maintenance of discipline, and law are their responsibility with their duty of care and governance.

Point 6. Each individual needs to learn and accept his or her place as a law-abiding and contributing member of the Social Family with necessary and relevant personal Responsibilities.

Assuming these points are in place, the schooling experience will be successful. Teaching, both developmental and learning, will be effective, for nothing succeeds like success. Respect and self-discipline, to name two socially useful conventions, enable programs like the rewarding success of 'Numicon', the highly productive 'Breakthrough to Literacy', the much enjoyed 'Oxford Reading Tree', and the now well-documented successes of 'THRASS' to be as effective as they certainly can. There should be no excuse for poor literacy and numeracy emanating from our schools. With regard to the general science course produced and promoted by Nuffield Foundation, any science teacher seriously following it would commend the enthusiasm and enjoyment it generates in pupils through an extensive scientific experience and knowledge outcome.

We all need to feel empowered through our knowledge and experience and enabled through a consequential energetic will. In this way we become creative, co-operative, and sustainable while developing a will for civic pride achieved through the valued Social Family: that elusive "WIN WIN" Covey position.

Life is Built on Memories

Wrong is understood through facial expression, voice tone, gesture, posture, accumulated sense-memory, and association. Wrong memories or wrong association when perpetuated clearly generate 'wrongness'. Learned 'inaccuracies of behaviour' or in work processes through omission or 'coincidence-failure' relate also to lack of relevant guidance experience (scaffolding) which is needed to both positively and accurately inform learning. Emotionally premature presentation of information causes insecurity. Occurrences outside experience can result in this with regard to breadth and understanding and can too easily produce wrong learning with rejection, corrupted understanding, and emotional turmoil. Further rejection or exponentially broadening networks of wrong processing of thought then ensue. These confused beliefs with more rejection produce violent or irrational responses, fixations, and partial inability to constructively function. For these reasons alone it would be better to revisit various approaches including political correctness by teaching 'all they have to know' in time to 'protect' them from going beyond experience. Sadly they can no longer choose regarding early sex education or learning about brutality exemplified by the Nazi attack upon Germans, Jews, Gypsies, Freemasons, Jehovah Witnesses, and so many others. There are few emotionally mature moments to open the "trap door" of understanding the workings of a mind. Get the moment wrong, and both balanced awareness and awakening are lost.

When questioning if there is a social and civic responsibility to educate children or if it is their Right results: outcome verifies the argument. An educated person can achieve more and become personally fulfilled in consequence. Education is a formalization of extending awareness. This is true of the good woodsman, mechanic, and farmer. If extending awareness is accepted as factually probable and is believed to be beneficial to all, it is an obligation of the wealthy to help in this mission. The Wealthy Western World helping with African Focused Aid through sponsored education is one example of accepting this mission. ISIS disagrees. The inter-tribal horrors of the Rwandan tragedy were and still are a human trauma. One wonders if some form of education could have helped avoid that tragedy. These images of evil affecting the minds of adults and growing children build upon earlier experiences with its dehumanizing anger, fear, hate, and resulting insanities. The whole business of nurturing our children, all children, leads to an inevitable conclusion that if driving a car requires training, an exam, and a licence, then possibly a review of how the Social Family may help prospective parents in their task is implied. A humorous mental picture of training required before a "child creation permit" is awarded springs to mind, but this is a valid message. The final years of schooling could include this parenting education to the advantage of a future filled with less 'frazzled' parents: the same could be said of citizen information and purposeful rewarding experiences. A better and fulfilling future for all should be the outcome of education.

What activities, unlike the movement of a falling stone, constitute life? Listening and having feelings comprise living. Trusting is social enrichment. This eases us regarding others: we cannot know, think, or do everything. Thinking and responding empower our lives. Consequently, actions and activity are the essence of experiencing and are the road to achieve a fulfilling life. Wanting and wishing are natural products of the intellect. These 'drives' can lead to life-changes following planning and projecting the probable outcome of taking action. Outcomes may not meet expectations, but there is a need to try. Sometimes this driving need leads to experiencing 'failure'. With a constructive view of failure, thanks to a security built through our early learning process, we can benefit greatly from so-called failure or learning opportunity. Since initiatives advance society, demonstrating initiative needs to be respected and constructively encouraged despite outcome; for INITIATIVE is having the courage and energy to take an optimistic step into the unknown with an expectation of benefit. Democracy is an attempt to enable all group members to take their own responsibility while informing others of a general agreement. Learning to fail and constructively move on is an important skill. We all 'fail' sometimes. Constructive objectivity is needed; it is a skill. We all make mistakes, but experience and maturity, with common sense, are acquired and add to an effective life through such learning.

Many schools work to encourage and promote leadership skills. Those can be well achieved in team games, school clubs, Prefect systems, student bodies, and through House/Pupil team competitions. Also, the importance of participating positively is welcomed irrespective of skill levels. However, the format and tradition need to be put in place. Our young need to learn how to organize, to develop awareness and valuing of 'people skills', and to build positive and constructive groups with self-respect. Schools, like the family, mean personal connection. They are 'community' where it is right and proper to expect and offer mutual support. Individuality, which can be one person's gift to the 'whole group', needs to be respected. It is a constructive trait springing from a personal awareness: respecting individuality which is reflecting a personality can prove mutually beneficial. The fact of "individuality" is important and relevant to personal development for others also, as it can lead the way. In the field of special education individuality can be the making for a better life chance. Extended families with broader interactions or the closer focused and far smaller numbered nuclear family both set the stage for social and emotional development. Members enjoy their mutual belonging, or if isolated can find warmth and contact in a group.

Yet there is a fear that we are choosing to develop into a more isolated people preferring an existence with headphones, computer games with computer tablets, and distanced communication via cell phones being permitted to dominate people's waking hours. The human spirit may yet rebel. For some reason we seem to be increasingly distancing ourselves from each other. Currently when we have to come together it seems to be more collision-like despite a mutual dependence upon people's avoidance: this is also adding to the dislocation of the Social Family with members feeling a growing isolation in a crowd. Loneliness is within the mind and may well be caused by insecurities leading to contact avoided. Media-fed insecurities lead to isolationism be this via diversionary activities, portraying violence, or other.

Efficient language-use is an enabling skill. That free-flowing meaning focused into spoken and written language are crucial tools of communication is a no-brainer: each is just one of several forms of communication which assist in confidence building. Banter, leg pulling, and games of the confident with discussion are personally enjoyable. Languages use varies from situation to situation in which demands and provisions also vary. In each of a variety of situations one form of language will be more "Fit for Task" than another. The use of wrong language upsets the success of communication and thus loosens shared understanding with lost emotional ease in both the formal and informal modes: the reverse is not so accommodating.

The use and study of grammar, précis, literature, structure, and inference, for example, will enable more focused and appropriate language use. Grammar is the whetstone for the blade of intent and meaning. With clear meaning there is little room for misinterpretation and so misunderstandings are avoidable. With effective language use there is a greater probability of peace, calm, and happiness for society. Through a better understanding this enables a freer acceptance of obligations and fulfillment of Responsibilities by the community. However, reasons for disagreement may be more constructively shown as well. When disagreement occurs, clarity is the friend of discussion.

SIMPLIFIED CATEGORIES OF NEEDS: <u>for you to add</u>

Personal needs:_____

Social needs: _____

Administrative and Governmental needs: _____

Language Dictates

Teaching of formal English, arguably for a few, enables the individual to think and express thoughts more broadly, efficiently, and in greater depth. I believe this is true for all. Informal forms of language also have strengths, not least of group identity, but language and vocabulary are firstly tools of interpersonal communication and thought extension. A smile can be a welcome and a warning depending upon what is occurring. The arrival of a loved family member brings a different smile to the face from that of the prevailing fighter just before the final winning blow. Likewise tears can be of sorrow, relief, and joy. These semiotics are full of power and memories. They are linked to the past, thereby enabling understanding and projecting into the future with its memories. Spoken language and conversation, though relying upon past uses and understanding, may be highly variable. The person best able to expound and expand their point of view with clear meaning can generally achieve far more information exchange than those with solely a limited informal style of language: this is due to functionality. Students should not be placed at a disadvantage. They are made for different purposes. The chainsaw is obviously completely different from the bench saw, although both cut wood: the time for using a chainsaw is not the same as the time for using a fine bench saw. So, it is suggested here that a failure to enable youngsters to have equal access and opportunity with regard to a broad command of their formal language forms, with exemplars in literature, is to knowingly do them a great disservice. It is education's responsibility to teach formal language skills, just as it is the job of education to teach a more responsive and adaptable pencil grip. Each skill and ability needs to achieve specific aims, 'fit for purpose' and so effective use. Neglect of this purpose and fitness, both broadly and specifically, is irresponsible for it will limit students' breadth of options and opportunities. In the same respect the ability to speak two or more languages or dialects increases the depth and breadth of language possibilities, but only when and where appropriate.

Work Value

Our corporate 'masters', for so I believe they see themselves, talk arrogantly of the "Pipeline of Skills" which they need in the workforce to ensure their wealth. Such is too prevalent and an unacceptable attitude behind and towards industrial labour (all contributors) building and leading to labour dissatisfaction and demands. The function of society is social: the function of successful production is to provide for people and society. To suggest that schools and further education establishments are simply a pipeline spurting out under some ungodly pressure and working labour like a crude oil for industry, again speaks for itself. 'Quality of life' seems to figure little here with its social relationships and Responsibilities. One could be forgiven for wondering if it is even considered. All that appears to be generally considered is protecting the further bloating of bonus bank accounts using this 'crude oil' of labour and workers' *essential* skills. As has been often written, money represents stored labour:

some take and store too much of it for themselves and at a cost to others.

Lending money is big business. $20 paid out to gain $200 has a starting point of 10% interest already paid. No way is this consolidating debts to a manageable level. There is seemingly not even one month to pay back and thus avoid the interest payment, as the $20 has been paid in advance, at the start. Does the interest stay at 10%, and is that monthly? And so again the vulnerable suffer. 'Bring us your gold and we will give you cash'! How sad it is that people are able to legally seduce others into parting with, for some, their last usable asset. Quantitative funding based upon expensive computer financial tracking systems is there for big funders; cash for debt is there for those in need. We are aware that what is both the cause and the outcome from these actions tends to be even more spending. A common consequence of 'easy money' is increased debt! National stimulus packages turn inactive money into cash through methods such as time based bonds issues, which need to be repaid. There is no such thing as a free ride. To avoid financial pain and despair, the general practice needs to return to "If you can't afford it now, don't buy it now: save up for it and then buy." Sadly, advertising pressure and so called 0% financing do not help such a resolve.

University and other forms of further training and education are all equally needed, and each needs to pass the UTILITY TEST of being fit for intended use. If the intended use is to use the worker's time, energy, and ability with a main purpose to 'line someone else's pocket', then we are talking about the wrong utility. Such almost criminal irresponsibility and greed would rob the very producers of the wealth of their right, and here I will use the word fully, their right to a fair share of the stored labour produced and available for their use due to their labour. Since we cannot do and know everything, money is a handy way of compensating others for their work, knowledge, and skills that are needed. Any business requires teamwork, also described as team input. Also needed is a financial cushion (savings) to survive and overcome difficulties. This fairer sharing is not to be confused with historical and present communism, which exchanged one form of autocratic dictatorship for another. This fairer sharing is concerned with natural justice, agreement, and the seemingly unobtainable Real Democracy based upon social responsibility: a fuller understanding of what Social Family infers and needs. Communism supported by armed forces is as damaging as 'democracy' based upon fooling and manipulating the people. The primary suppressive activity is often through emotion-provoking advertising campaigns. Manipulated political power can be directed and achieved by corporations and their paid for mouthpieces. To obtain wealth by stealth and exploitation of position is and I expect always will be evident and equally wrong. It is as evil and as wrong as anarchism, though anarchism can seem less harmful as it is seeming wrongly professes to actually support freedom. Oil spills, toxic waste, radiation, chemical leaks, insecticides, preservatives, and fear all cause great and long lasting harm. An exaggerated demand is met by industrial extremes because we have been indoctrinated to want too much: we expect and ask for too much. What we need matters more than what we would like. We seemingly can no longer sensibly distinguish between the two.

To provide for unreasonable demand and to feed the bloated appetites of this 'age of waste', we all have to pay the price. Smaller friendlier places of work or production related to local benefit could be the norm in providing for all our real needs with local demand ruling rather than corporate profits. Downsizing and upgrading both our quality of life and quality of need could provide far more time for the social part of life. Surely the rational, sensible, desirable, and health promoting way is *to work to live rather than live to work.* Such a due emphasis with its healthy gentler way of life embracing an associated flourishing level of recreational local crafts and activities would produce a kinder existence and stronger community. Right now this is still possible. At present the jigsaw pieces are still available. Yet both the active will and the philosopher-promoters to put the ideal, which it is, into words leading to action are missing. With the arrival of shared direction, a planned working together for the community would lead to a better quality of life. Cooperation, a will to share, good natured humour, and lasting focus on friendship would result. This is the time to look backward for inspiration and warnings and forward towards the achievable dream.

AT WORK

Beyond having an income, an interesting and rewarding occupation makes more of life through personally valued achievement which produces job satisfaction. In a good satisfying job we receive supportive feedback and praise. The question if the work is worth the rewards offered becomes a no brainer with happiness, satisfaction, and the meeting of our daily needs. When we fit our jobs we can say we 'feel at home'. What a compliment this homeliness is to colleges and friendly management which display confidence in what is being done as with those around us. In such a situation a contented staff member wanting to overcome challenges is more likely to be confident and competent. This is not exploitation in the labour sense, simply because the boot is on the other foot with the worker exploiting the perceived benefits of the work. Playing dumb at work, acting so as to seem unable to completely comprehend or to fully achieve just to have an 'easier' time is brain numbing. Just doing enough to get paid is such a waste of life. Work is generally what you make of it. By joining a group of workers one enters a micro-culture complete with security standards, shared tasks, and real rewards. It is naturally best to fit in with the group and so it is better to avoid what could be seen as unwelcomed behaviour. This social skill develops in the encouraging family and school experiences. Once in the world of work this reinforces the importance of reflective self-discipline. The workplace "well-poisoners", through their insecurity, unsympathetic manner, lack of self-discipline, and ill-advised actions isolate themselves more and worsen a sorry situation.

We do not all wish the same form of higher education, including apprenticeships. Clearly, we do not all need to be trained in the same way. Let the education and training fit the mind and skill, not the other way round. Let the work fit the preference: an unachievable ideal. How so? When combating conflict, as wars show, the unachievable becomes achievable because of unity and resolve. There is no reason why such huge efforts should be any less for the benefits of a happier and more satisfying life experience. Rather than being a bad memory for so many, education should be a real self-awareness builder, a finding and a preparation for some of our preferred possible futures. Similarly, such building of interpersonal awareness which usefully occurs in work Education should bring security, realistic success, and confidence. Some achieve this via university, others in the shrinking numbers of family businesses, and others through work participation and apprenticeships. One unfortunate side effect of costly university is compromise. Gaining the paper does not mean that preferred employment is available. Often a tiring search is needed to find a compromise while too many have to take a less preferred and suitable alternative. Apprentices seem more fortunate in this. Work experience is testing/experience by doing the job. Should this prove unenjoyable, then a change is possible before the loss of too much precious time, finance, and effort. Also, work experience through apprenticeships, if not purposely oversubscribed and improperly supervised, enables most to step into work for which they have proven suited and skilled, while also having the benefit of knowing the people who will be their colleagues. Apprentices are trained by experienced skilled 'practitioners' whom they respect as 'proven practitioners' knowing the better ways to work. With proper respect, acceptance of personal Responsibilities, and the importance of the Social Family concept, abuses should be avoidable and avoided. A work environment with an implied 'pack' structure will not do. Job environment is key to state of mind and quality of both work and life; thus, it is a very part of the individual.

Secure job protection enables confident forward planning, and if the work produced is up to a good standard, then the employee deserves no less as a result. Protection of employment is the administrators' responsibility. This is a social responsibility and demands commitment which is equally as important as sales, development, and investment and is therefore dependent upon them. Further, it is cost-effective to have an effective and dependable workforce who demonstrate pride in good work and loyalty 'to the firm'. This seems more easily achieved at a local level in smaller units rather than the ever-changing and growing units of the free-trade and job market reduction: the corporate world. Huge Japanese and Korean conglomerate Zaibatsu have achieved one form of worker centred industry, proving it can be done if the will is there. Further, national pride centres on well-run companies paid for and built by the nation. Examples are water, electrics, post, health, communications, and transport. These can become important national icons and part of a nation's identity. 'Foreign' buy-outs break this down. Today's new nation states or colonial empires have evolved because the corporate colossi, with absorption of larger portions of the market, creating fewer players, their practice of asset stripping, and the labour force's loss of job security have survived and are succeeding. They are increasingly becoming the dominant new way of community provision. It is the responsibility of national government to protect its nationals regarding this: in reality there are no relevant rights here.

· · · · · · · ·

CHAPTER 21:

BEING RESPONSIBLE

HEALTH:

It is the responsibility of the individual to maintain a healthy life relevant to their circumstances. The purpose of having a National Health Service is to maintain a <u>consistent</u> and high standard of health support for all citizens across the nation. This is generally reactive but would be better if it were more focused on being proactive. Recently it has been shown that Canadians spend an additional sixty billion dollars annually on topping up their health through paid for health care. Dental care and care of the elderly with high medication costs are major factors. In this context one can talk of rights until one is blue in the face, but this form of quality service can only be provided by people fulfilling their Responsibilities efficiently and fully. For them to do so consistently and dependably, clear known adequate funding is required with emphasis upon combined health provision. Administration is outside that direct activity but needs to be efficient and not bloated. This is not an industry, though some like to think so. It is a service provided by dedicated health practitioners and the rest are add-ons. Bonuses paid to chief managers should rather be paid into a reserve fund for emergencies. The nurses and doctors don't expect bonuses for healing or saving their patients; they do so as the goal of their vocation. What makes executive administrators so different? Their attitude! If extra money can be found then it should be used to support the actual provisions for those who work *directly* with and for the patient clients. Executives are paid well enough. Remember those wonderfully efficient ward Matrons? Fulfilling well one's Responsibilities is reward in itself if sufficiently paid.

Enabling the drug companies which produce our medicines to keep secret their medication testing processes, outcomes and so research finding seems a stupefying neglect of both responsibility and due diligence on our behalf. Independent corroboration and verification regarding benefit, dosage, and any unwelcome side effects seem axiomatic. It seems that the secrecy of a medical product testing, with patent protection safely in place, is far less important than the patient.

I cannot escape, nor do I wish to, my belief that the necessary health care and education should both as a priority be provided out of taxation for all ages. The "paid for" provision red herring is irrelevant, as it is too often intentionally used to confuse any failings of the national systems and those that govern. Being wealthy and paying more in taxes will help to provide for more people, and that is right. There are far more needing care than with great wealth. The wealthy and many forms of protected employment save the Health Services through insurance claims with their subsequent payouts. The reality of health care and educational waste can readily be objected to and huge savings achieved for reallocation by reducing such waste. By reducing unnecessary medication and avoidable waste of disposable articles, higher investment in pro-active preventative strategies significant savings could be made. Payment for band aids, cotton wool, antihistamines, and so many more could be met by most. However dentistry and eye tests with cost of prescription glasses and surgery are totally another matter. Health care 'regional only' purchases need to be replaced since they are more costly than national/federal bulk purchases of medicines and hospital provisions. Large bulk purchases would win larger discounts and reduce administrative costs. Subsidized but not free meals could provide greater variety and quality, especially called for by longer term hospital patients. Health care is a matter of setting priorities, being proactive, and providing good public information. So, there needs to be reviewed any health perks or loopholes that the unscrupulous seek out and use in the name of their Rights while conveniently forgetting their Responsibilities to others. No one has a right to abuse the system; it is not theirs, it is ours. No one has the right to needlessly drain finite resources. Many have horror stories of such abuses. One example I learned from a distraught Doctor (JP) friend was of an asthmatic patient 'wielder and dealer' who made her way to a funded new vacuum cleaner, then new carpets because of old dust, a refrigerator to store goat's milk amongst others, an air filter system, new bedding and sitting room furniture, and so on. She had support from another Social Body. I know from my own similar problem that completely removing carpeting, turning mattresses and using a duvet, purchasing second hand leather seats, buying fresh food every other day, and giving the home a good blow through with open windows achieves most of the effective changes required. As time passed, such savings achieved could possibly be used to purchase some extra luxuries as well as necessities. So much more could be done within our health services without the selfish drains upon the health-purse. So much dreadful suffering could be better treated if the administrators addressed this. Good health and education build a nation. Production improves with less working days lost, good health adds to imaginative creativity, and so development flourishes.

When patients have to go abroad for otherwise delayed necessary operations and treatment, something is badly wrong. Only those with the necessary finances or those who are prepared to impoverish themselves can take this option; the others are left to deteriorate, suffer, and not infrequently die. Lack of training in palliative care has led to some terminally ill patients being denied strong enough pain reduction since 'additional medication strength could result in addiction which is an avoidable outcome'...for a terminally ill patient AT THEIR END! When old funding practices are allowed to dictate and be continued despite new better treatments, denying the better form for some, this shows administrative negligence of care. When chemotherapy administered intravenously is better funded and more available than easier and improved tablet medication, then reorganization of the mindset is needed. Waiting lists could be addressed by ensuring the availability of more specialists thanks to free education, training, and funds gained from reducing top administrator numbers by removing bonuses and other waste. Part of this debate concerns the demand for a right not to have to suffer longer. The extension of personal pain to all involved goes against decency and is irresponsible humanity. Those who suffer needlessly are family, friends, sensitive caring nurses, doctors in a hopeless predicament, and the dreadfully sorry and suffering patient crying out for release. Further, the care consumes large amounts of those scarce resources totally against the wishes of numerous affected patients, which are totally ignored so far. *Further, a caring Government would ensure sufficient good purpose - designed* 'terminal homes', FULLY equipped and with FULLY well trained carers.

Another question is about being able to go to the hospital 'of choice'. If there were not a variety of provisions, one would assume there would be little need other than a clear necessity to be located at the nearest hospital to help those regularly visiting, especially when elderly. Some patients do not receive visits because of distance and travel costs. These are mostly husbands, wives, and or children. Assuming uniform care provision, an area with higher hospital demand due to several demographic factors would require and construct more local units. Cost of administration and information storage would presumably be reduced by being local and linked with known local GPs. A significant number of people from abroad use the British health service ("health tourism"). The appealing cost has been close to a free service: this seems to have become almost a National Health export industry. Ensuring good appropriate health establishment abroad through aid and education, paid for by a few less war machines, would probably reduce the need for these destroyers of life, utilities, communities and hope. Stability and community growth would improve international good will and interdependence and reduce Health Tourism. More resources for home and local health small scale care could well result, possibly enabling better prevention. In addition modern rooming houses available for all nurses and those overworked young doctors could be built. Unfortunately the previous provisions in the UK were sold to became lucrative new housing. Nothing to do with bonuses?

Encouraging healthy families is the responsibility of both education and health services. Good food and home life tend to produce healthy people. These are encouraged through good imaginative educational programs and role models. There is no complete protection from ill health nor from mental illness, but we can improve the odds. Sadly the most caring and loving homes and the super fit can suffer due to lack of information and 'bad luck'. When large numbers prove to be unhealthy, then something fundamental is wrong. When it was found that many English enlisting for the Boer War fell below the health requirement, changing the state of malnutrition of the labouring classes became a reform goal. However, such a situation is not just History. Dr. Simon Davidson on Jan 7th. 2010, CNN in the early morning section of the broadcast for any wishing to 'stream this' , observed that one in five future Canadian adults will suffer from mental illness: this is an alarm-call! It is a Primary Responsibility of all within the Social Family to reduce any known causes of mental illness. Studies have shown social causes, financial problems, medical treatments, substance abuse, life's pressures, and media are some of the avoidable causes. Somewhere in this mix comes the need for more funded research into diagnosis of the personal and federal high cost causes. Social Maturity is not inevitable and too many hours absorbing those more perverse forms of stimuli from the media must be one major cause. The opportunities for times of mind healing calm and relaxation are greatly reduced. A strong collection of incidents I remember is of a young colleague, in catering, who was drawn to watch many undead etc. films and shows. She blew the very wind out of me when meeting round some corner amid her surprise and following shrieks of terror. I naturally tried to quip, "Hey, I am not that ugly," etc. but it did not do much for me either! The example shown by so-called adults are too many, developing fears and insecurities via ever popular soap operas and (un)reality shows. Further, a failure of self-respect and self-discipline abounds and spreads simply put because society is clearly failing as it loses those practices of providing positive guidance with the creation of groups of community guiding spirits. We should be seeking the higher things of life, and not be wallowing in the excremental outpouring from the irresponsible, mentally arrested authors, script writers, actors, unenlightened directors, and producers with their socially immature and morally bankrupt sections of our so-called 'entertainment INDUSTRY'. Mind pollution is accepted too readily while political correctness numbs the openness of intellectual thought. Discussion is replaced with fear of an almost autocratic despotism of self-appointed and inadequate thought-police. This censorship, which is what it is, blocks proper discussion and reason. Reason and debate, which are the bedrock of social maturity, are sadly replaced with insecurity and a dictatorship of the immature. To return to holidays when all shops and businesses close seems a sensible course: there would be no fast food. Poorer members of society operating in low paid service jobs are once again exploited. These also need time out with their friends and families when others are doing so. Further, the increased number of 24-hour shops and businesses puts greater strain upon the workforce who are battling to make ends meet by paying for inflated housing prices, and so they are much more vulnerable. One fixed half-day closing a week, for all in one area, could give all there a break while still allowing for picking up of urgent shopping in the area next to these shops. This second area could enjoy a similar half day's break on another day This simple strategy worked well to the benefit of the workforce and business owners in England, UK: a gentler time. However I imagine frequent bus services and the use of automobiles helped. Now 24 hour services continue to expand as does the use of robot ordering and cash out tills.

'Grown up' children increasingly remain living with or returning to the homes of their now far more elderly parents due to lacking work or shelter or both. Some probably bring their own children with them which often the grandparents will care for daily. A number but not all are too lacking in 'grit' to sort themselves out from the problems of their own making. Parents, once ignored, become the safety net which resulted from their child's ignorance, lost education, and earlier disrespect. Let such sort themselves out and grow up. Those innocent of fault here are fortunate in their parents' loving support and so they appreciate and respect them. However, it is not a right that parents again accept a responsibility they feel towards their offspring during times of crises which are the result of bad national government and greed: it is a variable, but not a fixed point. Hopefully should there become a need for a reversal of these positions of care, the offspring will have the courage and decency to rise to the occasion.

Worldly pressures are another cause in need of support. Cortisol hormone, adrenaline, and several dozen other hormones (Ref: Layton, *How Fear Works*) are responsible for fight or flight. By repeatedly being present within our bloodstream, this 'hormonal cocktail' will affect health. This absolutely natural but harmful cocktail is caused by fear, anxiety, and insecurity.

> INSECURITY → STRESS → ANXIETY → IMMUNE SYSTEM BECOMES LESS EFFECTIVE → INCREASED ILL HEALTH → DETERIORATION OF LIFE'S QUALITY → ISOLATION → INCREASED ANXIETY AND DEPRESSION → SERIOUS ILLNESS, DEPENDENCE, SUICIDE OR FRANTIC AGGRESSION

PERSONAL RESPONSIBILITIES

A responsible community provides the conditions favourable to a feeling of security, enjoyed voluntary service, and contentment.

Parent and child each have their Responsibilities: both gradually have to learn what they are. Similarly, employer and
employee each have their similar Responsibilities. A system
of rights should infrequently be necessary because schooling has achieved that awareness-sensitivity. School informs,
develops skills, reveals innate abilities, explains, and socially
directs. Both parent and school have their Responsibilities to
each other as well as to the student. If the employee is experiencing problems beyond work, then that is not strictly an
employer's concern. However, many employers will see it as a
responsibility they take on to help employees if they reasonably are able. The worker has obvious Responsibilities regarding standards of work, punctuality, reasonable care, honesty,
and not causing harm while supporting the employer. If
things do not work out, then leaving is the option with whatever agreed upon form that may take. Responsible employers
provide work suitable to the time and the skills of the worker
with 'fair pay' for the hours put in. Time to eat and necessary
rest must be provided. Security of employment with time
for holidays is expected with allowances for family emergencies. Proper safe equipment is generally assumed. Hopefully
this will become true for the whole world in time. Sadly,
exploiting cheaper and less responsible producers abroad
is a common irresponsible course for too many 'Western'
companies to take. Though they are able, such companies are
unwilling to fulfill their responsibility to insist on better pay,
care, and working conditions. This is supposedly justifiable
in the name of cutting costs, competitive marketing, shareholder benefit, and the inevitable scourge of bonuses.

In foreign locations mining facilities have been permitted
close to hospitals and schools. Chemical and petroleum
production upwind of schools appears acceptable abroad
because of the financial 'benefits'. One example of 'constructed justification' is extraction from the oil sand and shale
of Alberta. Sadly one can multiply this many times over in

third world countries including the wanton destruction of vast swathes of forests - the lungs of the world including the Amazon, Central America, Asia, and Congo Jungles. What this will lead to eventually is anyone's guess. These and worse are to be found in so many other areas. Such abuse is clearly not necessary. People need to work together responsibly to ensure that the things we believe in occur. We must battle together peacefully but in strength. Our vote can do more than count, as they can add up to a whole new order and produce governments that are honourable, less self-interested, and not chosen by those self-interested big businesses or big unions who are ambassadors and priests of their relentless missions to gain greater power and make even more money.

Ever increasing housing costs need not be a given. Increased costs give realtors and estate agents' higher income and thus become an incentive to maintain this rise. While it is true that the markets can move in both directions, a fixed fee basis, not related to percentage rates, could be one factor in supporting stability. Further, if negative equity precipitated a housing crisis and a world financial and labour market meltdown, the "Bail Out for Banks" should have been more controlled and controllable in 'holding grants' for the house-holders or business affected via their existing mortgage or loan with a fixed percentage of any future sale price being paid back at a later stage when conditions had improved. One would hope this would have made payment of "fat cat" executives less likely since the money would have gone directly to where it was needed, which would have required government will and a new focus for lobbying. To calculate the finances a standard sales figure using building cubic footage or floor square footage base could be devised, with a built in 'inflation change' figure. Hopefully, if something like this were adopted in a future crisis, more businesses could then continue, less jobs would be lost, and fewer houses and even housing districts abandoned with less demand upon welfare and health care.

One assumes that employer/employee pension plans are for the future wellbeing of these **partner** wealth creators - one 'workforce'. Efficient pre-planning would benefit Social Family Members through reduced taxpayer burden. Income collected locally could be invested in local business 'stocks'. Such greater security would enable workers at all levels a better chance to plan for their future. Further, reducing state dependence would free up funds for other priorities. These pension funds should not be under government control. It is the Responsibility of all employers to enable and encourage this planning, just as it is the responsibility of all workforce members to make an honest effort in whatever their 'work product' may be. These products of savings need to be "at arm's length" and extend beyond any control by the employer regarding funds for personal use and investment. But why stop there! A small addition could make a great difference to those needing later the security and care in a nursing home, the funds having been taken away from the sticky fingers of government treasury: "robbing Peter to pay Paul". Pensions and future care are shared Responsibilities of the individual, law, places of employment, and government. The continuing role of maintaining good rather than barely adequate standards and security of investment remain. Such planning demonstrates society's recognized debt payment to its workers by showing respect and value of the elderly.

A Minority Voice Supported

In Canada a group of at least 12 Members of Parliament can form themselves into an official Political Party, thus enabling them to gain allowance from taxation to campaign during elections. This is seemingly a small matter. However, this enables a successfully planned and promoted pressure group to make an impression and produce changes of conditions or processes which could have huge significance for the ignored or disadvantaged. During a "hung-parliament", a minority group could achieve maximum input and influence, caused by voter doubt. Critical minority party support also enables the public or MPs to make a position become urgent in an area where government was hitherto 'hard of hearing', and so this can be a good thing. However, a firmly established and long term minority pressure group with such power also could endanger the principles of democracy.

TOLERANCE and CO-OPERATION

There is a responsibility to interact, to take part, and to co-operate. The importance of accepting this is an essential part of integration, especially when living as a guest in another community. Joining amicably with the community creates good social bonding. Anything else leads to separation, misinformation, suspicion, mistrust, and failed integration. The angry and embittered results we see travelling to join ISIS terrorists in Arabia and now also in Africa. Practicing tolerance is an equal responsibility for old and new citizens, whether nationals or immigrants. The only way to achieve this is by starting with clear ground rules, advice, and support when the two groups meet and so offer better likelihood of starting right.

Being isolated as a choice or outcome is to feel alone and disconnected. This results in stress which easily builds into a negative attitude and loss of any positive potential social interpersonal growth. *Dissociative relationships* lead to lone-liness. Isolation easily leads to fears which affect ability to rationally cope and therefore prevent a contented and happy state of mind. It may reasonably be concluded that people who 'get involved' in society, providing they don't 'overdo it' and exhaust themselves and all around them, will be happy and experience a feeling of constructive wellbeing. Feeling different is to be different.

SMILY Diagram

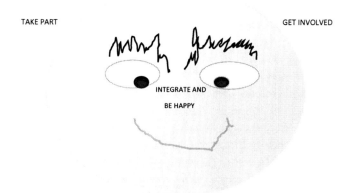

TAKE PART   GET INVOLVED

INTEGRATE AND
BE HAPPY

THE UNBORN and Unknowable

During this period of large scale population movements (2015/6 and beyond) due to famine, warfare, and economic optimism, there will be broad changes required. Emigrating unfortunate, damaged, traumatized, and miserable souls try to brave considerable dangers and hardships to escape threats, murder, torture, intimidation, rape, child recruitment, and abuse. When submerged in very different geography, culture, traditions, and languages there falls upon the generous receiving nations brand new Responsibilities which have to be coped with, similarly for the new arrivals. The hope is for a better future for all and their descendants.

We may ask if we have a responsibility towards those yet unborn, and if so, to question if they have rights over and above ours. If Responsibilities do not come first but Rights do, then the unborn, the unknowable, and the non-existent have greater powers than we imagine. This is less than logical and so the question stalls. A non-existence can only have an artificial existence and does so only by being a creation of the mind, thus it can have no position or form beyond imagination. This leads to discounting ideas, theories, aspirations, visionary revelations, and inspiration all of which clearly have effects which are 'worldly': their effect is their reality. So the discussion restarts. If these 'ideas' have actual existence, then they will do so because they act through or upon existing entities. These are the enablers of their 'idea relevance' and the enablers also of their purpose. The enablers take the primary role and position. So too, it could be argued, the living takes priority over the as yet non-existent. In the case of the unborn being a *reality concept*, they actually become purposeful. As yet they are without rights, for they do not exist, but we who do exist and acknowledge their approach will have put in place our Responsibilities regarding them. Because we may have elected for ourselves specific rights does not mean the non-existent have rights which can be exercised. However, we can and do exercise Responsibilities. Many women thinking of having a child give up smoking and drinking and adopt sensible rest as well as exercise. Funds are saved, books are read, and so on. All this for something which does not yet exist, but the Responsibilities do. Equally we have Responsibilities regarding future generations to come, and so must exercise due care of and for our planet. Rights can appear to have a more limited lifetime.

ABUSE and CARE

Regarding our children's credit/debit card behaviour, parents are unable to step in and stop them from self-harming. An artificial limit is imposed on an artificial situation despite the reality of damaging and growing debts. Some adolescents, not accepting their Responsibilities, abuse parental trust, amongst other things, through feeling free to take actions such as excessive use of the home telephone, having 'home alone' parties, stealing, and so on. Such will also be quick to quote their rights which undermine home discipline as well as their own social development: this is equally a problem in schools. Children do not ask to be brought into this world, but once here it is a primary concern and responsibility that they receive mature and measured care by being taught to be responsible people. If anything, it is people in general who should have a right to be protected from the Antisocial Family through firm state and societal support of the defective home and later with regard to school discipline. It is the proper regard for others, our actual caring, that results in good order, community, clean neighbourhoods, dependability, and caring enough to give time and money. These values all stem from respect, not abuse.

Medical research has well proven its value to us all, but funding is mainly left to private companies who go on to charge high prices for their products. These have benefitted from grants, loans, and tax breaks. Patents use these products for long periods of time which even results in some becoming unavailable through shortages. Fundraisers and charities slowly build their information data base to produce information resources because of their own research and development, such as cancer research, MS, and the British Heart Foundation. The industrial 'medicine' developers need to be profitable for their investing shareholders who also benefit from these medical innovations, research, and development.

In general new and improved medicines tend to be far more expensive than the ones that have more than paid their way - these are being replaced. Nations can find vast sums for warfare to cure a perceived social disease requiring drastic military surgery. Funds could be arranged and made available to remove wait times for urgent treatments and provide new and proven better treatments sooner.

Some members of rights movements use seemingly legal intimidation rather than correcting specific focuses on wrong and confused perceptions. The animal rights movement has some particularly nasty minorities as examples, which have resulted in media-directed abuse and resulting suicides. Farming is one area with such cases. These planned malevolent activities are often with forms of hidden abuse included while ignoring other rights of their victims.

CHAPTER 22:

THE WORLD FAMILY -
Definitions and Laws

<u>Respect</u>: a justifiable and warranted approach towards others earned by an individual or group based upon action and attitude. This tends to be caring in nature while showing deserved deference for past actions and achievements. Empowered by and of the mind, respect can often be linked with imitative behaviour.

<u>A Human Right</u>: a fixed, inflexible concept that is written and enforceable in law imposed upon society(s.) Its purpose is to function as a guideline to better safeguard perceived finite concepts of a state of existence preferable to alternatives seen and experienced. When empowered by and of the law as written, it is irrespective of other possible outcomes.

NATURAL RIGHTS,
Entitlements, and Abuses

Natural rights are conferred by agreement at the grass roots level: they are felt. Human Rights may start with these but states or ruling bodies do the fine political tuning with potential votes counting uppermost. They are made of and by design, needing to be universally agreed and acted upon to have validity. A specific right defines what it will probably cause (outcomes) and what it hopes to achieve (goals or target). The following need to be properly discussed and reviewed periodically regarding Human Rights:

1. INTENTION

2. OUTCOME

3. POSSIBILITIES of FAILURE

4. UNFORSEEN ADDITIONS and INFLUENCES

Knowledge is rooted in experience - a favourite theme of the Scots Philosopher (Hume). A free market (and not monopolies) provides market competition, as advocated by the Philosopher (Adam Smith), thus providing choice and less expensive commodities. The shrinking number of breakfast cereal producers seems to have gone hand in hand with rising costs for these over-advertised products. If most shoppers simply walked past these products, then probably their prices would soon fall. Competition of ideas is also the way to progress towards a better life environment if this occurs by the beneficial sharing of experience and knowledge. Imposed legalistic rights, in hand with 'political correctness' and some would add stupidity, are inventions and are not natural. Further, they are neither allowed to be found wrong and thus revised; nor are they always fair and right. It is being truly right which would reinforce a legal status. Further, it is worth restating that these rights have the tendency to be kept unchanged even when introduced to new situations. They seem to have little strength elsewhere. Their adoption or rejection should come from how they affect those places and pressure groups which promote them. What matters most is that there is active and effective safeguarding for those at risk: fit for purpose. A 14-year-old Bangladeshi girl who had rejected a suitor had acid thrown in her face to disfigure her, which it did. Tragically this is not a lone instance. A child bride bears a child which ruptures her womb and bladder. If she survives, she is now incontinent and is removed to the outskirts of the village. Her 'marriage' ends with any duty of care. One nation's, one region's, or one family's view of a right is not necessarily another's. Rights 'take' while Responsibilities support and give. At the time of writing, the so-called wealthiest nation in the world - the USA - reportedly has 40,000,000 people who are denied adequate health care and use of banking facilities. With the amounts found to bail out the corrupted banks and fight 'colonial wars', it seems indefensible that this situation continues. This poverty is not only maintained but is a political pawn of the unscrupulous and self-satisfied 'servants' of the people. Or maybe that will change. Hope springs eternal!

ATTITUDE decides the GOALS which contain specific AIMS working towards SPECIFIC OUTCOMES

The reality of money, which Karl Marx/Engels echoed from earlier writers, tells us that money is stored labour and is therefore power. The greatest value of money, I would suggest, is the very possible reduction of the effects of poverty which the poor are unable to 'buy out of'. That wealth accrued through brain, strengths, and self-discipline is a good thing: That the poor remain un-helped is not. More of this stored power needs to be 'unleashed' to enable these people to ultimately take care of themselves: a prerequisite of human dignity. This subsequent increase in purchasing power produced might just be good for the economy and further develop industries, produce new industries, and repair broken communities. Poverty means "actions needing to be taken": such national shame calls for action. By seeing or experiencing examples of the effects of poverty it is natural for the wealthier to store up and save money as planned self-protection. Ways can be devised to help the less fortunate save for those "rainy days." The Penny Fund Burial Societies, UK Co-operative Society, Building Societies, Prairie Co-ops, local Fire Fighters, insurance, and coastal life-boats are just some examples which show what can be done when we pool our resources and work together. However, we would need to ignore our advertising that induces consumers' impulse purchasing.

EUROPEAN CONVENTION OF RIGHTS: "Wider Public Interest"

Like love, rights demand a response to have value. It also shows growing needs suggesting associated fulfilment. Division of peoples is not fulfilment. Unfortunately the too frequent referring to and brandishing of Rights causes alienation between people. Required first is achieving a balance of differences to better facilitate the movement towards general good will. This demands self-control and patience.

Yes, we need space to live but with overpopulation compounded by too rapid population growth, planning becomes inadequate and downright impossible. Thus, the resulting increased competition leads ultimately to conflict. The only probable answer will be to reduce the breeding rate. Nature and human nature will take care of this in time, but by then it may well be too late. Our wish to own things is one way family size shrinks: more goods require less children and expense. Another is a growing worldwide perception of the strain of having many children: the wealthy nations' view is better to be avoid this and own more things.

There should be adequate access to open lands, parks, recreation, and I would add local meeting places like English pubs. The latter is not a problem with self-discipline and consideration of others in place. Providing protected local open spaces becomes a problem once building density reaches a specific level: few green areas are left unless they have been established before the building starts. London UK should be most grateful to those inspired women who insisted and battled for the establishment of parkland areas against the odds. These are places to relax and walk with room for children's safe play and paths to push a pram. These, along with their English Garden City movement, have changed the direction taken by the building industry. They had looked well into the future.

Rules of acceptable behaviour reinforced through home and schooling need to be clear, with censorship of the media to remove those times when producer self-controls fail. I know this protection may be unpopular with some (possibly those with hidden agendas), but it is life and so clear sanctions and scrutiny are needed. If such public action did not need firm handling, then there would be no need for building planning regulations, police, laws, law courts, Defense Forces, and so on. Further, all sorts of wrongs are changed into the seemingly acceptable by renaming them through misnaming or "New Speak" as outlined in the book called 1984 by George Orwell. This same New Speak is used to change the descriptor "filth" to "adult entertainment"; also rule-breaking to "professional fouls" perpetrated to engineer an unfair advantage. Another example is the spiteful, noisy, crassly engineered and self-indulgent stupidity that have become known as "reality shows". Again, we have the dysfunctional media and media's self-awards to thank for this downward spiral.

The Nature of Obligations

If we feel strongly obliged regarding some action, a demand of conscience becomes and is a duty with its fulfillment a priority. Obligations are deeply important to us: obligations being products of the internalized are part of our mindset and character and are a personally imposed duty and responsibility. Rights carry no such obligation to take action: one tries or quite naturally keeps clear of falling foul of them. Assumed codes of behaviour, once generally accepted, become part of the social form. They often develop into a part of cherished traditions. They are aspects of the social mind and call up individual emotions. This emotional human element makes each of them valid to the person and of value to many. Role-models are found and used to pass on the message, particularly to developing social minds: these obligations taught to the young are based upon reason and personal acceptance while Human Rights can be empowered by the processes of the law.

PARENTING

FAMILY: A household of individuals, generally related, from the same kinship, stock of preceding family. A single unit within a community of many units with shared customs and shared traditions. This term can refer to a race or clan.

NUCLEAR FAMILY: Consistent parent partners cooperating together with the young they provide for, support, protect, and socialize: a unit of two generations.

EXTENDED FAMILY: A larger group family composed of three generations or more with recognition of and inclusion of ancestors. A cooperative structure with many pooled resources.

These are my summary of points made by **Bottomore** (1962) and **Kingsley Davis,** Human Society

> *"Social structure influences population changes as well as being affected by them." p88 TB Bottimore*

At least one parent or guardian will need to have flexible work hours for times when their young child needs them. One example is when a child is ill and feeling very vulnerable. Returning home from school can be an exciting sharing-time for both the child and parent. Returning to an empty house or apartment is not the better way for a youngster to develop and feel wanted. A request for parent presence seems more a candidate as a Right with full legal and financial protection. Guidelines regarding employer responsibility could strongly assist this goal. Also, with the *extended family* as opposed to the *small nuclear* family, helping mom or dad is less of a problem. All of this has to be balanced with what the place of work or company needs, what is necessary for proper efficiency, and how much support can be afforded using judgements of criteria. Interestingly Toyota has reported this year's research which shows that reducing hours worked can significantly improve worker efficiency. Those unprincipled women who take away the opportunity of work for another intentionally to skim the company with maternity leave pay a few months later harm all. Just as antisocial are those repeatedly feigning illness or with five or more parents and in-laws whose funerals 'had to be attended'. All such activities breed the distrust affecting those following. *The Daily Mail* (UK) reported that £20,000,000,000 is stolen from the British people every year through fraudulent health care. It is proposed that passports will soon be a part of a security anti-fraud check. No doubt infringement of Human Rights will rattle around the matter. If funding savings are success-ful, then there are many legitimate needy beneficiaries in the line-up for help. In need are victims of conflicts overseas, also those upholding the laws, as well as care giving parents or relatives of people with serious mobility problems . Savings funds could also provide useful additions to health care and help for the very elderly and terminally ill.

Rights should only be extended to those who meet their obli-gations and are of good intent: those other 'despicable' anti-social people certainly won't respect any limitations we place upon ourselves to help out our moral principles or decency. They will continue their malpractices till caught and pun-ished. It continues to be necessary to make sure gangs, thugs, rapists, and confidence tricksters have the fullest reason to beware, which means removing loopholes in the law. The obligation to protect minors continues: what constitutes a minor in the case of crime needs to also be reassessed in the light of what they do, why they do it, and how they behave. If their crime was intentional, preplanned, and serious enough to be seen as an adult crime, then they need the same treat-ment. If forced into the situation, the forcing perpetrator should receive additional punishment without remission and the child should receive support. In many matters children are fully aware of what they do and why. If one chooses freely to appear in every way to be at or beyond the age of consent, then so be it. If one plans and intends to use a knife as a weapon, then so be it: full law and punishment. Again the 'crime of passion' needs consideration in this context. If one goes for a "joy-drive" and kills someone, then so be it: full law is appropriate. If one freely indulges in robbing the elderly, then adult punishment is again called for. Furthermore, any negative role a parent or relative might have played should be investigated as a matter of course.

Behaviourism teaches that a change of behaviour shows that a lesson has been learned. This seems almost obvious until challenged by knowledgeable educators. However, it cannot be denied that in the case of the disruptive and violent student, to successfully change such behaviour is the desired goal for the sake of parent, teacher, and other impressionable youngsters. Child-centred education and what has been described as 'social wets' appeared to produce some 50,000 truants, a rise in self-harm and in crime. This negative behaviour could be laid at several doors, but firmer educational discipline is a controllable starting point. Out of school targeted education for interest groups is a great way to bring together like-minded people. These tend to have similar group priorities (though differing skill levels) and are happily occupied. A danger to focus upon is shyness with isolation, loss of confidence due to taunting, and other real fears. Tolerant behaviour as a skill and as a social goal generally needs to be encouraged and taught. Avoiding abuse or countering it successfully is another valuable life-skill. History studies, human geography, and playing team games can all add understanding here. As a soccer goalkeeper I had to quickly learn how the goals that went into my net were not entirely my 'fault', despite what some ineffective team members might say. Also, respecting the skill of some particular attacking forward member of the opposing soccer team was a matter of survival through taking appropriate defensive action. Knowing more enables us to do more effectively. An essential part of learning is wishing to know. This is an appetite which needs to be fed. The shallow nature of early English National Curriculum permitted the loss of much "Value Added" educational content, with not a few valuable experienced teachers leaving with it. Defining detail can so easily lose the essence and spontaneous 'Golden Moments' which family can be so good at avoiding and educators so good at initiating in a calm, disciplined, and constructive environment.

The Nature of Respect

Respect is a valued behavioural outcome from experience embraced by reason and seen in others. Since it is valued, this respect often leads to imitation, which is why socially agreed upon good role models are so productive. Role models are an educational instrument, for better or worse, and are therefore socially significant: positive roles requiring positive support. Role play can be an investment in emotion. From what has been written before, I trust that the importance of change and progress is agreed upon. If the role model is bad, it will prove to be harmful and socially negative. Such role models need to be countered or made unavailable, especially to the impressionable young. As these negative influences appear, full use of social powers should be deployed to limit their harm. There are many changers of the world who have benefited huge numbers of others and hence our way of life. Respect unifies people, whereas the danger of legalistic rights is that they may also be used as a tool to gain advancement and thus divide.

Role of Patience

Quiet charitable acts and good works, so important to Sikhs and Muslims, provide life's 'value added' for many. To support 'small' people's businesses, filling gaps created by events, and giving with no expectation of getting back are important in Faiths: their focus is upon personally getting closer to God who provides all. We share what we have been given, emphasizing mutual support. This help is patient and undemanding; it facilitates relevant gradual natural growth. The good outcome from patient help and support is not expected to be achieved all at once. It is beyond charity and is also found in aspects of industry and commerce. One such example is the British supermarket chain, Waitrose, with their funded schools in Africa. The outcome of this good work will obviously require time and patience before the valuable return on that human investment matures, for the good of Africa.

CORPORATE POWER......
and Corporate-itis!

BUSINESS as the
Autocratic Monarchy

Modern transnational businesses have become an autocratic industrial monarchy: unfeeling and with an insatiable appetite for wealth and power unparalleled. National assets are bought by these business, thus feeding their insatiable appetites further. This national asset stripping is enabled by handpicked and funded politicians, neglectful of their primary obligations both to nations and to their electorates. Possibly it will end in open warfare between corporations using the nations and nationals they 'own'.

Four Cs in business

Command

Communicate

Collaborate

Conform goals, beliefs, and focus

Community in crisis generates a them-and-us attitude which does not bode well for the future. As consortia compete to take over smaller businesses, eventually a few super conglomerates will be in competition with each other without distraction from the less powerful. This will inevitably leave violence and industrial espionage as the future.

Dictatorships

Hopefully the United Nations has at last 'grown up'. The UN was called by troops fighting in action "The United Notions". This infantile squabbling babble has too frequently fallen short due to childish and short-sighted self-interest. It is now beginning to deal with the bullies within our worldwide Social Family. Hopefully this will be called by History 'The Age of Ending Dictatorship'. The peoples of the world deserved this of their leaders and are now better at demanding it. Might on its own cannot be right! The bigger the wrong the worse it is. In 2011 Tunisia, Egypt, Chile, Libya, and others were gaining support from world leaders making reprehensible, defenceless, and criminal allowance of over 50 years of atrocities in the once Belgian Congo or also Zimbabwe, as with far too many other locations. As "peace keepers", UN Troops have to follow written procedures. Approaching men who are carrying their guns have to be correctly challenged, or the soldiers will face murder charges if someone is killed. It is little surprise that these soldiers prove brave but ineffectual. That so many so-called freedom fighters and governmental troops can kidnap or else `arrest` and make the criminal INJUSTICE far worse, shows how feeble the UN is. Ask how it ever got to that state or condition. Simply, the answer is because it was allowed to happen. The list of Human Rights seems to have two main forms of existence. On the one hand, where they are generally accepted they too easily become a form of tyranny exercised by individuals and minorities divorced from other broader and key Responsibilities. Where they are tragically needed and not seen, they are knowingly ignored internationally and by those holding power locally.

A quieter and just as insidious autocrat is emerging, based on the worship of money, company profits, and the self-award of bonuses. As my dad said to describe such a corrupt belief system:

> For them, *"money is my god and my cheque-book is my altar!"*

In the past Canada "talked and so did not scream".....Michael Ignatius (CBC 18/11/12) who spoke of previous 'respect not arrogance' observed how now the "media thrives upon adversarial politics" leading to the stance adopted to achieve advantage and popularity being mistaken for strength. So there is a need "to feed the beast" or "lay the track". This may well not be good journalism, but it achieves the 'viewing' numbers in a downward spiral of The Public and Reporting standards.

Bribery and all sorts of corrupt practices increasingly 'feed the beast'. Technology is employed to break into the privacy of social media. Social media through to cell phone calls are no longer safe or private, thanks to the Rights devoid Techno community hackers. This type of governmental intrusion has been the case from well before the 1960s. The book by Watson and Hickman (2012) entitled *Dial M for Murdock* makes for chilling reading. If one believes that there are Rights, notice how far they do not go when big business comes into play. Dispossessed Natives of the Amazon Jungle are a prime example. You may think you own what you have, but if a conglomerate corporation wants it, see how long you last.... rights and all!

Of Facebook, Twitter, YouTube, etc. there is risk, or would it be better termed a hazard? Article 31 states support for the child's right to play. What form is this play and how far does the 'right' extend? What other rights can supersede this? What can be termed 'child abuse' due to limiting a child's exploratory play and confident development? What constitutes too great a risk to 'permit'? How to overcome the varied nature caused by and through differences in peoples' values? Possibly Risk Management Skills need to be taught universally in schools.

It would be interesting to see if the Three Points of Contact rule in mountain climbing has some equivalent in use of technology. Then again there arises that search for balance between safety and risk versus probable benefit. Every child and adult needs to EXPERIENCE regulation and prohibitions, with known sanctions, to become a co-operative member of the Social Family. Most will need far less regulation to quickly understand the needs and benefits.

In this time of great change, the active prevention and putting an end to the threat of big business dictatorships is needed. They can too easily make decisions which lead to disregard of both the environment and indigenous peoples. This results in evils of poverty, loss of hope, manic depression, and suicide: even their products may be second best with manufacturers insisting on 'a higher quality product' taking over while other products are `eradicated`. Some displace whole blocks of people for mining purposes, others through factory closures and relocation. They exploit the weak, for example through inflated prices of the very medicines the desperate need to survive or to lead a reasonable existence. Others are controlled and poorly paid due to their vulnerability; they may depend upon keeping hard-to-find unskilled work as they care for dependants. Those who put in the hours being the `wealth builders` are vulnerable. Work-dictators protect their own by publicising inventions to discredit others or by applying other financial pressures; they lobby to gain unfair advantages through the political system; they take over news media to control public information and therefore thought, moods, and awareness. Our governments are responsible for permitting and even encouraging this situation: they are well-rewarded.

It is the remit and duty of governments to enable the provision of essentials for all its people-clients. Essentials include food, clothing, shelter, protection, `quality of life`, and health. It is the duty of the people to enable this through honest performance of work suited to their abilities and proper payment of properly agreed upon taxation of their portion of the wealth created by their work. It is the duty of Education to ensure the safety of its pupils, high standards of discipline, respect, and learning (book and social) with an aim to promote each child`s skills and general society's well-being. `Quality of life` as an adult is one goal which can be achieved through a sound appreciation of obligations and Responsibilities to each other and the Social Family. A major reason for the continuance, protection, and promotion of industry and work WITHIN each nation is its benefit to those who work there. To protect local and national production and production jobs. Nations with their governments need to be protected from the power of corporations which are becoming increasingly immune to a single national demand.

These corporations are seemingly immune due to size, being international, and their vast wealth. It is essential to find means to reduce their power and their strength, for they have on too many occasions proven unworthy of trust. For example, mining interests sweeping aside indigenous peoples, mining side output creating spoil heaps, destruction of otherwise locally grown food production, sea fishing consortia's greed and ecological impact hillside timber extraction with landslides in addition, woodland areas removed, oil extraction and spillages, unhealthy additives in food, inflated medical expenses, bribery, spying and phone tapping, ecological destruction, and financial corruption of all sorts. The list is endless. Too much misery has followed the takeover of one by another as once essential workers see their jobs removed abroad or simply closed in order to provide an increased market share by another provider. One such glaring example is the threatened closure of the British steel mills by its Indian owner TATA, (April, 2016) with loss of 15,000 directly employed personnel with the surrounding businesses decimated. Mergers could be beneficial with the availability of investment and knowledge, but National Integrity and meeting its people`s needs should take precedence. Any merger conditions should be legally binding with the majority of management of the host nation; changes to the merged company would maintain the same workforce (security of labour) with guaranteed worthwhile retraining for new or displaced workers. Should this become international law, I fancy that far fewer relocations and closures would occur. A major concern remains of future falling populations with decreasing demand. In this case planned industrial shrinkage would be required. Franchises and apprenticeship could be two tools used to stabilize and protect the labour market jobs. Some corporations make a practice of stealing the development of agricultural products from poor nations, for example through DNA registration and patenting. Also, the innovations of their workers are under-rewarded through single payment rewards and loss of any patents control of their brain-child: an annuity of 1, 2, or 3% on every sale would be more just! Companies and governments cannot always be right: they do not know everything, but they can try to honestly live up to their full Responsibilities by making their best `effort.`

Any democratic government or constitutional monarchy is an employee of the people. Without the people, they have no purpose. The people pay them their wages via the agreed upon method of taxations. They are awarded gratuities such as pensions for life and are also cared for at the public`s expense with health care. They manufacture nothing. Enabling is a fine privilege, but it comes with clear Responsibilities. The following is taken from one of those e-mails that do the rounds (2015):

Salary of retired Prime Minister . . . . $450,000 for life

Salary of retired politician . . . . $174,000 for life

Salary of House Speaker . . . . $223,500 for life

Salary of Majority / Minority leader . . . . . $194,000 for life

Average salary of a soldier . . . . $40,000 a year

Average income for Pensioners . . . . $12,000 a year

UNITED NATIONS: 2014

United Nations' officials are unelected. Many of its members do not subscribe to real Democracy. Both situations are clear indication of the level of emphasis placed upon the democratic principle by its founders and today. Undemocratically appointed "nit pickers of international politics" seem to abuse their powers for 'national' interests and personal gain. They neglect the moral duty and Responsibilities by enabling autocratic totalitarian powers to deceitfully clothe themselves with the appearance of decency through the mirage of their form of due process and patronage within their United Nations membership. That there are some dedicated members is undeniable. Others should not be there, but have to be, due to the nature of the UN. Clear self-interest is seen to dominate on all sides. Similarly this appointment system is alive and kicking in the European Union. Unelected member ministers of the European Council of Ministers not long ago attacked the British Monarchy for being unelected like themselves.

Similarly, the United Nations continues to fail to put its own house in order. The Monarchy is a very popular institution in Britain and the Commonwealth due to their actions: they provide a focus and stability with so many other benefits for communities worldwide. The European Union (EU) does not provide a true democracy. It has been often correctly suggested that a constitutional reform to the autocratic EU is long overdue. Such reform should focus upon ending jobs for the boys as appointees and establish a democratically elected council, as practiced for their parliament. Since the Council of Ministers holds the major powers of the European Union's administration and law, immediate change is needed. Such reforms need to be so constructed to give the elected parliamentary member far more power and powers than the appointees in the Council. Only recently did Ireland honestly fulfil its promise of a referendum but has done so: others might iron out some of Europe's political formulation problems.

A glaring example of misinformation and misunderstanding is the Argentinean woman and her stooges' who shout about the UK and the Falklands. They forget that with a similar argument Wales (UK) could claim large sections of Argentina. Self-interested posturing rather than concern for the whole is yet again ever present in the supposedly bastion of world right, the United Nations. Like Argentina, if less ranting and posturing went on replaced by more mature constructive discussion, reconciliation and progress would be the outcome.

Company Profits

A concept of Responsible Profit guidelines seems to be much needed. The making of personal fortunes due to genuine brilliance and not inflated costs does not harm the Social

Family. Greed is a sad reality. The greedy do not make the most socially aware people, as their social duplicity demonstrates. The odd charitable donation from such, be it ensuring one is noticed in the glitzy 'right setting' or social networking 'nest', can pay back far more than it gives in the form of self-interested and self-rewarding charity. However, some fortunes have been made most honourably due to innovation and sheer hard work. The welfare and proper recognition of the workforce and their contribution are rewarded in context with early share awards and realistic bonuses called 'salary rises'.

> *Management* and production line ensuring efficiency → job security → obligations are met (home and work) → customers are satisfied → enabling continued work and security

Somewhere along the timeline there needs to be a way to gain a fairer balance between margins of profit with salaries and benefits. Such matters should look beyond market forces using realistic planning. The loss of jobs to machines seems illogical at first, until higher profit margins, management bonuses, and pressure from the competition are considered: 'if we don't, they will, and we will be gone with all our workforce jobs'. Also, with high unemployment when there are so many more people wishing and needing to work being added to the numbers, that high price we pay to keep the work-shy and manipulative-idle housed and fed is even more galling for they take away resources from those trying genuinely to return to work via retraining and such. Social costs grow and tax revenue sinks. None of this has easy answers; if it had I suspect it would have been tried and worked long ago. Outsourcing abroad is another bone of contention. A company built by the workforce should stay with that workforce. Nationally active worker boycotting could encourage less of this. Permanent or long term unemployment through fabrication of ill health, infirmity, age, or lack of suitable work will require far more public cooperation to improve. The Social Parasite does everything in its power to avoid work and gain the maximum available benefits while arrogantly contributing nothing meaningful for the wellbeing of others. Keeping social rules and taking a justifiable pride in doing so can be encouraged in schools building upon their initiation within a caring, disciplined home. Confidence and clarity of mind are needed to follow this route. Some are unfortunately the victims of a defective educational system and social development, but somehow many of firmer character overcome the same loss of direction, indiscipline, and wasted opportunity despite home and educational shortcomings.

How many are failed by teachers going on strike: an action which seems contrary to their stated concerns for their clients? Many teachers who would work on because of fear of retribution from union and bullying colleagues so join the strike. Such action denies the young their need for consistent good education at these times (a Right?) and most strikes unbelievably take place during scheduled examination times! How totally unprofessional is that! One wonders if these same pupils will ever be able to do what adults can and <u>sue for both distress and damages</u> where they could prove their case. Sue who, you may question and then answer, "Who else but the individual teacher for breach of the child's right to education and breach of the implied and moral contract with each child and their parents," Then parent blocks could go on to sue the union for being the pressurizing bully causing this form of action or rather inaction. Next, parents losing income for having to remain at home as a result sue the unions as a block to recover the lost wages. These unions plan, are accomplices, and are the organizers. One could understand it better if teachers were complaining about examination form, parent reporting, inadequate resources, pupil indiscipline, legal vulnerability, incidents of parent intimidation, or parent trustees endangering education quality within that school.

That the majority of teachers are very fine people and have a mission to help children grow is undeniable, but that can change through disillusion and the effect from the other sort of far less dedicated teacher.

. . . .

TABLE OF RIGHTS and OBLIGATIONS with the GLUE (touchstone) of RESPECT

Spaces have been left for you to fill in and add to. My inclusions are suggestions for consideration.

RIGHTS	OBLIGATIONS/ RESPONSIBILITIES	RESPECT
To learn and be taught	Be social, of a group, support governmentally organized	Mutual
To live	To consider and support others also living	Respect others' existence
To die	Pre-care and for loved ones. To remove needless suffering with safeguards..	Respect the person's own wishes
To own / ownership	Provision /safety and help others relevant to what is owned	Honestly acquired

RIGHTS	OBLIGATIONS/ RESPONSIBILITIES	RESPECT
To have a childhood, a time to 'grow'	Protection, to advise, provide correction, permit and encourage safe experimentation	Allow/accept that mistakes happen. Be firm but fair.
To enjoy the fruits of one's labour	Honestly acquired, with care of others	Respect other's will for peace, beauty, calm etc. Others have the same right.
Protection / to live in peace / to use self-defence	Share the defence and food, ensure political participation, play an active role, support government	Acknowledge our differences which do not cause harm or distress.
To worship	To protect ~ individually and in law	Respect differences
To give away what is yours, including money	To family, friends, others	Compliance
To breed / have children	Shelter, feed, protect, educate	Not exploit or over-discipline.
To enjoy, to have fun	Responsibility of employer, employee, client, maintain quality, respect others' needs	Not at the expense of others

RIGHTS	OBLIGATIONS/ RESPONSIBILITIES	RESPECT
To have one's own opinions	Be factual - research; speak from knowledge, not supposition	Understand that opinions will be shared with others and may be contrary.
To like and to love	Keep any promises made	Aim for mutual respect
To work	Trust and be trustworthy, to work well	Trust; fair reward; respect others' efforts and suggestions
To work	Quality/worker standards; safe and healthy environment	Mutually acceptable work with adequate rest.
To work	Stability of personal demands; honest absences; training	Fair treatment, security, safety

RIGHTS	OBLIGATIONS/ RESPONSIBILITIES	RESPECT
Freedom of the press	Watchdog versus privacy, verifiable research and data	Privacy times for all; accurate and honest reporting
Government re. Taxation	Purpose: to ensure funds necessary for the wellbeing of all; not inflated; accurate accounting	Honourable personal payment; consideration for those suffering problems
Taxation	Part of our social contract	A proportion for the vulnerable.
Armed forces	Pay, modern equipment, duty of care, good pension. Training and good information.	Their sacrifices, courage, long service, and old age

Local Government:
Add to or simply fill in the gaps

RIGHTS / Activity	OBLIGATIONS/ RESPONSIBILITIES	RESPECT DEMONSTRATED
Be socially involved/ community	Hosting and attending; support	
Forward looking	Conservation/Environment	

To ensure the provision of shelter (housing)	Controlled costs; building standards; access	
Protection~ law/ war/attack/privacy		
Efficient local services		
To be heard		
Avenues to appeal against unjust actions or laws		
Natural justice		
Operations abroad (surgical)		
Seek option to suffering	Emergency services and good care	

Accurate reporting		"Openness"
To buy and use energy	Ensure dependable provision	Elderly's lower income and greater needs acted upon
Personal Data protection versus Access	Provide clear guidelines and safeguards	
Choice of partner		
To be at home with young children		
To have peace and quiet		
	Sharing responsibility	

REALISM and FAILINGS

Dealing with upset and disappointment can seem very difficult at the time but this is a necessary life-skill. There is little hope of an alternative. Removing failure if possible would result largely in not being able to deal and cope with failure later and not being able emotionally to usefully learn from its inevitable occurrence. From childhood we need to learn how to *successfully cope* with failure and to essentially overcome difficulty. These childhood moments are generally minor, and are therefore less consequential or harmful. With these experiences we acquire a personal set of strategies of knowing when to take a chance and knowing when it is best to 'leave it'. We learn how to control upset and how best to prevent upset from controlling us. Learning such courage, self-control, and worthwhile response is developed over time, with experiences. The 'helicopter parents' who are always flying to their poor child's so-called defence are in fact a real danger to their child's development, their future, and their future happiness. They prevent necessary emotional learning with a sanctimonious blanket of unreal *dependant security*. It will end in tears or worse as fear, hysteria, and mistrust are handed down the generations. Such parents are often insecure themselves and pass this on while others are angry with the world. A very unfortunate few have been significantly scarred by life - this weakens their judgement. Though the strength of their care and love for their child is fear, they seem to believe there is a need to excessively cocoon and protect. Help is one thing, but the giving of unending and unnatural support is another. How our society as a whole deals with this debate appears, in part, to be unpromising.

POLITICS

POLITICS:

> **1c.** *The art or science concerned with winning and holding control over a government*
>
> **2** *Political action, practices, or policies*
>
> **3a.** *.....competition between competing interest groups or individuals for power and leadership.*

3c. Political activities characterized by artful and often dishonest practices

5a. Relations or conduct in particular areas of experience

......The art or sequence of government ....

.......concerned with guiding or influencing government policy.......

.... the art or science of winning control over Government.........

(Merriam Webster 11th Collegiate Dictionary)

For most ways of life, politics are relevant and exist at many levels. Actions which affect people demand a process and form of interaction, discussion, and agreement: change is better with the people's agreement. Consequently, the act of achieving a balance to produce an agreed outcome occurs through person-to-person contact. This requires organization and is political. When one will is imposed on others, the process has moved away from responsible politics to become simply the raw autocratic uses of force since *it no longer depends upon agreement* between those collectively valuing and seeking a desired outcome or vision. However, the autocrats responsible for imposing their will more than likely followed a political process to gain their own brand of agreement within their minority group. A measure or set of measures designed to progress to a predicted outcome is generally referred to as an 'instrument': and so one may speak of an instrument of or for change. The enabling of an instrument is in the agreement it achieves. It enables this measure to be activated, but its true value is found in what it does - its outcome(s) - not in what it promises. Again, the honesty and sincerity of politicians matter greatly in a healthy Social Family. Our politicians need to be believed worthy of trust to achieve social security and stability.

In a world that recently seemed to be financially falling apart and almost morally bankrupt, the need for something or someone to blame emerges. Lack of honesty demonstrates lack of respect for others. A democratic society with self-discipline, give and take, humour, and good governance, while being also wrapped in apathy and greed further confused by unrealistic expectations, all point towards us as the immature causes of THE problem. Corporations spread like a cancer throughout the world, gobbling up its 'production cells' while deciding for us the unopposed future. They trample upon individuals and smaller enterprises. They buy and use political power. Some feed wars and poverty. They pollute the atmosphere, the very earth we depend upon, and also our wills through the manipulative evils of advertising promoted by the media: ....'you owe it to yourself' ..... 'why wait; have it now' ..... 'this is better and it makes more of you' ....'buy one and get the other half price'.....'this could be your lucky day - buy a card.....' ..... 'Fracking companies take care of the environment'....

Not all is bad, but too much is clearly so. A ship with a hole in it is not all bad, but it still may sink. The disease of corruption spreads silently and steadily within. They say the Devil looks after his/her own and it certainly appears to be true. The list is endless with fat cat bonuses following bailouts, organized crime's involvement in politics, trade unions' activity with inter union 'take-overs', and organized crime's involvement in industry, arms supply, sport, corrupt religious administration, and news corporations. It could seem there is no hope; however, the planned and focused power of individuals all working together can be decisive in the overpowering of the powerful. Think clearly, focus, observe, recruit, refocus, evaluate, decide, plan, and only then act.

We, the people, need to clarify what we actually have acting on our behalf and what is so-called 'good for us' but is actually not beneficial. Analyze individually (one at a time) consumer protection bodies, government committees, boards of directors, religious leaders, educational inspectors, the charities we fund, vested interests in legislation, and government structures: all these need reviewing and not by the corrupted factions within the news media. Much is talked about 'openness', but its meaning is as nebulous as its reality for what is not known is very hard to 'open'. Also, so-called Independence is an illusion as we are all 'owned' by something and someone: owning enables deciding what happens to that entity. Once the entity is aware of the reality of that situation, it mostly gives in and cooperates. If a larger structure is broken into smaller parts, then new 'owners' appear. However, when less powerful they should be more open to scrutiny and consequently be less harmful to us.

There is no singular form of democracy: briefly look at British and American styles of government. The British model works on Cabinet Consensus. Its constitution is unlike the US written format. Britain operates largely on a constitution of precedent, what has gone before. All in government have been elected by the people. There are three main parties, but self-promoting independents are a strong feature at election time. Permanent professional civil servants provide continuity, advice, and report to the people's Members of Parliament. The Monarchy advises and signs into power Bills of Parliament, making them Acts after due discussion and agreement in Parliament. The understanding is that only under the most extreme of circumstances would the Monarch oppose the will of Parliament. Parliament could override such an action through special powers. Generally one political party 'wins all' at election time, thus removing much of the guesswork from policy produced unlike a later negotiated, messy, and less transparent coalition government. There are the Civil Servants and committees which advise and can offer checks for all parliamentary activities. The House of Commons (MPs) decide what to do regionally and nationally. Highly paid outsider lobbyists try to push, persuade, and even bribe these MPs into looking after company or national interests and make the election of some MPs financially possible. Some MPs and Lords become inside lobbyists. In the House of Lords are representatives of the very rich, belief groups, the aristocratic haves and not long to survives, political appointees, political spies, and rewarded political cronies. These Members of the House of Lords cannot stop the will of the Commons MPs, only advise additions or changes and slow the passage of the Bills which detail proposed government actions. They operate as a sort of quality control. Strangely the system seems to work freely and well, that may only be so until corporations step in more fully. In Canada, with their cap on election time spending, the obscenities and waste of USA elections south of the border are largely avoided. The process is less externally directed due to funding restrictions.

The United States draws from many aspects of British Government tradition. It has two houses, both elected by the people. Election occurs between two parties though others periodically appear. The presidential candidates, rather than a monarch, rely upon the US equivalent of royalty for patronage and a chance to stand for election by the people. The selected are preselected before the people have their say: the choice has been largely pre-chosen. The vast sums of money spent, with the underlying reasons, would probably be well-recognized in ancient Rome. Greater wealth pushes some candidates in front while others run out of funds: generally nothing to do with their quality. The status quo is protected once again: one may safely assume payback time comes later. Following the outcome of an election, Political Appointees drawn from supporting corporations, the wealthy, and also some with proven skills appear thanks to the Presidential Patronage. The President seems almost an Autocrat but is prevented from that possibility through the power of the vote, two administrations maximum, and impeachment. As seen at present in gun law reform, health care, and action against poverty, one "House" can block even the most necessary of reforms should the will of its majority wish. Individual will has fully been transferred. The President can be rendered almost powerless. Thus, action regarding the will of the people, the safety of the people, the health of the people, and the poverty of people could continue to be postponed for future consideration. Free speech is enshrined in the constitution so there is always Hope left inside the box.

The USA is a federation of states, each with its own powers while needing to abide by Federal Dictates. The United Kingdom is fast becoming a federation with the nations within gaining their own national powers and governments overseen by Parliament: it is yet to be seen if ultimately the United Kingdom(s) become disunited.

What is 'divinely' apparent is the absence of labour camps; frequent political beatings and widespread assassinations; exploitation of children; incarceration of those mentally at risk; torture; religious victimization; and suppressing the humanity of women. This is just a glimpse of the many benefits of democracy. However, equal opportunity of the peoples is somewhat elusive. 'Rags to riches' is the exception to the rule. Poverty and ill health are too often seen together contaminated further with the leprosy of organized crime.

To move on, change is not necessarily bad nor inevitably good. However, too much change occurring too quickly will destabilize. People need time to adjust. Governments of change can cost too much and change too many things too quickly to sufficiently become efficient. Too swift and broad change can become counter-productive, confused, and incomplete. It would be interesting to have a public debate centred on a right to hear from politicians in power EXACTLY what they plan, in advance, with greater influence and use of referenda and computer polling. This could include tax changes, pension and health provision, immigration, retrospective law, foreign aid with or without claw-back clauses, capital punishment, and inevitably - that other political football - education. Though more Democratic it would be impractical due to cost, inconsistent mood swings, and the provision of information with an ability to interpret it, which again is why there is a civil service. Politicians provide their outline policies in their manifestos, their five-year plans, to be ratified by our vote at referendum-election time. The way the intake of political candidates is organized is crucial. The political election campaign should demonstrate integrity, constructive character, and vision: otherwise why vote for that candidate! Local governments can play a key grassroots role as a proving ground for worthwhile elected members who move on to greater authority and power. Local government can prove to be both a limiting as well as informing factor for state and federal governmental. Local community powers are focused in local government centres, providing facilities and services and encouraging clubs and societies. Their membership tends to be proven by locally respected people. In these local-politicians trust and effectiveness are generally rewarded by being repeatedly re-elected, and so these qualities are an incentive to promote local 'social growth' and community. The evil of party politics in Canadian municipalities is mainly avoided enabling greater local democracy and variety. Personal involvement and local knowledge (not expensively and imperfectly gained by committees) prove less likely to contain misinformation leading to misunderstanding, though self-interest is still a factor for some. Calm thought, plenty of ground level experience, and good long-term planning work well while measures made in haste can too easily lead to repenting at leisure.

Little playacting is required in local elections such as braces, shirt sleeves, and tub banging seemingly so necessary for some to seal themselves with the people: many local people will remember that first date, cycling, skate boarding, and dancing at the proms. They all know or know of the candidates from way back, quite possibly from school and community events. So, the community stars can move from LOCAL to NATIONAL contribution and a well-won promotion to become politicians who are tried, tested, proven, and known.

CHAPTER 23:

GOVERNMENT

<u>Thomas Paine</u> (1996). *Rights of Man* p. 137

The good Government should be:

> ..."*no more than some common centre, in which all the parts of society meet*" *also in use a "representation ingrafted upon Democracy*" *concentrating "the knowledge necessary to the interest of the parts, and of the whole.*"

Representatives act in a position of trust. Having been entrusted they have the power to both change and demand due to the authority given them by, through, and with the consent of the people, being maintained by their continued support and will.

In the EU the government 'gives power to itself' via the Council of Ministers ...... this is not true representation any more than Democratic Government nor their expensive quangos. For true consensual government, maximum consultation is necessary with direct electoral acceptance from and by the taxpayers. Corporate political power is not Democracy.

Thomas Paine (1996). p. 147 rightly emphasized the following:

> "*A constitution is the property of a nation, and not of those who exercise the Government.*" In other words, power is controlled or restricted by the people.
>
> and therefore restrains abuse of power
>
> WHY HAVE A GOVERNMENT? ...Security......
> Making Laws and Executing Laws p. 153

A government which continues to need full popular support establishes the legitimacy of their use of power(s). It is understandable and accurate to feel that elected people are there on our behalf and are in fact taking our place through our agreement. They defend and hold the powers of a people, collectively acting and united as one. Once elected, hopefully they will continue to listen. A government acts as one voice with collective responsibility. Their value lies in being able to form this one voice reflecting an acceptable compromising consensus, reflective of the value and differences of many voices and minds, with due respect. If instead of representing us they arrogantly override, therefore indulging in dangerously ignoring the facts and their very real need for democratic agreement, they lose their right to govern because they have abandoned their primary Responsibilities. Such a betrayal of public agreement and support makes that government illegitimate, no longer acting through consent, and subject to legal ramifications. Such arrogant disregard will lead to conflict in general and possibly civil war.

Government standards and policy uniformity do not run services but do direct policy and funding.

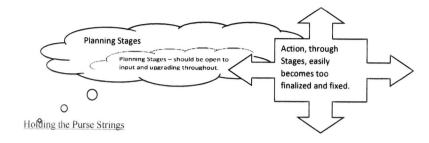

Holding the Purse Strings

Holding the Purse Strings

Governments through their control of resources and money exert clear social control. Its positive side is obvious, as are the alternatives when these powers are corrupted and abused. They may also be usurped by other agencies not subject to the people's choice. There are some natural born leaders who can empower the people and advance society with the strength, depth, and value of their ideas. They encourage us to be less selfish and to accept fund allocation for the betterment of others' lives. These philosophers are the golden essence of worthwhile politics. After our survival needs have been met, the importance of money becomes secondary and ideals rise to the fore, as they should. However, it appears that the public have developed a lack of guiding faith and beliefs, which includes loss of support for the community, growing multicultural fears, and multilingual distrust that fear and insecurity enter family life. The insecurity that is generated focuses on the accumulation of wealth and things which we view as essential to our protection: security, and survival. This is borne of induced insecurity and growing cynicism. Things owned replace personality strengths, even to the point of taking on crushing debt: a world gone mad fed by disinformation, multinational corporate greed, tyranny, and terrorism large and small. These many changes bring re-adjustment, both potentially positive or negative. Internationally trade-percentage protection could be established through agreement, warfare, or a return to autocratic dictatorships. The dangers grow daily, even hourly, as millions relocate too fast for them and for those who are receiving them.

Being prepared to recognize that our mistakes are our own fault and we consequently have Responsibilities to rectify them seems currently less accepted and evident. Blame and accusation smoke screening seem a too regular preferred alternative. It is common sense that this is not the way to go, but common sense is not so common anymore. Again, one problem is the proliferation of overprotective parents with their unreasonable approach consequently misinforming and mis-educating their children. Central Authorities necessarily taking actions may as a result have to go beyond any intended outcome. At times of potential conflict, mature and secure goodwill and common sense reduce or remove problematic consequences. The danger comes from a dissonance and disconnect developing between perceptions and reality. A one-to-one example is racial prejudice, in which the belief searches out supportive evidence for that belief using imagination and hearsay while avoiding positive traits or aspects.

Clash of civilizations or their successful merging is one of attitude and information. There is no reason to believe that successful merging cannot occur with the benefits of clear thought, self-discipline, and mutual respect. That so frequently this does not occur is the responsibility of a minority of self-interested and less mature individuals profiting from misinformation, exaggeration, and spite: often those shouters and screamers. I firmly believe that the majority need and wish for a peaceful life. Sadly, environmental and social conditions can and do interfere with this so it cannot be taken for granted. Intelligent and balanced vigilance is required, especially regarding current potentially traumatized and brutalized people who need considerable support, reassurance, and time to heal.

WAR: the definitive aspect of war, small or large, is its end. Endings occur when one or both parties have exhausted the will and so that fatally perceived need to continue the conflict ends also. Sad memories of exhaustion, destruction, and lost loved ones and comrades seem to reason eloquently for continued peace rather than the previous logic and warped reasoning which resulted in armed conflict. A tragic outcome of passing time and with passing generations is they proceed ever further away from the moment and realization of a need to end the war madness. So much costly structure and irreplaceable life has been lost. Avoidance of War is another argument for listening to the experiences and wisdom of the elderly added to and augmented with the study of relevant literature, with both history and its geography. At present most nations in the Western World are enjoying a long period of peace due to growing unity and successful politics. However, disunity grows and many other parts of the world seem to have to endure almost endless warfare due to corrupt governance and perversions of religious beliefs. The effect of these damaged and brutalized masses understandably fleeing from these regions added to which is growing climatic chaos are as yet to be appreciated, something London UK, New York USA, and Toronto Canada, for example, are well able to attest to. What may change or need to change with the huge isolated blocks of immigrants suggests the greatest caution, even strong well-considered opposition to ill thought out planning. There will be only one chance to make each arrival a successful event. As Churchill said earlier, "This is not the end. It is not even the beginning of the end. But it is, perhaps, the end of the beginning."

Election Manipulation
and The Senate

Ten percenters (counted voter "Don't Knows") have mis-stated their positions and situations purposely trying to gain a political edge, it is said. When asked, the reply can be blandly but honestly, "par for the course". Such efforts to sway voters are despicable. It is a betrayal of trust and disrespects democracy's ideal of speaking openly. Fanciful names may form a snappy title, but do not 'change the smell from the rotten carcass'. 'Wedge policies' are nailed into the brain of the listening electorate and are as potentially un-examinable as 'hot button issues'. Society believes it has safeguards in place, only to find out later that it does not as when a small minority of properly elected members of Parliament or Knesset or Senate etc. take control of a minority government. Currently Canadians are being asked if it would help or harm to abolish the Senate. The Senate contains political appointees, true. Some of these have long proven records of excellence in their field and so are an invaluable source of knowledge and guidance. To lose this resource would be foolish. Also, senators can act as a break on an overconfident and arrogant government or when a government is making a mistake. As governments proceed to form new laws or upgrade existing laws, they benefit from the scrutiny and input from both the civil service and the Senate. The problem lies in the regulation, scrutiny, overseeing of expenses, and human resourcing of the Senate. These are matters of detail: reorganization of these matters is called for. Senators could be elected by three or four constituencies acting together, thereby leaving some appointee specialist. Regulations stipulating specialist appointees should only include appointed senators with the power of the senate to reject an unwelcome appointee. The Senate could be divided into two parts with each having separate duties but all required at open debate of the full

Senate in clearly defined situations. The permutations are many and a referendum with a first and second choice system vote could decide from a shortlist of options. The different options would be debated with support being free and open on non-party lines by both the Members of Parliament and the Senate with a free vote.

CITIZENSHIP

There is that duty of every citizen, assuming they are able to think, talk, discuss, and be mobile, to be committed to taking effective action by voting. Some sadly find it too difficult even to make the effort to vote at election time and so fail this basic responsibility. More mature people value their privileges of citizenship.

> **Responsibility:** the outcome of experience and an awareness of 'basic decency' and needs. A belief in a code of Responsibility being agreed and used to meet the changes within life, to readjust social imbalance and better meet emergencies. Therefore responsibility is a concept of action-need which should morally and intellectually be addressed through positive action to the benefit of others: empowered by and of the mind remaining open to reason

It is the duty of all citizens within our Social Family to do what they can within their capabilities and particular gifts for the benefit of the Social Family while also benefitting themselves honestly. It is additionally important to appreciate that by making a social and civil contribution we can cement a feeling of belonging and worth, and this perception needs to be community supported. Happiness and contentment result with an extended network of worthwhile supportive friends. The group will appreciate that creative support is to their advantage as well. It is no longer *them and us* but rather the far stronger us and ours:

Data Collection

Electronic communications, defensive surveillance, interrogation, and simple snooping appear to disregard what some would term our privacy RIGHTS. Opposing such collection of personal information could suggest a right to plan harm undetected. This shows the need for careful definition with effective checks and balances. Freedom to think and communicate does not appear to be so free. Dossier collection and building related to individuals and groups is a fact both regarding national security and potential sales. What is more of a worry is seen in the USA where data collected is owned by the collector and thus 'private'. Hopefully this will change and there will be better laws made in Europe and beyond. It should be fully debated as a central election issue, thus making our collective will clear.

'Thought architecture' is structured externally by education, media, experience, conversation, and external custom, and internally by our physical state, emotion, and memories. Our own mental state and structure can now be defined via data collection of our purchases over time and our computer usage. Currently much daily conversation is electronic and increasingly so. Conversations and debate between 'friends' adds to thought building. Identification through 'TRIGGER WORDS and PHRASES' has initiated a closer monitoring of our activities. Our ideas proceed through these processes. Illustrative examples are established within us and shared through e-mail, Facebook, Skype, YouTube video clips, and so on. These do not necessarily form the final thought or belief, but may well inform others what the belief-structure becomes and thus direct commercial actions. However, if printed or saved, they suggest a fixed fact: hence the 'witch hunts' of the unwary by such as the media and Political Correctness Brigade. The ability to monitor audiences and identify the different sites visited with their content gives a considerable amount of user information. In turn, this opens up users to manipulation and tailored sales pitches. Using a store or bank card provides considerable information to the store or bank which is stored and 'safely' accessed by them. In the everyday condition of 'conversation', we need to exercise judgement and Responsible behaviour, for there is "no knowing who is listening" in or how we influence others. The promoters of the various media and information services; the educational learning pursuits; and advertising, including television clips of upcoming broadcasts, all have ways of collecting data. This may be used irresponsibly or in hidden opposition to any Rights concerns, but the collectors in the USA are the sole owners of the data.

Feminism and Myth

Feminism is the intellectual result and natural outcome of an active reaction against sexist injustice and role protectionism which has existed through the ages. Unfortunately such injustice cannot be corrected at large until a social climate will allow it and suggest need for forceful demonstrations. There can be no reason to push second class citizenship on one sex, or worse to deny their dignity and humanity. Think of the slums that have existed throughout time, when slavery and exploitation of people were generally commonplace. Philanthropy and unionisation were essential to adjust the indefensible injustice, and they did. For these problems to be solved, fuller social balance and real universal justice had to be achieved and with it new 'traditions' added. However, the respect deserved between the sexes needs to be fully accepted and demonstrated by both sexes. I fear there will probably always be detractors of both, but this will hopefully be stopped from getting out of control by the awakening of more enlightened and reasonable attitudes of the detractors and abusers to be found in the different sexual categories. We each are equally important. Some may sadly view themselves as 'small cogs', but all the cogs in a machine are needed if it is to work correctly. Each cog was placed there as is each person. Personal choice is having that freedom to choose and that means a preference to live as that person wishes within the Social Family context and not necessarily as some might prefer. It is a bit like the difference between needing and a wish list. Today, the confrontational feminist can do more harm than good just as the dictatorial and violent male or female can. If I am not physically or mentally harming anyone, then let me lead my life in my way. Agreeing to disagree intelligently can so simply remove the potential to cause harm. That is an essential part of family living and also of the Social Family. However, injustice must be addressed and resolved as we accept our Responsibilities within the Social Family. Also, it becomes the duty of each member to ensure active responsible action to address injustice using their own abilities or gifts legally. Cast back and remember some of the informative protest products of the 60s: songs from Pete Segar, Joan Biaz, Donavan, Bob Dylan, and well before that Woody Guthrie. Earlier Picasso's artistic scream regarded the Spanish Civil War, and still circulates the globe. As demonstrated, even a footballer can use his fame to make a valid point about the "bloated bankers' bonuses" following the recent crash. It may reasonably be suggested that in almost all situations if one has objections then speak up, but with consideration and balance. If someone is being deeply distressed or being harmed by your approach, just 'don't go there'; leave it, for nothing positive can be achieved! Treat it, as the Arabs say so brilliantly, as if "It is just dust in the wind". It can often be more important to appreciate when not to speak as knowing what could be said. Such display true intelligence while supporting 'social glue'. Bear in mind this does not remove a better and more constructive moment later.

Immigration and Culture

There is a growth developmental process in cultures within which are a multitude of subtle differences. Dislocation may be pivotal at times. There are also aspects of survival which may have evolved. Members of a culture generally value and understand the cultural process which transmits unity while also providing security which members of that culture have "bought into". Naturally different geographical, historical, and economic factors produce differences of culture. Climate, vegetation, and topography will all have an influence. Population size and pressures along with local dangers or shortages will produce times of group stress which may again provide new customs. In short, customs will vary greatly.

I as an immigrant to Canada am doubly grateful for those abilities, values, and beliefs I live by and which balance my life, given to me by family, faith, and one section of the society I have left. I am an accumulation and amalgamation of my forbearers and most particularly my parents, their friends, and my education. I am now freely accepted by this nation and I wish to both identify with its spirit and culture. If this were not so, then I would not remain, for there would be no point. I owe it to my adopted home to maintain and promote what I have observed and to accept its beliefs and ways, for these are what make Canada. These have made this nation's people so welcoming and generous: its established people are what the nation is. Outsiders trying to change this wish to destroy the essence of that nation by arrogantly inserting their own version, are only a product of what they may well have been leaving in the first place. Accepting additions to a culture takes time but frequently occurs through general agreement. Canadian culture is based on the past looking towards our view of the future: pioneer spirit, damned hard work, sacrifice, trade, mutual support, and Christian ethics gradually and gently expanding beyond. A nation needs to be both proud and confident of all these things and confident enough not to follow the current British example of self-doubt. There they seem to be discarding the old and trusted ways for no good reason. Many now seem to feel a need to offer excuses for their praiseworthy achievements, forgetting the sacrifices of the resident peoples responsible for the success of that nation. A slave had value to its master, but members of the British workforce and armed forces simply died for oh so many visions and individual fortunes. Some local communities have lost their self-respect and political voice as they have been combined. The smaller, interested, and active political municipalities have been compressed into great big impersonal power blocks. There is a perception that this produces a greater efficiency. However, that efficiency is of the financial accounting kind. It is dead money, lifeless for their benefit, and dictated rather than agreed. This 'conglomeration' or 'concretion' is not at the personal level and benefit to those submerged local communities: small is beautiful and also accessible. Thrown aside and ignored are local belief systems which generated empathy and a community with heart. The enlarged block applies the brakes which slow or stop. It begins the decay of locally initiated responsible behaviour and constructive local control.

One Australian example of the unfeeling action of bigger administrative power blocks was the expulsion to the UK of a man raised in Australia and at over 50 years of age knowing nowhere else: no roots in the UK, no memories in the UK, and no place in the UK. Having applied for Australian citizenship, the Social Servants, dealing with his case, became aware of a past crime committed in Australia way back when and one assumes, since it was a matter of record, was punished: citizenship being denied he was deported! He had been resident from the age of six; his character had been moulded by the Australian Education Services. Having a family, with all that involves, he was kicked out! Political motive can be the only reason for such a crass outcome unless those involved were too 'stupid' and totally unsuited to be left with adult Responsibilities associated with holding down such a responsible administrative job. If removal was required, it should have been at the time of the breach of law: this bears all the indications of retrospective injustice. There is no 'natural justice' here nor consideration of so-called Human Rights to protect those at risk! The broader looking and more flexible nature of Responsibilities should almost inevitably remove such incidents. There unfortunately can be no full protection against 'limp brained, uncaring petty officialdom' who serve their own vanities and power-need before properly serving the Social Family. Further, if there were recent eventualities to justify such draconian measures, then the 'free' press and communication networks should and would have made that clear at the time they CHOSE to report this aberration. This was reported from Australia (18/04/2011) and defies the national responsibility and decency regarding a long-time resident.

All societies have their Mavericks and also their thugs but the essence of each different society is what it and its people are and so need. For the Hindu, Jew, Muslim, Buddhist, Christian, etc. society differs, but the aim must be the good of the people and not finance, big business, or politicians. Our varied ways of living differ, but their road is the same goal. Sadly, with modernization there seems to be a growing number of the ignored.

REGRETTABLE FAST PACE OF LIFE

With the spread of technology and achieving almost immediate international communication links, hopefully there
will take place a convergence of our awareness. Humanity
is becoming increasingly one. Interconnected and interdependent we should look for and find the more harmonious
way. A global unity of ethics is evolving and being accepted as
was 'to do unto others as you would wish them to do to you'
central to many belief systems and much sanity. The benefits
of unity and acceptance of core Responsibilities will enable
long term peace and prosperity for all. The underlying reality
that the other person is human and we are responsible to and
for each other will be undeniable. JOHN TEMPLETON
suggested that upon waking we should think of five things
to be thankful for. Since life for far too many can become
too rushed and overfilled to have time to quietly think, to
care, and to experience a meaningful life, it is time to slow life
down. Robotics could well facilitate this if not subject to and
dominated by accumulated wealth. We are becoming awash
with information but shallow in thought: the fast, shallow,
and easy way is unrewarding and pointless, even destructive.
This slowing down would enable us to find more personal
space in our lives and enable us to again think deeply and
understand rather than reflex-react.

INFILTRATED DEMOCRACY

Ask yourself who really chooses the politicians. Then
remember how the political units are getting larger and fewer
with the powerful growing more powerful as a result. Once
politicians sprang from local roots; now they spring more
from industrial and financier shoots. It is obvious which is

better for us as individuals. The clock is turning backwards. Our selective process has been taken over and submerged by very large interest groups with their own agenda and we as individuals within the process tend to be just tolerated, at present. The debate has been emasculated as far as the individual is concerned; decreasingly ideas focus upon the individual's level of benefit. Human Rights are a form of political shop window dressing. They work where they were working due to traditions or Responsibilities towards others and they continue to be worthless elsewhere.

There is always a role for conscience to mediate and add humanity when others insist upon following the letter of the law, even when conditions or circumstance suggest differently. In France the sensible acceptance of a 'Crime of Passion' and in Scotland 'neither has the case been proved nor disproven' shows the way.

Films can burn people: reportedly there were 196 murdered homeless people in 12 months for 2005/6. In USA and Canada these were real fights promoted for filming using cell phones and the like to record and send them. One cries out, "How can such happen?" What sort of minds need this sort of thing? Children are less liable to differentiate between reality and staged incidents - this is emotionally damaging for them. It is a matter of record that children rescued from war zones have considerable difficulty recovering. The violence and extremes of horror available via the media are seen by some children and the damage caused can go deep inside as mind pollution. Bull baiting, cock fights, and dog fights are all banned and these forms of gambling and vicarious gratification are shunned by the mature and well adjusted. However, violent and perverse media are being allowed to poison the minds of our Social Family. For many, laughter seems to legitimize the abhorrent, even if canned - recorded over. Gladiatorial games of ancient Rome promoted brutality as entertainment. No doubt they laughed too at gross outcomes of barbarity: those immobilised by fear about to be attacked; the fleeing and hapless and hopeless about to be savaged; and others writhing in pain. Physical and mental distress were very close. What can be the excuse in today's more 'civilized times' for actually enjoying the discomfort, embarrassment, and misery experienced by others? This is in no way a sacred right or freedom, and it occurs far too regularly.

Difference of Time and Character

With the development of mutual respect comes convergence. The 1960s were the experimental years which brought fast change along with social experimentation. Social walls fell and conventions tottered over: a new confidence was evident in which hope abounded. Much of class disappeared. Difference produced interest. People grew closer. Both sympathy and empathy blossomed. Happiness and peace were a central theme and freedom another: a time of rejection and strangely also of consolidation. It was 'the time of change', which later politicians would use as a useful slogan. The Western World was going through a rethink and was reinventing itself. I imagine modern China is experiencing some of the same. Being there was liberating and inspiring. Swinging London and the music-theatre scene blossomed, and then something happened - intangible with its own cold and damp feeling. Vietnam (1955), Tibet invaded (1959), The Belgian Congo War (1960), Mao's Red Book (1966), Northern Ireland Troubles (1968), Tiananmen Square (1989), famines reported, Chechnya (1994). What happened to it all! Now it seems more like I was a passenger standing on the wharf watching my cruise liner going towards and beyond the horizon.

The HANDICAPPED and the ELDERLY

Hopefully life is getting better. Yet again the litmus test must be those with problems who are less able to help themselves, thereby extending awareness and learning Responsibilities for the fit. Handicapped volunteers organize fun outings, shopping trips, rides to hospital for appointments, hot dinners, seasonal celebrations, home improvements and decoration, visits to reduce isolation, and so much more. Some enjoy having different companions every trip, while others prefer and enjoy a predictable uniformity. These provide cherished memories, demonstrating and teaching that we all matter and people do care. It sends a strong human message with no force included or needed: it is a free gift.

In my time there seems to have been a great increase in asthma, eczema, other allergies, nervous disorders, nerve damage, and cancers. The role of the mind regarding our immune systems has been compounded by drifting chemicals in the air and manipulation of our food's primary sources - this is not yet understood. Fortunately medical treatments have vastly improved thanks to dedicated and imaginative people. Hopefully the African contribution will provide more affordable technologies and medicines, thus bringing down costs and increasing treatments. This growing African promise is thanks to responsible inward investment by company charities of the West and the phenomenal enthusiasm, inventiveness, and hard work of Africans. One just prays that the recent growing warfare on the continent and next-door will shrink away, thus giving the old, the young, and the handicapped a future more in tune with Western expectations - a future that is now becoming more probable.

European Convention of Human Rights: Nos. 9 and 14

<u>ARTICLE 9</u> Freedom of thought, conscience, and religion 1. Everyone has the right to freedom of thought, conscience, and religion; this right includes freedom to change his religion or belief and freedom, either alone or in community with others and in public or private, to manifest his religion or belief, in worship, teaching, practice and observance. 2. Freedom to manifest one's religion or beliefs shall be subject only to such limitations as are prescribed by law and are necessary in a democratic society in the interests of public safety, for the protection of public order, health or morals, or for the protection of the rights and freedoms of others.

<u>ARTICLE 10</u> Freedom of expression 1. Everyone has the right to freedom of expression. This right shall include freedom to hold opinions and to receive and impart information and ideas without interference by public authority and regardless of frontiers. This Article shall not prevent States from requiring the licensing of broadcasting, television, or cinema enterprises. 2. The exercise of these freedoms, since it carries with it duties and Responsibilities, may be subject to such formalities, conditions, restrictions, or penalties as are prescribed by law and are necessary in a democratic society, in the interests of national security, territorial integrity, or public safety, for the prevention of disorder or crime, for the protection of health or morals, for the protection of the reputation or rights of others, for preventing the disclosure of information received in confidence, or for maintaining the authority and impartiality of the judiciary.

<u>ARTICLE 11</u> Freedom of assembly and association 1. Everyone has the right to freedom of peaceful assembly and to freedom of association with others, including the right to form and to join trade unions for the protection of his

interests. 12 13 2. No restrictions shall be placed on the exercise of these rights other than such as are prescribed by law and are necessary in a democratic society in the interests of national security or public safety, for the prevention of disorder or crime, for the protection of health or morals or for the protection of the rights and freedoms of others. This Article shall not prevent the imposition of lawful restrictions.

ARTICLE 14 Prohibition of discrimination The enjoyment of the rights and freedoms set forth in this Convention shall be secured without discrimination on any ground such as sex, race, colour, language, religion, political or other opinion, national or social origin, association with a national minority, property, birth or other status.

ARTICLE 15 Derogation in time of emergency 1. In time of war or other public emergency threatening the life of the nation any High Contracting Party may take measures derogating from its obligations under this Convention to the extent strictly required by the exigencies of the situation, provided that such measures are not inconsistent with its other obligations under international law.

Hopefully Canada's C51 will soon be fully revised and ready to initiate an overhaul or removal of these matters seemingly set in stone.

FRANCIS BACON: Law of Nature

The concept that the 'law of Nature' can be attached to the human condition for Responsibility is a perception led by both tradition and, more essentially, experience. The 'confirming spirit' from experience does that since it confirms and reaffirms Responsibilities, but from within those being well aware of a very personal conscience. The laws of Rights come from without and are external to us, and consequently need the implied 'follow-on responsibility' as well as a pattern which is acceptable to the Social Family group. All this needs be viewed from the base of individual Responsibilities. The dangers and snares of confused meaning in language use were highlighted by Whitgenstein and this very mistakenness being frozen and enshrined in law can, for one, be used to achieve or retain political power as emphasised by *Nietzsche*.Such is amply demonstrated in history and the almost hysterical worship of Human Rights. Further, there tends to be recognizable a certain instability, often suspect, seeming always outside the law and frequently inside a wrong 'political correctness'. The outcome so often brings social sanctions and isolation (punishment) without any properly balanced hearing, debate, or responsible consideration, way beyond what is reasonable or deserved. When responses are seen as finite and single-edged, are termed self-evident, and are politically backed, then they become empowered 'truths'. However, these expressions of 'ideas' may or may not be based upon truth, but rather a strongly held opinion filled with emotional confusion - many relevant observations can be attached from the Nazi regime through to fighters for 'freedom' and are often, too often, limited to their own point of view. Once power has been achieved, then the new way may be easily portrayed as Right by the new writers of history.

Even the simple concept, idea, or statement needs to be clear. It is the essential essence of any resulting social or national construct. Clarity needs simplicity. This cannot be said of Rights when related to their interpretation, depth, breadth, and width of use. Too often they cannot be seen as producing Responsible Behaviour and can be full of 'confusables'.

WITHIN A MORE PERFECT WORLD

……. Thoughts

Promises once made would be remembered and kept.

All people would respect the preferences of other ……. Even to abstinence.

Starvation and abuse would be viewed as unacceptable and lead to 'universal' action.

Age would be respected for its experience and insightfulness or understanding.

All laws would be forward looking and never retrospectively spiteful.

Public servants would have learned that they are servants first and would thus better earn respect right up to Prime Ministers and beyond.

Illness would strike the evil and miss the goodly.

Lengthy periods of quiet and calm would be viewed as a human necessity.

Travel would not be an invitation to overindulge, cause noise, and speed dangerously, all at a cost to others.

Schools would successfully teach respect for others and responsibility towards others.

Schools would educate in recognizing 'true friendship' and how to find 'your' way to choosing a partner.

'Believe in it', check if there is anything wrong in it, and if everything is OK, then 'Go For It'.…… do it!

There would be general recognition that losing can often be a stepping-stone to success: it depends upon you.

Being reasonable would not need a descriptive preamble.

Sirens would not need to be heard.

Television programs and entertainment would be filled with minds big enough and able enough to see and use material unsullied by filth and the sordid side of life.

Documentaries would progressively focus upon social needs and the improvement of shortcomings.

People would think first and chose what benefits beyond themselves.

The Word War would mean worldwide coordinated attacks upon diseases of both mankind and society.

All drug peddlers would swallow their entire stock.

Religious leaders would all promote the open responsible mind capable of thoughts and the actions which could happily be shown to be from a God who hates spite, arrogance, anger, war, violent death, poverty, injustice, and corrupt self-interest.

There would be an accepted need for well-trained religious leaders.

This view would not differ much regarding politicians.

TERMINUS

This work, for that is what it has been as well as a labour of love, stems from my belief in all kinds of people and in their collective constructive kindnesses and values. Around

us are destructive self-interested forces rotting and moulder-
ing what is good. The exceptional resources of spirit demonstrated every day by individuals and groups are amazing.
Their strength and goodness do not depend upon gender,
race, age, or orientation. All have been outstandingly 'golden'
and will continue to be so. Society's great responsibility to
our children's future is to encourage and support all those
whose will and strength of awareness lead them to work for
their own betterment *with* that of others. This acceptance
inevitably means and leads to change. This betterment
means and requires difference. The ever-changing and
adapting 'spirits of community with individual and group
Responsibilities are paramount to achieving civility and a
basic and stable society.

Future is a product of choice.

We are the product of freely made commitments.

*What we each need is a warming of within from our active
warming of the world outside.*

Prejudice can so easily lead to the sadness and waste of
knowing and not achieving, but this cannot be worse than
realizing too late the pain associated with and from not
trying. Each person needs an opening of and to their own
personal way. We grow in perceiving and understanding
what is around us and what is and could be. So, each person
needs instruction and support to discover possibility, from
those who have gone before. Old age is experience waiting to
be shared. To not share is to extend ignorance with experience un-extended and thus wasted. All peoples of all 'chosen
formalities' require the freedom to expand their humanity
and give in a constructive way. Different can never be automatically wrong; quite frequently different is needed and is
therefore right. If difference is not intent upon the harm of

others, then it is an opportunity, an insight, and a probable step forward.

Support of others goes beyond the use‿u‿all and the abandonment of wasted opportunities of the un-used‿u‿all. We are all able to support and encourage others to TRY. Only this way will humanity progress and deepen. It is everyone's 'Responsibility' and could never be defined as or in a rigid and time-based defined system of invented Rights.

Since you have reached this point, my sincere thanks to you for your perseverance. I said at the start that I am no wordsmith, however, I do hope you have found the piece thoughtful and thought-provoking with interesting additional information. Please forgive the shortcomings. You will have become aware that I do believe there is a battle going on, one which if we could be persuaded to recognize and follow our Responsibilities would end the very real conflicts. Hopefully this piece will encourage others better suited to champion that essential need to return to respect; to further the cause of empathy and good manners; to resurrect hospitality and thoughtful conversation; to restore a commitment to establishing and fulfilling our Responsibilities; to expand and successfully eloquently return us to the ideas expressed above. Such a situation would remove the need to strong-arm so-called Human Rights upon the unwary. It is best to ensure fair justice by promoting a happy future for all through a healthy caring Social Family. Limited I am, but strong can be the many. During World War II, whilst walking in the garden at number 10, Sir Winston Churchill saw one of his aids trip and fall into a rose bush. Looking upwards he loudly proclaimed, "O Lord, the foolish Thou shendesht me to win thish war!" I hope true warriors for community and society will be forthcoming. We all have limitations, but hopefully our visions are unlimited.

Remember the banking executive who refused to accept his bonus due to the layoffs he saw taking place with other cuts as a result of the financial crisis? He was such a breath of fresh air: a thoroughly responsible act at a time of uncertainty for many. Today (15/4/2015) I heard some great news on BBC World News. A chief Executive in his thirties, CEO Dan Price, learned through reading that to be happy an individual should receive $70,000 a year, no more and no less: the average for his staff was $45,000 with most below $40,000. He had built the company Gravity Payments from scratch. True to his new belief and thus responsibility he reduced his large salary to $70,000 and raised all 120 staff salaries to the same $70,000 figure, no matter the job description. With emotion and as a child of the 60s I knew this dream, and this dream of the 60s has now arrived. God bless him!

THE GREATER FACT of RIGHTS

Since people have rights, these extend throughout the family and into the nation and beyond. This nation of people has a right to expect that those who would CHOOSE to ask to join and become part of their proposed adopted nation would accept the need and obligation to follow its norms and expectations, thus becoming one with the 'national identity'. The nation's identity is what identifies and unites that nation and so to act against that identity is to purposely and with premeditated intent attack and endanger the nation. That these applicants or even simple visitors have a responsibility to take reasonable care to understand and live within the national norms is axiomatic... a no-brainer. Each is providing for themselves while contributing to the whole, abiding by the nation's laws, and respecting beliefs and traditions - those aspects which make up the spirit and essence of that nation which is a unity of its identity and comes with Rights (Article 14) which are un-abused. The couple who were naked at the top of a sacred mountain need not be surprised at the offence it caused and the reaction they experienced (2015).

Too frequently it would appear that rights are initially there for the comparatively rich, as with the Magna Carta meaning The Great Charter of the (Lords') Liberties, and increasingly diminish and fade with the growth of poverty. Juxtaposed with gained riches and wealth is a greater responsibility for the poor: a far greater productive force than legalistic rights since Responsibilities are written within ourselves and so develop. These are part of our worth and our being, and we carry them with us freely choosing to act upon them wherever we go: in response to needs. This is what Jesus taught and what was taught by other great teachers also in other religions. Each family and nation should be similarly respected and respectful.

Though it may be said that everyone has a right to their opinion, this may seem a bit silly because everyone has the opinions they have, irrespective of any fanciful right. Is this some form of external take-over movement? What occurs will either confirm or deny that we all have this right or that the right does not matter a damn. There are different 'flavours' of opinion: some are apparently acceptable while others are not. Why? Opinion hopefully comes from experience. So, do some experiences count less than other experiences? It would seem so. The reality is that an "unacceptable" opinion is one which has become actively viewed as intentionally harmful. Freedom of conscience can be crushed. Conscience is supposed to be one of the highest mind 'reflexes'. Reasoned and calm discussion needs to be open to <u>all</u> opinions without screaming opposition. If a position is feeble it will fall to logic and a well-reasoned debate, no need to scream and shout. Opinions will only be internally altered by the individual accepting another position which has been listened to thoughtfully and understood. The fact that some opinions appear not to be generally or mildly acceptable illustrates the previous and following position that 'everyone' does not necessarily have a right to their own opinion due to and because of the harm they produce, including government. Also, by saying, "I have a right ..." does not make it an active fact; it simply remains an opinion. It may be a heartfelt product of belief or even the result of a misplaced sense of fun; this proves to be irrelevant. Being such there is no Right there. Peace of mind or state of peace will not of necessity be found in Rights, for in a recourse to law legalistic rights are the essence of legalistic conflict and so can make matters worse. In legal action positions become ever more entrenched, moving individuals and groups in tragically additional directions they likely would not have chosen. Thus, conflict grows.

Ashley Smith's solitary confinement was for four years. Another unfortunate was so confined for fifteen years. They were unable to have any conversation. They were denied any physical contact. Food arrived through a gap in the wall. Their opportunity for moving outside of their cells was "possibly" for one hour a day!

On 29 January 2006, Ashley Smith turned 18; on 29 July a motion was made under the Youth Criminal Justice Act to transfer her to an adult facility. Smith hired a lawyer to fight the transfer, but was unsuccessful. On 5 October 2006, Smith was transferred to the Saint John Regional Correctional Centre (SJRCC). Due to her behaviour at SJRCC, Smith spent most of her time there in segregation; she was tazered twice and pepper-sprayed once. On 31 October 2006, Smith was transferred to the Nova Institution for Women in Nova Scotia (a federal institution). [1] Through 2007, Smith was transferred a total of 17 times among the following 8 institutions during 11 months in federal custody:[8] While at Grand Valley Institution for Women in Kitchener, Ontario, on 16 October 2007,

Smith requested transfer to a psychiatric facility; she was placed on a formal suicide watch on 18 October. In the early hours of 19 October, Smith was videotaped placing a ligature around her neck, an act of self-harm she had committed several times before. Guards did not enter her cell to intervene, and 45 minutes passed before she was examined and pronounced dead.[1] (Wikipedia)

The Fifth Estate Report:

On 8 January 2010, **CBC News Network's The Fifth Estate** broadcast a documentary about the case titled "Out of Control". In the documentary, reporter Hana Gartner describes Smith as a **fourteen-year-old** placed in a youth facility **for one month** in 2003 after **throwing crabapples** [my emphasis] at the mailman. Smith was placed in solitary confinement after disruptive behaviour on her first day. Her initial one-month sentence would last almost four years, entirely in isolation, until her death in 2007............
The frequent "use of force" reports required to document responses became a source of concern for facility officials. According to an internal document obtained and partially read aloud by Gartner, eventually Corrections Canada administrators instructed guards and supervisors not to respond to self-strangling attempts by Smith, "to ignore her, even if she was choking herself."

On 25 October 2007, three guards and a supervisor at the Grand Valley Institution for Women were charged with criminal negligence causing death in relation to Smith's suicide; the warden and deputy warden **were fired**. The criminal charges were later dropped. On 8 October 2009,

Smith's family launched a wrongful death lawsuit against the Correctional Service of Canada, demanding C$11 million in damages; the suit was eventually settled

out of court in May 2011 for an undisclosed amount.
[3] (Wikipedia)

> *The true nature and reality of Human*
> *Rights is seen when observing*
> *their effect on behalf of the*
> *powerless and impoverished.*

INDEX

References

Abrams, D. (1990). *Social identifications: A social psychology of intergroup relations and group processes*. London, UK: Routledge.

Allen, D. M. (1994). *A Family Systems approach to individual psycho-therapy*. Northvale, USA: Jason Aronson Inc.

Arberry, J. A. Translated and Intro. (1983). *The Koran, interpreted*. Oxford: OUP, World's Classics.

Bales, K. (2012). *Disposable people: New slaves in the global economy*. University of California Press.

Barry, V. E., & Soccio, D. J. (1988). *Practical logic* (3rd ed.). Orlando, USA: Holt, Rinehart & Winston, Inc.

Blatz, W. E. (1966). *Human security: Some reflections*. Michigan, USA: University of Toronto Press.

Booth, W. (1890). *Darkest England: The way out*. Revised: Salvation Army Press.

Bottomore, T. B. (1971). *Sociology: a guide to problems and literature* (2nd ed.). London, UK: George Allen & Unwin Ltd.

Buzan, T. (1984). *Use your perfect memory*. Plume.

Buzan, T. (2002). *Mind mapping*.

Caden, C. (1908). [Social] context of learning to read. In *Language and Literacy*, Volume 2. Open University Press: Mercer

Cobley, P., & Jansz, L. (2003). *Introducing semiotics*. Royston, UK: Icon Books.

Cronbach, L. J. (1963). *Educational Psychology* (2nd ed.). USA: Harcourt, Brace & World, Inc.

Crooks, R. L., & Stein, J. (1988). *Psychology: Science, behavior and Life*. New York: Holt, Rinehart and Winston, Inc.

Compiler, D. E. (2001). *The wicked wit of Winston Churchill*. Croyden: Michael O'Mara Books Ltd.

deBono, E. (2000). *Six thinking hats*. Penguin.

Eagleton, T. (1983). *Literary theory....an introduction*. Blackwell, also John Wiley & Sons.

Eckerman, P. (2004). *Emotions revealed:Understanding faces and feelings*. Holt, Henry & Co. Inc.

Fisher, H. (2004). *Why we love*. Holt Paperback.

Goleman, D. (1995). *Emotional intelligence. Why it can matter more than IQ*. Bloombury.

Goleman, D. (2004). *Destructive emotions: How can we overcome them: A scientific dialogue with the Dalai Lama.* Bloomsbury.

Goleman, D. (2007). *Social intelligence: The new science of human relationships.* Arrow.

Hansem, E. (2006). *The New England transcendentalists.* History Compass.

Johnston, P. (2010). *Bad laws imposed by the Nanny State.* Constable, London.

Lebdoff, D. (2004). *A new Civil War: How a new elite is destroying our democracy.* Taylor Trade Publ.

Lotman, Y. (1972). *The analysis of poetic text.* Ardis.

Marx, K., & Engles, F. (2010). *The Communist Manifesto.* Artous.

McKenzie, E. (1980). *14,000 quips and quotes: For writers and speakers.* Greenwich House.

Mordiston, G. (2009). *Stones into schools.* New York: Viking Press.

Mosley, J. (1999). *Quality circle time: The handbook.* David Foulton Publ.

Naitoh, P., Kelly, T., & Englund, C. (1990). *Health effects of sleep deprivation: Navel Health Research Centre.* Reprinted from OCCUPATIONAL MEDICINE: State of the Art Review. Henley & Belfast.

Orwell, G. (1949). *1984.* Seeker and Warburger.

Pain, T. 1996). *The rights of man.* Wordsworth Classic of World Literature.

Pease, A. & B. (1981). *Body language ... How to read other's thoughts by their gestures.* Orion.

Pier Beaver, R., et al. (1993). *The World's Religions.* Lion.

Resnic, L., & Weaver, P. (1981). *Theory and practice of early reading.* Lawrence Earlbaum Associates Inc./Routledge.

Rogers, B. (1997). *You know the fair rule: Strategy of making the hard job of discipline in schools easier.* Prentice Hall.

Smith, A. (1998). *Accelerated learning.* Network Educational Press Ltd.

Smith, A. (2002). *Behind the brain.* Network Educational Press Ltd.

Strathclyde. (2011- August). *Strathclyde Report.*

Stubbs, M. (1983). *Discourse analysis: The sociolinguistic analysis of natural language.* University of Chicago Press/ Basil Blackwell.

Thorp, M. (Ed.) (1956). *Ladder of bones: A history of Nigeria 1853-1953.* Jonathan Cape.

Thrasher, M. (1925). *The Gang.* Doctorial Dissertation. University of Chicago.

Thrasher, M. (2013). *The gang: A study of 1,313 gangs in Chicago.* University of Chicago Press.

Toffler, A. (1970). *Future shock.* Random House/Pan.

Toffler, A. (1980). *The third wave.* Pan.

Various Editors. (1993). *The world's religions. A Lion Handbook.* Oxford UK: Lion Publishing.

Vygotsky, L. S. (1978). *Mind in society: The development of higher psychological processes.* Massachusetts, USA: Harvard University Press.

Walkerdine, V. (1990). *The mastery of reason: Cognitive development and the product of rationality.* London, UK: Routledge.

Ware, J. R. Translator (1964). *The sayings of Confuscious.* USA: Mentor.

Watson, T., & Hickman, M. (2012). *Dial M For Murdock: News corporation and the corruption of Britain.* London, UK: Allen Lane.

Wells, G., & Nicholls, J. (1985). *Language and learning: An interactional perspective.* London, UK: Falmer Press.

Festinger, L., & Carlsmith, J. (1959). *Classics in the history of psychology. Journal of Abnormal and Social Psychology,* 58, 203-210. A 71-male student sample from Stanford University was used in this 1954 Cognitive Dissonance Study.

FT Magazine. *The NatWest one:* Gary Mulgrew by Ginny Dougary.

Google: *Friends Extradited 2014*

Wikipedia. *NatWest Three.*

OTHER WRITINGS worth a visit

Davis, G. (1961). *My country is the world.*

The adventures of a world citizen, Putnam, in which he outlines his experiences battling for world government and world citizenship as an outcome of his World War II experiences.

Gladwell, M. (2013). *David and Goliath*. Little Brown & Co. The underdogs can win and so the unconventional successes.

Englel, F. (1844). *The condition of the English working class*. The work that inspired Marx.

Sandel, M. (2013). *What money can't buy: The Moral Limits of Markets*. Penguin. Moral Strength versus Market Power: it is wrong that everything is for sale.

ARTICLE 13(2). Universal Declaration of Human Rights.

· · · · · · ·

·

CPSIA information can be obtained
at www.ICGtesting.com
Printed in the USA
LVOW12s0139080916
503643LV00002B/8/P